MW01033988

The Fundamentalist Mindset

satran@umich.edu

The Fundamentalist Mindset

Psychological Perspectives on Religion, Violence, and History

EDITED BY

Charles B. Strozier, David M. Terman, and James W. Jones, with Katharine A. Boyd

Foreword by Martin E. Marty

OXFORD
UNIVERSITY PRESS

2010

OXFORD
UNIVERSITY PRESS

Oxford University Press, Inc., publishes works that further
Oxford University's objective of excellence
in research, scholarship, and education.

Oxford New York
Auckland Cape Town Dar es Salaam Hong Kong Karachi
Kuala Lumpur Madrid Melbourne Mexico City Nairobi
New Delhi Shanghai Taipei Toronto

With offices in
Argentina Austria Brazil Chile Czech Republic France Greece
Guatemala Hungary Italy Japan Poland Portugal Singapore
South Korea Switzerland Thailand Turkey Ukraine Vietnam

Copyright © 2010 by Oxford University Press, Inc.

Published by Oxford University Press, Inc.
198 Madison Avenue, New York, NY 10016

www.oup.com

Oxford is a registered trademark of Oxford University Press

All rights reserved. No part of this publication may be reproduced,
stored in a retrieval system, or transmitted, in any form or by any means,
electronic, mechanical, photocopying, recording, or otherwise,
without the prior permission of Oxford University Press.

Library of Congress Cataloging-in-Publication Data
The fundamentalist mindset : psychological perspectives on religion, violence,
and history / edited by Charles B. Strozier, David M. Terman, and James
W. Jones ; with Katharine A. Boyd ; foreword by Martin E. Marty.
p. cm.
ISBN 978-0-19-537965-5 – ISBN 978-0-19-537966-2 (pbk.)
1. Religious fundamentalism—Psychology.
2. Fundamentalism—Psychology.
3. Psychology, Religious. 4. Violence—Religious aspects.
I. Strozier, Charles B. II. Terman, David M.
III. Jones, James William, 1943– IV. Boyd, Katharine.
BL238.F8496 2010
200.1'9—dc22
2009034142

Printed in the United States of America
on acid-free paper

This book on religion and violence
is dedicated with love to:

Cathryn Compton
Mari Terman
Kathleen Bishop
Karen and Kevin Boyd

Contents

Acknowledgments

This book has deep roots in the individual scholarship of its authors and editors, but the project that became *The Fundamentalist Mindset* began with an online discussion created by Daniel Hill. In 2003 Hill recruited Charles B. Strozier, Ruth Stein, James W. Jones, and Richard Koenigsberg to present brief papers on aspects of fundamentalism for an online conference produced by PsyBC, a professional development website that, among other things, is concerned with the application of psychology to social problems. The PsyBC discussions of fundamentalism consisted of two month-long dialogues with others, who paid a minimal fee to participate. The first such discussion took place in the early summer of 2003 and the second a year later. We are grateful for the incisive comments of participants in those forums.

In February 2005 David M. Terman and Strozier organized a conference on the psychology of fundamentalism at the Chicago Institute for Psychoanalysis. That well-attended, day-long event brought together, besides Terman, Strozier, and Jones, individuals who stimulated our thinking, including Martin Marty, Ruth Stein, Scott Atran, Jessica Stern, Tanya Luhrmann, Harry Trosman, Robert Galatzer-Levy, Bertram Cohler, James W. Anderson, and Eva F. Lichtenberg.

In September 2006, through May 2008 Strozier hosted a monthly seminar in New York City at John Jay College on the psychology of fundamentalism that continued the conversation of those committed to the project. The intellectual leadership of the seminar was provided by Strozier, Terman, Jones, and Kathleen Bishop. The idea from the beginning of this monthly seminar was to provide a forum for deepening our understanding and to collect papers to publish as a book. Every author in this book presented his or her work to that seminar at some point. The conversation was enormously stimulating and the seminars were always followed by friendly dinners with good bourbon, acceptable wine, and outstanding conversation.

We are particularly grateful to those who joined the seminar in an active way but did not contribute papers, including Bill Blakemore, Kathleen Bishop, Michael Flynn, Matthias Beier, Michael Teitelman, Gavriel Reisner,

Richard Raubolt, Benjamin Orr, Scott Atran, Shuki Cohen, Itai Sneh, Walter Davis, Richard Koenigsberg, Prudence Emery, and Nina Thomas. Other guests attended at least one meeting and contributed much, including Arthur Pressly, Claude Barbre, Catherine Keller, Peter Heltzel, Donald Shriver, Doris Brothers, Jack Sherin, Ian Hansen, James Gilligan, Jill Berke, Lee Jenkins, Peter Romaniuk, Harry Paul, Sue Boland, and Susannah Heschel. We apologize if we have failed to mention a guest.

The coordinators of those seminars were, first, Stephanie Heller, then Benjamin Orr, and finally Katharine Boyd, who of course also played a central role as editorial assistant for this book.

Once papers were written for this volume, most authors met in New York in September 2008 for a day and a half to critique each other's work and give shape to the volume as a whole. Authors then revised their papers in the fall of 2008 and submitted final versions by January 2009. We are grateful to all those who provided comments and suggestions on those papers.

Several special people provided additional assistance. Scot Ausborn, the librarian of the Chicago Institute for Psychoanalysis, was indefatigable in tracking down materials for David Terman. Andrea Fatica, the assistant director of the Center on Terrorism at John Jay College, helped a great deal in organizing the monthly seminars in New York.

Charles B. Strozier
David M. Terman
James W. Jones

Contributor Biographies

Katharine A. Boyd is a PhD student at John Jay College of Criminal Justice. She was awarded a graduate assistantship from the Department of Homeland Security, allowing her to participate in this collaboration. Besides her coauthored contributions to this volume, she has written two other articles on religion and violence (with Charles B. Strozier).

Daniel Hill is a psychoanalyst and educator and a leading proponent of the paradigm shift to affect regulation theory. In addition to his private practice, he has taught courses for more than twenty years at various psychoanalytic and psychotherapy institutes. These include courses in adolescent development, psychopathology, and the clinical use of multiple psychoanalytic models. Hill's publications and presentations include topics ranging from the erotic transference and the clinical use of multiple models to the influence of the Internet on psychoanalysis and the possibilities and limitations of video-mediated therapy. In 1996 he founded and continues to direct PsyBC.com, which provides online and face-to-face education of mental health clinicians. For the past three years he has conducted conferences and private study groups focused on a detailed understanding of affective processes and their regulation in normal development, pathogenesis, and treatment.

James W. Jones has earned doctorates in both religious studies and clinical psychology, as well as an honorary doctorate from the University of Uppsala in Sweden. He is a distinguished professor of religion and adjunct professor of clinical psychology at Rutgers University, a lecturer in psychiatry and religion at Union Theological Seminary, and a visiting professor at the University of Uppsala. He is also a senior research fellow at the Center on Terrorism at John Jay College. His most recent book, *Blood That Cries from the Earth: The Psychological*

Roots of Religious Terrorism, was published in 2008 by Oxford University Press. He is the author of eleven other books, including *Terror and Transformation: The Ambiguity of Religion* (Routledge, 2002), *Contemporary Psychoanalysis and Religion* (Yale University Press, 1991), and *Religion and Psychology in Transition* (Yale University Press, 1996), and more than twenty professional papers and book chapters. His books have been published both in the United States and Europe and translated into Japanese, Korean, Chinese, and Portuguese. He serves on the editorial boards of several publications both here and abroad. He is a Fellow of the American Psychological Association, and at their annual convention in 1993 he received an award for his contributions to the psychology of religion. He currently serves on the governing board and as the vice president of the International Association for the Psychology of Religion. For six years he was cochair of the Religion and Social Sciences Section of the American Academy of Religion. He also maintains a private practice as a clinical psychologist. Dr. Jones has been invited to lecture in Europe and the United States on the psychological roots of religious terrorism.

David P. Jordan is the Distinguished Professor of French History, Emeritus, at the University of Illinois at Chicago. He was born in Detroit in 1939 and educated at the University of Michigan and Yale University. He is the author of books on Edward Gibbon, Maximilien Robespierre, the trial of Louis XVI, and most recently Baron Haussmann and Paris. He is currently at work on a book about Napoleon.

Farhad Khosrokhavar is a professor at Ecole des Hautes Etudes en Sciences Sociales in Paris. His main fields of study are Iranian society after the Islamic Revolution and Islam, in particular its radical forms in Europe and the Middle East. He has published sixteen books, three of which were translated into seven different languages, and more than seventy articles, mainly in French. He has been a Rockefeller fellow (1990) and has presented at conferences in a number of European and American universities (Saint Antony's College in Oxford, Princeton, New York University, Columbia, UCLA, University of Southern California, Stanford, Harvard, Yale, and Texas University at Austin) and many think tanks and other institutions. He was a Yale Visiting Scholar in 2008 and a Harvard Visiting Scholar in winter 2009. His latest books are *Muslims in Prison: A Comparative Perspective between Great Britain* *and France* (with James Beckford and Danièle Joly, Palgrave, 2005); *Suicide Bombers: The New Martyrs of Allah* (translated from French; University of Michigan Press, 2005); *Quand Al Qaeda Parle: Témoignages derrière les barreaux* (Grasset, 2006); *Inside Jihadism: Understanding Jihadi Movements Worldwide* (Yale Cultural Sociology Series, Paradigm Publishers, 2009); and *Etre jeune dans le pays des ayatollahs* (in cooperation with Amir Nikpey, Robert Laffont Publishers, 2009).

David Lotto is a licensed psychologist, psychoanalyst, and psychohistorian. He received his PhD in clinical psychology from York University in Toronto in 1974. He received a certificate in psychoanalysis from the Westchester Center for the Study of Psychoanalysis and Psychotherapy in 1982. He has been in full-time clinical practice in Pittsfield, Massachusetts, since 1978. He has been an active member of the International Psychohistorical Association for more than twenty years and has been a regular contributor to the *Journal of Psychohistory* and *Clio's Psyche*. He has also published in the *Journal of the American Psychoanalytic Association*, the *American Journal of Psychoanalysis*, and the *Journal of the American Academy of Psychoanalysis*. He has written about war, nuclear war, the Manhattan Project, revenge, sacrifice, fascism, political conservatism, ritual cult abuse, Freud's Irma dream, and Republicans.

Martin E. Marty is the Fairfax M. Cone Distinguished Service Professor Emeritus at the University of Chicago, where he taught from 1963 to 1998. The American Academy of Arts and Sciences appointed him to direct a six-year, five-volume *Fundamentalism Project*, which he did, with R. Scott Appleby as associate. He has written more than fifty books, most of them dealing with the history of religion in America, but in retirement he has shifted focus to study interreligious issues and the relation of religion to violence and the search for peace. He was awarded the Medal of the American Academy, the National Humanities Medal, and other honors, including the National Book Award.

John R. McLane received his bachelor's degree from Harvard College in 1957 and his doctorate in South Asian history from the School of Oriental and African Studies, University of London, in 1961. He spent his professional career at Northwestern University, where he is currently Professor of History Emeritus and associate dean for faculty affairs in the Weinberg College of Arts and Sciences. He edited *The Political Awakening in India* (Prentice-Hall, 1970) and wrote *Indian Nationalism and the Early Congress* (Princeton University Press, 1977) and *Land and Local Kingship in Eighteenth-Century Bengal* (Cambridge University Press, 1993). He is now studying the rise of the Hindutva or Hindu-ness movement that promotes Hindu nationalism.

Bettina Muenster has worked as a research assistant for Scott Atran and Charles B. Strozier on various studies relating to terrorism. In June 2006 she graduated from John Jay College with a BA/MA in forensic psychology and a master's certificate in terrorism studies. She is a lifetime member of Psi Chi and Phi Eta Sigma National Honor Societies and has won numerous scholarships and awards, including the Women's Forum Scholarship in 2003, the University Student Senate Scholarship in 2003, and the Thurgood Marshall Scholarship in 2003. During her undergraduate career her paper "State-Sanctioned Killing" was published in the annual *John Jay's Finest* edition of 2002. Upon graduation in 2006 she won the Arthur and Elaine Niederhoffer Undergraduate Prize for her thesis "Humiliation, Shame and Aggression: The Role of Humiliation and Shame in the Genesis and Perpetuation of Politically Motivated Violence."

Lee Quinby is the inaugural visiting professor at the Macaulay Honors College of the City University of New York. She was the distinguished chair on the millennium at the Rochester Institute of Technology, the Harter chair at Hobart and William Smith Colleges, and most recently the Zicklin chair in the Honors Academy at Brooklyn College. She specializes in the study of apocalyptic and millennial belief in American society. The author of three books, *Millennial Seduction* (Cornell University Press, 1999), *Anti-Apocalypse* (University of Minnesota Press, 1994), and *Freedom, Foucault, and the Subject of America* (Northeastern University Press, 1991), she is also the editor of *Genealogy and Literature* (University of Minnesota Press, 1995) and the coeditor of *Feminism and Foucault* (Northeastern University Press, 1988) and *Gender and Apocalyptic Desire* (Equinox Publishing, 2006). Her essays have been published in *American Historical Review*, *Constellations*, *ESQ*, and *Signs*, and she was the guest editor of the *Women's Studies Quarterly* special issue *Women Confronting the New Technologies* (2001).

David Redles received his PhD in history from Pennsylvania State University and is currently associate professor of history at Cuyahoga Community College in Cleveland. He is the author of *Hitler's Millennial Reich: Apocalyptic Belief and the Search for Salvation* (New York University Press, 2005, paperback 2008). He also contributed "The Millennial Reich as Induced Apocalypse" to *War in Heaven / Heaven on Earth: Theories of the Apocalyptic*, edited by Glen McGhee and Stephen O'Leary (Equinox, 2005); "Nazi End Times: The Third Reich as Millennial Reich" to *End of Days: Essays on the Apocalypse from Antiquity to Modernity*, edited by Karolyn Kinane and Michael A. Ryan (McFarland, 2009); and "National Socialism" to *The Oxford Handbook of Millennialism*, edited by Catherine Wessinger (Oxford University Press, forthcoming).

Charles B. Strozier was educated at Harvard (BA) and the University of Chicago (MA, PhD), was a research candidate at the Chicago Institute for Psychoanalysis in the 1970s, and finished his clinical training at the Training and Research Institute for Self Psychology (TRISP) in New York City in 1992. He is currently a professor of history and the director of the Center on Terrorism at John Jay College, CUNY, and a practicing psychoanalyst in the city. He has published scores of articles and book chapters on aspects of history, psychoanalysis, religion, and violence and has written or edited nine books, including *Lincoln's Quest for Union* (Basic Books, 1982; revised edition, Paul Dry Books, 2001); *Apocalypse: On the Psychology of Fundamentalism in America* (Beacon Books, 1994; revised edition Wipf & Stock, 2002); and *Heinz Kohut: The Making of a Psychoanalyst* (Farrar, Straus & Giroux, 2001; revised edition 2004, nominated for a Pulitzer Prize). His forthcoming book, based on in-depth interviews with survivors and witnesses of September 11, is titled *New York City and 9/11: A Psychological Study of the World Trade Center Disaster.*

David M. Terman is the director of the Chicago Institute for Psychoanalysis, where he has been a training and supervising analyst for the past thirty years. Dr. Terman had his undergraduate and medical education at the University of Chicago and his psychoanalytic training at the Chicago Institute for Psychoanalysis. He is one of the analysts who helped develop the work of Heinz Kohut and what has become known as self psychology. He has contributed to several central aspects of clinical and developmental theory. He reconceptualized the Oedipus complex in self psychological terms, and he was one of the first to note the importance of positive experience in forming psychological structure in development. He has also explored the history of anti-Semitism from a self psychological perspective. His current work on the psychology of fundamentalism and other political and social forces has grown out of a reconceptualization of the nature of paranoia.

Foreword

The Settings of Mindsets

Martin E. Marty

Eugen Rosenstock-Huessy gave authors and editors sound guidance when he contended that one book is about one thing; at least the good ones are. On his terms, and numerous others, this strikes me as a good book. It is clearly about one thing, the mindset of fundamentalists, especially those of militant and malevolent sorts. There are other kinds, of course, as the authors in this book all know and show. The friendly neighborhood fundamentalist at the checkout counter, in the airport line, or studying the Gospel of Luke at a nearby Bible church would be upset to be thought of as malevolent or militant, though she might grit her teeth in anger and be tempted to take a swing at you for making even a mild comment about her choice of church friends, pastors, holy book, and way of life. She may admire the National Rifle Association and its love of guns, but blandishes none herself. She may consider a bomber of an abortion clinic to be consistent and more admirable than are obstetricians who perform abortions, but would shudder if asked to be part of a bombing conspiracy. On many terms she is quite different from most of the subjects in this book.

Students of fundamentalist mindsets, like our authors, might say "Not so fast!" to anyone who, reading that paragraph, would be ready to sever all conceptual connections between the milder neighbor and the member of a fundamentalist sect in open war with others. Subjecting those milder examples to careful examination can reveal aspects of the mindset that will not hold still for close-up study when missiles fly between Shi'ite and Sunni Muslim militants or when Muslims and Hindus in India engage in wars that are more than tribal. In medical laboratories scientists examine bacteria and viruses that cause a single individual to be in the hospital for treatment in order to understand the kinds of viruses and toxins that can kill millions in a plague. It is possible to speak of syndromes, spectra, or scales along which one can find all kinds of fundamentalists without suggesting that all those "others" are all alike.

So, back to Rosenstock-Huessy: this book is about that one thing, the mindset. Yet the philosopher knew that "one thing" did not mean that an author had to be obsessive, repetitive, or minimalist. I pull his *Out of Revolution: Autobiography of Western Man* off the shelf and find myself holding a 795-page book that includes forty-four columns of index, where "shirts, brown, black, etc." nestle, thanks to alphabetical neatness, next to "shop keeper," "Siberia," and all the other *s*'s. Look up the index references within the book, however, and you will find that they elaborate on the single theme of "revolution." The same is true of this book, whose authors range widely, as they should, the fundamentalist mindset being complex, its reaches into the brain and out to the world being protean.

The initial illustration of the amplitude and scope of the book is evident in the first paragraph, where Charles B. Strozier and Katharine Boyd set forth a clear thesis which I will reproduce here:

> The fundamentalist mindset, wherever it occurs, is composed of distinct characteristics, including dualistic thinking; paranoia and range in a group context; an apocalyptic orientation that incorporates distinct perspectives on time, death, and violence; a relationship to charismatic leadership; and a totalized conversion experience.

There you have it. Those five lines provide direction for all the contributors and can serve as an outline for follow-ups, as in college classes or discussion groups. As a lead-in and sample, I'll travel with the reader through the first seven chapters. Commenting thus along the way will be one way for me to point to features of what I regard to be an excellent book without writing bumper-sticker-length blurbs.

The coeditors immediately address the first theme in their definitional thesis, namely, dualism. Those who view fundamentalism only from the distance of headline references may not begin by thinking about the concept of dualism, so they will be informed or will have their thinking refreshed by the opening chapter. The authors are not conceptually provincial or sectarian, as if needing to protect their own choice of key terms. Thus in this first case they generously bring up other helpful references, such as Manichaeanism and binary opposition, which have their place elsewhere but do not capture the nuances to be noted in this book. A few paragraphs later one will have been introduced to condensed versions of a variety of definitions that will get elaborated in later chapters: paranoia, apocalypse, the charismatic, and all the rest.

Advertising this list of mindset subtopics, the contributors have to follow through, and do, beginning with an essay by David Terman, who shows how dualistic thinking relates to group psychology and how it can issue in paranoia and rage. Here we are on familiar soil, even when observing less than lethal forms of fundamentalism. An array of television evangelists may be seen addressing tidy middle-class audiences whose members seem to "have it made" in relative suburban comfort. Yet the evangelists invoke bogeys, from the secular humanists to the armies before Armageddon, and they do so with a fervor that shows them reflecting or stimulating paranoia. During political campaigns right-wing talk-show callers regularly demonize "the other" and spit and spout rage in efforts to quicken rage in others. To note that is not to defame them or distort their intentions; they advertise that such demonizing is what they are doing and claim that they are serving God, country, and citizens by dividing the world as they do.

By mentioning the right wing, by the way, I do not mean to suggest that all fundamentalisms are on the right. Some versions of liberation theologies were articulated and stimulated by leaders on the left who let paranoia take over and who then themselves take over the ranks of the ragers. Dr. Terman draws on psychoanalysis to connect individuals and groups, confirming the observation that threats to the group's "history, values, and goals" easily get fired and fused into actions that are self-protectively lethal.

Fundamentalist mindsets may be evident in expressions such as Buddhism or Eastern philosophies held by groups that are "fundamentalist-like," but they come naturally to many adherents to faiths such as Judaism, Christianity, and Islam. This is the case because these prophetic faiths are based on scriptural revelations involving God and humans and they form movements that look toward a future and an end, be it paradise, heaven, sheol, or "new heavens and a new earth." Time matters greatly to them, and the movement of time, as experienced in a group context, inspires urgency and a sense of mission among the members. They are ready to suffer in many ways and to experience setbacks along the way because the final outcome of history is assured in their favor and will work against the varied "others."

We recognize this apocalyptic stress as a corollary or outcome of dualistic thinking. In many cultures, including North American, this apocalyptic note can be muted, as in paranoiac mutterings, or noisy, as in sputterings of the enraged. Observing the hold of apocalypse on so many can be confusing to experts in psychology, and certainly to the rest of us. How, one asks, can wealthy Texans who enjoy country club life ship themselves off on Sunday to hear the threats preachers make against everyone else as Christ is to come again, coupled with the promises to us, who are saved in Christ? Yet fear of being "left behind," as a book series and films have it, or the promise of being lifted to a new realm with a returned Christ accompanies such apocalyptic thinking. The grand version appears on a different scale and with a different choice of weapons among overtly militant groups, as they are observed regularly in Islamic fundamentalisms in our time. Editors Strozier and Boyd return to discuss how, as groups need a narrative, the apocalyptic serves to fulfill the need: "The apocalyptic provides fertile soil for the violent potentials in the fundamentalist mindset."

They also link with author James W. Jones as they introduce another term, *totalism,* which they see as a key element in or outcome of fundamentalist conversions. One can read, and many of us have read, conversion stories that reach back to the Torah, the New Testament, the Qur'an, and all the stops along the way. Some are accounts that feature a blinding moment of truth that leads the convert into battle for God. But just as many are more gradual, tentative, and exploratory, and they also lead to drastic new interpretations of life. Such an experience is satisfying to the convert, who becomes ready to witness to the benefits of conversion but who would not think of taking up the sword to induce conversions. The fundamentalists as described in chapter 3 do not always take up the sword either, but they are ready to do so because their conversion is "totalistic" in character, and it has to lead to outlets and action.

Of course some leader has to take up old texts, foster aggressive impulses, and use them for renewal, rebirth, and commitment. Theoretically this can all be done quietly, as when a scholarly inquirer in the library gains a spiritual insight. Normally, however, and almost always when a group is involved, there has to be a charismatic leader. The authors of chapter 4 suggest that research on this subject is only beginning, that more has to be learned about the transactions that go with charismatic leaders and groups who come to share their vision of history and personal destiny.

A fresh and even dramatic feature of *The Fundamentalist Mindset* is the concentration in part II, "Motivations for Violence." Many fundamentalists manifest a potential for individuals and groups to turn violent. In such cases the "other" is perceived as a threat to "our" existence and purpose, so we are called to thwart them. Such thwarting can come electorally in republics or commercially in societies where the fundamentalists can afford television, radio, print, and electronic media. Thus censoring of voices uncongenial to fundamentalists may not look like violence, but it does violence to freedoms. In other-than-republics or when faith in the republican process has broken down, fundamentalists can be led to engage in violence. The reasoning or resolve then is "I must blunt, harm, or kill to end the threat of the other."

In chapter 5 David Terman reappears to turn attention to what has to be a central concern in any book that deals with a mindset, namely, *mind.* He is interested in the extreme versions of fundamentalism, in the form of the "paranoid gestalt." One reads magazine features with headlines such as "Inside the Mind of a Suicide Bomber" only to experience frustration that results from the inability to get inside such a mind. What begins as a very technical essay in phenomenology takes on graphic life when Dr. Terman focuses on, for example, the horrors of anti-Jewish paranoia in Christian and finally in Nazi history as well as in case studies such as those in the book *What's the Matter with Kansas.*

Strozier follows up with a far-reaching essay on the general characteristics of the psychology of fundamentalism as it relates to violence. It was his expertise in this field that first drew my associate R. Scott Appleby and me to him as we embarked on a synoptic study of fundamentalisms. His reference to his own clinical practice adds a personal touch to his scholarly summaries. Theological treatments of suffering, hope, and more make their way into this psychological study in ways that should inspire other such explorations. For those who are ready to lie awake at night, his closing lines should stir restlessness or nightmares, as he pictures how "in a world of rising and often raging fundamentalisms there emerges a dangerous potential nexus of paranoia and strong faith that embraces nuclear weapons." One wishes that the U.S. Department of Defense leadership had had this kind of chapter available before the invasion of Iraq: "We can guard against [the dangers just mentioned] only by first becoming acutely aware of their dynamics."

Bettina Muenster and David Lotto elaborate on the power of humiliation to spark violence in the fundamentalist mindset and conclude with a provocative reflection on the United States.

In our time jihadi violence receives the most press, but it is by no means confined to the extremist Islamic factions and factors to which Farhad Khosrokhavar brings informed comment.

In an earlier draft of this foreword I got so carried away by what I read and the reflections such reading prompted that I went on too long. Now I have been cautioned to be more restrained, hard as it is for a historian to skip the historical studies in part IV, for an Americanist to resist commenting on part III, "Christian and American Contexts," and for an amateur theoretician to keep to myself any comment on theories and concepts. Providing such comment would be satisfying to me, but should be unnecessary for readers. My interests were born of the Appleby-Marty project that occupied so much of my attention for so many years.[1] Though I have moved on to other studies, I have to say that this book not only refreshed my memory about what we knew then, but it also offers information enriched by expertise in psychology, and does so in ways that some of my colleagues and I were unable to do a dozen and more years ago. Note that the references in this book show both how expert the contributors are and also how rich are the fields for readers of all sorts to explore.

The Fundamentalist Mindset

Introduction

Charles B. Strozier and David Terman

Before 9/11 one could be merely startled by the rise of fundamentalism in what seemed a secular world. It has been widely noted that as many as 30 percent of all Americans, or well over a hundred million people, are some form of evangelical Christian whose boundaries often blur with what, more strictly speaking, might be called fundamentalists. Garry Wills some years ago noted that it was careless of scholars to keep losing track of so many people.[1] Nor is fundamentalism a purely Christian phenomenon. There are "furiously religious" people here and abroad in many faiths; one might even talk of a "global epidemic" of fundamentalism.[2] *The Fundamentalism Project* that began in the late 1980s and was led by Martin Marty was the first major scholarly response to what was generally perceived in academic circles to be the astonishing rise of fundamentalism in America and the world.[3] Marty and his colleagues wisely spoke of "family resemblances" between seemingly different fundamentalisms in their comparative global study and carefully distinguished the object of their concern from orthodoxy. They took pains to describe the positive ways strong belief can bring meaning into people's lives, while at the same time capturing some of the more malevolent influences of fundamentalism on all world religions. We are now more keenly aware of these malevolent influences, and this book attempts to focus especially on the relationship of fundamentalism to violence.

It is our premise that there is a psychology of fundamentalism, a mindset that transcends its particularity in contemporary religious movements. Islamists, for example, have fueled the global jihad of Al Qaeda; evangelicals have pushed Christianity to the right in this country; and the settlers in Israel have evoked a new millennialism about Jewish land not seen in centuries. Such religious fundamentalist movements can be quite noisy and seem to define the phenomenon. But the mindset of fundamentalism is something more deeply ingrained in the self that finds expression in a variety of human institutions, including religion but by no means restricted to it, and has a history that gives it protean meanings over many centuries. Norman Cohn has described cultic groups at the fringes of society in the Middle Ages. The Terror of the French Revolution realized the paranoid and destructive potentials of a revolution that expanded human freedom. Nazism was undoubtedly the most important fundamentalist, millennial movement in the twentieth century, if not in human history. The individual and the collective, that is, psychology and history, work synergistically to create, diminish, aggravate, and heal the many forms of fundamentalism in religion, politics, and culture.

As scholarly observers examining fundamentalism from a clinical and psychological point of view, we recognize that in our focus on the violent potentials in all forms of fundamentalism it is necessary never to fall into our own false and rigid dichotomies. We studiously seek to avoid using our analytic categories as sticks with which to beat those with whose beliefs and politics we disagree. Much of the rich sociological and religious data in Martin Marty's five volumes of *The Fundamentalism Project* describe people whose lives have been saved and enriched by their experience of deep immersion in reborn faith.[4] New religious movements, often derided as cults, can provide meaningful communities of support for troubled souls who are thus kept out of hospitals and off debilitating medicines.

One of the interesting aspects of the essays in this volume is the diverse ways the authors approach their subject. Some rely on clinical psychoanalytic data as their point of entry to the problem of fundamentalism. Several have actually been in the field interviewing fundamentalists in a variety of contexts. Many rely on some form of lived experience. Some focus on historical texts. Others value the interview. It is an open question which approach should be privileged in this field of inquiry, though one has to suspect that it is the very diversity of method as represented in this book that creates part of the excitement in the inquiry.

One issue of method is more general, however, and needs to be noted carefully. In this kind of analysis one inevitably generalizes from insights derived from individual psychology to that of the collective. Those of us in this field would lose important insights if we did not boldly reach out from what we learn in individual psychology to more general concerns. But we must avoid being simplistic or mindlessly reductionistic. The challenge is to speak about the general mostly using data from the individual, while always keeping in mind the necessity for subtlety and nuance in such conceptual explorations.

Marty's *Fundamentalism Project* clarifies many important aspects of the phenomenon as it has taken shape in contemporary religious movements. He (and his many colleagues) clarify that fundamentalism is sharply different from orthodoxy (e.g., the Amish). The orthodox seek to preserve;

fundamentalists seek to change. Fundamentalism challenges the landscape of secularism. It is a phenomenon strongly threatened by and in response to the modern. Fundamentalists' primary impulse is to take back what they often see as an idealized past. In that process they conceive of the struggle as an ultimate one. There is nothing trivial about their encounter with the modern secular world; it is a titanic struggle for all true believers. In that process, however, they search in decidedly idiosyncratic ways for ideas to ground their reimagining of faith in what can only be called a process of "selective retrieval."

This book supports and builds on these (and other) findings of *The Fundamentalism Project*. But in several important areas we go beyond that earlier work.

- First, we stress the centrality of the psychological tendency toward dualism and paranoia so central to the fundamentalist mindset. To understand the Manichaeanism of the mindset is to enter the inner experience of belief and to grasp in new ways the central importance of fundamentalists' anxious vigilance that often verges on actual paranoia.
- Second, our work emphasizes the apocalyptic character of all fundamentalists who live for the end of the world and their own redemption in a reborn one. They embrace, in this sense, a survivor mission. Their apocalyptic narrative defines their story.
- Third, this book places a great deal of emphasis on the intimate relation between fundamentalism and violence. There are other dimensions of the fundamentalist experience in the world that are worth studying. Our approach makes violence and violent potentials in all fundamentalisms our central concern. The one word never mentioned in all of the five volumes of *The Fundamentalism Project* is *terrorism*.[5]

This emphasis on violence and terrorism deserves further explanation. There is no question that fundamentalism is psychologically complex. There is no obvious or direct link between its varied forms and violence. The yeshivas in Israel produce the Haredi, but the settler movement has different roots altogether. Hamas is much more religiously fundamentalist than the PLO but is also very political, with secular, authoritarian themes. The madrassas in Pakistan produced the Taliban, who took over Afghanistan but have nothing directly to do with Osama bin Laden and Al Qaeda. And closer to home, the readers of the *Left Behind* series are often products of hermetically sealed Christian schools or home schooling but are not the same as those who kill doctors who perform abortions.

This book is systematically and unabashedly psychological in its approach to the problem of fundamentalism. The language, indeed the discourse is within a definite frame of reference. The problematic issue is that of violence. We argue that there is a potential for violence that is at the core of the fundamentalist mindset. At the same time we seek assiduously to avoid pathologizing the many scores of millions of believers in faiths large and small around the world who consider themselves strong in their beliefs and derive much meaning from their religious commitments. We use the construct *fundamentalist mindset* as a neutral descriptor. Labeling can be corrosive. The very term *fundamentalism*, given its vague definition, can be used to denigrate those believers other than oneself who follow a spiritual path alien to one's experience. Many people around the world with strong religious faiths find salvation in the path they have chosen, personal meaning from their specific commitments, and solace from the valley of tears in which they wandered before being reborn in their new faith. Respect for difference is a necessity for anyone who dares to study the world of fundamentalists.

There are also aspects of the fundamentalist mindset that can be highly positive psychologically in the experience of those with strong religious beliefs. What we call *dualistic thinking*, for example, is often subjectively experienced by a believer as merely a sharp marker of the boundary between his or her faith and a corrupt world filled with sin and violence. A trip to your local multiplex movie theater is enough to make you empathize with the passionate disdain of fundamentalists for the pornography of contemporary life. Consider as well the experience of being reborn in faith—whether its literalized form among Christians or its more symbolic form among Islamists, or Haredi, or Hindus, or many others—as the crucial moment of conversion from an old to a new self that opens up possibilities, both psychological and spiritual. Even when we talk of paranoia in this book one must remember that for many fundamentalists a heightened sense of danger and victimization supplies the necessary passion to resist evil and explore new pathways to redemption. The paranoid merges with the prophetic. Finally we must note that apocalyptic energies fuel much that is hopeful and redemptive in the world. The antislavery movement in the United States was thoroughly grounded in millennial rhetoric and motivations; our "redeemer nation," as Timothy Weber called it, has often employed the apocalyptic to oppress, as with our imperial project, but has equally inspired much creative social change, as with the idealism of the civil rights movement and the Peace Corps. An important psychological dimension of the environmental movement today infuses activism with green apocalyptic energies in ways that draw from the curious comment in the Book of Revelation that "[God] shouldest destroy them who destroy the earth" (11:18).

The way to sort out much of this seeming conceptual confusion lies in understanding the significance of the underlying psychology of those who fall into this loosely defined and very large category of fundamentalists.

Christianity, for example, is by definition teleological and millennial.[6] The millennialism of the faith can be ignored but not denied, and it may be fervently embraced in ways that motivate creative social change. Apocalyptic Christianity, however, death-drenched as it is, welcomes a violent end to human history and relishes visions of sinners swimming in the lake of fire.[7] Most Islamists, to take another example, find peace and comfort in the safe, if secluded, world of family and mosques. Jihadis, on the other hand, radically twist the words of the Qur'an and grasp aspects of the hadith tradition to make Islam serve their wildly apocalyptic and paranoid world of violence. The paranoid and the apocalyptic, it can be said, in general motivate the fundamentalist mindset, opening it to the possibility of violence. That underlying psychology is quite different, it seems, from the psychology of those believers who are more empathic, grounded, hopeful, and drawn to loving their neighbor as themselves, even when they embrace millennial and utopian dreams.

We are mostly concerned with extremists and fanatics, just as the historical events we describe are those of crises, from the French Revolution to Nazi Germany to post-Partition India. These historical events have often been described as totalitarian. Our goal is to delineate the contours of the psychology of such fundamentalists in ways that allow for conceptualizing their potential for violence. A quite different psychology motivates millennialists seeking to end slavery in America or save a choking planet, just as utopian dreamers such as Martin Luther King make for good neighbors and the intense desire for the coming, or return, of the Messiah can enrich the life of an individual and a community. Our focus on the paranoid and the apocalyptic should not obscure our respect for the utopian and the hopeful.

The fundamentalist mindset is also not restricted to religion. One can easily find atheistic psychologists and secular bricklayers who fit our ideas about the fundamentalist mindset. In fact some chapters in this book explore realms far removed from religion, such as the French Revolution and the Nazis. But it happens that religion is the human institution assigned the task of providing answers to the ineffable questions of beginnings and endings, both of which fall well outside of social science. Religion attracts humans with an inclination for pondering ultimate questions; some are extremists. To explore the fundamentalists' mindset is therefore inevitably to study mass religious movements, including contemporary Islamists, Christian fundamentalists, and Hindu nationalists, among many such examples. But our goal is to name the contours of a fundamentalist mindset that transcends the particular and the religious. That project, we argue, is the beginning of an attempt to understand the deeper meanings of the violence that haunts our lives.

Part I

WHAT IS THE FUNDAMENTALIST MINDSET?

1

Definitions and Dualisms

Charles B. Strozier and Katharine Boyd

For the most part observers of fundamentalism skirt absolute definitions. The word was coined by Curtis Lee Laws in 1920 in relation to developments in Christianity in the second decade of the twentieth century.[1] Many feel it is absurd to extend something so specifically Christian to analogous developments in other faith traditions. In *The Fundamentalism Project* Marty and his colleagues try to solve this issue by talking in their massive study of "family resemblances" between movements in often strikingly different traditions. Their approach is comparative and phenomenological; they believe there is something important happening in the world that sharply differentiates such movements from traditionalism, conservatism, and orthodoxy.[2] But it is dangerous to be more concrete. Given its protean and elusive nature, a simple definition of fundamentalism risks being simple-minded. The movement of those we call fundamentalist is too new historically for there to be a clear and agreed-upon definition. In fact we argue in this book for the benefits of ambiguity, which makes for a larger conceptual umbrella. Fundamentalism is clearest in context. There are a variety of behaviors, attitudes, beliefs, rituals, and so on that fit underneath that umbrella. It is our contention, however, that the underlying psychology of fundamentalism is what unites these varied manifestations of the phenomenon. Defining that psychology is the task of this book.

The fundamentalist mindset, wherever it occurs, is composed of distinct characteristics, including dualistic thinking; paranoia and rage in a group context; an apocalyptic orientation that incorporates distinct perspectives on time, death, and violence; a relationship to charismatic leadership; and a totalized conversion experience. It is useful for heuristic purposes to make these distinctions, and yet one must be aware of the enormous overlap between these categories. Dualistic thinking, for example, can be apocalyptic; paranoia determines the way others are constructed in general; and the apocalyptic narrative overlaps other characteristics of the fundamentalist mindset. One also returns frequently in the literature to psychological themes of shame and humiliation, to the need for simplified meanings, and most of all for the absolutist and totalized way things get structured in the fundamentalist mindset. It has often been difficult to know what not to include in this discussion. Some of the literature on shame and humiliation, for example, is only tangentially relevant for our purposes, though we are keenly aware that such issues are vital for understanding the fundamentalist mindset. In this and other areas we have sought a balance between comprehension and excess.

Our concern in this book, however, is with the more malevolent expressions of the fundamentalist mindset that is prone to violence. We must first discuss how writers have conceptualized these characteristics in an effort to generate a comprehensive theoretical framework regarding the psychological understanding of the fundamentalist mindset. The theology, or ideology, ultimately depends on the underlying psychology. Dualistic thinking is grounded in a rigid psychology that denies the possibility of error. The psychology behind utopianism is more hopeful and is grounded in a human future. In comparison, the paranoid gestalt often works with the apocalyptic. Violence pervades such a mindset. In the next section we describe the contending constructs used by different authors to describe the facets of the fundamentalist mindset, which enables us to analyze comprehensively the psychological spectrum of related ideas.

CONTENDING CONSTRUCTS

People who write about the fundamentalist mindset use a variety of closely related terms. Many writers use the phrase *dualistic thinking* to depict the conflicted or opposing nature inherent in absolutist ideology. Michael Barkun uses the term *Manichaeanism* to describe the "tendency to view the world as a battleground between pure good and pure evil."[3] Similarly *binary oppositions* reflects the conflict between two ideas. Stanley Schneider uses the term *paranoia* to describe how the fundamentalist mindset interprets opposing points of view as a threat.[4] Eric Hoffer uses the term *suspicion* to describe the "pathological mistrust" that contributes to conformity within a mass movement.[5]

Robert Jay Lifton talks about the *end times* to mean the end of the world by undefined means, though he is mostly concerned with nuclear annihilation.[6] When using an adjective to describe apocalyptic group formations, Norman Cohn and Bryan Wilson use the term *millenarian*; Richard Landes and Wilson use the term *millennialism*; and some, including David L. Miller and even Richard Landes in another context, use the term *chiliasm* to emphasize the thousand-year cycles so often mentioned by apocalyptic groups. Bernard McGinn distinguishes the term *apocalypticism* as a more radical form of *eschatology*, which is the theology of last things.[7] *Utopianism* describes an ideal community and is often associated with millennialism as well as political ideologies.[8] More psychologically one should note that because we all die everyone reflects at some point on individual and collective endings, but *endism*, or the location of self in some future, ultimate narrative pushes such reflection into a profoundly different realm, wrapping the future in magical projections that isolate it from meaningful, human connection with the past.[9]

Many writers use the term *charismatic* to describe the appealing personality style of fundamentalist group leaders. Lifton uses the term *guru* to describe the more malevolent side of charismatic leadership. His favorite example of what he calls "attack guruism" is Shoko Asahara, the leader of the Japanese cult Aum Shinrikyo, which sought to bring about Armageddon through the use of ultimate weapons.[10] Many authors use the term *conversion* to address a change in religious belief or orientation. Similarly authors writing about Christian fundamentalism often use the phrase *born again*, which stresses the disconnect between one's former life and a new religious identity.[11] In comparison *radicalization* describes a fanatical change in self for multiple fundamentalist venues, both religious and political.

Authors contributing to this volume recognize this diversity of language but for the most part settle on key terms. For instance, we refer to *dualistic thinking* because it suggests the psychological conflict embedded in such cognitive orientation. Similarly *paranoia* suggests the malevolence in the fundamentalist mindset better than mere *suspicion* and incorporates the psychological dimension that may be a way of organizing the world. The *apocalyptic* connotes the end of the world (unlike *utopianism*) and applies generally across faiths as well as in the secular world. Additionally the apocalyptic represents a psychological orientation that is more profound than, though often encompassing, eschatological theology. We prefer the phrase *charismatic leader* as it applies more generally and suggests the relationship between leader and followers. *Conversion* applies to those changing faiths, and we also use it to describe those changing in degree of faith. *Radicalization* may incorrectly suggest that violence is inherently associated with the fundamentalist mindset rather than a potentiality.

We now turn our attention to explore the psychological characteristics of the fundamentalist mindset described by these terms. First we explore the relationship between the dualistic cognitive orientation and the potential for violence.

DUALISTIC THINKING

Authors who write about fundamentalism often treat dualistic thinking as a primary characteristic of the mindset. One might even say that for some the centrality of binary oppositions defines the fundamentalist mindset.[12] Robert M. Young, for example, argues that psychological anxiety due to perceived threat or uncertainty results in a tendency to simplify: "To simplify in psychoanalytic terms is to regress, to eliminate the middle ground, to split, dividing the world into safe and threat, good and evil, life and death." Dualistic thinking causes one to "see others in very partial terms—as part-objects," such that fundamentalists "lose the ability to imagine the inner world and humanity of others."[13] These dualistic categories force the experience of others into group structures. Such thinking provides a moral framework that differentiates good from bad, and then totalizes the difference. The "totalistic moral thinking" associated with these groups appeals to some people, particularly among young individuals who display weak identity formation.[14] Such strong conviction is more easily generated when the message promoted resonates with people's preexisting beliefs and stigmas regarding the other. Eric Hoffer suggests that for a doctrine to be effective in generating and maintaining a mass movement, the belief in the certainty and truth of the doctrine is more important than its actual meaning. A true believer is not baffled, frightened, or discouraged by obstacles; his faith makes him secure. In fact the greater the obstacles, the more secure his faith becomes.[15]

Dualistic thinking is inherently related to paranoia and the apocalyptic. Paranoia is a specific cognitive orientation that stimulates dualistic thinking. The apocalyptic serves to organize such thinking. Dualistic thinking becomes apocalyptic because "locating evil also presumes the possibility of salvation, or an escape from evil."[16] The struggle between the forces of good and evil requires destruction and eventually the end of the world. People who perceive themselves to be joining a righteous cause, thereby opposing the evil other, can then form a fundamentalist group. "Apocalyptic logic" organizes dualistic thinking by establishing an ideology of "redemption and demonization" which ultimately "polarizes camps between a victimized elect and an odious enemy."[17] Chip Berlet stresses that dualistic thinking is not forced upon people but is embraced willingly by those who believe their apocalyptic ideology is the absolute truth.[18] Dick Anthony and Thomas Robbins argue that "moral, eschatological, and cosmic polarities" create the psychological context on which "hinge the millennial destiny of humankind."[19]

Such belief systems limit personal judgment and variation of opinion within groups. By defining those who are not in the group as evil, the fundamentalist mindset reduces, and can eliminate, empathy for the other and ultimately dehumanize the out-group. The oppositional nature of dualistic thinking provides a foundation for the potential of a group or individual to rationalize the use of violence toward "the other."[20] It is the violent potentials in fundamentalist thinking that is at times actualized that is so often overlooked or minimized by most scholarly observers.

2

Theories of Group Psychology, Paranoia, and Rage

David M. Terman

This volume is concerned with understanding the psychology of the fundamentalist mindset, and most of this psychology is derived from the theories of psychoanalysis. Psychoanalysis does not speak with one voice, however, and, as in any scientific endeavor, many of the concepts have changed since Freud first formulated his pathbreaking insights into the human mind. A brief and necessarily incomplete review of the history of the central concepts I use in this book follows; they are (1) concepts of the group, (2) the nature of paranoia, (3) the understanding of rage, and (4) the relationship between religion and violence. But first a cautionary tale.

Eric Marcus, among many others, has cautioned against applying to groups ideas derived from the psychoanalytic study of individuals. He holds that it is particularly hazardous to apply psychoanalytic metapsychological theories that have been developed in the study and observation of individuals to the understanding of groups. The group does not have a psychological structure, nor does it have some kind of instinctual nature.[1] The group is not the individual writ large. Kurt Lewin has noted that "the organization of the group is not the same as the organization of the individuals of which it is composed," nor are the goals of the group the same as the goals of the individual.[2]

The problems of method in the psychological study of groups are profound. For example, groups are able to act with great violence. I customarily speak of the anger or rage of the group, but it must be understood that such terms are metaphors. Organized social or political groups may do horrendous deeds, but it would not be accurate to say that (for the most part) the individuals who do the violence are animated by a lived rage. Rather, they are acting in accordance with a complex structure of group ideals and norms. War, terrorism, and genocide can only be group activities that are executed with a great sense of righteousness and often excitement but not rage or even anger as it is thought of in individual psychology. Nonetheless groups seem to react with a kind of collective rage to actual or perceived injuries to the group self.[3] It would appear that such sense of injury leads to what I describe as a paranoid organization of the group, which also *appears* to function, in part, as an expression of such rage, but this is a matter of considerable complexity that I think merits much further exploration.[4]

Indeed *all* affect states in an organized social or political group require careful consideration and qualification. Hence the same caution and distinction between individuals and groups should be observed in the understanding of shame and humiliation. These affects or states arise in reaction to the damage to the individual's or group's self-esteem. I usually speak of shame in relation to the individual. When trying to conceptualize analogous affects in groups, some have argued that it is more meaningful to speak of humiliation.

Though the individual and the group are not synonymous, each profoundly affects the other. For example, deeply held aspects of the individual self are invested in the group self, and it is evident that intense affects are generated in the individual when the group is perceived as threatened with extinction or humiliation. At the same time one must not conflate individual pathology with group processes. In an extensive recent review of theories of the psychology of terrorism, Jeff Victoroff is quite critical of various psychoanalytic formulations that explain individual psychology as a cause of terrorism.[5] Childhood antecedents are difficult to prove, he asserts, and there is no evidence that particular pathologies "explain" the acts. Attributing the group mindset or the acts that grow out of it to individual psychopathology is mistaken. Still, there is something to be gained conceptually in extrapolating themes of individual psychology for understanding the dynamics of group behavior, if done cautiously and in a nuanced way.

THEORIES OF GROUP PSYCHOLOGY

The history of psychoanalytic thinking about groups begins with Freud's first speculations about its nature in 1921.[6] He hypothesized that groups are bound together when the members have replaced their own ego ideal with the person of the leader. This process allows members to identify with each other, and that creates a common bond, an important element in the formation of the group. The identification with the leader also releases members from the strictures of their own conscience (not yet conceptualized as the superego). Freud also theorized that the group feeling—the identification with one another—occurs in reaction-formation to the hostility and envy members would naturally feel toward each other. Further Freud thought that groups regress. Taking Le Bon's descriptions of large groups, Freud held that groups function at a lower intellectual level, are labile and easily swayed, and that they long to be led by a strong leader, a chief. He likened the relationship between a member of the group and the leader to a patient and a hypnotist; just as the patient gives up his own judgment and especially his own moral and ethical standards and limitations and unquestioningly allows the hypnotist to be his guide, so the member of the group may give up his own morals and can be led to do what he would never do as an autonomous person.

English analysts after World War II pursued work with groups and developed extensive theories about the nature of the psychology of groups. Basing their approach on the metapsychology that Melanie Klein was then elaborating, they began working with small, unstructured groups.[7] Wilfred Bion pioneered experiments in which the leader or therapist intervened only to interpret what he or she believed the group as a whole was experiencing.[8] In those groups the leader gave no guidance, and there was no defined task. Under these conditions, Bion postulated, the group becomes organized by three kinds of "basic assumptions" that are counter to rational expectations. These assumptions, he argued, are unconscious organizations that are both regressive from the "work" of the group and are expressions of primitive developmental anxieties and conflicts in the individuals in the group. Bion labeled these assumptions *dependency, fight-flight,* and *pairing.* The dependency group is characterized by the collective fantasy of the leader's ability to provide everything for the group in a magical and omnipotent way. In the fight-flight assumption, the group organizes around the conviction that there is an enemy who must be attacked or avoided; a paranoid leader often rises to lead this type of group. The pairing group hopes that there will be a couple in the group who will solve the group's problems in some sort of messianic way. Bion saw the group as a whole as a collective expression of unconscious individual developmental needs. The type of group organization comes from the conflict between the collective unconscious of the group and the individual's needs. He saw the basic assumptions as based on the individual's primitive and intense emotions that are expressed in shared fantasies of an omnipotent or magical variety that will allow the group to achieve its goals and satisfy its desires. Though Bion did not comment on the significance, he did observe that the fight-flight group often comes into being when the dependency group fails to get the leader to respond to its dependency wishes. One might interpret this sequence as a collective response to the frustration of a group's reasonable wish to understand what their work is and how that can be facilitated by the leader. That is, the very restricted responsiveness of the leader is not at all a neutral experience for the group but can easily be experienced as withholding and hostile. Though Bion inferred that the organization of the group comes from deep, primitive intrapsychic processes, one can alternatively infer that the group's response is reactive to the reality of the group's situation: the members need some sensible direction and become frightened and enraged when none is forthcoming.

Kleinian French analysts developed Bion's ideas further. Didier Anzieu saw the group as the individual writ large. He wrote, "The group psychic apparatus is constructed on those of individual members and a specific socio-cultural environment. . . . The group psychic apparatus tends to be formed around the super-ego, the ego ideal, etc."[9] The group has an unconscious, constructs a fantasy reflecting the unconscious wishes and/or defenses, and even becomes the form of a psychical agency (id, ego, superego). Groups exhibit all the psychological mechanisms one may see in the individual, such as regression, repression, denial, and splitting.

René Kaes, stressing another aspect of group structure, pointed to the importance of ideology as a binding force in groups.[10] He added this idea to Freud's focus on the centrality of the leader. Kaes saw ideology as arising from the unconscious needs of the group's members. It is an *un*conscious organization of the group. For Kaes these unconscious fantasies or ideologies serve both infantile wishes and defenses of every psychosocial developmental phase.

Anzieu and others underlined the distinction between the psychology of small and large groups. Anzieu thought that his theories applied to small groups, those having fewer than eighty members. He labeled groups over three hundred "a crowd" and held that such groups could not be understood with his own explanatory framework. This restriction, of course, limits the applicability of his theories to the understanding of history.[11]

Otto Kernberg, however, is quite explicit about the nature of large group psychology, which he calls "mass psychology." He sees its foundation in the individual's fear of the loss of autonomy and boundaries as a function of being in a large group. From this fear he postulates a regression in the individual to early psychological organizations that are characterized by what he considers the nature of such early life, that is, to "primitive object relations, primitive defensive operations, and primitive aggression with . . . pre-genital features." The result of the individual psychological regressions is a group organization that reflects the individual and is ascribed to the group. The *group* itself may often regress to several kinds of organization. The natural tendency of groups is to regress and evolve into either a "narcissistic-dependent" or a "sadistic-paranoid" configuration. Kernberg sees the development of the group as a whole more or less as a sum of the individual psychological needs. These are "regressed," "primitive," and suffused with "primitive aggression." Following a leader whose own tendency is to regress to narcissistic or paranoid organizations is one way to protect the individual from the aggressions that arise in the group. Kernberg holds that this tendency to organizational regression is inherent in the nature of mass psychology.[12]

It is often difficult to tell in Kernberg's writings whether he is in fact describing the individual in the group or some collective psychological structure. This confusion is compounded by the fact that the conceptions of the group are heavily weighted with an emphasis on the assumed inherent propensity of both individuals and groups to function in accord with presumed anxieties and defenses that Kleinian psychology attributes to the earliest phases of individual development. He does, however, give an account of the dialectic between the members of the group and the group as a whole and/or the leadership. All groups are prone to stimulating transferences in their members that are derived from every stage of psychosexual development. That is, members may feel needful, competitive, or envious or feel the need to idealize the leader. The leader in turn may be stimulated to respond with narcissistic inflation or paranoid fears of the group.[13]

There are a number of difficulties with the formulations of the English and French Kleinians. First, their description of the dynamics of groups is derived from the individual and epitomizes the critique of writers such as Marcus. For example, one might ask, What is the meaning of *regression* as applied to a group? What is the group regressing from? Implied in this notion is a kind of normative maturity. This idea also implies that there is some kind of ideal form of group organization that develops over time, suggesting that groups grow up, like individuals, and have "mature" qualities from which they regress.[14] But such a concept is highly questionable when applied to human groups. A group may have various kinds of organization, and one might judge them by a variety of criteria depending on one's political or moral values. But it seems unlikely that there is an epigenetic sequence in the development of a group, and that makes it difficult to judge a group in terms of its maturity. Maturity judgments are in fact value judgments. Second, the group itself is seen mainly in terms of its postulated inner psychological forces. Though it is reasonable to argue that the psychology of the group is an important determining factor in its perceptions and actions in the world, the almost exclusive focus on these postulated inner forces does not adequately account for the real-world tasks of the group nor the role of events in the external world and their effect and meanings for the group. Third, it is problematic to attribute a structure or quality of an *unconscious* to the group. Where would such an unconscious reside? How would it be maintained? That there are implicit assumptions, myths, and self-perceived attributes of a group can readily be seen and understood, but the concept of a repressed, dynamic unconscious is a misleading idea to apply to a group. A group cannot have a psychological apparatus. Finally, these authors see the psychological characteristics of the group almost entirely as a defense against internal anxieties—both within the individual and attributed to the group as a whole—rather than as an effort to engage and organize the world. In this vein Marcus has pointed out that Bion has described universal group fantasies, but "[Bion and those who follow his theories] related these fantasies to the vicissitudes of group process and to leadership, but without relating this to the adaptations required of natural social groups."[15] Ideologies, for example, while surely and significantly reflecting the groups' psychological organization, also integrate the activities of a social or political group and organize its patterns of action in terms of the future or in accord with a structure of values and beliefs. Ideologies are a part of the group self.[16]

One possible bridging concept between the individual and the group is the "group self" that Heinz Kohut described.[17] Like an individual, the group organizes itself with core ambitions and ideals, and these account for the sense of continuity and cohesion of the group. They determine the nature of its most important actions. Kohut hypothesized that some kind of basic self of a group jells at some point in history, and that self points to the future. One expression of the central constituents of the group's psychology is its ideology, for ideologies may carry both the ambitions and goals of the group and its ideals. These elements give the group its cohesion, strength, and ability to act in the world. Further, these elements can be examined as they relate to the organizing psychological aspects of the group without postulating the kinds of complex drive-defense structures that arise in a single individual in the course of a development that is shaped by a helpless infancy and powerful caretaker; nor do they require the assumption of a group unconscious.

The group self includes collective constructs of its nature that are partially composed of events in the history of the group. These are given meaning both by the real consequences of those events and by the meanings ascribed to them by historians, political leaders, cultural figures, and, in modern times, the popular media (and now by the Internet).[18] These events and their meanings become important parts of the group's self and vital determinants of its self-esteem—its sense of strength, power, and goodness. They might stimulate the formation of certain ideologies or become parts of them. I hold that such structures in the group may and do have important conscious and unconscious meanings for the *individuals* in the group, but I maintain that they are either conscious or *implicit* in the group.[19]

The work of Kernberg, Bion, and the French theorists clearly highlights the importance of ideology in group life and the political phenomena that are the subject of this book. Their work also underlines the phenomenon of the paranoid configuration of both small and large groups. Regarding large groups (masses, in Kernberg's terms), Kernberg writes, "The large group evolves into a dynamic mob characterized by predominantly paranoid features and the selection of paranoid leaders: it is typically represented by the mass psychology of revolutionary movements with totalitarian ideology."[20]

PARANOIA

An understanding of paranoia is essential for comprehending the fundamentalist mindset.[21] Though the term dates back to antiquity, the modern theory of paranoia as a clinical entity was formulated in Germany in 1818 by Johann Christian Heinroth and later by Karl Kahlbaum. It has had a long and interesting history in psychiatry, where its precise meaning and place has been the subject of periodic reevaluation. Voluminous writings in both the psychiatric and psychoanalytic literature have attempted to define and clarify the construct.[22]

The classic psychoanalytic understanding of paranoia is Freud's explanation of the German jurist Daniel Paul Schreber.[23] Schreber had written memoirs of his life that vividly showed his paranoid psychosis.[24] Reading those memoirs, Freud attempted to explain the reasons for Schreber's illness in psychoanalytic terms. The central construct of his formulation was in terms of repressed homosexual desire: I (a man) love him; no, I hate him (for loving him is an intolerable homosexual wish); no, he hates me (for it is also intolerable that I am angry). The central intolerable wish is homosexual; it is reversed into hatred (also unacceptable), and then the hatred is projected.

Melanie Klein, an early and influential psychoanalytic theorist, privileged paranoia as a phase of normal human development. She developed the idea of a "paranoid-schizoid position" that she believed was the earliest phase of infant development.[25] In this phase infants project their own sadism onto the breast (both when they are frustrated and as a necessary discharge of their inborn aggressive drive). The breast is then experienced as sadistic and malevolent. On the other hand, good experiences with gratification are associated with a "good breast," or good object. The good and bad are kept apart in the psyche and in the perception of the object. (This is referred to as the splitting of the self and the object.) Both the perceived sadistic object and the good object are taken back into the psyche. Both are said to be "introjected," and once inside one's mind they become a part of one's own perception of oneself and the world. If the split object is not integrated in a later developmental phase (the "depressive position"), whether because of excessive aggression in the self or inadequate containment by the object, the aggressive and libidinal drives remain split, and aggression may escalate. Klein posited five central ideas about this aggression: (1) the origin of hostility and sadism is internal (derivative of the death instinct); (2) the feelings manifesting this aggression are hostility, rage, and sadism; (3) these feelings are projected onto others; (4) these hostile others are then re-internalized as hostile and severely judgmental aspects of oneself; and (5) they are then reprojected onto the "other," who is then seen as sadistic and judgmental and inspires rage and fear. Klein called this process projective identification. She argued that these mechanisms are all present in the very earliest stage of infancy and, if they are not balanced by sufficient good experience, are the basis for paranoia and schizophrenia later in life.

Freud's idea about the homosexual drive as central in the initiation of paranoia has not survived subsequent scrutiny except as it became redefined, but his and Klein's emphasis on projection, and especially the projection of hostility, has blossomed into one of the defining characteristics of paranoid thinking. (However, Freud's idea of the restitutional function of paranoid delusions has also remained important in many theorists' understanding of the symptoms of paranoia.)[26] The elaboration of theories of paranoia in development has been an important component of the Kleinian understanding of groups. Projection has not, however, been confined to hostility. Many aspects of self have also been deemed to be projected: unacceptable weaknesses, defects in moral character, and severe judgmental attitudes as well as anger and deprecatory attitudes.

Harry Stack Sullivan, lecturing in the mid-1940s, postulated that the most basic issue underlying paranoia is the feeling of inferiority. What is transferred to the other is *blame*: "One is the victim, not of one's own defects, but of a devilish environment."[27] John Frosch later elaborated on the importance of humiliation for the pre-paranoid child at the hands of the same-sex parent.[28] Hence any passivity was equated with humiliation. William W. Meissner tried to combine the ideas of projection as elaborated by the Kleinians with the centrality of weakness as articulated by Sullivan. He added the idea of loss and used a complex set of internal operations to explain paranoia. He postulated a process he called "paranoid construction" in which all perceptions are rigidly screened in relation to threats to or maintenance of self-esteem and the preservation of the self.[29]

Increasingly, contemporary theorists have focused on the issue that Sullivan first pointed to: the relationship between paranoia and self-esteem and humiliation. After an extensive review of the history of psychoanalytic concepts in paranoia, John Oldham and Stanley Bone also found that "self-esteem regulation and fear of humiliation are central issues in paranoid pathology." They noted that "self referential grandiosity is a manifestation of sensitivity to humiliation. Furthermore, this enormous sensitivity to humiliation makes these patients unable to be indifferent to the implications of anything in the world around them."[30]

David Shapiro goes further. He deconstructs the mechanism of projection and even more strongly emphasizes the importance of self-esteem and especially the sense of weakness and humiliation. Likening the paranoid character to the obsessive-compulsive in its rigidity, Shapiro holds, "When one imagines the more severely rigid person . . . who is cut off from and cannot tolerate conscious awareness of weakness or of feelings of inferiority and shame, the picture changes from stubbornness and imperturbability [the obsessive character] to defensive sensitivity."

> Any treatment at the hands of another person that may seem coercive or disrespectful—anything that resembles being "pushed around," a rebuff or other insult or indignity, particularly from a person of superior rank; sometimes the mere presence of figures who are respected, often grudgingly respected—any such circumstance will threaten to remind the grandiose person of his smallness, that is, will humiliate him. Respected figures, superiors, will therefore regularly become objects of prideful, defensive sensitivity and antagonism. I am proposing that a defensive and antagonistic relationship to the external world or, at least, to certain kinds of figures in it, is intrinsic to the severely rigid character and is *independent of and prior to* projection.[31]

Shapiro specifies what that projection is about, and like Sullivan, he points to threats to self-esteem: "In other words, the projective threat will be constructed, not simply out of repudiated impulses and feelings but out of the particular anxieties generated in the rigid person by repudiated impulses and feelings. Altogether, therefore, I reverse the usual understanding: instead of saying that paranoid defensiveness is the product of projection, I say that the projective process is the outcome of the rigid character's defensive mobilization."[32] The character Shapiro describes is rigid out of extreme narcissistic vulnerability. What must be protected are the senses of weakness and inferiority and experiences of humiliation. This construction is consistent with Sullivan's view that blame is projected for the internal sense of weakness. As I show in a later chapter, self psychology offers a theoretical framework that links these elements in group psychology in an understandable structure whose components can be observed.[33]

RAGE

The psychoanalytic understanding of individual rage and aggression begins with Freud's postulation of a death instinct in 1920.[34] For Freud all humankind had to discharge some quantity of this in-born drive. His discussion of the social problems in the regulation of this and the sexual instincts led to his formulation of the inherent conflict between individual happiness and the requirements of civilization.[35] In his exchange with Einstein about the reasons for war, Freud underlined the use of aggression and force to maintain power and dominance, both within and between social and political groups.[36] The chief reason for the group's acquisition of power is to prevent the domination of a single individual. The institution of law is a means of perpetuating the power of the ruling class, and the development of notions of justice serves to rationalize and justify the current distribution of power.

Mid-twentieth-century psychoanalytic writers later identified a particularly problematic variety of aggression. Erich Fromm described what he termed "malignant aggression" or "vengeful destructiveness" as a particularly intense form of aggression. It differs from normal defensive aggression, for it is characterized by a "thirst for vengeance" and is "cruel, lustful, and insatiable." He observed that cruelty stimulates the desire for such vengeance.[37] Anthony Storr also associated such cruelty and the wish for vengeance with the experience of helplessness against a superior force. Attributing the experience of such humiliating tormentors to paranoid projection, Storr captured the psychological state of such individuals in the grip of feeling persecuted by powerful, malignant others when he wrote, "No torment is too extreme for those who have tormented one; no humiliation is too great for those who have exploited one's own impotent helplessness." Like Fromm he linked cruelty and the desire for revenge and the pleasure of power with "those who have felt themselves to be insulted and injured."[38]

Heinz Kohut labeled this kind of aggression "narcissistic rage." His phenomenological description also emphasized its boundlessness and its unrelenting need to right the wrong of narcissistic injury. Kohut did not see this rage as growing out of a drive; instead he understood it as a reaction to damage to the self.[39] The source of narcissistic rage must then be located both in the external reality of the situation and in the internal meaning and state of the individual who experiences the injury.

Turning now to the phenomenon of violence and rage in the group, I see that the narcissistic injuries that characterize the occurrence of such rage in the individual are also present in the group. The midcentury analytic writer Jerome Frank noted that the "greatest threat to human survival is not selfishness, but altruism. It is the threat to the group of which one is a member, not to oneself, which evokes the most powerful aggressive response." Specifically Frank pointed to the fact that the group "embodies and preserves certain ideals, values, and symbols."[40] These are the narcissistic structures of the group and are carried in its ideology. The loss of the ideology is worse than biological death. The work of Friedland and Juergensmeyer has shown that these essential constituents of what I am calling the group self, when threatened or damaged or seen by the group to be so endangered, are the stimuli for the most violence-prone mindsets and the most violent and cruel group actions.

STUDIES OF RELIGION AND VIOLENCE

Most authors who have studied terrorism emphasize the group nature of the phenomenon.[41] Nehemia Friedland underlines the central role of ideology for the group and for the individuals in the group for whom ideology is extremely important, especially when the group or individual perceives that the ideology is threatened.[42] He calls attention to the fact that ideology can be as "real" a source of deeply felt anger or frustration as conflicts of interest that are conventionally understood (i.e., economic or power issues). Mark Juergensmeyer strongly agrees with this emphasis on ideology.[43] He points out that the individuals in a group of religious terrorists sincerely believe that their ideals are under siege. The cultures (in the sense of a social group with an ideology) have the perception that their communities are being violated, and their acts are simply a response to the violence they have experienced. Humiliation and revenge are key motivators. Martha Crenshaw also underlines the importance of vengeance in the motivation of terrorists.[44] Such vengeance is directed to those who have been thought to perpetuate injustices. She notes that terrorists see themselves as both heroes and victims but are able to have a sense of superiority as they exercise the power that their acts have over others.

Jerrold Post, who has interviewed many incarcerated terrorists, classifies terrorist movements into three types. One concerns "nationalist-separatist" movements, examples of which are the secular Palestinian Liberation Organization and the Irish Republican Army. The second type is "social revolutionary terrorism," examples of which are the Red Brigades in Italy, the Shining Path in Peru, and the FARC in Colombia. The third category is "religious extremist terrorism," examples of which are all of the religious fundamentalist movements. Each of these is characterized by a particular variety of social and personal history. The first carries out the grievances of the parents' generation, righting the perceived wrongs that their generation experienced at the hands of nationalist conflicts. The second rebels against the parental generation and comes out of the protest of the New Left. The last arises from religious ideology. Post emphasizes that these are group activities and cannot be understood as individual pathologies, only as "collective identities." He lays particular stress on the role of the leader in the formation of these groups.[45]

In contrast, Marc Sageman emphasizes the *absence* of well-defined leaders or leadership. In his study of the Muslim diaspora in Europe, he examined the relationships between the peers who were involved in terrorist activities. He found that these men feel alienated in their host countries but have long-term affectionate bonds with each other. Sageman describes the men turning to one another, becoming isolated from the surrounding dominant social groups, and finding out-groups to hate. One of the crucial elements in the transformation of these men is a sense of moral outrage, especially in regard to the treatment of the Muslim community. Such incidents evoke anger and a strong desire for revenge.[46] Another essential element pushing these men to terrorism is their linking of injustice and their reactive outrage to some aspect of personal experience. Instances of discrimination in their everyday lives are examples of such a personal connection. Linking up with like-minded peers—people with whom they had grown up in their countries of origin, fellow students, coreligionists who attend the same mosque—helped cement a cohesive group whose membership became contingent on their willingness to execute violence.

Vamik Volkan, who has explored ethnic violence and terrorism, maintains that understanding what he terms the "large group" is key to understanding the nature of this kind of conflict.[47] The large group—the nation, an ethnic group—is bound together by a shared history and shared values.[48] There are two important components of a group's conception of itself. One is what Volkan terms a "chosen trauma"; the other is the "chosen glory."[49] Each is an amalgam of historical fact and elaborations of fantasies and meanings that the group develops. Clearly the latter boosts the group's self-esteem, but the former, the chosen trauma, may also play an important role in the pride of the group, if not in its definition of its essential character. Volkan hypothesizes that those who become terrorists have personal experience of victimization or trauma in their developmental history and become active as they identify with injury to the large group, the ethnic or national group.

CONCLUSION

The fundamentalist mindset is situated in a group psychological context. In reviewing much of the psychoanalytic theory of groups, I found some conflation between the psychology of the individual and that of the group. I have tried to establish clear distinctions between their underlying structures. Several trends in research are evident. The group's history, values, and goals are central to the group's concerns, and threats to these elements—experienced by the group as assaults on its self-esteem—are increasingly cited as the source of violence. The history of the theory of paranoia shows the same direction: there is more recognition of the problems of fragile self-esteem, shame, and humiliation in the genesis of the paranoid structure. Intrinsic to the structure is dualistic thinking and the Manichaean view of the world. Work on violence in groups shows analogous psychological organization: great investment in the ideology of the group that contains its goals, values, and sense of group self-esteem. An injury to those goals and values produces a paranoid organization and an analogy to rage in the individual (though I point out the problems of attributing individual affects to groups) and subsequent violence. Both the paranoid organization and the apocalyptic aspect of the mindset are further explored in chapters 3 and 5.

3

The Apocalyptic

Charles B. Strozier and Katharine Boyd

Strictly speaking, *apocalypse* is the transliteration of the Greek word *apokalypsis*, meaning "to uncover or disclose." In the Judeo-Christian tradition *apokalypsis* has always meant the specific ways God is revealed to humans. Such "revelation" of God and a new beginning, however, requires the end of the human experiment, or the death of everyone.[1] Collective endings in this narrative are the precondition for heavenly new beginnings. Violence is always redemptive. An ethical and spiritual ambiguity lies at the heart of any apocalyptic drama. The strictly religious (and mostly Western) context in which most apocalyptic stories have been told, however, should not obscure the more psychological ways in which thinking about collective endings and radical new beginnings has inspired political and social movements for millennia and become woven into the fabric of what we mean by the fundamentalist mindset.

The literature on apocalypticism is itself further divided into several subheadings we will consider, though we stress that such distinctions can become somewhat arbitrary and that there is a good deal of overlap between the conceptual categories.

TIME

The experience of time is a fundamental factor in apocalyptic thinking. Bernard McGinn emphasizes the appeal of the apocalyptic as an explanation for one's personal history, as well as the larger context of world history.[2] In the theory of premillennial dispensationalism that is the ideological basis of Christian fundamentalism, present time constitutes the last dispensation before the end of the world.[3] The apocalyptic provides an understanding of history, "its unity, its structure, its goal, the future hope which it promises."[4] McGinn says that such Christian groups believe "they have been given control over history, even a blueprint allowing them certainty regarding the signs of the times and the approach of the End."[5] We argue that in comparison to other cultures that experience time as moving through cycles of birth, destruction, and rebirth, the Judeo-Christian tradition simplifies its conception of time as linear and teleological.[6] There is only one birth and rebirth. Fundamentalist Christians radicalize this teleology; they believe in one creation, which will be followed by the end of the world and will conclude with the rebirth of the righteous few. Stephen O'Leary argues for the need to distinguish apocalyptic ideology from conspiracy. Although both utilize dualistic thinking, the apocalyptic "locates the problem of evil in time and looks forward to its imminent resolution."[7] Apocalyptic time is kairotic. Such time is not linear or homogeneous but is weighted by value and experienced in an uneven, discordant fashion. Like trauma experienced by an individual, such experience of time is psychologically and spiritually different from history as we know it. The apocalyptic is psychologically grounded in kairotic time, for the only meaningful future event is the transformative end of the world, followed by salvation. Apocalyptic believers are not living within time but rather "escape history by destroying time," thereby freeing themselves of responsibility for the world. Kairotic time is always running out, and urgent expectation of the end frames believers' logical, spiritual, and ethical deliberation.[8]

Richard Landes argues that millennialists experience "apocalyptic time" when they expect the end to occur, though he believes they are able to reenter "normal" time following disappointment. Landes says that prior to apocalyptic time believers see signs of the end everywhere, and "such arousal, precisely because it believes that the future will be radically discontinuous with the present, liberates believers from any earthly inhibitions. . . . No fear of future consequences (except from a judging deity) restrains the conscience of apocalyptic actors."[9] Jean Baudrillard describes how the perception of time relates to violence. He argues that apocalyptic groups believe that salvation has not yet occurred in history, which leads to feelings of extreme tension.[10] People in apocalyptic groups sometimes experience great stress and anxiety that often are displayed in acts of violence or mass suicide in hopes of precipitating the end. Salvation was prophesied to occur at the end of time, and these individuals wish to take the initiative and end time themselves.[11]

DEATH AND VIOLENCE

The psychological embrace of an apocalyptic order compels individuals to reconceptualize death, for both the individual and the collective.[12] It is human nature for one to imagine one's own death; the apocalyptic perspective extends that image to include collective death.[13] Such imagining is highly motivated. The apocalyptic narrative provides purpose, direction, and imagery for one's conceptualization of death and ultimately stresses the transcendence of death.[14] Many authors emphasize that the perception of death and violence is drastically reoriented in the fundamentalist mindset, where the day of destruction is "not one of terror but one of vindication."[15] Hoffer argues that a mass movement can transform death and violence from a frightful or unjust event into "an act of make-believe and a theatrical gesture" such that participation "seem[s] easy when [such events] are part of a ritual, ceremonial, dramatic performance."[16] The books of Daniel and Revelation embrace end-of-the-world imagery in ways that require violence, blood, fire, and total destruction. The imagery provides a plot for collective death, though the narrative requires that a righteous few survive. One can say in general that apocalyptic myths are always survivor stories.

Although most authors agree that the apocalyptic narrative has been associated with violence, Mortimer Ostow and others argue that it can manifest in two ways: in a passive form or in a more militant form.[17] Those who embrace a passive apocalyptic are much less inclined to inflict violence against those outside their group.[18] The preferred term in this context, used by both Ostow and Samuel Heilman, is *quiescent* rather than passive. A quiescent apocalyptic group may not participate in violence, which is Ostow's point, but it is not actually passive in its ideology because salvation is ultimately dependent on violent destruction. In fact destruction in the apocalyptic narrative is depicted as a form of punishment and a method of cleansing, which adds moral credence to violence and ultimately world annihilation.[19] Some suggestion of this active relationship to violence even among those ostensibly quiescent lies in the politics of apocalyptic groups, which, for example, look more favorably on corporal punishment and a "willingness to inflict pain on children in the name of discipline and see punishment as a proper means of upholding order and obedience."[20]

The move toward violence can then be enthusiastically embraced. A group's commitment to the apocalyptic emboldens personal conviction in the group's righteousness, which then facilitates violence. Militant apocalyptic groups rationalize their activism by reframing the concept of renewal so that "rebirth, just as literal birth, can be induced rather than awaited passively."[21] At the same time most fundamentalists do not believe humans can intentionally act to compel the end to occur.[22] This shift in agency from the individual to God characterizes apocalyptic thinking in general. The resulting lack of personal agency is a powerful tool to repress desires or urges to act violently. However, strong commitment to a religious cause, in addition to relinquishing personal agency, is often associated with feeling relieved of guilt or responsibility for one's own actions. This combination may enable the true believer to rationalize acting on his or her violent urges. Dualistic thinking, an inherent part of apocalyptic thinking, makes one view "the rest of the world's religions as satanic strongholds—not as the cultures of people with the right to live and worship as they please."[23] Consequently an otherwise passive community may justify preemptive violence against the other if it feels threatened.[24] Robert Jay Lifton suggests that religiously motivated violence requires the group to experience an aggressive numbing that results from total ideological commitment to a dualistic doctrine.[25] Aggressive numbing, in the context of the apocalyptic transvaluation of time, undervalues the present and yet is able potentially to mobilize violence to inaugurate an apocalyptic future.

Nuclear weapons fundamentally alter images of death and violence for all humans. Humans now have the capacity to execute totalized destruction, a capacity previously held only by God. The existence of ultimate weapons means that all people can imagine collective death and that "it takes an act of imagination, or a numbing, *not* to think about it."[26] Few scholars discuss the effect of nuclear weapons on the apocalyptic beyond mentioning that nuclear weapons have been included in the end-times scenario.[27] O'Leary argues that these weapons make the apocalyptic a much more credible concern for more people. He points out that Hal Lindsey, the author of the well-known apocalyptic text *The Late, Great Planet Earth* (1970), and others have incorporated the development of ultimate weapons as one of the "signs" of the coming end.[28] Similarly Landes writes that the "cloud of nuclear destruction . . . has proved a breeding ground for apocalyptic and millennial themes."[29] The existence of ultimate weapons has dramatically altered the psychohistorical context of the modern apocalyptic. Humans are affected spiritually and psychologically by nuclear weapons. As a result the apocalyptic has evolved into a new dimension that intensifies the potential for violence in apocalyptic groups.[30]

MANIFESTATION OF THE APOCALYPTIC

Social Context

Apocalyptic groups can be differentiated by their historical context.[31] Frank Kermode, for example, argues that apocalyptic narratives in history are distinguished by the interaction of three characteristics: the "apocalyptic 'set'" creates the potential for apocalyptic ideation to be accepted; the "canonical apocalypse" is apocalyptic religious doctrine; and the "interpretative apocalypse" is writing and materials that have become associated with the movement but are not canonical.[32]

Kermode's apocalyptic set stresses context in determining the relation between ideology and a mass movement. Bryan Wilson emphasizes that a movement is "strongly characterized by the prevailing cultural tradition of the society in which it occurs" and that "cultural responses, [such as] mythical themes [and] patterns of action . . . are often re-structured in the context of millennialism." Wilson argues for the importance of studying such movements within their appropriate cultural context.[33] In a similar vein O'Leary argues that apocalyptic narratives contribute to and react to their historical context. He analyzed "how the form and symbolism of apocalyptic discourse are shaped by and in turn help to shape the collective behavior of, its historical audiences." By focusing on the rhetoric of the end-time Millerite movement of the 1840s and of Hal Lindsey, for example, O'Leary shows how both of these narratives utilize the "social knowledge base that enables apocalyptic movements to appeal occasionally to a wider audience." For example, the Millerite movement that drew in thousands of members in the 1830s and 1840s utilized the socially accepted premise that the Bible is divine authority; it needed no additional argument. O'Leary shows how the Great Disappointment of October 22, 1844, when William Miller's prediction of the end did not occur, contributed to general social knowledge. Following this event groups that predict dates for the apocalypse generally do not appeal to the mainstream public. As a result the evangelical apocalyptic espoused by Lindsey never actually specified a date for the end. Lindsey suggested only the immanence of the end due to "signs" that cause the public discomfort.[34]

Speaking in general terms Ostow describes three types of apocalyptic discourses created to address specific social group formations: those created to provide hope for the oppressed; those created by authority figures to maintain proper order by threatening the populace with ideas of destruction; and those created to encourage people to take up arms against the enemy.[35] Norman Cohn, who describes the millennial movements in medieval Europe from the eleventh century through the sixteenth, suggests that certain sociological preconditions must be present before an apocalyptic movement can flourish.[36] There must be a large group of impoverished people who are unorganized and not well integrated into society. Such groups are more likely to form if the individuals in them are not able to further their interests through secular means. In addition there must be a significant event that changes the state of societal life, such as population displacement, the growth and expansion of the economy, or new forms of trade. Apocalyptic groups often flourish among people who fear catastrophe or after a major disaster, such as a famine or plague.[37] Often such traumatic events are interpreted as signs of the end. Cohn suggests that many, if not all, humans desire salvation from suffering, which is further amplified in times of crisis.[38] He stresses that apocalyptic movements require the population to feel a generalized anxiety and uncertainty. Ultimately apocalyptic group movements are potentially dangerous and difficult to control because of the multiple avenues along which people arrive at such thinking.

Psychological Context

To address the general psychological orientation of apocalyptic groups, Ostow emphasizes mood as the determining factor for how one perceives and rationalizes people, things, and events.[39] He suggests that the apocalyptic is the projection of internal mood onto the societal landscape. Ostow evaluates mood in relation to the apocalyptic on two levels: the individual and the society. He describes the predisposition for end-of-the-world thinking that exists in some individuals as a "personal apocalyptic complex" and proposes that this complex has the potential to become an illness, an "apocalyptic syndrome."[40] One's inability to control rage, particularly if it is amplified by feelings of humiliation, can combine with a predisposed apocalyptic complex to generate the syndrome. With regard to the psychology of society, Ostow claims that the "apocalyptic mood" can become prevalent in a society and draw on people who individually experience the apocalyptic complex.[41] The predisposed individuals form a cohesive collective that is bonded by the apocalyptic, whereby the population's visions are reaffirmed by the nature of the group. The apocalyptic paradigm can also be generated by stress in those who are otherwise not prone to such thinking.

Anxiety, insecurity, and uneasiness are common sentiments among the dispossessed. It follows that the apocalyptic narrative is often associated with poor, oppressed, and disenfranchised populations that are in need of hope for salvation and an idealized future, as well as the satisfaction of vengeful fantasies that target their oppressors.[42] Hope, however, is a universal human yearning that cuts across class lines.[43] One finds apocalyptic ideology in times of crisis as well as prosperity, which generates "excessive narcissism and a concurrent loss of the sense of communal obligation."[44] But apocalyptic thinking is not limited to the poor and needy.[45] Cohn discusses the Free Spirit heresy, which did not come from the poor segments of society but rather sprang up among mystics from the upper class who believed in removing social distinctions and living in communal settings.[46] Similarly Lois Ann Lorentzen describes the members of the apocalyptic group Earth First!, a radical environmental group with apocalyptic beliefs, as being members of a rather privileged class.[47] It is also important to note that people from all levels of education are found among fundamentalist group members.[48]

Philip Charles Lucas emphasizes the psychological attraction for millennialists to the "sense of security and consolation in their assumption that the millennial scenario they embrace transcends the venality and uncertainty of secular history."[49] O'Leary suggests that the apocalyptic is created to help "explain and justify the phenomenal realities of evil, to locate humanity within a cycle or progression of cosmic time, and to legitimate or subvert the structures of existing power through the resources of sacred myth."[50] When discussing fundamentalism many writers believe that humans have a general, universal need to be connected to some cause that endures beyond one's lifetime and offers a semblance of immortality.[51] Other authors emphasize the social aspect of a group that involves one's friends and kin, or the heroism perceived among group members as primary motivating factors for joining a movement with a cause.[52] A mass movement, such as a fundamentalist group, can provide a venue to fill both of these needs. Additionally the nature of the fundamentalist mindset generates similar behavior among individuals who join such groups for other reasons.

Acknowledging the problems of applying individual psychoanalysis to groups (described in depth in chapter 2), we cautiously refer to Benjamin Beit-Hallahmi, who uses psychoanalysis to examine the nature of the apocalyptic for the individual and the group.[53] He suggests that the violent imagery in the apocalyptic narrative may be created to maintain or achieve psychic balance and prevent one from conducting such actions. Images of destruction and violence may offer an outlet for aggression and frustration. The period of salvation in the future appears to represent a desire to be freed from the burdens and urges of the body.[54] He suggests that a militant apocalyptic group that acts on violent or aggressive urges is struggling outwardly against a perceived enemy while also struggling within itself "against a powerful tendency toward self-destruction," often finding that its pursuits result in its own destruction.[55] This struggle is compounded by an attempt to deny reality while maintaining the limited amount of reality necessary to continue their pursuits. The denial of reality has been alluded to by Festinger, Riecken, and Schachter as a reaction to cognitive dissonance, a manner of reconciling contradictory beliefs.[56] This skewed perception of reality among members of the collective is what causes such groups to be likened to those suffering from schizophrenia and other forms of mental illness.[57]

Ultimately the apocalyptic narrative has an appeal beyond alleviating socioeconomic distress.[58] Incorrectly assuming that such factors fully explain the appeal of the apocalyptic limits our capacity for responding to and preventing totalistic violence.

Apocalyptic Discourse and Interpretation

O'Leary stresses that not all disasters and ills are followed by an increase in apocalyptic tensions but that "only rhetoric can turn any disaster, real or perceived, into a sign of imminent end." He studied the manner in which the apocalyptic narrative, or discourse, is interpreted and how it "operates rhetorically by linking the 'rational' with the 'ocular' voice." Argument and interpretation take place in the evolution of the discourse in ways that show how apocalyptic narratives generate a thought process. Apocalyptic narratives exist "as a social process, a cooperative interaction between rhetor and audience." Using Burke's psychology of form, O'Leary argues that the response of an audience is a function of its expectations.[59] Ultimately it is through this social process of argument and interpretation that the apocalyptic acquires the group's understanding and meaning of symbolic myth.

Ostow describes three social formations of apocalyptic groups, differentiated by the manner in which doctrine is articulated.[60] In one version an apocalyptic narrative is created for the oppressed that emphasizes the rescue of the righteous from oppression. The second form, often issued by the ruling power to control the masses, stresses punishment of the sinner. The third form is generated to promote militancy by focusing on the oppressed fighting the oppressor to achieve salvation. To formulate these different interpretations fundamentalist groups often utilize "selective retrieval" from assorted canonical and noncanonical doctrines.[61] This process enables the group to draw from sacred doctrine to formulate a specific dogma that suits the leaders' agenda.

Funkenstein describes the process by which apocalyptic doctrine becomes the formative ideology of a mass movement. He calls the leader or the individual who brings the apocalyptic literature and ideas to public consciousness an apocalyptician. This character undergoes a standard process by which he (hardly ever a she) proves his claim of new knowledge regarding the end of times. First he uncovers prophecy, often from canonical literature combined with another source. Following his discovery he creates a new method to decode the prophecy, which implies subjective interpretation. Finally the apocalyptic formulates a way of interpreting history to create a meaningful account of the coming end of the world. Funkenstein implies that feelings of tension and fear are generated from subjectively interpreted doctrine that claims the end is imminent.[62] Hoffer, on the other hand, suggests that fear of the future does not mobilize people, but that faith in the future can enable or provoke collective movements.[63] Fear of the end, which is dependent on the interpretation of the narrative that claims the end is imminent, combined with hope in salvation is how the apocalyptic narrative facilitates group formation.

It is a mistake to assume that apocalyptic narratives are permanent and do not change. Focusing specifically on new religious movements, Lucas examined how "articulation, elaboration, and modifications of millennial visions" changed over time. He argues that such visions are "fluid and adaptable configurations of mythic, symbolic, and ideological elements" that change "in response to shifts in the larger culture, changes of leadership, and contact with new and more attractive teachings."[64] He argues for a symbiotic relationship between the historical setting and the interpretation of the apocalyptic narrative that enables an absolutist doctrine to be protean in action. The narrative's ability to transform enables one to see how a passive group may become violent and how a violent group may become passive.

Others stress that apocalyptic thinking contributes to violent action.[65] The behavior of apocalyptic groups can be affected by the degree to which the movement interprets apocalyptic narratives and generates end-of-the-world imagery literally rather than symbolically.[66] The literal interpretation of the apocalyptic narrative can mutate millennial thought into violent action. Mason suggests that it is the "narrative quality that can divest apocalypticism of passivity."[67]

CONCLUSION

The apocalyptic provides a specific narrative with historical continuity. That narrative may also include a group ideology, particularly one that is paranoid. The apocalyptic indulges in dualistic thinking, violent images, and a desire for the end of the world, a discourse wherein one's paranoia and rage are explained, justified, and given direction. The apocalyptic provides fertile soil for the violent potentials in the fundamentalist mindset.

4

The Charismatic Leader and the Totalism of Conversion

Charles B. Strozier, Katharine Boyd, and James W. Jones

CHARISMATIC LEADERSHIP

Paranoid and apocalyptic mass movements that defend and provide affirmation for the fundamentalist mindset are often associated with charismatic leaders. History is full of leaderless mass movements, but many groups formed in the context of what we are calling the fundamentalist mindset coalesce in relationship to a charismatic leader, often in a cultic context, in ways that direct and shape the group itself.[1] Hoffer argues that the effectiveness of the group is dependent on members' conviction in the cause rather than the cause itself, and that the effectiveness of the leader is dependent on his self-confidence rather than his message.[2] Leaders sometimes claim to be the messianic figure of prophecy; at other times a leader mobilizes the masses by claiming to be a seer or a prophet of the coming revelation. Although it is not entirely correct to say that charismatic leaders are always frauds, most are what Anthony Storr has called saints, sinners, and madmen.[3]

O'Leary argues that "charisma is best conceived as a property *attributed by the audience*."[4] This quality signifies the synergistic nature of the leader-follower relationship. The leaders exert a powerful influence by expressing ideas with assured, intense conviction.[5] At the same time most charismatic leaders are psychologically paranoid, which is the source of the certainty with which they speak.[6] Such leaders attract and captivate disciples, not friends. Followers are attracted to such a strong personality and conviction. A leader is better able to assert that his claims are legitimate if he adopts "culturally established styles of leadership."[7] Cohn stresses that a charismatic leader is most successful when he adapts traditional cultural ideas, stigmas, and lore to his particular fundamentalist ideology. He emphasizes that this process of creating an ideology has the potential to become a movement if the leader "possesses a suitable personality and is able to convey an impression of absolute conviction."[8] Lifton adds that charisma includes the "ability to instill and sustain feelings of vitality and immortality, feelings that reach into the core of each disciple's often wounded, always questing self." He warns that such emotions "can be as fragile as they are psychologically explosive."[9] Hoffer argues that "one of the main tasks of a real leader [is] to mask the grim reality of dying and killing by evoking in his followers the illusion that they are participating in a grandiose spectacle."[10] Paranoid groups often use the apocalyptic to mobilize people.[11] Margaret Thaler Singer suggests that leaders use the threat of the end to generate anxiety among followers wishing to leave the group.[12] Cohn asserts that apocalyptic groups in medieval times arose out of revolutionary sentiments among the oppressed and that leaders would embark on a social movement utilizing the apocalyptic as an ideological structure. Often the leaders were intellectuals, most commonly former priests who had a history of interest in mysticism. Such charismatic leaders (called prophetae by Cohn) formatted apocalyptic visions (from different sources, including the Book of Daniel, the Book of Revelation, Sibylline oracles, the works of Joachim of Fiore, and the Doctrine of the Egalitarian State of Nature) to suit their own interests. By emphasizing the distressed state of society, the leader was able to impress upon the people their role as the righteous, while demonizing the enemy.[13]

The apocalyptic provides the narration for leaders to exploit. However, it is worthwhile to note that not all leaders are fraudulent; some indulge in the illusion as well. For example, describing the psychological makeup of Shoko Asahara, the leader of Aum Shinrikyo in Japan, Lifton writes, "The guru and the world become combined. But instead of the self becoming . . . a part of the world, the world becomes an aspect of the self." He says that the visions of the end are "a projection of the self and an assertion of the self." To comprehend the violent actions of a group, one must recognize "the state of the guru's self. A totalistic group process develops, but it is the guru who takes the group into the Armageddon-like series of events."[14]

The relationship between the charismatic leader and the members of the group emboldens both parties' conviction and reaffirms each individual's sense of group self. The charismatic leader plays an important role in determining the degree to which the fundamentalist mindset may actualize its potential for violence. The leader has the ability to formulate the ideology in accordance with paranoid and apocalyptic tenets and direct the group self to support and partake in violence. To fully understand how the charismatic leader can direct a group, however, we must address how the individuals come to identify with, adhere to, and compose the group self.

THE TOTALISM OF CONVERSION

Many psychological observers have discussed religious conversion. The story begins, of course, with William James, who regarded religious conversion as normal and therapeutic and as the transition from a "divided self" to a "united self." Sigmund Freud, on the other hand, saw religious conversion as a neurotic regression to infantile needs. Carl Jung, returning to James's approach, considered conversion potentially transformative and profoundly curative. It was not until Erik Erikson that this debate became a more fruitful one that distinguishes totalism from wholeness. Erikson states that wholeness is "an assembly of parts . . . that enter into fruitful association and organization" such that "as a Gestalt, . . . wholeness emphasizes a sound, organic, progressive mutuality between diversified functions and parts within an entirety, the boundaries of which are open and fluid." In contrast, totalism "evokes a Gestalt in which an absolute boundary is emphasized. . . . Nothing that belongs inside must be left outside, nothing that must be outside can be tolerated inside. A totality is as absolutely inclusive as it is utterly exclusive." Erikson emphasizes that the psychological need for totality is due to the loss of wholeness from "accidental or developmental shifts," causing one to "restructure [oneself] and the world by taking recourse to what we may call *totalism*."[15] The fundamentalist mindset is grounded in the psychology of totalism and is based on a paranoid psychology. In conversion to a fundamentalist mindset, a new self forms and the old is discarded as despised. Rituals such as baptism may celebrate the new self, which is then reinforced in personal behaviors and markings, such as the beards adopted by newly minted jihadis. The totalized community strongly reinforces the newly converted with its own participatory rituals that strengthen individual and collective identities and sharply distinguish the reborn from the outside evil world. An absolutist conversion process grounds the fundamentalist mindset.

Conversion is a complicated psychological and spiritual process, and our analysis in no way seeks to pathologize the experience, which is, in any event, a multidimensional phenomenon: "No one process of conversion applies to all conversion motifs."[16] Most of the literature on conversion is from within the field of religion and purely descriptive. Lewis R. Rambo, for example, describes five types of conversion: (1) an intensification of faith; (2) new affiliation with a religious community; (3) an institutional transition between similar faiths; (4) conversion from one type of faith to another; and (5) departure from a religious tradition.[17] Others have shown that some conversions, regardless of type, are spontaneous and unstructured. But when carefully analyzed even those conversions that on the surface appear most spontaneous always have some antecedent event or process leading up to them. Still, conversions need not necessarily be sudden, spontaneous, or dramatic in order to produce major changes in a person's life.[18] There is little difference in the effects and outcomes of conversions that are dramatic and those that occur more gradually. In fact most observers of conversion stress that it is a "gradual, rational process of active search and self-realization."[19]

Our concerns in this book, however, lead us to probe a less empirically demonstrated aspect of a certain type of conversion. Some studies suggest our line of inquiry. Several observers have noted the relationship of trauma and personal crisis to the conversion process. Prior to conversion there is almost always some antecedent or precipitating stress, crisis, social influence, personal struggle, or trauma.[20] Raymond F. Paloutzian summarizes this common finding in the research: "A key element in any conversion or transformation process must be some element of doubt, pressure, or motivation to change: there is no reason to change one's belief system or worldview if one has no doubts whatsoever about them or if circumstances have not confronted the person's religious beliefs or practices sufficient for them to be called into question."[21]

Conversion experiences often serve as the solution to an identity crisis, though they may also serve to alleviate chronic depression, loneliness, and alienation.[22] Allen E. Bergin writes, "Conversion and intense religious experiences can be therapeutic with respect to a variety of symptoms."[23]

Conversion as a response to trauma or depression may lead the vulnerable to adopt an apocalyptic ideology. Beit-Hallahmi argues there is a sequence in conversion: first, one experiences an event or trauma that causes one to reassess priorities; second, one adopts a variation or substitute identity; third, one establishes a break or disconnect from the past.[24] This process fosters higher self-esteem and the formation of a new identity; likewise, the new identity generated with the conversion engenders high self-esteem. The certainty of conviction empowers the new self and provides hope despite the perceived corruption and chaos of the surrounding world.

Carol Mason writes about the conversion experience of the apocalyptic believer.[25] The conversion process, she says, is initiated when one reads the apocalyptic narrative in a sympathetic fashion, suggesting that one is predisposed to apocalyptic ideation or shares a similar attitude toward the group identified as the other. This attitude enables one to identify with the message and affects how one interprets the prophecy and reacts to the narrative. This process of involvement with the narrative is the evolution of the self, a transformation of one's identity. The narrative also designates identities for those deemed the opposition, which restricts a believer's ability to perceive the opposition except through the confines of the narrative. Ultimately, in this sense, conversion is an apocalyptic event in which the old self is destroyed and the righteous self is reborn.

CONVERSION TO THE FUNDAMENTALIST MINDSET: CASE STUDY EXAMPLES

In *Apocalypse* Strozier describes the conversion experience of a fundamentalist in New York City whom he refers to as Monroe. Monroe's doubts in life that contributed to his conversion worked their way into his vision of the end. He "had to tie down the apocalyptic" with concrete images and expectations, avoiding issues of uncertainty "because everything else closer at hand was so problematic." While he lived what appeared to be a successful, happy life, Monroe was unsatisfied and troubled. Conversion offered him a complete sense of self and hope in his new life. He "discovered . . . the power of Jesus and the mastery of death," an issue that particularly concerned him following his father's passing.[26] Although his father's death was very difficult for him, the personal crisis that ultimately resulted in his conversion arose from his feeling of emptiness, lack of motivation, and feeling that he had already wasted half of his life.

When speaking generally about fundamentalists, observers have found that conversion serves to unite the split self as experienced by the believer. Strozier's interview study found that in various ways each fundamentalist had a history of trauma that dealt with "real or symbolic death" that contributed to radical divisions within the self. The born-again experience is a profound claim that one has found salvation from suffering, thereby healing the broken narrative. This process is described as "a direct religious response to our common traumas." The fundamentalist group possesses the psychological power to nurture conversion by "using the human need for love and acceptance."[27]

Another example comes from the world of new religious movements. In *Destroying the World to Save It*, Robert Jay Lifton describes some of the totalistic conversion experiences of Aum Shinrikyo members. A young Japanese woman named Iwai found Aum when she was seeking a Buddhist sect that would satisfy her spiritual and intellectual needs. She describes her generation in Japan as by being dissatisfied with the economic privilege and success that had fulfilled her parents' generation. During the social changes of the 1960s and 1970s, she says, her generation "longed for the ideal father or ideal mother," and she describes "the gap between the way society actually works and the way the immature mind perceives it." Aum satisfied her with a rational explanation of karma, and she grew to appreciate Asahara as a mentor who was farther along on his path of spiritual enlightenment. Her experience in Aum made her feel free and happy. Iwai experienced a totalistic conversion such that she ultimately became a strong supporter of *poa*, the Buddhist principle perverted by Asahara to justify killing people. Lifton suggests that it was "both her anger and her need for 'logic' and a rationale

[that] contributed to her embrace of Aum's violent perceptions of bad karma." Iwai went through the initiation process, where she enjoyed the "the absence of discrimination against women, the opportunity to leave behind the angry conflicts, . . . [and] a chance to pursue her spiritual quest without restraint." However, she was isolated in the totalistic environment of Aum, which caused her to experience a psychological struggle between submission and resistance, dependency and autonomy during her conversion. Throughout the conversion process her relationship to the guru became unyielding. An example of her devotion was her support of Asahara's use of prophecy to manipulate disciples regarding the end of the world. Lifton quotes Iwai: "I simply thought that the idea of Armageddon was handy for organizing followers and I was kind of sympathetic to Master, who had so many followers to deal with."[28]

As these examples suggest, there may be a nearly universal experience of a certain form of totalized conversion that is a precondition for the easy adoption of paranoid and apocalyptic ideologies. Certainly the relationship between conversion and the potential for violence is neither necessary nor proven by examples that may be idiosyncratic. Much more empirical research is needed. But there does appear to be a suggestive link between the way some who later turn to violence in the name of religion first turn to God with a passion and enthusiasm that hides darker and more malevolent inclinations.

Part II

MOTIVATIONS FOR VIOLENCE

5

Fundamentalism and the Paranoid Gestalt

David M. Terman

I have discussed the history of psychoanalytic theory about the nature of groups, the theories of paranoia, and the theories of rage and violence.[1] My own ideas differ from much of the work that I have reviewed. Though my theoretical framework is derived from the psychoanalytic tradition, I have tried to carefully maintain the distinction between individual psychology and the cognitive-affective organization of groups. In this chapter I begin with a phenomenological description of behavioral psychological properties of the fundamentalist mindset. I am aware of the large volume of work and thought that other psychoanalytic theorists have given these matters, but I think my approach may be more amenable to empirical observation and better able to develop connections to the disciplines of history and sociology. I hope to offer an additional perspective with which to examine these phenomena.

PHENOMENOLOGY

I propose a theoretical framework with which I believe we can best understand the underlying psychological structure of fundamentalism. I call this structure the *paranoid gestalt*. It is a general perceptual, affective-cognitive organization in individuals and an analogous, shared cognitive structure in groups. Its pattern and specific terms are similar in individuals and in groups. The pattern is quite stereotypic, and this invariant regularity is most evident in groups. I speculate that this cognitive gestalt has a neurobiological foundation, like the fear of snakes. One can imagine its origins in some proto-human built-in invariant reaction to large animate masses. (Better watch out, that thing wants to eat me!) With further evolution it has become a way of experiencing and reacting to power, power differentials, and threats to one's physical or psychological existence, especially when one feels less powerful than another. It can be described as follows.

In individuals there is a range of cognitive states. (1) The mildest is a fleeting feeling that "the world is against me." (2) The next is the conviction that "they" have control over jobs, money, power, and so on. (3) More severe are the entrenched feelings of victimization by a person or groups; these feelings may be accompanied by hostile suspiciousness and general wariness toward most of the world. (4) Finally there are the frankly psychotic states of pure paranoia or paranoid schizophrenia with delusions and hallucinations of persecution. Over the whole range of these states there is the conviction that someone or some group is very powerful, hostile, and malevolently intended. Distrust is the hallmark of most relationships, for even apparent surface benignity or neutrality masks underlying malevolence. When the source of hostility and threat is seen to be a group, then the belief is that there is a group of individuals who are not only malevolently intended, but are also interconnected in their activities and intentions against the victim; that is, they share a conspiracy in which the chief object is the harm of the victim. More common is a conviction that there is a group whose clandestine, powerful, conspiratorial malevolence is directed against the group of which one is a member. For example, two sets of commonly held beliefs (perhaps from a bygone era) are that the rich guys (or capitalists) are against us (the common people) and that the communists are against patriotic Americans.[2]

The perception of an imbalance of power is a very important part of the gestalt, for the malevolent forces are always very powerful, and the victim is undeservedly and unjustly weak. The persecutor is only and always concerned with increasing his or her power at the expense of the victim. There is also a moral quality to the paranoid gestalt: the enemy, of superior force, is bad, and oneself, the besieged, is good. This moral quality is less prominent in individual psychology than it is in groups.

In groups the pattern is even more stereotypic. There is an aggrieved in-group, the group that is organized by the paranoid gestalt, and there is a feared, hated group that is seen as destructive, that is the paranoid object. The paranoid group is suspicious of the destructive group's intentions and purposes in a fashion analogous to that in the individual. The designated destructive group is the chief source of danger to the paranoid group's well-being or welfare. Even more crucially, the destructive group is the chief and determined obstacle to the achievement of the ideal state that the paranoid group is trying to establish. This ideal state is a very important element of the gestalt for the paranoid groups. It is the carrier of the moral superiority of the group, and it serves as a cohesive force binding the group together. But inextricably intertwined with the ideal state is the destructive force that opposes it, and that usually is seen to be demonic. The ideal state can be achieved only with the destruction of the destructive force, almost always the members of the destructive group. This dynamic is the source of the Manichaean worldview that is characteristic of the fundamentalist mindset. And it is often a moral imperative, indeed a moral virtue to eradicate, kill, those who want to prevent or destroy the establishment of the ideal condition; in fact that destruction itself is often seen to lead to the ideal state. The paranoid group believes itself far superior morally but far weaker in any dimension of temporal power than the destructive group. Indeed the designated destructive group may seem to be almost omnipotent or omniscient—hence its demonic quality. It is this combination of characteristics that virtually defines the fundamentalist mindset as we see it manifest in both religious and secular contexts throughout history.

Given this schematic, one can easily categorize political and social groups throughout history.[3] Many revolutionary movements follow this prescription. The French and Russian Revolutions, for example, fit this model well. Each had its version of the perfect society. The French believed that they would establish the perfect Enlightenment state that would be liberal and absolutely egalitarian, embodying liberté, egalité, fraternité. The communists in Russia believed they would establish the worker's paradise: from each according to his abilities, to each according to his needs. And each had its destructive group. Among the French, Robespierre and the Committee of Public Safety saw the aristocrats and the Royalists trying to subvert and undo their new order and saw them in ever-widening groups, and the Russians targeted all the wealthy and privileged groups in Russia, from the aristocrats to the capitalists to the rich peasants. Each group was driven to self-righteous excess in its will to exterminate the evil members of the group they designated as demonic and destructive. The Reign of Terror in the French Revolution and the never-ending terror of the Soviets are classic examples of the violence and the attempt to exterminate the destructive group that the gestalt dictates.[4]

The Nazis were prime examples of the schema.[5] Their utopia was the Thousand-Year Reich, which was synonymous with its being *Judenrein*, free of Jews. The destructive group's extermination equaled the achievement of the utopia. In the case of the Nazis, the choice of the Jews as the destructive group was consonant with at least a thousand years of European history. From the Crusades onward, paranoid groups varying from bands that proclaimed the imminence of the second coming to the rulers or groups within various small principalities found that the obstacle to their well-being or the fulfillment of their ideals were the Jews, the destructive group of choice.[6] It is important to note that when such sentiments were not deliberately fomented, they usually arose in connection with some group trauma, such as social dislocation or the Black Death.

The choice of the Jews as the destructive group in Western history bears some relationship to the issues under consideration in this chapter. In a contribution to the dynamics of anti-Semitism I hypothesized that one of the reasons for the choice of the Jews as the paranoid object was their position in relation to Christianity as the nonvalidators or debunkers of the central Christian ideal.[7] By their historical refusal to recognize Jesus as the Messiah, the proper and true carrier of the Judaism from which he arose, they called into question the divinity of Jesus. This undermined the central binding ideal of Christianity—no minor challenge! The epithet that often initiated the pogroms on the Jews was "Christ killers," usually meant literally by the populace that invoked it, but having a larger metaphoric truth for the historical and social forces that produced it. The reasons for that position were well described by Rosemary Ruether in her tracing of the intense anti-Semitism of the early Christian Church, most of it arising after the excommunication of all non-Pharisaic sects after the fall of the Temple in 70 CE.[8]

There have been smaller currents in history that have emphasized the dangers and perfidy of the destructive group but have not been clear about their own utopian vision. Richard Hofstadter describes numerous instances of paranoid beliefs among segments of American society.[9] At the end of the eighteenth century, for example, many conservative New England clergy expressed great fear of a destructive group called the Illuminati, a group of Enlightenment thinkers who lived in Bavaria. One New England preacher wrote a book in which he warned that the group was formed "for the express purpose of rooting out all the religious establishments, and overturning all the existing governments of Europe." Clearly the destructive group is omnipotent, but the danger to the paranoid group is not so much to the utopia that it espouses as to the existing values and structures with which the paranoid group is identified.

The phenomenology of fundamentalism clearly conforms to this pattern. The Abrahamic religions show each of these elements. The paranoid Islamic group holds and is working to establish its utopian vision of the perfect world under Islamic law, Sharia. Its destructive group is the West, Christian or Jewish or both, and it is holy and sacred to try to exterminate the Western infidel. This is a classic paranoid gestalt.

The emphases in Christian fundamentalism are somewhat different. On the one hand, it appears to be a pure culture of paranoid gestalt in its most basic form. The world is neatly divided in two: the devil is evil, and his destruction, with the destruction of the world, will allow the establishment of the ultimate good open to the select who are good.[10] The accent, however, is different from other political paranoid movements, for the destructive group is everyone in the world who is not part of the paranoid group. And the destruction of the destructive group will be accomplished by God.[11] The paranoid group has no active role; at least this is true for the majority of the American group. Instead the emphasis is on personal salvation: being on the right side and being saved. Perhaps it is the culture of hope and optimism that is the American wont that makes the mainstream fundamentalist accent more positive—at least for now. However, there are sects that see themselves as having to actively eliminate various destructive groups. These conform more closely to the paradigm.

Jewish fundamentalists are divided into several groups. Most subgroups, such as the Haredi and the B'nai Yeshiva, like their Christian counterparts are passive in their awaiting the Messiah at an end time. Their job is to study and wait. But the activist group of settlers, the Gush Emunim, fully conforms to the gestalt. Their utopia is the reestablishment of Israel as God gave it. Their destructive group is the Palestinians who live on the land they deem must be inhabited by Jews (as God commanded). It is their moral obligation to kill or drive off those Arabs.

A DYNAMIC THEORY OF THE GENESIS OF THE PARANOID GESTALT: A SELF PSYCHOLOGICAL APPROACH

How can one understand the dynamics that stimulate the formation of such structures? I think one can get some clues from the understanding of individual psychology. At the same time that one must be mindful of the caveat that the group is not the individual writ large, one may gain more understanding of the phenomena because of their remarkable similarities.

Paranoia is an essential component of the fundamentalist mindset, but initially remaining with a descriptive approach to observed behaviors and attitudes, I have not used the rich, but speculative, connections with many of the commonly postulated mechanisms that have evolved in psychoanalytic theory. Along with the more recent work on paranoia, I have placed much less emphasis on projection and have given much greater attention to the issues of shame and humiliation. I will consider the importance of damage to the individual or group self in the genesis of the rage that is part of the paranoid gestalt. I have noted the emergence of the awareness of a different variety of rage and aggression in analytic work in the late 1960s and early 1970s. It is especially intense, cruel, and relentless in its aim to annihilate the offending other. Labeled "malignant aggression" by Erich Fromm, it was systematically elaborated by Heinz Kohut as "narcissistic rage."[12]

Kohut's seminal work on narcissistic rage began to suggest an explanatory framework.[13] He held that narcissistic rage occurs when the individual is unable to control the person that is supposed to properly function as a part of the person's self, what he called the *selfobject*. It is akin to one's assuming that the "other" is as much a part of one's self as one's finger. If one cannot move one's finger as one expects to, catastrophic fear and rage result. Kohut underlined that it is the lack of *power* over the other that leads to the catastrophic, relentless, boundless rage that he labeled narcissistic rage. Ahab's pursuit of the whale that had taken his leg—that integral part of his body—is the quintessential example of such affect.[14] Kohut offered the beginning of an explanation of paranoia: "The ego . . . increasingly surrenders its reasoning capacity to the task of rationalizing the persisting insistence on the limitlessness of the power of the self, but attributes its failures and weaknesses to the malevolence and corruption of the uncooperative archaic object."[15]

I would add several elements to this formulation to construct an explanatory hypothesis concerning paranoia. First there is the dimension of the importance of the perception of power—efficacy, in Ernest Wolf's terms—for the maintenance, cohesion, and vitality of the self.[16] The affirmation of that efficacy may come from the caretaker, who must validate the efficacy (the *mirroring selfobject*), or it may come from the awareness of mastery of the task.[17] The converse of the experience of efficacy is that of helplessness, which may come about simply because one is inadequate to the task or as a result of the actions of another (i.e., defeat). Defeat is most humiliating, for that is helplessness at the hands of another agent. Kohut did highlight the genesis of narcissistic rage in conspicuous failure or humiliating defeat, but the lack of control of the selfobject does not quite explain the nature of the transaction that causes the humiliation. Rather, an important part of the genesis of the humiliation is the comparison between one's own power, or helplessness, and the power of the other. If, further, the victor has, or is perceived to have, pleasure in the defeat of the vanquished, the humiliation and rage are greater.[18]

The concept of the *negative selfobject* also helps explain some of the trauma.[19] In this case one is defined as the despised weakling that the laughing victor creates in his or her victory. The sense of contemptible helplessness is compounded and aggravated by the inability to effect a response that reasserts one's power or dignity. Further, if power is a particularly valued attribute of the self, the shame and threatened fragmentation are still greater. Finally, in childhood loss of power and the thwarting of one's will may occur on moral grounds. The parent often disciplines the child with the admonition that the action is not right or good. The child may experience this assertion of parental power and the thwarting of his or her own will as a moral defeat, with the parent asserting moral superiority. The parent is the representative of "right" and "good," and the child is in the position of "wrong" and "bad."

I have added several elements to the factors that Kohut suggested. One is the narcissistic value of the experience of power per se as an attribute of the self. The second is the understanding of the nature of the transactions that humiliate by defining the self as weak and contemptible. There are several aspects to the latter. One is the disparity in relative power; the other is the affect or the perception of the affect of the victor. The degree to which pleasure or exultation is displayed may reinforce the sense of helplessness and contemptibility of the loser.[20] Finally, there is the moral dimension: one is not only weak, one is also bad. Here too the power of the negative selfobject is great, for there is no escape from such a definition of self. The badness is intrinsic to the being, for one is defined in the selfobject evaluation that constitutes the response to the forming self.

Thus the step from humiliation and defeat to the paranoid gestalt is relatively small. The experience of weakness or defect is so intolerable that it cannot come from oneself; it must come from the outside (as it did, in fact, in the initial traumas). I would postulate, following Sullivan, that the transfer of blame for the defect or weakness is to the other. Any subsequent situation that might lead to the experience of weakness or defect cannot be permitted or endured. It is the doing of the "other."[21] This becomes the gestalt of "I am not weak or defective, it is others who prevent my strength and success," or, in more archaic terms, "my greatness and omnipotence." The narcissistic rage mobilized in this position is expressed in the hatred and wish to destroy the malign other, and this becomes a kind of negative empathy, the opposite of understanding the subjectivity of the other. The stance toward the other is not to see him or her as separate and with complex sets of motivations and needs, but as a being who is organized only around the destruction of one's self and whose essence is essentially evil. So the paranoid object is not just a flaw in the narcissistic universe that must be obliterated, but an evil whose existence threatens one's destruction.

The concomitant polarity, the greatness, even divinity of the self, has been understood as the revival of archaic grandiosity. In schizophrenic paranoid psychoses, delusions of being God are quite common. One root of this delusion is defensive: "I am not the inferior weakling that I fear I am. I am great and powerful." One root is regressive. I would suggest that another root is derived from the relationship of morality to power. The experience of power seems to require the conviction of righteousness. Perhaps it originates with an archaic sense of entitlement: "What I want to do and can do is right." The moral dimension—the declaration and assertion of righteousness—is also defensive against the deep feeling of badness that the punishing experience has engraved on the self.

Applying these formulations about individual dynamics to groups yields several hypotheses. As I noted in chapter 2, one must exercise caution and be ready to alter one's theories with further investigations and concrete evidence. The group does not develop in the same way an individual does. The group has no childhood, nor did it have parents; hence the traumata one postulates for the individual in his or her vulnerable childhood cannot be said to have occurred in the group and therefore cannot be the nucleus around which later injury blossoms. However, as Kohut hypothesized, there is a way in which a group may be thought of as having a "group self."[22] That is, in analogy with individuals, groups may have a pole of the group self that consists of its goals and ambitions and another pole that consists of its guiding ideals. There are also sets of qualities that the group sees as uniquely its own and that give it a sense of continuity with itself.[23] Corresponding to the "grandiose self" of the individual is the group's sense or experience of power, and corresponding to the individual's need for both ideals and idealizable figures are the ideal visions of the group and the need for idealized leaders. Again like individuals the group may hold its greatness in either or both constellations of the group self. As Volkan, De Vos, Loewenberg, and others have observed, the group has a shared history and develops collective perceptions of its characteristics. These include its power vis-à-vis other groups, its notions of greatness and goodness, and its values. And values and virtues are embodied in ideologies.

The work of René Kaes points to the importance of ideology in group cohesion, and the implication of the work of Nehemia Friedland and Mark Juergensmeyer also points to the importance of ideology, for they have shown that the damage to ideologies or threats of such damage in the perception of the group or its members is a key source of terrorism.[24] Analogous to the findings of Katz regarding "righteous slaughter" in individuals, groups develop murderous violence when their ideologies are seriously challenged.[25]

Ideologies are largely (though not entirely) the embodiment of the group's ideals, and the importance of the ideals of the group deserves some emphasis. It forms one of the links between individual psychology and the psychology of the group. One of the transformations of one's investment in oneself is identification with the larger group.[26] This larger group may be one's ethnic group, nation, state, religion, or a general sense of the universe, meaning the state of being when experiencing a merger with a larger entity.[27] The ability to invest in the existence and goodness of the group permits the individual a better psychological balance in his or her own life, and it can aid in the acceptance of one's mortality. It also reinforces the investment in one's ideals, for the group is an extension and validation of those ideals. In the realm of the idealizing part of the *individual* self, the investment in the *group* and its ideals is a crucial developmental achievement. Hence the integrity and existence of both are of vital concern for each member of the group—often more important than his or her own life! The ideals of the group and its ideology are essential to the *group* as well. That importance may arise from its being a collective result of the importance that this aspect of the group has for the individuals who compose it.

The importance of some kind of utopian vision for the group is an extension of its idealizing needs and tendencies. Ideals are an expression of the way that things should be, and a logical extension of this organization of goals is the development of models of a perfect world. As I have noted, all of the fundamentalisms have such models of perfection.

Having described the nature of the self structure of the group, we may now consider the kinds of events that constitute the trauma that gives rise to the paranoid gestalt. One kind of injury is to the "grandiose self" of the group, its sense of power and greatness. The perceived loss of such attributes engenders humiliation and the need for revenge. There are numerous examples of such traumata throughout history. Two widely documented instances are the Germans after World War I and the Treaty of Versailles and the Muslim Middle East after the nineteenth-century decay and collapse of the Ottoman Empire. The Germans felt humiliated by the terms of the Versailles Treaty, which stripped them of all their colonies, imposed heavy sanctions, and forbade their having an army. After the crushing and humiliating military defeat, these decrees further destroyed central sources of pride and power. The humiliation of the state could not have been more complete. The economic collapse that followed also left individuals feeling defeated and helpless. The paranoid organization offered by the Nazis reclaimed German glory and power and proposed an evil "other" to blame for their collapse and to see as the barrier to the establishment of the German millennium.[28]

The collapse of the Ottoman Empire as the last vestige of pan-Muslim temporal power was an enormous blow to Islamic teaching and history.[29] With the additional humbling of any pretension to power and greatness by the colonial experience under Western nations, the Muslim Middle East was humiliated further, and it turned to visions of secular utopias to restore its sense of power and pride. But those also failed. Their sense of power was traumatically damaged further by the establishment of Israel, and yet again in their defeat in the 1967 war. Combined with the failures of the Arab governments to create societies in which educated people could meaningfully work, the humiliation of both the individual and the group was complete.

Damage to the other pole of the group self, the locus of its ideals and their embodiment in its ideology, may be even more powerful in its capacity to stimulate humiliation and the paranoid gestalt. The selection of the Jews of Europe as a demonic threat to the Christian community is an instance of such perceived damage. The wars of religion, though determined by a multitude of factors, were driven by the conviction that each party's religious truth was in mortal danger.

The threatened damage to ideologies and their utopias may not necessarily arise in conflict. The disillusion in their power and perfection might occur as a function of events in the real world that reveal them to be weak. The collapse of the attempts to realize secular utopias of the twentieth century, communism and Nazism, was one of the factors leading to the rise of the religious utopias embodied in the fundamentalisms. The demise of the Soviet Union and the failure of the communist vision may be the more powerful factor in the upsurge of the fundamentalisms, for communism held the hopes and the prospects of empowerment and righteousness for both intellectuals and impoverished masses throughout the world. One of the factors that led to the widespread paranoid organization in so many social and political groups in revolutionary France was the total collapse of all guiding ideals, as embodied in the Church and the monarchy.[30] In the context of our study, Farhad Khosrokhavar has shown this dynamic in his interviews with Al Qaeda prisoners in France, in which some of them spoke of their feelings of alienation and loss with the fall of communism.[31]

The disillusionment with the promises of perfection and individual empowerment of secular societies may be another consequence of the collapse of communism. Though liberalism in the United States was certainly not communist, the utopian vision enunciated by the communist ideology may have been a wellspring that also underlay the liberal aspirations for equality and concern for the "common man." Thomas Frank and Kevin Phillips have documented the puzzling phenomenon of midwestern Americans voting against their own economic interests because of their religious ideologies.[32] These voters have turned away from this world to look to the next; the kingdom of heaven beckons, and its promises of ultimate perfection are alluring even if, and perhaps especially if, the cost is the neglect or destruction of this world.

The combination of a perceived assault on the group's power and on its ideals may be especially potent in fostering the rise of more rageful and violent paranoid groups. The Arab Islamic fundamentalists—or rather, the global jihadi group—arose from the damage to both the power and ideal structure of the group as a group. I have already discussed the loss of power and hegemony to the West. The popularity of Western cultural values and norms have been seen by many as a threat to and destruction of their most deeply held religious traditions and values.

Finally, the experience of *personal* injury to the self, especially when one views that injury as a function of hostility to the group of which one is a member, certainly stirs up both humiliation and rage in the individual, who then contributes to the group sense of humiliation and makes the resultant paranoid gestalt more likely. The experience of both Muslim citizens of corrupt and frustrating regimes and Muslim citizens of European countries who feel alienated and that they are denied status as an equal and integral part of European society has been vividly documented by Khosrokhavar.[33] Because they are unable to fit in they feel intensely ashamed and inadequate and become the perpetrators of the terrorist actions in the West.

The sum of these traumata—to the group's sense of power, to the group's ideals and ideology, and to the individual members of the group—make a paranoid gestalt with its Manichaean dichotomy and need for revenge and violence almost inevitable. The Islamic fundamentalists arise from all of these factors. In Khosrokhavar's chapter he outlines the central role of humiliation in individual experience, which becomes transformed from individual criminal acts to jihad by virtue of the person's becoming part of the jihadi group. The jihadi ideology has created a group that permits the self-righteous reversal of humiliation into the humiliation and extermination of the evil other. That other is seen as the source of the individual's traumatic loss of self-esteem and power.

The American Christian fundamentalists still view the destruction of evil as God's prerogative, but with the traumatic injury to the American sense of power from 9/11 and the economic dislocations that have followed, there was a disturbing rise of the popularity of the political positions espoused by these groups. It is not impossible that if they were to gain power they would transform our country into a paranoid structure, and we would become a totalitarian society. Some have been concerned that the Bush administration was already on the road to a fundamentalist mindset.

The relationship between the narcissistic vulnerability of *individuals* and the nature of the group bears further examination.[34] As we have seen in the case of the jihadis, if individuals feel vulnerable or humiliated in their personal lives, they are more likely to respond to the paranoid organization of the group. Some of the more violent American Christian fundamentalist groups show this combination of group and individual sense of injury. The Aryan Nations was extensively investigated by Raphael Ezekial.[35] It consists of a group of men who were deeply scarred in their individual development and experience themselves as weak and helpless. They have joined a group whose doctrine is Christian white supremacy, with all the elements of the paranoid gestalt. The individuals in this group find restitution for their personal feelings of inadequacy and humiliation in the group's paranoid gestalt. (This group is also led by a paranoid leader who espouses the doctrine and has a relationship to the members.) The trauma to these men's sense of power did not, however, occur as a *group*; rather, each member seemed to develop his sense of weakness *individually* in the course of his personal development. Once individuals joined the group, they shared the group's sense of damage to the group's ideology. However, it should be borne in mind that, unlike the Islamicists, many, if not most, of the individuals in the white supremacy group adopt the gestalt, not out of a sense of *personal* injury in terms of the group's ideology, but out of their identification with the group, now the carrier of their dignity and their transformed ideals.

Finally it is important to note that a group with a paranoid gestalt has a variety of individuals as members. Particularly when the paranoid gestalt is the organizing structure of large groups, such as German Nazis, Soviet communists, and American fundamentalists, the members have the mix of character and psychology that is true of all large groups. Those who are particularly fervent participants are more likely to share the sense of humiliation and need for revenge, but that is not necessarily true of many members of the group.

THE PARANOID CREATORS OF PARANOID IDEOLOGIES

One aspect of the relationship between individual and group psychology is the creation of the paranoid ideological structure that the group adopts and that comes to characterize its cognitive-affective organization. Not surprisingly the individuals who create paranoid ideologies are paranoid. There are three striking examples of this phenomenon: Paul de Lagarde, one of the precursors of Nazi ideology; Sayyid Qutb, the Islamic theoretician; and V. D. Savarkar, the founder of Hindutva.[36] The psychological development of each of these men showed signs of a paranoid personality organization that began to manifest in their early twenties, and each experienced a strong sense of humiliation at some point in their development. In de Lagarde's case it occurred very early in his childhood with a cold, martinet father. In Qutb's case it seemed to arise in connection with his response to the demands of a masculine role. We do not know enough about Savarkar's early development to say. But each man, out of his personal experience of humiliation and rage, constructed a paranoid ideology. De Lagarde's, published in 1853, presaged the Nazi ideology; he called for a new, perfect Germany that was purged of all traces of Jews. Qutb called for an ideal Islamic state in accordance with Sharia that was to be established by jihad against the West in general, the Jews in particular, and the impure Muslim societies in the end. For Savarkar, it was a Hindu fatherland purged of rapacious, exploiting Muslims. Both Qutb and Savarkar endured sadistic, deeply humiliating treatment in the prisons they were sent to as a result of their political positions and activities. The works that grew out of these experiences, Qutb's

Milestones and Savarkar's *Hindutva: Who Is a Hindu?*, were insistent on the presence and extermination of the evil other.

The paranoid gestalts that arose from these sources were alike in many ways. Each saw his own society as contaminated and impure; each sought to restore an earlier purity; each promised a redeeming superiority to those shamed by the corrupt society in which they lived; each dichotomized the world; and each elevated the destruction of the contaminating other as a virtue. For de Lagarde that other was the Jew; for Qutb the other was the *jahiliyyah* world, that is, most of the world; for Savarkar the other was the Muslim.

The effect of these ideologies varies according to the nature of the social, historical, and political context in which they become dominant. The congruence between personal experience and conflict and that of the group—the need to deal with a sense of intolerable shame in either the individual or group self—determines the power of the constructs. Clearly when a group is under the stress of deep narcissistic injury the paranoid gestalt is a frequent default organization.

THE PARANOID GESTALT AND THE APOCALYPTIC

We have extensively described and discussed the importance of apocalyptic thinking in understanding the source of the fundamentalist mindset and its tendencies to violence. The apocalyptic narrative spells out a kind of ideology that is the template for Christian fundamentalism in the Book of Revelation.[37] As the first clear statement of the paranoid gestalt in human history, it has both a special importance and a special place. Written by John of Patmos in 95, it follows the destruction of the second Temple and fall of Jerusalem in 70 and the consequent excommunication of the Christian sects (along with all other non-Pharisaic sects) from Judaism in 90. The Gospel of John was written right after the excommunication, five years before the Book of Revelation. And John, Ruether pointed out, was the gospel that most clearly accuses the Jews of the death of Christ.[38] The narcissistic rage toward the Jews who had excommunicated the Christians and the Romans who were persecuting them may have found its most vivid expression in the images of Christ returning to torture and exterminate sinners. The apocalyptic reflects both the degree of narcissistic rage and the anxiety about the total extermination of the group. The fear of destruction would certainly be understandable as a reaction to the destruction of Jerusalem and the active persecution of the Christians by the Romans following their excommunication. So the particular cast of the apocalyptic—the total destruction of the world and all the nonbelievers in it—makes sense in the historical context in which Revelation was written.

This paranoid ideology has become part of the cultural heritage of the West. It is the vocabulary in which the psychology of the paranoid gestalt has been expressed in many periods in the history of the Christian West. The millennialists of the Middle Ages as described by Norman Cohn, the Americans of the Great Awakening, the present-day Christian fundamentalists have all been shaped by the ideology of Revelation. The apocalyptic shading of Nazi ideology also arises from this aspect of Western culture.

The current upsurge of apocalyptic Christian fundamentalism in the United States has been extensively documented by Strozier.[39] He and Lifton have connected this apocalypticism with the development of the atomic bomb. It is the human capacity to destroy itself that has fueled the apocalyptic solution. Group extinction is even more frightening—and more narcissistically damaging—than one's own death. For group death means that the expanded individual self—in the group and in one's children—also dies. So group death is both a physical extinction and a psychological annihilation. It may be the ultimate narcissistic injury. Indeed one may speculate that it was just this kind of supra-individual extinction with the consequent rage that inspired the original composition of Revelation. The perception of ultimate psychological annihilation may occur not only in reaction to the reality of physical extinction.

It is paradoxical, however, that the apocalyptic coloring of the paranoid gestalt of American fundamentalists has not led to overt violence (except in certain groups). Comparing the current Islamic and Christian fundamentalist groups, one would say that the Christian is far more apocalyptic than the Islamic, yet it is not as overtly violent. This fact may argue for the importance of the degree of humiliation at the hands of other groups in the real world. This raises questions about the relative importance of a group narrative as such and the group's experience and history in determining the shape and violence of the group's psychological organization. But that must be left to another work.

SUMMARY

I have described a cognitive-affective pattern of individual and group psychological organization that is the essential structure of the fundamentalist mindset. I call this pattern the *paranoid gestalt*. My thesis about the underlying dynamics that give rise to the paranoid gestalt in groups derives from a self psychological understanding of the genesis of the gestalt in individuals. I find cognitive-affective organizations in the group analogous to those one sees in individuals. The concept of a group self with a need for power and a unique character and as the source of ideals and values embodied in ideology usefully focuses our attention on the issues of group self-est and its converse, its destruction by humiliation. The humiliation arises f the damage to the group self in its notions of power, greatness, or pe tion. And from the sense of humiliation arises the narcissistic injury group and the consequent narcissistic rage (analogous to, but not the as, that in the individual). This then gives rise to the group's claims t valed greatness, its visions of utopia and the malignant evil other who in the way of achieving that vision and who therefore must be extern The analogy between the factors that lead to "righteous slaughter" b dividual and the righteous slaughter of the evil destructive group by noid group is quite striking. For the group, this is also the sou Manichaean division of the whole world into the righteous "we" a "other." The same sense of narcissistic injury animates both. Th gestalt is often embodied in the ideology of the group, and perce to the validity or practice of the ideology are important sources o iation of the group. These are the essential dynamics of the fur mindset.

I have described some of the relationships between the ir the group. The idealizing needs of the individual play a very la nature of the relationship to the group. Individuals norma idealizing needs and wishes in the group, so when the group attacked, individuals may feel even more humiliated and enr they are personally shamed. Those individuals who have enced personal humiliation—either in their personal lives a group—are more prone to greater narcissistic rage. The such individuals may then make the group with a para prone to violence.

Paranoid ideologies are often created by paranoid examples of that phenomenon were discussed.

Finally, the importance of the apocalyptic was discu ideology of Christian fundamentalism, was the first wr ment of the paranoid gestalt. Its cultural and psycho made it a component of many subsequent such group history and now in the Muslim world as well.

6

The Apocalyptic Other

Charles B. Strozier

The apocalyptic is the death-drenched dimension of the fundamentalist mindset. Among religious fundamentalist believers there is nothing more basic to their belief system than hope for the coming (or return) of the Messiah. For secular millennial movements, such as the Nazis, the redemptive goals are rather more vague but equally central to their aspirations. There can be ultimate salvation only with the absolute destruction of the world and its evils. The end of death overcomes death itself, however, in a remaking of the world that brings with it powerful hope. This transcendent process totalizes the other, requiring radical dualisms and evoking evil in paranoid ways. This remarkable link between paranoia and the apocalyptic gives us insight into the violent potentials in the fundamentalist mindset.

There are many different expressions of the apocalyptic in the individual nd throughout history. Many yearn for the radical remaking of the world ithout any dream of violence; indeed the apocalyptic can inspire progressive ocial change. Paranoia exists on a psychosocial continuum that moves from latively mild forms of a sense of victimization to hallucinatory images of il influences on behavior. I am talking about the more extreme examples of e apocalyptic and paranoia, those cases in which both are totalized and ade absolute. Such a radicalizing process is not a necessary ingredient in world of fundamentalism; I would argue, however, that there is an erent tendency toward totalizing the apocalyptic and paranoia within the damentalist mindset. That tendency may remain merely a potential for historical periods, but various kinds of crises can readily set in motion move to extremes. Malevolence lurks in the intimate relationship of noia and the apocalyptic.

begin with paranoia, which exists ontologically as a potential in the self can be actualized in moments of historical crisis. David Terman in ter 5 describes this ontological potential as a "paranoid gestalt" that he s a given in the self and in the group. I tend to think of paranoia as a bit more elusive, as embedded in our psychology but readily evoked and part of our individual and collective experiences. I think this sensitivity to the historical moment underlay the approach Richard Hofstadter wisely took half a century ago in his essay on the paranoid style in American politics—even though he uses different language—and explains why his essay has been so enormously influential.[1] Within psychiatry there is a mostly irrelevant literature on paranoia that is concerned with the choice of appropriate drugs for treatment. The more psychological literature, especially within psychoanalysis, got off to a bad start with Freud's 1910 explanation of paranoia's basis in repressed homosexuality.[2] It continues in the margins, since few psychoanalytic psychotherapists actually treat paranoids for the simple reason that they respond very badly to the prolonged experience of inquiry into motivations. The work of the Kleinians in psychoanalysis (as described in chapter 2) and their emphasis on the "paranoid position" has focused some attention on the issue among clinicians. Among other observers, Jerrold Post has written about narcissism and paranoia; Vamik Volkan has been concerned with what he calls the "second skin" of nationalism; Joseph Berke and his colleagues have put together a valuable collection of essays on paranoia called *Even Paranoids Have Enemies*; Robert Jay Lifton, as always, is excellent on the subject, but a lone voice and somewhat idiosyncratic; and I have written one book and edited several others relating to the subject.[3] But for such a vital subject that is so important if we are to understand contemporary violence, we are left with a surprisingly thin literature.

Certain things are clear. The paranoid lives in a world of heated exaggerations, in which empathy has been leached out and which lacks humor, creativity, and wisdom.[4] The paranoid lives in a world of shame and humiliation, of suspiciousness, aggression, and dualisms that separate out all good from pure evil. The paranoid is grandiose and megalomaniacal and always has an apocalyptic view of history that contains within it a mythical sense of time. Many paranoids are very smart, and I have long felt it may be the pathology of choice for the gifted. There is no question that paranoia focuses all of one's cognitive abilities in ways that can make one's schemes intellectually daunting. Some have noted that a heightened degree of suspiciousness bordering on mild paranoia can be adaptive in situations of real chronic danger, as many African Americans experience in the ghettos of American cities or as Palestinians feel about their lives in the West Bank or in Gaza. To talk of "adaptive paranoia" in this way, however, is tricky and often emerges with a political agenda in mind, such as clarifying the identity of the evil persecutor. Such formulations also usually fail to recognize the serious deformations in the self that come with any degree of paranoia, for its sufferers relinquish much to its pathology. In paranoia everything is intense and of the moment, and time is forever running out. The paranoid's understanding of history is truly diseased. Great forces are arrayed against the paranoid; in fact virtually the workings of the cosmos itself are aligned to punish and persecute the victim. One is helpless and beaten down, but this keen sense of victimization and what can be seen as negative grandiosity ("No one has suffered as much as I have in the face of this persecution") readily turns positive in its most malignant and psychotic form ("I am actually greater than my tormenter"; "I am the creator"; "I am Napoleon"; "I am Jesus"). The conspiracies that abound in the mind of the paranoid are not just isolated events that affect him or her, but are actually the very motive force of history. There is nothing of consequence to understand in the world except how these large conspiracies work, which explains why paranoia is so totally self-absorbing.

The instrument of the conspiracies and the source of dread is a large figure, or a conglomeration of figures or even forces, that psychological observers have always agreed is a projection of the paranoid's own inner sense of evil. What makes psychotherapeutic treatment of paranoids so difficult is that the therapist usually becomes rather quickly established as the persecutor in the mind of the patient. For our purposes it is worth noting that the paranoid's subjective images of evil that are rooted in trauma become distilled and institutionalized into collective imagoes (unconscious idealized mental pictures) of designated victims—Jews for Europeans over many centuries, Westerners now for Muslims in the Middle East (the "Zionists and Crusaders" in the discourse of Osama bin Laden), blacks and Jews for American radical racists—that in turn intensify the paranoid potential in the self. Such imagoes may exist in very different ways for different individuals and even groups. They are, however, embedded in the collective or group self and are capable of assuming virulent form in moments of historical and social crisis.

This experience of the apocalyptic other thus grows out of confused and ambivalent but deeply personal knowledge. What gets established is a kind of paranoid projective feedback loop. The awful and disgusting evil other, who is created from within the self of the paranoid, serves as an objective correlative to stir desire and fantasy deep within the paranoid, who in turn strives to find relief by intensifying the imago of the evil other through more projection. The apocalyptic other is objectified as the subjective self in this way, becoming in the process a ludicrous tangle of desire, power, and malice. Hofstadter made the astute observation of the pedantry that always makes a mockery of paranoids' attempts to describe the conspiracy they face.[5] In the literature of those who deny the Holocaust, for example, one finds that some of these tomes have literally thousands of footnotes and other academic trappings, which unconsciously imitate the best of Jewish learning. Timothy McVeigh, in his letters to upstate New York newspapers after his return from the Gulf war but before he embarked on his murderous project, talked vaguely of understanding the big picture that no one else could see or understand, but he sounded like the intellectuals he seemed to mock.[6] The paranoid knows the evil other because it is his own creation. When asked to describe that other, a look of horror will come over the face of a paranoid, a look that comes from a place of secret awareness. It is really very striking. Sometimes, indeed often, he will tilt his head slightly, jut his chin, perhaps turn somewhat sideways to look askance, and smirk with a knowing smile that can become a terrifying and haughty laugh.

The paranoid is a haunted soul. Although Freud got the homosexual angle wrong, his most profound insight into the psychology of paranoia was its restitutional character. The actual psychological illness and collapse in paranoia is rooted in some deep and abiding trauma that is usually beyond the reach of a clinician to analyze in any meaningful way because paranoids are so resistant to psychotherapeutic investigation. But what we can surmise is that the paranoid's response to the crisis of fragmentation is a frantic attempt to stave off what he or she inevitably experiences as the psychological equivalent of death by constructing an alternative universe of imagined dangers populated with projective imagoes of inner experience. That new reality fills in for the old. The new reality is bursting with terror and is not a stable terrain—paranoia, like anxiety, spreads—but at least this new world of malice is familiar. It cannot be taken away, and if one can just understand it properly, maybe, maybe it will not cause more misery and torment.

I cannot stress enough the suffering that lies beneath the often angry, arrogant, and superficially confident exterior of a paranoid person. I have encountered it often in my clinical practice, but usually fleetingly for the reasons I have mentioned. For the past four years, though, I have had a fully paranoid patient in my practice. Harriet is a seventy-five-year-old woman whose neighbors send poison gas into her house through the air vent, whose colleagues in her local Greenwich Village AA meetings are conspiring to turn her into a "lesbian, drug-addicted slut," and who can barely recover during the night from the pains in her neck from the Tasers that are used against her by the local police, trained by Bernard Kerik, then New York City police commissioner. Her landlord, who works closely with Rudy Giuliani (who keeps a secret apartment in her building), sneaks in at night to do unspeakable things to her sexually, and once she woke up with a large, growling German shepherd in her bed. Karl Rove, when he was in power, was the ultimate engineer of her suffering, though he worked in concert with Giuliani. As public figures change, so does her explanation of the ultimate source of her suffering; needless to say, her theories are all undergoing transformation since the election of Barack Obama and the Democrats and the defeat of Bush, Rove, Cheney, and Giuliani. Her theory in this sense is malleable, adjusting inner reality to the changing face of history, though she is smart enough (and just sane enough) to question her constantly shifting paranoid explanations. The question she keeps asking is why people of such power care about someone so insignificant. The world makes absolutely no sense to Harriet. All she really knows is that she suffers.

There is visible rage that surfaces in Harriet's experience. She reports that in her apartment she often starts yelling at those who torment her, those malevolent figures who are either listening in at the door, or through a microphone in the fan, or outside her window. Sometimes she throws things out of frustration and anger. She would kill, she says, though such violent fantasies usually get turned on herself, reducing her to despair and suicidal ideation, and she collapses on the floor in tears. She screams out in fury, which once led to her arrest, when annoyed neighbors called the police. I have often tried to get her to a psychiatrist and on some medicine, but she adamantly refuses, and of course to push any harder than I have risks undermining my strong but inevitably tenuous therapeutic alliance. Once in St. Vincent's Hospital, where she was taken after a fall, two German twin female psychiatrists performed an operation on her head, removed part of her skull, and implanted a device that continues to torment her. Besides, she fears taking in any substance that will surely be a toxin and intended to cause her more harm.

The most important point for our purposes here, however, is that Harriet experiences her fantasies of violence against those who torment her, from neighbors to Rudy Giuliani, as ethically justifiable. There must be a way of vindicating what she feels she has been forced to endure. The daily punishment, the Tasers, the attacks, all are part of a scheme that is fluid and confusing in their meaning but not in their effect on her. She cannot say why Giuliani insists on hurting her, but she is absolutely certain subjectively of the effects of his malice. Ethically he therefore deserves punishment, either by her, by the police, or by some outside authority whom she constantly implores me to help her identify. In her experience her feelings of extreme victimization that are so embedded in the template of her paranoia turn to fantasies of killing her oppressors.

Let us consider this extraordinary sequence from victimization to violence. The paranoid intimately understands the secret world of evil he has created in his projective schemes. The rigid dualistic outlook further protects against the malice and loads the self with virtue and righteousness. The other then becomes the embodiment of evil and not only can but must be dispensed with. In its more extreme cases, when fantasy turns to action, the paranoid feels more than simply an allowance to kill. Killing becomes an obligation. And because in the paranoid world one acts on behalf of absolute righteousness, killing becomes healing, as Lifton wrote so eloquently about the Nazis, or as Aum Shinrikyo, the apocalyptic Japanese cult in the early 1990s, sought in its wild schemes to carry out Armageddon.[7]

The violence of the paranoid, in other words, exists as a potential in its very nature and can be turned into action, depending on the moment. Violence is intrinsic to paranoia, at least in fantasy. Such violence is often described as counterphobic, that is, the feeling "I must strike out at the evil other before it attacks me." In other words, even in fantasy such violence is experienced by the paranoid as self-protective. But given the rigid dualistic world that the paranoid inhabits, to act against the perceived tormentor in the name of self-protection is to become a savior. Violence heals and redeems. The evil of the world threatens our very existence. The paranoid becomes the vehicle of totalized salvation and redemption, which is why, I think, paranoia plays such an important role in religious fundamentalism and the apocalyptic.

In its deeper (and totalized) meanings paranoia thus becomes apocalyptic. Apocalyptic ideas are of course rampant in the culture and by no means restricted to religious fundamentalism. Everywhere there are images of Armageddon and the end, from Homer Simpson, who works fitfully for the local nuclear power plant, to Schwarzenegger's *Terminator*, to the banal *Left Behind* series.[8] Sometimes a genius like Don DeLillo explores apocalyptic themes in ways that bring new meaning to old forms. In *White Noise* (1991), for example, a professor of "Hitler studies" moves through traumatic history to nuclear threat, and in *Mao II* (1992) the narrator joins the cultic frenzy of the Moonies with immersion in the Beirut terrorism of the 1980s. Some of our most perceptive contemporary philosophers are equally drawn to the power of the apocalyptic. How can they not notice it, since it defines the most terrifying and yet sublime levels of contemporary existence? It is not surprising that a new shelf of books on the September 11 Al Qaeda attacks appeared in 2002, including works by Jacques Derrida (*The Work of Mourning*), Paul Virilio (*Ground Zero*), and Giovanna Borradori (*Philosophy in a Time of Terror*).[9]

Nor is the powerful idea of totalistic redemption without its element of hope. Our own successful nineteenth-century experience of abolitionism would have been inconceivable without its apocalyptic undertow.[10] In Christian theology people as diverse as Daniel Berrigan and the liberation theologians Allan Boesak, Elisabeth Schüssler Fiorenza, and Pablo Richard read the Book of Revelation as a call for the oppressed to remake the world in their own image.[11] Lois Ann Lorentzen describes the apocalyptic nature of the environmental activism of Earth First!,[12] and one could add the People for the Ethical Treatment of Animals, as well as the very interesting and hopeful movement of antiglobalists among young people all over the world.

Even on the wacky edges of this movement, among the millions of those who either believe they have been abducted by UFOs or have faith in the truth of the phenomenon, are many who are certain that, as the late John Mack described it, alien beings outside of our familiar Cartesian world are attempting to save us from our path of destruction toward collective death.[13] The German theologian Jürgen Moltmann in *The Theology of Hope* argues for a renewal of Christian eschatology in his reading of Revelation, and Catherine Keller, a theologian at Drew University, argues passionately in *Apocalypse Now and Then* and in many subsequent essays that Revelation is a text of hope, filled with dark and ominous images, especially of women, but that the wild and poetic flux of end-time images must be yoked to our salvation.[14]

Nor can we ignore the malevolent power of the apocalyptic and its role in the creation of "atrocity-producing narratives."[15] Personally I am impressed (and appalled) by the Revelation images of blood running up to the bridles of the horses, of seals opening to death, of trumpets blowing violence, and of vials pouring forth destruction in three great sequences of sevens, each linked forward and backward at the endpoints of destruction. As I describe in much more detail in chapter 10 of this book, Revelation is a story of biblical genocide, with God acting, in the words of James Jones, as a "Divine terrorist." The text is presented as a dream, which is why John wrote it in the past tense, and it moves quite logically from the release of great violence at the hands of an angry God to final redemption in chapters 19 through 22. Revelation is also a survivor narrative, for the text proves simultaneously the death and torment of the other and the salvation and redemption of the elect. There are, of course, many survivor narratives, and some can become paradigmatic of the hopeful for all time. But in the apocalyptic the survivor narrative gets corrupted and turned into violence as it gets totalized, or turned into an absolute story of redemption.

Sadly, we also must understand that the destruction of the apocalyptic other, even if the agency is switched from humankind to God as in Revelation, is subjectively experienced by those who become violent as serving the highest of purposes. Endism, or the location of self in some future narrative, as I called it in 1994, is highly motivated. Dispensing of the other in collective ways, something we call genocide, grows out of an intensely felt idealistic and moral commitment to make the world better.[16] People commit individual violence for all kinds of idiosyncratic reasons, but it is the deeply idealistic goal of changing history, of correcting it, of purifying it racially and ethnically that leads to genocide. And for the most part those who carry out extermination projects believe they are acting on behalf of a messianic goal, on behalf of God's end-time purposes in the world, or some variation of these motivations.

Finally, and most generally, the endist narrative is also not one thing, but has itself evolved historically, from the Egyptian *Book of the Dead* in the thirteenth century BCE, to the early Zoroastrians some six centuries later, to John of Patmos in 95 CE, and to Joachim of Fiore (1135–1202) in the Middle Ages. In no way, however, is this evolution more important than in our recent historical discovery of the ultimate power of destruction with nuclear weapons and increasingly with biological agents. In fact nuclear and other weapons of mass destruction have changed us psychologically in ways we are just beginning to understand. We don't need God anymore, as we have since the beginning of culture, to carry out the end. The agency shifts. The ultimate power of destruction is now in human hands. It changes our world of desire. Nuclear and other ultimate weapons are, of course, dangerous in and of themselves in the hands of wild, apocalyptic groups below the level of the state, such as Aum Shinrikyo, or in the hands of new, religious terrorists like Osama bin Laden. But the more important and subtle psychological point is that the very presence of nuclear weapons in the world evokes the existence of murderous cults and new terrorism, indeed of fundamentalism itself. Robert Jay Lifton defines *nuclearism* as the "worship" of nuclear weapons for the power of God that they possess. As Lifton put it in 1979, "The ultimate contemporary deformation is a condition we may call *nuclearism*, the passionate embrace of nuclear weapons as a solution to death anxiety and a way of restoring a lost sense of immortality. Nuclearism is a secular religion, a total ideology in which 'grace' and even 'salvation'—the mastery of death and evil—are achieved through the power of a new technological deity."[17]

Nuclear weapons represent the religion of our age. They define our politics and values and most of all set forth the end-time narrative by which we live. Failed states such as North Korea yearn for and acquire the weapons, as do problematic regimes such as Iran. Most informed observers believe that if bin Laden had had access to a nuclear weapon and the operational ability before the September 11 attacks, he would have placed one or more on the planes that struck New York and Washington; he did obtain a fatwa (a ruling on a point of Islamic law given by a recognized authority) from a radical cleric in 2003 to allow for the use of such weapons in the future.[18] Does he imagine wiping out New York City or ending human history? Such a question in his case is almost certainly hypothetical but may not remain entirely fantastical for other figures in future decades. But we must also remember our own deep and obsessive involvement with nuclear weapons. We joined with the Soviet Union for half a century in an extermination project over ideology that at several points nearly brought about the end of history. We have pulled back from that brink, but now proliferation to other states and probably in the future to terrorist groups has made the world even more unstable. Yet we cling to the weapons and their power. As others do, we worship them in our own peculiar way. It is no longer, if it ever was, an issue of freedom or democracy. Nuclear and other ultimate weapons and all they mean call forth human desire to possess that power, to own it, to make it our own, to reverse the divine sequence, to make ourselves gods.

By this extraordinary psychohistorical turn of events the apocalyptic other transforms personal suffering into a collective worship of nuclear weapons. It is a dangerous sequence. Paranoia is hardly new in human experience; it probably emerged countless thousands of years ago as adaptive in an evolutionary sense (like fear of snakes). But paranoia in the contemporary era has perhaps long outlived its useful adaptive meanings. Paranoia, as I have tried to make clear, is inherently apocalyptic, and its tendency to construct the other in these terms opens the self to violent fantasies and sometimes violent action. In a world of rising and often raging fundamentalisms there emerges a dangerous potential nexus of paranoia and strong faith that embraces nuclear weapons. We can guard against such dangers only by first becoming acutely aware of their dynamics.

7

The Social Psychology of Humiliation and Revenge

The Origins of the Fundamentalist Mindset

Bettina Muenster and David Lotto

In April 2007, on a seemingly normal day for college students at the Virginia Polytechnic Institute, a young man of Asian descent, Cho Seung-Hui, decided to kill as many people on campus as he could. He was determined, fully prepared, and utterly devoid of doubt about the moral implications of his actions. In fact the slaughter was so calculated that the twenty-three-year-old scheduled time to videotape himself for forty-five minutes in a van outside the shooting range when he practiced there a month before the shootings. After killing two students on the early morning of April 19 he returned to his room to access some photo files, then decided to walk to the local post office to overnight a rather comprehensive package of videos, photographs, and statements to the NBC news network. About two and a half hours later he resumed his rampage. In four classrooms he killed another twenty-five students and five teachers, firing 175 rounds of ammunition.

The costs of the murders to Cho were high: he spent thousands of dollars, according to the *New York Times*, and sacrificed much of his time and finally his own life. But to him it was all worth it. Consumed by rage over the way society treated him and evidently feeling like an outsider who did not get the respect he deserved, he chose solitude and seemed invisible for most of his life. In fact he had no social bonds whatsoever—no friends, girlfriend, or close connection with relatives. The statements he sent to the media and the world are particularly disturbing:

> I didn't have to do this. I could have left. I could have fled. But no, I will no longer run. . . . You have vandalized my heart, raped my soul, and torched my conscience. . . . You had a hundred billion chances and ways to have avoided today. But you decided to spill my blood. You forced me into a corner and gave

me only one option. The decision was yours. Now you have blood on your hands that will never wash off.[1]

How can someone who callously killed thirty-two innocent people claim that others are at fault? In terms of blame attribution, Cho's rationalization of his actions sounds exactly like that of the terrorist Osama bin Laden, who justified the September 11 killing of some three thousand civilians by arguing that he felt similarly cornered: "The Western regimes and the government of the United States of America bear the blame for what might happen."[2] Recent studies on school shootings reveal some astonishingly common characteristics: except for one of fifteen investigated, all shooters were male; a majority experienced chronic or acute humiliation, mostly through more or less cruel rejection and social exclusion by others; many exhibited narcissistic tendencies; and most had an obsession with firearms and explosives. The authors of one study concluded, "The typical shooter is a male student who has been ostracized by the majority group at his school for some time, and has been chronically taunted, teased, harassed, and often publicly humiliated."[3] Social humiliation is associated with retaliatory behavior, even at additional cost to the retaliator, as has been demonstrated by Brown in his classic study.[4] When humiliated, individuals and groups seem to have a particular appetite for revenge. The self, it is feared, will never be the same unless such injustice is appropriately addressed. What renders humiliation such a dangerous source for generating violence is the fact that such experiences are often fueled by long-lasting and extremely negative emotions. To exemplify the complexity of the humiliation phenomenon we present a brief review of the concept of humiliation using a number of theories from social, existential, and psychoanalytic psychology, and then demonstrate how cultural, social, and psychological forces may combine to trigger the fundamentalist mindset.

HUMILIATION, SHAME, EXISTENTIAL THREAT

The subjective experience of humiliation is clearly a major force mediating retaliation. Several authors have recognized the impact a humiliating experience can have on a person, frequently leaving him traumatized for life if the humiliation is severe. Baumeister recognized the power of psychological scars resulting from interpersonal violence: "A characteristic of these scars is that victims lose faith in their basic beliefs about the world as fair and benevolent or even in themselves as good people."[5] Margalit refers to humiliation as "mental cruelty," more specifically describing it as "the extension of cruelty from the physical to the psychological realm of suffering."[6]

The devastating power of overt derogation is also highlighted by victims of torture, who expressed a preference for death rather than a life of humiliation.[7] Gilligan interviewed prison inmates who frequently expressed a preference for death or mutilation over a life "without pride, dignity, and self-respect." He asserts, "The death of the self is of far greater concern than the death of the body. People will willingly sacrifice their bodies if they perceive it as the only way to avoid 'losing their souls,' 'losing their minds,' or 'losing face.'"[8]

Every human being can identify with another's humiliation. We all fear humiliation and do what we can to avoid the experience.[9] Jackson argues that three factors characterize all experiences of humiliation. First, the locus of control lies entirely with the perpetrator, while the victim feels helpless. Second, the victim must perceive the treatment he receives as unjust and undeserved as it involves "excessive overt derogation" through the exposure of the victim's weakness, vulnerability, or flaw. Third, the humiliation must be public; the effect is strongest when a large audience is able to witness the act and weakest when the only observer is the humiliator himself.[10] Prevented from acting on the fight-or-flight response, which is naturally activated when perceiving a threat to the physical or psychological self, some individuals experiencing humiliation plot to strike back.[11]

Control has been identified by Silver et al. as the most important defining characteristic in the generation of humiliation as either a state or an emotion.[12] Because individuals who experience an event or act as humiliating lack control over the situation, their freedom to remove themselves from an environment of pressure and coercion is seized along with their sense of agency and ability to influence interpersonal interactions. The loss of control and power in interpersonal situations thus prevents the victim from having an impact on others. His self-image as a person worthy of belonging to the group is destroyed. Because an individual's feeling of a stable and healthy sense of self is based on trust grounded in a complex interdependency with other humans in the community or culture, humiliation is a powerful threat to one's identity as well as to the bond between the individual and his social world.

Both Swift and Scheff claim that in its most basic form humiliation presents a threat to the core psychological existence of the victim. The survival of the self is in jeopardy as the threat of isolation from the group triggers a fundamental fear of annihilation of one's identity, which had been painstakingly built on an accepted conception of a healthy social bond.[13]

Miller argues that humiliation deflates the individual's pretension to owning some quality or being of some status in the eyes of others.[14] In the most severe cases of humiliation the trauma experienced may be so great as to prevent the person from developing trust in others, instead becoming ever more suspicious and paranoid of others' intentions. Thus the person isolates himself emotionally from others and frequently dissociates from his own emotions as they may expose potential vulnerabilities to the outside world. Gilbert notes that patients with extremely traumatic experiences of humiliation exhibit "fear of closeness [and] intimacy and may even fear being understood."[15] Underlying the fear of exclusion and loss of control is thus the realization that a fellow human being deliberately aims at negating the victim's right to exist as part of the group in question.[16]

Whatever the nature of a particular grievance, what determines anger and blame attribution is the extent to which such grievances have been experienced as humiliating by the person or group in question. Anger and blame have been shown to be in a reciprocal causal relationship, and both predict retaliation.[17] "Anger reactions are judgments of moral culpability," according to Quigley and Tedeschi.[18] Because angry people have more power and energy than fearful people, victims are easier to control and oppress as long as they are kept in a state of fear.[19] The initial shock from a betrayal of trust through rejection usually results in a state of paralysis, until anger emerges and reactivates the system. Blame also mediates the level of experienced shame versus humiliation, which can be seen on a continuum. The more one blames oneself, the more shame one experiences; the more one blames the other, the more humiliation one experiences. Although theoretically possible, it is realistically inconceivable that only one of these emotions is present at any given time. Most often one is clearly felt stronger than the other, which determines consequent reactions to any offensive experience. Specifically, shame usually constitutes the core weakness within a humiliating experience; thus if aggression is the result of humiliation, this is because the shameful weakness was forcibly exposed.

A crucial point distinguishing shame and humiliation relates to the threat of rejection and social exclusion. When one is shamed and feeling shame a solution or alternative is provided, which allows one to regain social respect and redeem oneself in the eyes of others and to oneself. As a result of accepting the punishment imposed by the group, which is a condition of reintegration, feelings of guilt and shame are decreased and eventually disappear completely if the group offers absolute forgiveness. The purpose of humiliation, as opposed to shame, is to send the clear message to the victim that he does not deserve to belong to the group and is not wanted. Accordingly the act of humiliation emphasizes characteristics of otherness in order to rationalize exclusion. If such characteristics do not sufficiently exist, as is often the case, they can easily be created within the coercive environment, in which humiliation always takes place. As opposed to shame, the emotional response to humiliation focuses on "feelings of hatred" toward and "desires to retaliate" against the other.[20]

REJECTION, SOCIAL EXCLUSION, COGNITIVE RESTRUCTURING, MORAL DISENGAGEMENT, SELF-DEFENSE

According to Leary, Twenge, and Quinlivan, "Rejection may be one of the most common precursors to aggression. . . . Social rejection (conceptualized as weak social ties) was the most significant risk factor for adolescent violence, stronger than gang membership, poverty, or drug use (according to the Surgeon General) and has been implicated in an array of aggressive behavior in everyday life, including domestic violence and school shootings."[21] During rejection the person is faced with relational devaluation, which, if perceived as undeserved, is humiliating, sometimes excruciatingly, in particular when done publicly. Rejection is clearly much more than a mere social discomfort. Gardner, Pickett, and Brewer argue that an individual's need to belong is so strong that a blurring of boundaries between the self and the other occurs. Thus a loss of the relational bond simultaneously constitutes a loss of a part of one's identity.[22]

Moreover the experience of emotional pain extends into the physical and physiological regions, as MacDonald and Leary point out. These researchers have shown that, just as physical pain disrupts cognitive functioning, a "response to social exclusion appears to have a similar effect."[23] Thus the emotional pain resulting from social exclusion and rejection causes a "sweeping shutdown of the emotional system," followed by a loss of control and self-regulation, as exemplified in DeWall and Baumeister's lab experiment with subjects who were rejected.[24] As a result one response to social or physical pain appears to be a heavier reliance on more automatic cognitive processing, a characteristic of the fundamentalist mindset.[25] Following humiliating social exclusion the person feels trapped, becomes emotionally numb and detached, begins a process of cognitive deconstruction, and exhibits the exact same responses that can be seen following an experience of physical pain.[26]

"A sense of injustice—the basis of all revenge—is a primary cause of anger and rejection."[27] Perpetrators who retaliate perceive the self as victimized in order to conjure up a solid justification for violent conduct. Certain psychological processes must be activated to disengage an individual from the "mechanisms by which people come to live in accordance with moral standards."[28] In exploring these psychological processes it is important to remember that feeling threatened, humiliated, victimized, deprived of alternatives, and even powerless are all subjective experiences. They may be based on some realistic evaluation of facts and circumstances, but ultimately they are cognitive decisions made by a particular individual in a particular situation with a particular life history and genetic predisposition who is in a particular affective state. The combination of diverse circumstances and individual differences will therefore always thwart our efforts to develop a surefire profile or category of those who become violent versus those who do not.

What we do know, though, is that at some point a rationalization process must take place if moral disengagement from killing is to be justified. The most effortless way to rationalize wrongdoing is by arguing that one's safety is at stake; few question that human beings have the right to kill in self-defense. Consequently all that is needed to disengage morally is an explanation validating that one's safety is threatened. It has been shown, for example, that those with low levels of moral agency, who are therefore more likely to disengage morally, are also more likely to act on aggressive impulses when given the opportunity. These high disengagers are also less prosocial, which has been identified by Twenge et al. as a mediator for aggressive tendencies.[29] They are more likely to be rejected by others, which has been similarly identified as leading to violent retaliation. If group acceptance is not possible, self-segregation is the only option left, as the case of Cho demonstrates. Once blame is placed, anger increases and moral disengagement is facilitated, allowing for a counterstrike while rationalizing the behavior by telling oneself that there was no alternative. Throughout this process, blame attribution is influenced by the type of injury inflicted and the degree of intent to hurt as perceived by the victim.

NARCISSISTIC RAGE, HUMILIATION, AND THE FUNDAMENTALIST MINDSET

Psychoanalysts writing in the late 1960s and 1970s began highlighting the importance of humiliation in the generation of rage (as opposed to the more traditional concern with aggression). Anthony Storr, Erich Fromm, and especially Heinz Kohut in his classic paper "Thoughts on Narcissism and Narcissistic Rage" present a model for understanding the relations between injury, pain, humiliation, and shame on the one hand, and the unrelenting desire for revenge on the other. Kohut describes the paradigmatic sequence as follows. First there is a traumatic event leading to a narcissistic injury. Second, the victim of the traumatic event experiences it as a profound insult to the self, resulting in fragmentation, or the sense of disintegration of the self. In a retributive sense the byproduct of the fragmentation is rage, which knows no bounds, has vague and shifting objects, and is prone to violence in the frantic effort to right the flaw in the self.

Kohut argues that narcissistic rage involves "the need for revenge, for righting a wrong, for undoing a hurt by whatever means, and a deeply anchored, unrelenting compulsion in the pursuit of all these aims which gives no rest to those who have suffered a narcissistic injury."[30] He sees this progression from injury to revenge as operating in all people who experience narcissistic injury, but it is also clear that some individuals or groups are more narcissistically vulnerable and hence more likely to react with narcissistic rage when they have been narcissistically wounded.

Kohut's discussion of Hitler's rise to power, for example, stresses the injury suffered by Germany in its humiliating defeat at the end of World War I. A proud and mighty nation newly constituted after 1870 sought its place in the sun. Germany seemed unconquerable, which of course was the case in the east against Russia. Germany, however, lost the war in the west and had to accept humiliating defeat at the treaty of Versailles. That loss generated the "stab in the back" myth that Jews were responsible for the humiliation of Germany.[31] It is important to note that it is the group that is humiliated, either in its sense of power or its ideal systems and ideology, as described by David Terman in chapter 5 in relation to the "paranoid gestalt"; in different but entirely complementary ways by Farhad Khosrokhavar in relation to jihadis in chapter 12; by David Jordan in chapter 14 in relation to the wildly exaggerated attempt during the French Revolution to eliminate all internal enemies of the Revolution in the face of external military threat; and by John R. McLane in chapter 15 in relation to the Hindutva movement in India.

Humiliation is the motivational basis of the fundamentalist mindset. Humiliation is everywhere in the themes discussed in this book. Dualistic rigidities, for example, serve to protect the self from fragmentation in the face of slights and injuries, real or imagined. A disparity in power may also contribute to the genesis of humiliation; the greater the helplessness and the more powerless the individual feels, the greater the humiliation. This effect is multiplied in the social setting by the group, whose power to stigmatize and exclude is even greater than that of any single individual.[32] The effects of such humiliation and shame stir paranoia and violence and prompt much of the apocalyptic rhetoric so typical of the fundamentalist mindset. In the apocalyptic God redeems the great suffering of the martyrs and rains down violence on those who brought about the dreaded humiliation.

EMPATHY, APOLOGIES, FORGIVENESS

Whereas revenge is a primitive emotion, quickly accessible by the brain and a natural state of mind with which every human being can undoubtedly identify, a tendency to forgive is easily obstructed by anger and even more solidly blocked by rage resulting from humiliation. To forgive means to cancel a social debt. Forgiveness can be seen as the opposite of revenge, which, ironically, has historically been equated with justice.[33]

One variable found to be important in determining a tendency to forgive is empathy. In particular cognitive empathy, the ability to take the other's perspective, has been shown to promote forgiveness, whereas affective empathy, the ability to share an emotional experience, may promote forgiveness only for members of one's group but not for those outside the group. Affective empathy may thus be very important for group cohesion, but without cognitive empathy boundaries between groups may be strengthened, thereby promoting hostility toward those who offended.[34] Individuals observing a severely humiliating offense may show affective empathy for the victim only because they prefer to identify with the sufferer rather than the one who inflicts the suffering. Members of a fundamentalist group are not likely to exhibit perspective-taking empathy if they have been traumatized through humiliation themselves, experiences that already decreased the level of trust in others and triggered cognitive rigidity.

What is needed subsequent to an offense is a deeply meant apology, evidenced by signs that the perpetrator feels ashamed of his acts, and followed by actual compensatory gestures and behaviors indicating that such acts will not be repeated. This response will help the victim regain a sense of safety and psychological balance and reaffirm his worldview. An apology is also invaluable because, as Zechmeister et al. show, victims place great importance on receiving apologies and amends from the offenders before forgiving.[35] The only caution is that paranoid groups may not expect or accept forgiveness; it may not be enough to overcome the dualistic, apocalyptic, paranoid ideologies for such absolutist thinkers. Still, there may be something to learn from individual psychology in addressing such larger issues of healing the fundamentalist mindset. It is clear that nothing is free, least of all forgiveness. Grudges and grievances must be overcome in order to replace desires to retaliate with desires to conciliate and forgive. Because forgiveness is the biggest factor preventing aggressive retaliation, it is important to note that incomplete forgiveness, or pseudo-forgiveness, may be worthless at best and dangerous at worst. Just as pseudo-apologies are seen as hollow attempts to pretend to feel sorry, fake forgiveness or forgiveness for selfish reasons, such as to appear morally superior or gain power, may not lay to rest resentment and grudges.

Forgiveness following extreme humiliation may be particularly difficult to implement. If the humiliating act is one of extreme cruelty, such as the torture at Abu Ghraib prison in Iraq, victims may not be able to identify with the perpetrator because they cannot imagine engaging in such behavior themselves. Thus feeling empathy for the perpetrator is next to impossible. It becomes easier for the victim to portray the offender as the "evil other" and rationalize moral disengagement and violent retaliation. The more victims can identify with the type of offense on the basis of having committed similar offenses themselves in the past, the easier it will be to forgive the offender.

US

If revenge equals justice, violence can be easily rationalized, especially if such an understanding is shared with one's culture and society. A vengeful act may be considered a moral duty to restore justice. Punishment must be meted out, and if it is not forthcoming society as a whole may demand an additional punishment for whoever refuses to punish.

Though we are strongly inclined to search for evil fundamentalist dispositions in others, an uncomfortable reality is the extent to which America has adopted a fundamentalist mindset and attitude following September 11, 2001. The attack on 9/11 was unexpected, and the entire nation felt victimized and experienced the event as a humiliating existential threat. The country responded in ways characteristic of a fundamentalist mindset, with violent retaliatory actions directed toward both foreign and domestic "enemies." There was a cognitive restructuring, with dualistic thinking, externalizing anger and blaming others exclusively, moral disengagement, an absence of empathy toward the perpetrators, and a show of military might in the Afghanistan and Iraq wars.

And all of this in the name of justice.

8

Fundamentalist Faith States

Regulation Theory as a Framework for the Psychology of Religious Fundamentalism

Daniel Hill

The overarching aim of this chapter is to introduce the emerging regulation theory as a framework for understanding the psychology of rank-and-file religious fundamentalists. I will attempt to demonstrate that regulation theory explains both the fearful state that we observe in fundamentalists as well as problematic psychological characteristics that we have come to associate with them: Manichaean thinking, undue submission to and idealization of authority, a lack of curiosity and doubt, dissociation, and reliance on projection and splitting. Charles Strozier in his fieldwork among fundamentalists in the early 1990s details these psychological traits in the lives of a diverse group of believers in New York City.[1] James W. Jones in his 2002 study emphasizes especially the role of idealization and its distortions in understanding fundamentalists.[2] Such attributes, it should be said, are state dependent and do not constitute what we commonly call character. Fundamentalist psychological attributes are furthermore manifestations of a transient mental state in which their god assumes the characteristics of a caretaker who generates an insecure state of anxious attachment in those who are dependent on him. This anxious state of mind with respect to attachment accounts for the characteristics observed in religious fundamentalists.

REGULATION THEORY, ATTACHMENT TO GOD, AND CHARACTERISTICS OF THE RELIGIOUS FUNDAMENTALIST

Regulation theory is an interdisciplinary approach to the body-brain-mind that integrates attachment theory, neurobiology, psychoanalysis, psychiatry, cognitive science, evolutionary biology, and infant developmental psychology.[3]

The theory provides an understanding of how mental states are organized around affect regulation, which involves the modulation of levels of arousal and maintenance of the organism in a homeostatic state in which the brain-mind can function optimally. The theory takes seriously the idea that the mind, brain, and body are mutually influencing subsystems of the organism. To function adaptively the organism must be regulated. The regulation of affect is the regulation of the organism. The capacity to regulate affect is developed in the attachment relationship to the caretaker.[4] Patterns of affect regulation are activated each time one is involved in an attachment relationship.

The attachment function of the caretaker is to regulate the infant's affect, that is, the quality of the emotional tone and the level of arousal. Different patterns of affect regulation evolve as adaptations to the affect regulating patterns of caretakers. Such a pattern of affect regulation is imprinted onto the developing brain of the infant; that is, the regulatory style of the caretaker is internalized by the infant. Consistently sensitive caretaking generates secure attachment patterns in which affect is regulated and the brain-mind-body maintains a homeostatic state. Inconsistent or neglectful caretaking generates insecure attachment patterns in which affect is dysregulated and the organism functions suboptimally.

The brain-mind-body requires regulation to function optimally. There is nothing more basic to the development of an organism. When the system is stressed beyond a certain point (dysregulated) it must be able to return to a regulated, homeostatic state where it can operate adaptively. There is a range constituting an optimum level of arousal, a "window of tolerance" in which the system is regulated enough to remain flexible and stable. There is also optimal "response flexibility" to internal and external stimuli. In dysregulated states the system is either hypo- or hyperaroused and becomes organized into either a rigid or a chaotic state. Response flexibility is lost under these circumstances, and one becomes overly dependent on the internal or external constraints on the system. Adaptive capacities suffer accordingly.

MENTAL STATES

In regulation theory "mind" functions as a correlate of the brain, a vast system of highly specialized, information-processing modules, operating simultaneously and in interaction with one another. Each module is specialized to process different kinds of information coming from within and outside of the system (sight, sound, touch, proprioception, body state, etc.). The variety of specialization ranges from the simple perception of vertical lines to the processing of implicit, nonverbal, emotional communications, such as facial displays or tone of voice, to abstract conceptualization. When the system is well regulated there is an integration of mental processes. Under this condition all modules are available for processing information. They are functionally linked and reciprocally influence one another in order to assemble coherent internal and external realities.

When the system is dysregulated various modules of mental processes are deactivated or the integrative processes are overwhelmed. When the subsystems of the brain-mind-body are not all working together, when they are not integrated, the system is understood to be in a dissociated state. Things that should be operating in concert are not. The system is functioning suboptimally.

Such a mental state is the aggregate of mental processes. In the hyperaroused, preoccupied state with respect to attachment, the corticolimbic-based modules responsible for processing socioemotional information such as facial displays and the higher cortical processes mediating abstract thinking and the capacity for self-reflection may all be deactivated. Attention is hyperfocused on the attachment relationship as a source of safety.[5]

This state, involving the deactivation of self-reflection and the processing of socioemotional information, precludes the possibility for optimal mental functioning. The ability to think about one's own and others' mental states in terms of causal motivations, intentions, beliefs, desires, and emotions is compromised. We are in this state when afraid and simply reacting. Subcortical processes mediate survival modes (fight, flight, freeze). The positive or negative tone of the affect and the way one regulates the level of arousal at any given moment determine mental states. In such a preoccupied state our sense of self and autonomy are diminished in relationship to an idealized object whose needs must be satisfied to maintain the relationship. A hypervigilance to the needs of the object forces submission to it. The perceptions that are selected for attention, the memories that are activated, and the thinking that occurs are bent to these purposes. Such is the state of the religious fundamentalist in relationship to God.

MODERN ATTACHMENT THEORY AND THE PREOCCUPIED STATE OF MIND

Classic attachment theory argues that attachment evolved as a survival system across species to keep infants close to their caretakers and protect from environmental dangers. At the behavioral level the key is proximity. Distance from the caretaker regulates the behavior. Bowlby understood the mother as providing a "safe haven" to which the infant returned for protection and comfort and a "secure base" who watched over the infant and who could be referenced as the infant explores the environment. (The infant looks back to monitor if the mother thinks moving away from her is safe.)[6]

The exploration system is in a direct relationship to the attachment system. That is, exploration is an indication of a secure attachment state, which is organized around a sense of safety and well-being. From a psychological point of view, exploration involves curiosity and doubt. Throughout life we are curious and can question beliefs only when we feel safe. If one is in an insecure state the exploration system is deactivated.

Modern attachment theory takes a psychobiological perspective that argues that the attachment system is primarily a means for regulating affect.[7] As such, states of mind with respect to attachment are psychobiological adaptations to varying kinds of caretaking and their styles of affect regulation. Attachment states are context dependent. Different ways that attachment figures treat us and are expected to respond evoke correspondingly varied states.

Fear activates the attachment system. What matters is the arousal level and the regulation of the organism. For example, when people are scared they enter into a hyperaroused, dysregulated state, thereby activating the attachment system. One runs or looks back to the attachment figure for a sense of safety and well-being in order to return to a regulated, homeostatic state in which the brain-mind-body can function optimally.

Secure attachment involves a psychobiological capacity to regulate affect when under stress. When dysregulated, the securely attached individual expects to return to a homeostatic state. Furthermore secure attachment allows one to self-regulate flexibly, either dyadically with an attachment figure or alone. The avoidant attachment pattern relies on autoregulation. The preoccupied attachment pattern leaves one overly dependent on attachment figures for self-regulation. Both involve a lack of flexibility and both are dysregulated, psychobiological states. The avoidant attachment style tends toward depressive, hypo-aroused states. The preoccupied style leans toward anxious, hyperaroused states. We see in the internal working model of the preoccupied attachment state parallels to the religious fundamentalists' relationship to God.

The key element in the ontogeny of the relationship between self and object structures of the attachment system is the empathic availability of the attachment figure. In the preoccupied state one is dysregulated. One needs constant reassurance about the status of the attachment relationship and is shamefully overly dependent on the attachment figure for a sense of safety and well-being. The sense of self is state dependent and therefore diminished. This deficient sense of self requires that the believer cling to the attachment object in order to maintain a sense of coherence, continuity, and self-esteem.

MENTALIZATION, SPLITTING, AND ATTACHMENT

Fonagy and his collaborators argue that the most important representational system developed out of the attachment relationship involves the capacity to understand self and other in terms of "intentional mental states," that is, a capacity for "understanding of the psychological characteristics of other people (inferring and attributing causal motivational mind states, such as desires and emotions, and epistemic mind states, such as intentions and beliefs) and differentiating these from those of the self."[8] He calls the ability to know others and our self in these ways "mentalization" or "reflective functioning."

Fonagy demonstrates that the ability to think of other minds in terms of putative mental states is associated with a capacity to distinguish between one's own psychic reality and the actuality of the outer world. He calls the inability to distinguish between the representation and its referent "psychic equivalence." It is typified by thoughts being projected into external reality in a manner unmodulated by awareness that the experience of the external world might be distorted in this way.[9]

Fonagy and his collaborators have a robust set of empirical findings supporting the idea that the capacity for mentalization is associated with the kind of attachment state that is activated. Mentalizing is possible in secure, homeostatic states but is severely compromised in insecure states of hypo- or hyperarousal. Insecure states deactivate mental processes mediating mentalization, and psychic equivalence becomes a problem. The capacity to differentiate self from other is compromised. Projective processes are unimpeded.

Schore depicts a cascade of events associated with the activation of insecure attachment states when the system becomes dysregulated.[10] Cortico-limbic structures that process socioemotional information are deactivated, and one is essentially under the dictates of systems evolved for survival, subcortical systems generating processes producing fight, flight, or freeze responses to threat. The brain-mind-body has evolved to react automatically when the attachment system is mobilized. Mental processes mediating mentalization are deactivated because they slow the process.

Fonagy's research indicates that "splitting . . . is an important marker of insecurity." In insecure attachment states "the bad gets worse and the good becomes increasingly idealized."[11] A concomitant to such part-object representation is the attendant dualistic thinking in which insecure attachment states seem to generate the same defenses against integrating the good and bad aspects of an object: manic denial, contempt, and obsessive reparation. Here we see the underpinnings of the projection, splitting, and Manichaean thinking associated with religious fundamentalists.

THE INSECURE STATE OF THE RELIGIOUS FUNDAMENTALIST

The problematic "fundamentalist faith state" is a *state of mind generated while experiencing an attachment relationship to a particular version of God.* God, in this view, is an attachment figure to which one turns when afraid. The fear-activated survival system is basic to survival. In attachment theory terms, optimally God functions similarly to our caretakers from infancy and throughout the life span, providing a safe haven that comforts and a secure base from which to explore. Optimally such a relationship involves a reliably sensitive, accepting, understanding, and empathic (good enough) attachment figure that generates a sense of security. But it can be the case that the god is inconsistently and only conditionally available as an attachment figure. In such cases insecure attachment patterns are activated.

It is important to keep in mind that we all develop a variety of experiences with primary attachment figures and therefore a variety of attachment patterns. Religious fundamentalist groups are not made up of a particular personality. But they are immersed in a relationship to a God with particular characteristics, a relationship that generates a particular state of mind to which we are all vulnerable.

The fundamentalist faith state is insecure with respect to attachment. It is a state of mind that may be adaptive for maintaining a relationship with an attachment figure (God) that is inconsistently and only conditionally available. Such a state is considered a preoccupied pattern. As with a primary caretaker who generates an insecure attachment, the preoccupied pattern of the fundamentalist involves a relationship to a God who sometimes supplies all that a secure attachment requires. But this same God can also be one who is demanding, whose own putative needs intrude on the attachment functions, and whose demands must be propitiated to maintain the relationship. As a result of the inconsistency and conditionality, the preoccupied attachment state is marked by extreme attentiveness to the attachment relationship itself, especially to the state of mind of the attachment figure. This defensive adaptation develops as a means of reducing abandonment anxiety. One becomes preoccupied with whether the attachment figure will be available to serve as a safe haven and secure base. Such a relationship to God may be adaptive for survival and yet come with conspicuous costs.

The preoccupied attachment pattern, a defensive, suboptimal adaptation to a demanding and conditionally available attachment figure threatening abandonment, results in a hyperaroused, dysregulated state that compromises mental functioning. There are a variety of terms for this insecure state of mind in respect to attachment: preoccupied, anxious, ambivalent, resistant, and enmeshed. Each refers to characteristics of the mental state. I am using *preoccupied* to emphasize the hyperattentiveness paid to the attachment relationship and state of the attachment figure.

Another important aspect of this kind of insecure attachment relationship is that the attachment figure and the dependent member of the dyad share the preoccupied pattern. Both are concerned with abandonment. But because of the asymmetrical nature of the dyad, the needs of the attachment figure must be satisfied to maintain the relationship. The attachment figure is also insecure, and her peremptory needs must be met before she can provide a sense of security for the dependent member of the dyad. When the demands are not met the attachment figure is prone to states of anger. Idealization of the attachment figure and submission to her demands are key components of the relationship.

Abrahamic religions recruit the attachment system and insert God as a primary attachment figure. Some insert a version of God that generates a secure attachment relationship, whereas other versions of God generate insecure attachment relationships. Fundamentalist religions chronically activate the preoccupied attachment system through their depiction of a conditionally available God and continuous reference to the apocalypse, with its threat of abandonment. The fundamentalists we encounter are typically those in whom a preoccupied attachment pattern has been activated, who are dysregulated, and whose mental functioning is temporarily compromised. I have called this a fundamentalist faith state with respect to attachment.

GOD AS AN ATTACHMENT FIGURE: SECURE AND INSECURE

There is extensive empirical research demonstrating links between attachment patterns and religious approaches to life.[12] Mainstream Abrahamic faiths experience God as a reliably sensitive and available presence, comforting believers and serving as a reassuring or inspiring referent for exploration of the environment or their own mental states. In these faiths God is a secure attachment figure. However, for adherents to fundamentalist sects the attachment relationship to God generates a preoccupied pattern. In contrast to a continuously available, nonthreatening God, the God to which fundamentalists are attached is only conditionally available and easily angered, with needs that can intrude at any moment and with demands that must be propitiated. Thus fundamentalists experience an anxious attachment organized around a fear of abandonment.

Images of God as benevolent and caretaking are not orthogonal with images of a God that is controlling, demanding, and even punitive.[13] Indeed these images may reinforce one another, as with children who are very strongly attached to parents who act in disparate and inconsistent ways. Attachment to a fundamentalist God alternates conditionally between being available to provide a safe haven and being demanding and evoking a preoccupied state of mind in the believer. Interestingly a characteristic of adults tending toward preoccupied attachment is to remain tenaciously enmeshed in distressing relationships. In analogous ways fundamentalists cling tenaciously to their intrusive, conditionally available, angry, and vengeful God. We have much more to learn about fundamentalist faith states in our quest to understand the fundamentalist mindset.

CONCLUSION: SOME THOUGHTS ABOUT FUNDAMENTALISM AND VIOLENCE AMONG THE RANK AND FILE

What can my analysis of the fundamentalist faith state offer to an understanding of the psychology of fundamentalist violence?

In the opening chapter of this volume Strozier and Boyd caution about how to incorporate shame into our understanding while appreciating that it is vital to our understanding. The preoccupied state involves the incapacity to regulate shame and relies on rage as a defense against shame. It would be convenient to use this conceptualization to support the understanding of humiliation as a precursor of fundamentalist violence, as discussed, for example, by David Terman in chapter 2. One must be mindful, however, of a distinction between a hot-blooded and a cold-blooded violence. The preoccupied state involves a state-dependent, immediate reaction to shame as opposed to a premeditated response to shame. This is not to say that the immediate reaction cannot evolve into a delayed response but rather to caution against making a facile connection between the difficulty of regulating shame and violence.

Strozier and Boyd also state, "The theology, or ideology, ultimately depends on the underlying psychology." With regard to the perpetuation of violence some individuals may be particularly drawn to the role of perpetuator. However, such an analysis suggests that an ideology organized around an apocalyptic narrative and a fundamentalist God may activate states that render most members of the rank and file of fundamentalist groups vulnerable to becoming violent or tacitly or actively supporting violence by others in the group if the charismatic leader to whom one is attached promotes it. Invulnerability to the charismatic leader may be the exception.

Among its characteristics mentioned above, the preoccupied pattern with respect to attachment involves a dependence on dyadic regulation and a concomitant deficit in autoregulation, in this case an overdependence on God or the charismatic leader of the group for affect regulation. (By way of contrast, the secure pattern includes a flexibility to alternate between autoregulation and dyadic regulation.) This dependency on dyadic regulation, from a regulation theory point of view, can be understood as an underlying factor in the external locus of control and associated authoritarianism found in fundamentalist groups. Coupled with the need to please and the fear of abandonment by attachment figures, the rank and file are highly vulnerable to influence and manipulation by their leaders and the perceived wishes of their God. This would include the sanctioning of and, in some cases, the perpetuation of violence.

How does this fit with the effect on mental processes of hyperaroused, dysregulated, affect states amplified by fears of the apocalyptic narrative and threats of abandonment by God? I have argued that when in a fundamentalist faith state one's capacities for mentalizing are compromised, projection is unimpeded, and part-object thinking, including idealization of attachment figures and demonization of "others," dominates—the stuff of which the vulnerability to violence is made.

Part III

CHRISTIAN AND AMERICAN CONTEXTS

9

Eternal Warfare

Violence on the Mind of American Apocalyptic Christianity

James W. Jones

Ten or twelve clean-cut American men and women, boys and girls pray together in a basement room. Suddenly a group of fierce, heavily armed soldiers burst into the basement and threaten these innocent, pious folk. Soon you can save them. Join an underground Christian army and with a click of the mouse you can soon kill the invading soldiers.

—Description of an opening scene in the video game "Left Behind: Eternal Forces"

I need to begin with an explanation for the provocative title of this chapter—"The Divine Terrorist—Religion and Violence in American Apocalyptic Christianity." Ironically, I was reading *Left Behind* (the first volume in the *Left Behind* series; it describes the "rapture") on 7/7/05, the day of the terrorist bombings in London. I could not help but notice the parallel between what I was hearing about happening in real time in London as the result of a terrorist attack and what I was reading about happening as the result of God's rapturing his chosen people from the earth. Many of the scenes described as the result of the rapture had an eerie and sickening resonance to terrorist attacks. I could not help noticing this as one who lived through the 9/11 attacks up-close and was personally touched by them, as well [as one] who followed closely the reports of the Madrid train bombing and who has friends in England and so closely followed the reports of the London subway bombings. Planes crashed to the ground or smashed into buildings, trains wrecked and piled into each other, cars smashed up,

> first responders had trouble getting to the scene, chaos ruled, in grief and panic people searched desperately for missing loved ones. Except this was supposed to be an act of God, not of a fanatical terrorist group.
>
> —James W. Jones, *Blood That Cries Out from the Earth*

How does violence get into the minds of American apocalyptic Christians? One way is through violence-laden Christian literature—for example, the phenomenally popular *Left Behind* series of novels—and violent Christian video games that are the equal of any of the violence-saturated secular video games. I will briefly review research on the psychology of violence and the connection between violent media, particularly video games, and violent behavior. I will also briefly review some of the psychological themes found in violent religious groups across religious traditions. This will be followed by a description of some of the violent imagery found in the *Left Behind* novels and the video game "Left Behind: Eternal Forces" based on the series. This will underscore the thematic similarities between these examples of Christian media and the texts of violence found in violent and terroristic religious groups.

THE PSYCHOLOGY OF VIOLENCE

Like all human behavior, violent behavior is complicated and multidetermined. There is no single cause or single explanation. Research has identified many different psychological processes that are involved in violent behavior. Neurobiological factors such as weaknesses in frontal lobe functioning, dysfunctions in the serotonin metabolism, and poor impulse control have been associated with violent activity.[1] A history of childhood abuse and neglect and insecure and anxious attachment states in early life appear predictive of later violent behavior.[2] Experiences of shame and humiliation have been identified as major precursors to violent behavior.[3] Several studies have found that the violence prone are characterized by high levels of narcissism and grandiosity rather than low self-esteem, and that threats to narcissism and grandiosity appear likely causes of recourse to violence.[4] There are also sociocultural factors such as growing up in a culture of violence, initiation in a violent group or organization that leads to de-individualization and a diffusion of responsibility within the group, and being raised in an authoritarian family or culture.[5]

Research also supports the claim that viewing violent media increases violent behavior, especially in adolescents and more especially in adolescent males.[6] A review in the *American Psychologist* concludes that "since 1975, the scientific confidence and statistical magnitude of this link [between media violence and aggression] has been clearly positive and has consistently increased over time."[7] About this there is very little dispute in the research literature. The only disputes are about how long these effects last and the mechanisms through which they are effected.

There is much less dispute (although there is some) about the violence-potentiating effects of playing violent videogames, especially first-person games where directly engaging in violent behavior is part of the game.[8] Such games totally immerse players in a world of violence. On average violent video games are associated with an increase in violent behavior and a desensitization to violence. One review concludes, "An updated meta-analysis reveals that exposure to violent video games is significantly linked to increases in aggressive behaviour, aggressive cognition, aggressive affect and cardiovascular arousal, and to decreases in helping behaviour."[9] These effects appear robust even when trait hostility, empathy, and suspiciousness are controlled for. Much research supports the desensitization effect of exposure to violence (in the media and in real life) and ways that such desensitization leads to violent behavior. There are reports that the training of elite special forces in the U.S. Armed Forces includes the use of violent video games.[10]

Given the complexity of violent behavior, there is no simple one-to-one correlation between violent media and violent behavior, and I am not arguing that the games discussed here always lead directly to violence. But there are, on average, strong connections.

RELIGIOUS TERRORISM

For the past four years I have been involved in an elaborate research project on religiously motivated terrorism. Looking at writings, statements, and interviews with religiously motivated terrorists from across the religious spectrum, especially the Muslim jihadists around the world, Aum Shinrikyo in Japan, and right-wing Christian groups in the United States, I have found the following religious-psychological themes characteristic of all these groups.

Profound experiences of shame and humiliation either generated by social conditions outside the group and potentiated by it or generated from within the group. Feelings of humiliation on the part of Arab populations have been one of the most frequently cited root causes of the turn to fundamentalism. One Palestinian trainer of "human bombers" said, "Much of the work is already done by the suffering these people have been subject to. . . . Only 10 percent comes from me. The suffering and living in exile away from their land has given the person 90 percent of what he needs to become a martyr."[11] Forensic psychology has emphasized connections between shame and humiliation and violence. Forensic psychologists cite numerous studies correlating conditions of shame and humiliation with increases in violence and crime, especially among males.[12]

Splitting humanity into all-good and all-evil camps and demonizing the other. This demonizing of enemies is a major tactic of fanatical religious movements. Ayatollah Khomeini proclaimed the West the "Great Satan." Shortly before his assassination I heard a group of ultraorthodox rabbis on a New York radio station calling the late Israeli prime minister Yitzhak Rabin a traitor to the nation and an enemy of God who should be removed "by any means possible." Which of course he was, when an ultraorthodox Jewish student shot him. Militant Hindu nationalists have burned mosques and churches. In the United States physicians have been murdered and family planning clinics bombed. As one commentator on fanatical religions wrote, such groups "paint the world in black and white, creating radical polarities between good and evil."[13]

One of the most widespread beliefs of violent religious movements is their apocalyptic vision of a cosmic struggle of the forces of the all-good against the forces of the all-evil. Osama bin Laden says it clearly: there are "two adversaries: the Islamic nation, on the one hand, and the United States and its allies on the other. It is either victory and glory or defeat and humiliation."[14] Virtually all religious terrorists agree that they are locked in an apocalyptic battle with demonic forces. Shoko Asahara, the founder of Aum Shinrikyo, is reported to have shouted again and again at his followers "Don't you realize that this is war?" and to have insisted that his group existed "on a war footing."[15] Rev. Paul Hill, who shot and killed a physician in front of a family planning clinic in the United States, wrote, "The conflict is between God's will and kingdom and Satan's opposing will and kingdom."[16] Mark Juergensmeyer concludes in his investigation of religiously sponsored terrorism around the globe, *Terror in the Mind of God*, "What is strikingly similar about the cultures of which they [religious terrorists] are a part is their view of the contemporary world at war."[17]

A wrathful, punitive idealized deity or leader. The image of a vengeful, punitive, and overpowering patriarchal divine being is found in virtually all religious texts of terror. The believer must find a way to relate to an omnipotent being who appears to will the world's destruction. The believer must humiliate himself before this demanding figure, feeling himself profoundly worthless and deeply guilty. And the punitive, omnipotent being must be appeased, placated. A bloody sacrifice must be offered. Here the psychologist of religion can contribute to the discussion by pointing to some of the correlates of such an image of God. There is research that suggests, at least for religiously committed populations, that punitive and wrathful images of God are associated with an external locus of control, anxiety and depression, lack of empathy, and less mature interpersonal relations.[18] Thus it makes theoretical as well as empirical sense that a person who envisions God as wrathful and punitive would also be inclined toward a more rigid dichotomizing of the world and less capacity for empathy, traits that appear to characterize many religiously motivated terrorists.

The conviction that purification requires the shedding of blood. In many religions the theme of purification is linked with the theme of sacrifice. The Latin *sacrificium* means "to make holy." Sacrifice is a way of making something holy, of purifying it. Sacrifices are offerings to the divine and to the community. But they are a special kind of offering, for what is given is destroyed. And not only destroyed, but it (or something related to it, such as the religious community) is also transformed. Something is offered; something is made holy. This connection between purification or redemption and the shedding of blood appears central to so much religiously motivated violence.

The theme of bloody sacrifice is not traditional in Islam, but it often appears as part of the larger religious context from which the Muslim human bombers emerge. In reference to this theme of sanctification by self-sacrifice, Strenski writes, "The 'human bombers' are regarded as 'sacred' by their communities of reference. They have been 'made holy' in the eyes of the community that 'accepts' them and their deed. They are elevated to lofty moral, and indeed, religious levels, as sacrificial *victims* themselves or as kinds of holy saints."[19] Hassan reports that in Palestinian neighborhoods

> calendars are illustrated with the "martyr of the month." Paintings glorify the dead bombers in Paradise, triumphant beneath a flock of green birds. The symbol is based on a saying of the prophet Mohammad that the soul of a martyr is carried to Allah in the bosom of the green birds of paradise. . . . A biography of a martyr . . . tells of how his soul was borne upward on a fragment of a bomb. . . . [An imam] explained that the first drop of blood shed by a martyr during jihad washes away his sins instantaneously. On the Day of Judgment, he will face no reckoning. On the Day of Resurrection, he can intercede for several of his nearest and dearest to enter Heaven.[20]

Scholars familiar with the hagiographic traditions of the world's religions will see many common themes here, for example, the images of Christian saints and Buddhist Bodhisattvas borne up to paradise and ensconced in the highest heavens where, purified and sinless, they can intercede for others. By their offering and sacrifice the human bombers and other martyrs have indeed become holy. It must be noted that this understanding of martyrdom and self-sacrifice is not traditional in Islam, and it has been condemned by many leading Muslim clerics and scholars around the world. It represents a major theological innovation on the part of radical Islamicists like bin Laden and it requires a very selective reading of traditional Islamic texts. The discourse of the human bombers is not a martial discourse of anger and revenge but a spiritual discourse of redemption and purification.

Often a fascination with violence.[21] A team of psychologists who interviewed incarcerated Palestinian militants reports that "their acts were in defense of their faith and commanded by their faith, and they received religious absolution for the acts." One said, "A martyrdom operation is the highest level of jihad, and highlights the depth of our faith. The bombers are holy fighters who carry out one of the most important articles of faith." Another reported, "Major [martyrdom] actions became the subject of sermons in the mosque, glorifying the attack and the attackers." And another said simply, "Those who carry out the attacks are doing Allah's work."[22] A graffiti in Gaza reads, "Death in the way of Allah is life."[23] This too is not unique to Islam. A book by a Christian clergyman in the United States uses biblical and theological arguments to justify killing physicians at reproductive health clinics and is titled *A Time to Kill*, a title that says it all. One of the killers influenced by this book reports that, on the way to commit the murder, he opened his Bible and found a verse in the Psalms that he interpreted as justifying his actions.

Religions, however, do not simply justify violence the way other ideologies do. For religiously motivated terrorists violence takes on a sacred purpose. Violence and genocide can become religious imperatives, with a cosmic or spiritual meaning beyond that provided by any political or legal authority. This inevitably leads to a significant reduction in the usual restrictions on the deployment of violence, thus opening up the possibility of full-scale, unrestricted genocidal campaigns with weapons of mass destruction. Abu Musab al-Zarqawi, Al Qaeda's chief of operations in Iraq, proclaimed one of Al Qaeda's basic doctrines:

> Allah commanded us to strike the Kuffar (unbelievers), kill them, and fight them by any means necessary to achieve the goal. The servants of Allah who perform jihad to elevate the word (laws) of Allah, are permitted to use any and all means necessary to strike the active unbeliever combatants for the purpose of killing them, snatch their souls from their body, cleanse the earth from their abomination, and lift their trial and persecution of the servants of Allah. The goal must be pursued even if the means to accomplish it affect both the intended active fighters and unintended passive ones such as women, children. . . . This permissibility extends to situations in which Muslims may get killed if they happen to be with or near the intended enemy. . . . Although spilling Muslim blood is a grave offense, it is not only permissible but it is mandated in order to prevent more serious adversity from happening, stalling or abandoning jihad that is.[24]

Continuing jihad takes precedence over any other moral or theological imperative, including the traditional prohibitions against killing fellow Muslims and innocent noncombatants. For Al Qaeda jihad means total, all-out, unrestricted warfare. This mixing of religion and violence with the increasing sophistication and lethality of modern technologies of killing results in contemporary terrorism's increasingly deadly results. This transcendental legitimation of killing is another way that religions create and maintain a culture of violence out of which terrorism and genocide can easily emerge.

THE *LEFT BEHIND* SERIES

Since 1995, when the first volume in the *Left Behind* series, entitled *Left Behind*, was published, these books have become a publishing sensation among American evangelical Christians. They are based on the idea of the Rapture, when, before the battle of Armageddon at the end of time, the true believers are to be lifted up into heaven to escape seven years of tribulation during which take place the various plagues, battles, violence, and bloodshed described in the Book of Revelation. After this seven-year period, when most people left on earth will die vicious and terrible deaths while the raptured saints look on, Jesus returns and brings in the millennium, a thousand years of peace and joy before the final resurrection and last judgment, when the true believers are at last ushered into heaven and the unbelievers are resurrected from the dead in order to be cast forever into a lake of fire. This is the theology that has been fictionalized in the *Left Behind* series.

Since 1995 twelve volumes in this series have been published and two more are on the way, a sequel and a prequel; more than sixty million copies have been sold. A survey in 2005 found that 19 percent of Americans had read the *Left Behind* books.[25] A survey done in 2004 found that 38 percent of all Americans said they believe that the "Bible is the literal word of God and is to be taken literally word for word" (a conviction on which the *Left Behind* series is premised).[26] Evangelicals are not the only readers of the *Left Behind* books. According to one survey, 84 percent of readers describe themselves as "born again," 72 percent attend church at least once a week, 14 percent are members of mainline churches, 8 percent are Roman Catholic, and surprisingly 16 percent say they are not Christian.[27] This suggests that the majority of the readers identify themselves as "born again" and attend nonmainline or non-Catholic evangelical and nondenominational churches.

From the beginning there is violence, blood, and gore. The following are a few of the many quotations that describe the results of the Rapture.

> Even the newscasters' voices were terror filled, as much as they tried to mask it. . . . Thousands were dead in plane crashes and car pileups. Emergency crews were trying to clear expressways and runways, all the while grieving over loved ones and coworkers who had disappeared. . . . Cars driven by people who spontaneously disappeared had careened out of control, of course.
>
> Some of the worst disasters in the city were the result of disappearing motormen and dispatchers. Six trains were involved in head-ons with lots of deaths. Several trains ran up the back of other ones.
>
> The news was full of crime, looting, people taking advantage of chaos. People being shot, maimed, raped, killed. The roadways were more dangerous than ever. Emergency units were understaffed, fewer air- and ground-traffic controllers manned the airports, fewer qualified pilots and crews flew the planes.[28]

Remember that all this disaster, death, loss, and grief is presented as the actions of God. What sort of God would do this to His creation? And presumably the truly pious are watching all of this from their front-row seats in heaven. In fact in the last volume, *Glorious Appearing,* when all the holy people are reunited, it is suggested that the raptured saints watched while their loved ones died in plane crashes, were incapacitated in train wrecks, were crushed by colliding cars and collapsing buildings. How is that psychologically possible? What were they thinking as they watched from the safety of paradise this divine carnage heaped on those they cared about?

This theme of blood and gore intensifies throughout the series. In his wrath Jesus, the Lamb of God, causes an earthquake that wipes out a third of the world's population (*Soul Harvest,* published in 1998). Hail, fire, and blood rain down on the earth; one third of the planet is burned up. The horrors are described in excruciating detail. In the next volume a plague of scorpions is "so horrifying that men try to kill themselves but are not allowed to die" (from the book jacket for *Apollyon,* published in 1999).

All of this reaches its climax in *Glorious Appearing,* which describes the final return of Christ and the climactic battle of Armageddon against the forces of the Antichrist. The Antichrist is the secretary general of the United Nations, who has established a stronger world government with the promise of world peace and collected an army of millions to fight for world unity. The idea of world government as an agent of Satan has a history in American apocalyptic Christianity, and it has often focused on the United Nations. In his study of evangelical Christianity in New York City in the 1990s, long before the *Left Behind* series popularized this idea, Charles Strozier found it pervasive in evangelical circles. He writes, "In the scheme of things, Antichrist makes world peace, including peace with Israel, before revealing himself in all his horror. . . . The greater the world leader, and the more he speaks to global issues of peace . . . the more he is ultimately to be feared as the probable Antichrist." As Strozier comments tersely, "The subtextual message is beware the peacemaker."[29]

In volume after volume the *Left Behind* series dramatizes the satanic machinations of this world government as it rises to power. Parallel to this, the blood and gore increase, climaxing in the battle of Armageddon described in *Glorious Appearing.* Jesus himself viciously and mercilessly slaughters his opponents: "And with those very first words [from Jesus], tens of thousands of Unity Army soldiers fell dead, simply dropping where they stood, their bodies ripped open, blood pooling in great masses."[30]

Most glorious to the authors and their chief protagonists appear to be scenes of slaughter and bloodshed:

> As Rayford slowly made his way down to the desert plains, though he had to concentrate on missing craters and keeping from hitting splayed and filleted bodies of men and women and horses, Jesus still appeared before his eyes—shining, magnificent, powerful, and victorious. (208)

> Rayford watched through his binocs as men and women soldiers and horses seemed to explode where they stood. It was as if the very words of the Lord had superheated their blood, causing it to burst through their veins and skin. (225)

> Tens of thousands of foot soldiers dropped their weapons, grabbed their heads and their chests, fell to their knees, and writhed as they were invisibly sliced asunder. Their innards and entrails gushed to the desert floor, and as those around them turned to run, they too were slain, their blood pooling and rising in the unforgiving brightness of the glory of Christ. (226)

Animals are not spared the most cruel and hideous of fates:

> The riders not thrown leaped from their horses and tried to control them with reins, but even as they struggled, their own flesh dissolved and their eyes melted, and their tongues disintegrated. . . . Seconds later the same plague affected the horses, their flesh and eyes and tongues melting away, leaving grotesque skeletons standing, before they too rattled to the pavement. . . . First blindness and madness on the part of the horses, then the bodies of the soldiers melting and dissolving. Then the falling and piling of bones. (273–74)

Throughout the battle narrative special attention is lavished on its bloodiness. For example: "The great army was in pandemonium, tens of thousands at a time screaming in terror and pain and dying in the open air. Their blood poured from them in great waves, combining to make a river that quickly became a swamp" (249). So bloody is Jesus' victory that it results in a river of blood wider by far than the Mississippi: "Mile after mile after mile [they] drove next to a river of blood several miles wide and now some five feet deep" (258). The scene ends with the victorious Jesus walking across the battlefield sloshing around in the blood of his enemies: "Bodies were strewn for miles and the desert floor was red with blood. . . . Jesus dismounted.

The army of heaven . . . following as He strode through the battlefield, the hem of His robe turning red in the blood of his enemies" (228)

Even before the *Left Behind* series dramatized it so graphically, Strozier commented on the high level of violence in evangelicals' discourse:

> There is . . . a potential for violence in fundamentalism that I found troubling. As we have seen, violence often defines their discourse. They talk of washing their robes in the blood of the lamb (Revelation 7:14) and warm to the cascading images of destruction and death in Revelation as trumpets are blown, seals opened, and bowls emptied in the heavens. These waves of violence form a rising and interconnected spiral. . . . The churches themselves are awash in this imagery.[31]

The potently violent imagery of the *Left Behind* series as well as that of a string of Christian movies and violent video games (one Christian video game is entitled "Eternal Warfare") fill the heads of Christian readers with scenes of barely imaginable blood and gore.

THE VIDEO GAME

"The Rapture is headed for New York City, and just in time for Christmas," proclaims an advertisement in October 2006 for the video game "Left Behind: Eternal Forces." It opens with a tableau of smoke rising from the New York skyline, an image that is absolutely always identified with 9/11 by those I show it to, thus exploiting that national and personal tragedy for commercial and sectarian purposes. In stunningly realistic graphics Christians remaining on earth battle the Antichrist's army of Global Community Peacekeepers (that is to say, UN peacekeepers), bodies pile up on the streets of New York, and angels carry the good guys up to heaven through fluffy white clouds.

An early review of the game reported, "Evangelical videogame makers are praying that *Eternal Forces* will finally enable them to tap into the $25 billion global videogame market. They hope their 'Christian' values-themed game will capture the same audience that has made bestsellers out of violent standards like *Grand Theft Auto* and *Halo 2*." The reviewer suggested that the game's "Praise the Lord!" battle cry is not far from the "God is great!" words of the World Trade Center terrorists.[32] "Eternal Forces" is marketed by an advanced distribution through megachurches and pastoral networks, a strategy that has been employed in the past few years with Christian books and movies, resulting in record-setting sales.

Commentators note the games' "indoctrination in Christian supremacy because the game rehearses and instructs children in the mass killing of New Yorkers for the sake of Christ." One said he was appalled that in "Eternal Forces" corpses are left on the streets: "It's outrageous that this game has a feature to allow cold corpses of New Yorkers to pile up on the streets. No one gives them a decent burial." The game's makers agreed that LaHaye's antigovernment philosophy had found its way into the videogame: "The Antichrist's forces are on the warpath, actively hunting down and exterminating all resistance to his one-world government. This includes the good guys—the Tribulation Force—defending themselves against Satan." A review questions "whether Left Behind can justify its videogame violence with the Bible. If a player's only penalty for killing New Yorkers is a loss in spiritual points, then violence actually goes less punished in *Eternal Forces* than in seemingly more violent competition like *Grand Theft Auto*, in which homicide results in being pursued and arrested by the police. And in *Grand Theft Auto*, bodies disappear shortly after being killed."[33]

The game's makers chronicled the company's development:

> When we started Left Behind Games 5 years ago, we had a dream. It was a noble dream, to build the most successful "inspirational and family" video game publishing company in the world. Everyone knows that the entertainment industry, especially video game publishers, create dark content . . . and the idea to create games with positive morals and values is an aspiration almost everyone can get behind.
>
> In just 2 months, we have received word that our first product, LEFT BEHIND: Eternal Forces, the PC Game, is changing lives. Not only have individuals cheered us on with remarkable care and support, but now churches are joining in. Mega-ministries such as Focus on the Family, Promise Keepers, Women of Faith, Concerned Women for America and numerous others are all endorsing our efforts and our products.
>
> And like all worthy endeavors, opposition always rears its ugly head.
>
> LBG is developing products to include the same types of compelling elements that have made interactive games popular for years, and yet offer a less graphic experience to the sexual themes and gratuitous violence currently found in many titles. We plan to make all games visually and kinetically appealing. We anticipate our titles will be classified as both action, strategy and adventure genres, and will likely receive either an "E" rating (appropriate for ages 6 and up) or a "T" rating (appropriate for ages 13 and up).[34]

The game is described on the company's website this way:

> LEFT BEHIND: Eternal Forces is a real-time strategy game based upon the best-selling LEFT BEHIND book series created by Tim LaHaye and Jerry Jenkins. Join the ultimate fight of Good against Evil, commanding Tribulation Forces against the Global Community Peacekeepers!
>
> - Lead the Tribulation Force from the book series, including Rayford, Chloe, Buck and Bruce against Nicolae Carpathia—the AntiChrist.
> - Conduct warfare using the power of PRAYER and WORSHIP as more powerful weapons than guns.

- Recover ancient scriptures and witness spectacular Angelic and Demonic activity as a direct consequence of your choices.
- Fight against negative spiritual influences against the Antichrist and his forces.
- Command your forces through intense battles across a breathtaking, authentic depiction of New York City.
- Control more than 30 units types—from Prayer Warrior and Worship Leaders to Spies, Special Forces and Battle Tanks!
- Enjoy a robust single player experience across dozens of New York City maps in Story Mode—fighting in China Town, SoHo, Uptown and more![35]
- Play multiplayer games with the Tribulation Forces or the AntiChrist's Global Community Peacekeepers with up to eight players via LAN or over the Internet!

"Left Behind: Eternal Forces" is not a first-person shooter game (other Christian video games are, for example one called "Catechumen"). Still, its stunning graphics certainly served to immerse me in a world of violence. A player can direct various armed antagonists and send them on violent missions; cars explode and people are blown to bits; corpses pile up on the streets of New York. And it is important to keep in mind that an adolescent from an American apocalyptic Christian church who is playing this game may well also be hearing a message of violence and bloodshed from the pulpit, in hymns, and in church teaching. All this would serve to normalize and sanctify such violence. Thus it might have more impact on such a person than it would on an adolescent who plays the game in a different religious milieu, or a secular one, where the violent images are not reinforced and sanctified.[36]

The *Left Behind* books and video games graphically illustrate the clear and final demarcation of the saved and the damned, of good and evil. Such splitting and dichotomizing is found throughout other religious texts of terror, and many have commented on its salience in American apocalyptic Christianity. Many writers have noted that this splitting is central to the apocalyptic vision.[37] For example, Strozier writes that apocalyptic Christians believe that "nonbelievers are rejected by God and thus in some inexplicable way are only tentatively human." He then adds, "As such, nonbelievers are dispensable. If they intrude in the believer's world, the psychological conditions exist to make it possible for believers to accommodate violence toward nonbelievers."[38] This is one of the major the sociopsychological conditions that facilitate the move to violence. This same ferocious lack of empathy for potential victims can be found in every instance of religiously motivated violent and terrorist groups. In this way the ideology of American apocalyptic Christianity, and especially the *Left Behind* series, reiterates what one finds in virtually every religiously motivated text of terror: that religion contributes to what James Waller calls the "social death" of the other and so makes the other available as an object of violence.

What sort of God is it that presides over all this torture and bloodletting as described in *Glorious Appearing*? Clearly a God of wrath and vengeance. The authors leave no doubt that all these lakes and rivers of blood, this spilling of entrails, these hideous ways of dying, these melting eyes and bursting bodies were God's doing. A Jesus who rips open the stomach of his opponent and a God who mercilessly deprives men and women of the ability to repent and change certainly fit the image of the wrathful, controlling, and abjecting deities that psychological research has found associated with diminished empathy, authoritarian tendencies, and hostility, and that, not surprisingly, can be found in virtually all the texts and discourses of religiously motivated terrorists.[39]

What are some of the psychological processes by which religion might make someone violent? My own review of the material produced by religiously motivated terrorists from many different traditions suggests that universal religious themes such as purification and the search for reunion with the source of life can become subsumed into unconscious dynamics such as splitting and a Manichaean dichotomizing of the world into all-good and all-evil camps or the drive to connect with and appease a humiliating or persecuting idealized patriarchal other. The result is the psychological preconditions for religiously sponsored terrorism and violence.[40]

How does the *Left Behind* series fit in with other violent religious writings? *All the themes common to the language of religiously motivated terrorists are present in the* Left Behind *series*: (1) the sense of shame and humiliation at being left behind and the image of humanity as itself shameful; (2) the dichotomizing of the world into a war of the totally pure against the totally demonic; (3) a wrathful, punitive God; (4) a connection between purification and bloodshed; and (5) a fascination with and sanctification of violence. Given these parallels, the obvious question is the possible connection between this violence-soaked discourse in preaching, hymnology, and most graphically in the *Left Behind* series and games and the possibility of violent terrorist actions in the name of apocalyptic Christianity and its vengeful Jesus.[41] That question is beyond the scope of this chapter. But I can say that right now in the United States a whole generation of Christian adolescents is learning how to kill non-Christians, UN peacekeepers, and Christians less evangelical than themselves in the name of this apocalyptic Jesus.

10

Opening the Seven Seals of Fundamentalism

Charles B. Strozier

THE TEXT

The Book of Revelation poses unique challenges for anyone interested in fundamentalism. It is the paradigmatic text for endist Christians and indirectly stirs apocalyptic passions in countless millions of others, even those in faiths far removed from Christianity. In the world of fundamentalist churches a preacher earns his legitimacy (and it is almost always a "he") by demonstrating his deep knowledge of Revelation and his ability to convey that knowledge in meaningful ways to his congregation.[1] In the more totalistic communities of faith Revelation is at the center of their theology; for example, David Koresh would preach to his followers near Waco his "theology of the seven seals" for hour after hour in the blistering heat of Texas. In the general population, more than 25 percent are evangelicals, charismatics from Protestant denominations and especially from among Catholics, Pentecostals, and a host of nonaffiliated, mostly storefront, churches, gather in weekly prayer and Bible study that is grounded in the themes of the Book of Revelation, even if sometimes muted and by allusion in hymns sung lustily about being washed in the blood of the Lamb (12:11).[2] Such apocalyptic enthusiasms reverberate in contradictory ways in the culture. The media—including movies, television, and 24/7 news stations in many venues—feed on the apocalyptic. The more seemingly rational and reflective recoil in disgust and fall back on irony to grapple with such vulgar enthusiasms, without recognizing the authentic feelings of confusion about a human future that serve as the basis of all expressions of the apocalyptic. In a world of nuclear weapons we are all unsteady, including myself. There is no escape. The best one can hope for is some measure of understanding.

The Book of Revelation is more quoted than actually read, absorbed rather than studied, and evoked more in stirring hymns, in Handel's *Messiah*, and in the allusions of Martin Luther King Jr. than directly encountered. Revelation has always been hugely controversial. Writing in 95, John of Patmos is almost certainly not the John of the Gospels, but one cannot be absolutely sure of his identity. For many centuries the Church fathers tried to keep Revelation out of the canon, but its popularity with ordinary believers finally forced them in the ninth century to accept it as the last book of the New Testament. It is a confusing book, equal parts exhilarating and infuriating, hopeful and full of despair. But it is not without meaning and certainly not an aimless drift of mystical images. There is, for example, a coherent structure to the book. Overall Revelation consists of three waves of violence—seals that are opened, trumpets that are blown, and vials of wrath that are poured—each of which unfolds in a series of seven events. Each seventh opens to the next cascading wave of violence, so that, for example, the opening of the seventh seal releases the trumpets:

> And when he had opened the seventh seal, there was silence in heaven about the space of half an hour.
>
> And I saw the seven angels who stood before God, and to them were given seven trumpets. . . .
>
> And the seven angels who had the seven trumpets prepared themselves to sound. (8:1, 2, 6)

The major structural complication to the text is that inserted into the unfolding of the various sevens of seals, trumpets, and vials are seven digressions or "parentheses" on obscure subjects, such as the Whore of Babylon (17:3–6). The narrative culminates in the dramatic chapters 19–22 that include the final judgment, the second death for sinners, and the creation of a new heaven and earth for the redeemed, all in language that has seared itself into the imagination of the West.

The introduction to the basic story of the Book of Revelation takes up the first three chapters. Some general statements lead into our meeting of John of Patmos in 1:9, who becomes the narrator: "I, John, who also am your brother and companion in tribulation and in the kingdom and patience of Jesus Christ, was in the isle that is called Patmos for the Word of God and for the testimony of Jesus Christ." John reports, "I . . . heard behind me a great voice" who proclaims himself the Alpha and Omega, the first and last (1:10–11). This crucial passage establishes the Revelation of John of Patmos as a vision or dream. That is why the text is written in the past tense and more psychologically establishes at the outset that the book takes us into a spiritual dreamscape, legitimizing all the wild mysticism of its symbolic world but also opening the text up to a kind of analysis with which psychoanalysis has some familiarity. After the Alpha and Omega figure orders John to write to the seven churches in Asia, or Anatolia in what is now western Turkey (1:11), John turns to the voice and and sees seven golden lampshades and in their midst one who is the son of God, with a golden girdle and hair white like wool and eyes flames of fire and feet like bronze, and out of his mouth sticks a suggestively phallic sharp, two-edged sword (1:12–16). John falls at the feet of the mysterious figure, who tells him:

> Fear not; I am the first and the last;
> I am he that liveth, and was dead; and, behold, I am alive for ever more, Amen, and have the keys of hades and of death. (1:17–18)

For the next two and a half chapters John writes to the churches on behalf of the mysterious figure, who is generally taken to be the resurrected Jesus, though that is not clear in the text. The tone is scolding and angry. The churches are commanded to return to the way of God and stop their blasphemy. They are told that as Christians they need to steel themselves to suffering and martyrdom (even though "ye shall have tribulation," remember, "be thou faithful unto death, and I will give thee a crown of life" [2:10]), but most of all they must stop their sinful ways, their foul eating, their worship of idols, and their fornication. Otherwise they will be cast into tribulation and the children who issue forth from their fornication with Jezebel will be "killed with death" by Jesus himself (2:23). It is clear this Jesus is a very different kind of Christ from our familiar, loving one in the gospels, especially the Sermon on the Mount:

> Blessed are the poor in spirit; for theirs is the kingdom of heaven.
> Blessed are they that mourn; for they shall be comforted.
> Blessed are the meek; for they shall inherit the earth.
> Blessed are they who do hunger and thirst after righteousness; for they shall be filled.
> Blessed are the merciful; for they shall obtain mercy.
> Blessed are the pure in heart; for they shall see God.
> Blessed are the peacemakers; for they shall be called the sons of God.
> Blessed are they who are persecuted for righteousness sake; for theirs is the kingdom of heaven. (Matthew 5:3–10)

Chapter 4 of Revelation begins with John reporting that he heard a voice from heaven, "as it were" a trumpet, ordering him to "come up here" so that he can be shown things "which must be hereafter" (4:1). Such is the nature of the apocalyptic, those things that must be hereafter. The apocalyptic, derived from the Greek word *apokalypsis*, means "to uncover or disclose" and suggests a lifting of the veil to reveal a future God has already made happen, a future he knows but has yet to convey or let happen but will in good time, in his time and according to his whims and depending mostly on his anger. Such ideas about the future and God's role in it differ rather sharply from the more familiar prophetic tradition of the Old Testament and much of the Christian writings by Paul and others. In that prophetic tradition we are called to a change of heart, to repentance in the present, to a new way of living in anticipation of an end that will bring ultimate renewal and the Messiah (or his return). Prophecy in this sense is a call to efficacy and a challenge to change so that we can avoid catastrophe. In the apocalyptic, on the other hand, or the already determined future, hope is deferred. As a consequence the verb tense switches from the present to the future, which John experiences in his dream in a mystical present that he reports in the past tense, often using the conditional ("as it were" and "as though" are frequent textual insertions). This confusion of time and tense defines an important dimension of the apocalyptic.

Having been summoned to heaven John sees "in the right of him that sat on the throne a scroll written within and on the back, sealed with seven seals" (5:1). An angel asks who is worthy to open the seals, and John weeps because he knows no one is worthy. But he is told not to weep, for "behold, the Lion of the tribe of Judah, the Root of David, hath prevailed to open the scroll, and to loose its seven seals" (5:5). John sees a Lamb "as though it had been slain" with seven horns and seven eyes (5:6), who opens the first seal: "And I saw when the Lamb opened one of the seals, and I heard, as it were, the noise of thunder, one of the four living creatures saying, Come. And I saw and, behold, a white horse; and he that sat on him with a bow; and a crown was given unto him, and he went forth conquering, and to conquer" (6:1–2).

Each seal that is opened escalates the violence. The second releases another rider on a horse, though this one is red and has the power to "take peace from the earth, and that they should kill one another" (6:4). The third seal sends forth a black horse, and its rider holds a pair of balances (6:5); the fourth issues a pale horse with a rider whose very name is Death, "and Hades followed with him" with the power over a fourth of the earth "to kill with sword, and with hunger, and with death, and with the beasts of the earth" (6:8); the fifth reveals hiding under that altar "the souls of them that were slain for the word of God, and for the testimony which they held," crying out, as Martin Luther King Jr. was to ask in his last great and tragic speech, "How long, O Lord?" (6:9–10); and the mere opening of the sixth brings about a "great earthquake, and the sun became black as sackcloth of hair, and the moon became like blood" (6:12).

The principle of escalating violence continues in the text as trumpets are blown and vials of wrath are poured out. The blowing of the second trumpet releases "as it were" a "mountain burning with fire"; "the third part of the sea became blood" and all the creatures in it died and the ships were destroyed (8:8–9). The fourth trumpet leads to the opening of the bottomless pit; from it arises a smoke "like the smoke of a great furnace" that darkens the sun and spreads locusts and scorpions (9:1–3). Somewhat later the second vial of wrath pours into the sea "and it became like the blood of a dead man; and every living soul died in the sea" (16:3), while the wrath from the third bowl (the alternate word for vial) turns the "rivers and fountains" to blood (16:4). And so on.

Inserted in this story line are some very important digressions—seven of them, not surprisingly—that add texture and drama to the narrative in exactly the way dreams insert illogical images into their landscape to create complexity, meaning, and significance. The digressions bring into the story some of the best-known images from Revelation. In the middle of chapter 7, for example, John reports seeing the 144,000 of the "tribes of the children of Israel" who are "sealed" (7:4–8), an image that has prompted all kinds of exotic exegesis over the centuries. In chapter 11, speaking in the future tense, uncharacteristically as dreams sometimes do ("And I will give power unto . . ."), John says "two witnesses" will prophesy for 1,260 days "clothed in sackcloth" and with great power until the beast will ascend from the bottomless pit and slay them. The two witnesses will lie in the street for three and a half days, after which they will be resurrected and taken up to heaven (11:3–12). Marshall Applewhite and Bonnie Lu Nettles of the UFO cult Heaven's Gate (whose members committed collective suicide in 1997) called themselves "The Two" after these witnesses.[3] In chapter 13 we meet the beast that "rises up out of the sea, having seven heads and ten horns, and upon his horns ten crowns, and upon his heads the name of blasphemy," who "causeth all, both small and great, rich and poor, free and enslaved, to receive a mark in their right hand, or in their foreheads," and that mark is 666 (13:1–18). Finally one has to mention the Whore of Babylon, "with whom the kings of the earth have committed fornication" and who is arrayed in purple and scarlet and "bedecked with gold and precious stones and pearls, having a golden cup in her hand, full of abominations and filthiness of her fornication," drinking the "blood of the martyrs of Jesus" (17:2–6).

The climax of the book begins with chapter 19, when John reports hearing great voices from heaven saying "Hallelujah! Salvation, and glory, and honor, and power, until the Lord, our God" (19:1), words picked up by Handel in *The Messiah.* This heavenly multitude gathers for the marriage of the Lamb (though it is unclear what that means), and the heavens open to behold a white horse with a rider called "Faithful and True": "In righteousness he doth judge and make war." The rider's eyes are like flames of fire, and he is "clothed with a vesture dipped in blood." In a burst of phallic sadomasochism, out of the rider's mouth comes another mighty sword that he will use to "smite the nations," which he will rule with a "rod of iron" while he "treadeth the winepress of the fierceness and wrath of Almighty God" (19:11–16). The remaining verses 17–21 of chapter 19 are usually taken to be a description of the Battle of Armageddon, though the text does not call it that. Here the Great God eats the flesh of kings and captains and of mighty men and horses, making war on the beast, who, together with all those who received the mark, are thrown in "a lake of fire burning with brimstone" (19:20).

The violence cascades as the narrative erupts in a flurry of confusing images and events. An angel appears with a key to the bottomless pit. He lays hold of the Devil and binds him for a thousand years and casts him back into the bottomless pit. In that thousand-year period the souls of those who "were beheaded for the witness of Jesus, and for the word of God" reign with Christ (20:4). At the end of the thousand years for some reason Satan is "loosed out of his prison" and goes out "to deceive the nations which are in the four quarters of the earth, Gog and Magog, to gather them together to battle." God in rage sends down fire to devour them and sends the devil who deceived them (who may or may not be Satan) into the lake of fire, where they will be tormented forever.

At last comes hope and redemption. On a great white throne appears God, "from whose face the earth and the heaven fled away." He opens the books, including one that is the book of life: "And the dead were judged out of those things which were written in the books, according to their works" (20:11–12). The sea "gave up the dead that were in it," along with death itself and Hades. All are judged "according to their works." Death and Hades are cast into the lake of fire, along with all those not found listed in the book of life. "This is the second death," John says ominously (20:14). But John then sees a new heaven and a new earth and a holy city, a new Jerusalem, come down from heaven, "prepared as a bride adorned for her husband" (21:1–2). A voice from heaven tells John that God will wipe the tears from those who suffer and that there will be no more death, sorrow, crying, or pain. God is the Alpha and Omega. For one last time John is reminded of the awful fate that awaits "the fearful, and unbelieving, and the abominable, and murderers, and fornicators, and sorcerers, and idolaters, and all liars," for they "shall have their part in the lake which burneth with fire and brimstone, which is the second death" (21:8). That last reminder of the costs of unbelief and sin allows for an opening into a glorious description of the new Jerusalem, with its great wall of jasper and twelve gates leading into a city of pure gold, garnished with all manner of precious stones and a temple for the Lord God Almighty and the Lamb (21:10–27). In the final chapter John reports seeing a pure river and on its bank the tree of life with fruits and healing leaves. There is no day or night, "and there shall be no more curse, but the throne of God and of the Lamb shall be in it, and his servants shall serve him"

(22:1–5). John falls down to worship after seeing all this and is reminded by an angel of his duty to spread the word of his vision: "Seal not the words of the prophecy of this book; for the time is at hand" (22:6–11).

THE FUNDAMENTALIST MINDSET

This amazing text that has had such profound influence for nearly two millennia allows access to the inner workings of the fundamentalist mindset. Its deeper meanings can be grasped by opening our own seven seals to reveal this psychology.

One: Violence

The violence of the Book of Revelation is quite astonishing. Hail and fire mixed with blood are cast upon the earth, burning the mountains and turning the sea bloody (8:7–9); an angel pours wrath on the sun and scorches men with fire (16:8); strange riders of death prowl the land (6:5, 8); beasts wreak havoc (13:1–18); and the mighty whore drinks "abominations and filthiness of her fornication" from a golden cup (17:4). Destruction is everywhere, on the earth, in the seas, and in the mountains, and no living thing escapes God's wrath. The violence is exterminatory, or totalistic in nature, as it escalates toward apocalyptic forms.[4] The destruction unleashed by the opening of the fourth seal wipes out "a fourth part of the earth" (6:8); the blowing of the first trumpet wipes out a third part of trees and all green grass on the earth (8:7); the blowing of the second trumpet kills a third of all the living creatures in the sea and a third of all the ships upon it (8:9); and the blowing of the sixth trumpet releases four angels who assume responsibility for slaying a third of all men (9:15).[5] This widespread destruction culminates in the final judgment and the death of death itself, which God hurls majestically into the lake of fire (20:14). The fundamentalist mindset is drawn to such final answers, and the best construct for understanding the violence of the Book of Revelation is as a kind of biblical genocide. It is furthermore a genocide with agency from a very angry God, whom James W. Jones, in his contribution to this book, appropriately names a "divine terrorist."

There is, of course, a biblical context for the violence of Revelation. In Genesis, for example, God often exhibits his wrath at the sins and ingratitude of the humans he has created. He turns Adam and Eve out of Paradise for eating the fruit of the tree of knowledge (3:22–24), and later he wipes out all living things, except for Noah and his family and two of each of the animals in the ark (6:5–7). God is often angry at other points as well in the Hebrew Bible, but in general he betrays a definite sadness and regret and even a sense of empathy for those who suffer from his violence. When the Lord says before the flood, "I will destroy man whom I have created from the face of the earth," the text notes that the destruction of man "grieved him at his heart" (Genesis 6:5–7). In other places in the Hebrew Bible the violence that results from God's anger can be great but not genocidal. Deuteronomy reports, "We took all [Sihon's] cities at that time, and utterly destroyed the men, and the women, and the little ones of every city" (2:34), and Joshua is commanded to "smote all the country of the hills" and leave "none remaining" (10:40). In both cases, however, the destruction, though great, is localized and therefore highly circumscribed. Nothing in the Hebrew Bible, except perhaps the destruction described in the Book of Daniel, prepares one for the totalism of violence in Revelation.

The consequence for fundamentalist Christians, wallowing in the genocidal violence of Revelation, is what Garry Wills has described as an "embrace of death." It is really quite striking to hear a leader of the movement such as Pat Robertson escalate those whom he regards as nonbelievers into evil figures who implicitly can be dispensed with. For Robertson Episcopalians and Presbyterians thus carry the "spirit of the antichrist," which by definition makes them instruments of the devil. Fundamentalists' embrace of death extends in all directions. The completely misnamed pro-life ideology becomes not an ethical argument for life but gets yoked to policies opposing family planning, contraception, and sex education for young people.[6] Fundamentalists' embrace of death extends as well to their strong support for the death penalty, which is perhaps the most odious of all their enthusiasms, though what may turn out to be their most important position is their strong and unquestioned support for a robust foreign policy, war, and nuclear weapons. Together with their disregard for the earth and a human future, fundamentalists seem to live out the line from T. S. Eliot's poem *The Hollow Men*: "This is the way the world ends / Not with a bang but a whimper."

Two: Time

Time comes in many shapes. In the Cartesian world of rationality, a world in which science and progress seem immutable, time is evenly segmented and predictable. We know we ate lunch five hours ago and that tonight we will sleep another seven. In 2007 we knew Napoleon marched into Russia 195 years earlier, Columbus descended on the new world 515 years earlier, and Caesar became dictator of Rome 2,055 years earlier. Chronological time is so well ingrained in our unconscious that under hypnosis we know precisely when four days, six hours, and nineteen minutes have passed. Nothing more exactly captures chronological time than the precise calibration of the clock, which technology has pushed to new limits of precision in recent years. In atomic physics it can be calculated how long it takes for a quark particle to circle inside the proton of an atomic nucleus (10–22 seconds) and for an electron to orbit a proton (10–16 seconds), just as in cosmic time rules of calibration govern how fast the galaxies are moving away from each other since the Big Bang fourteen billion years ago.[7] It is psychologically comforting to trust the certainty of time unfolding in a predictable way. It would also be inconceivable to imagine the modern project, the scientific revolution, not to mention cities, roads, planes, and cars without a firm confidence in the predictability of time. Most of us embrace the modern world with varying degrees of enthusiasm, rejecting only pieces of the whole (for example, the pornography of violence that comes at us from the media), recognizing that we could never, and honestly would never want truly to reverse history and undo modernism. More conservative people in the culture, including those drawn to orthodoxy in many faiths, wish to slow down what they experience as a mad rush forward. Sometimes that resistance can be very determined, as with the Amish, but in all cases the yearning of the conservative and orthodox is for a real past, an actual past that existed and can, imaginably, be recovered, recreated, reinstituted.

Time, however, can also be kairotic. The Greek word *kairos* refers to qualitative time. The shape of this time is uneven and weighted for value, prized in psychological experience for its specific qualities, broken down, disjointed, and entirely unpredictable. Even in the rational world of modernism most would agree that time is accelerating in the objective sense that change in all areas of life occurs ever more rapidly. In the more specifically psychological realm Freud's proposal that the Oedipus complex is present in us from four to six years of age describes a quintessentially kairotic time, just as he argued in 1893 with Joseph Breuer that "hysterics suffer mainly from reminiscences."[8] More generally one can understand trauma only if one grasps the way it inserts itself as kairotic time in the self. Such moments of suffering in the past continue as though in the present, denying the past as it is relived, seeking fitfully and in despair a future with hope. Trauma forces a new kind of salience about time, bending it back on itself. In the dark tunnel of trauma one never knows how long it takes to travel to the light, or even whether one may trust that there is such a light, though the redemptive hope for the faithful lies in that imagined future, that moment when God acts, as in Mark: "The time [kairos] is fulfilled, and the kingdom of God is at hand; repent, and believe the gospel" (1:15).

Apocalyptic time is a totalized version of the kairos. In the apocalyptic, time is forever running out, which accounts for the terrible urgency one finds in Revelation and in the lives of fundamentalists in all faiths. This kind of experience of time has almost nothing to do with an actual past, which is to say with history. Apocalyptic time in fact reverses past and future. In the apocalyptic, time is idealized and diseased. John's vision in Revelation becomes the reported past of an imagined future. It is a call to faith now so that the inevitable future can be deferred. Such radical reversals, so common in mysticism, define this aspect of the apocalyptic mindset. An important consequence psychologically but also politically is to free fundamentalists from an obligation to the actual past and present, that is, the world as we know it. They are defined spiritually *and* ethically only by their relation to an imagined future. What they know best and really care about is the return of Jesus, their reading of John's version of tribulation, and their redemption when that book of life is opened at the final judgment.

To live psychologically as endists in this way is more than a retreat from history or a quiet rebellion against it. Endists, on the contrary, escape history by destroying time. Not to live within time is to be free of responsibility for the world and for the earth itself. Such freedom from time furthermore allows for an idealized future to be projected back into a mystical past. Fundamentalists have no desire to slow down time; they want it created altogether new. Christian fundamentalists, for example, do not experience Israel as a real place. It is God's land, and in their minds exists only as it is described in the Bible. Palestinians for all intents and purposes literally do not count. Jews are there to "ingather," as they say, and somehow influence the return of Jesus to Jerusalem.[9] The settler movement in Israel, growing out of the millennial movement Gush Emunim, or Bloc of the Faithful, that took shape in the wake of the victories in the 1967 war, is intensely apocalyptic and is filled with loose talk about God's gift of the land to Abraham as his covenant and quotes from Genesis about the boundaries of that real estate stretching from the "river of Egypt unto the great river, the river Euphrates" (15:18), which is to say all of the Middle East. And Osama bin Laden and the Islamists in general yearn in wildly mystical ways to re-create the world as they imagine it was at the time of the Prophet rather than its state of *jahiliyyah*, or ignorance, the state it was in before the Prophet and into which it has again fallen.[10]

The desire to kill time in this way arises out of a deep confusion about death. As Frank Kermode has noted, of all the world's religions Christianity is the most anxious about death, but it is not the only one.[11] Death (and mystical rebirth) is at the center of everything to do with fundamentalism, which then extends this anxiety in extreme ways. In Robert Jay Lifton's terms, fundamentalists totalize death.[12] Dread of endings becomes a denial of death in the myth of the final judgment that kills death, and time, while bringing eternal, and timeless, life to the faithful. God is not just angry at a specific group of sinners—homosexuals, idolaters, fornicators—who will suffer in the end time. They are only markers, or signs, of a more general descent into sin. God is enraged at absolutely everyone except those martyred saints huddling under the altar when the fifth seal is opened. God has no remorse. In fact he gleefully smites the nations with his "rod of iron" and seems glad to turn the rivers red with blood. He sits on his mighty throne with a smirk of paranoid certitude as all sinners and nonbelievers are cast into the lake of fire. The end is absolute. Time melts off the table, as in the Dali painting, then ends completely in the totalistic resolution of eternal suffering for sinners and eternal bliss in the new Jerusalem for the redeemed.

Three: Revenge

The theme of revenge against sinners dominates Revelation. It has its own dialect. From the very beginning, John reports in his letters to the churches God's angry language for their sinning ways, with references to killing their children with death (2:23), ruling them with a rod of iron (2:27), and how the devil "shall cast some of [them] into prison" (2:10). Much of the rest of the violence throughout the book centers on the specific theme of revenge on those who have made the redeemed of the earth suffer. For example, the martyred saints huddling under the altar when the fifth seal is opened crying out "How long O Lord?" continue, "Doest thou not judge and avenge our blood on them that dwell on the earth?" (6:10). In a very real sense all of the violence that constitutes the biblical genocide of Revelation is purposeful and aimed at those who have fallen away from the path of righteousness. The story of the two witnesses turns on the ridicule heaped upon their dead bodies following their murder by the beast. After their resurrection, however, God makes a great earthquake to slay the seven thousand who had mocked the two witnesses (10:11–13). The parenthetic story of the beast whose mark the sinners must have planted on them sharply demarcates those who are not redeemed and will of course suffer greatly at the end (13:17–18). The Whore of Babylon, an exotic figure who feeds off the blood of the martyrs, suffers terribly for her sins: "And the ten horns which thou sawest upon the beast, these shall hate the harlot, and shall make her desolate and naked, and shall eat her flesh, and burn her with fire" (17:16). And of course in the final judgment this process of revenge reaches a totalistic culmination, as *all* sinners, along with death itself and Hades, are thrown into the lake of fire (20:14). The absolutist idea of a final judgment emerges out of a fundamentalist notion of total revenge toward sinners. It is not surprising that apocalyptic characters in history, such as the Nazis, embraced a project like the "final solution," their genocidal attempt to annihilate every single Jew in the world.

One of the most curious constructs in the Book of Revelation, one that has burned itself into the imagination of fundamentalists, is the idea of the second death that enters into the discussion in chapters 20 and 21. This mystical image of a second death has a very long lineage in religious thought. It seems to have begun with the ancient Egyptians, who enshrined the concept in the *Book of the Dead* around 2000 BCE. For the Egyptians the first death is carried out by Seth and consists of dismemberment and isolation. Many of the elaborate funerary rituals of the ancient Egyptians were grounded in honoring the dismemberment and isolation that Seth inflicts, and many stories describe attempts by Osiris and others to prevent a further annihilation. It is this ultimate annihilation that constitutes the second death, which, as Jan Assmann notes, "had by all means to be warded off." Everything had to be mobilized to repel, humiliate, condemn, and punish Seth, precisely to prevent him from carrying out his further annihilation, which meant warding off the second death. As Assmann makes clear, "The first death was a transition into an immortality that immunized [men] against that further, ultimate death."[13]

The idea of the second death worked its way into Zoroastrianism and Judaism (e.g., the Book of Daniel), though very much in the margins until John of Patmos picked it up in Revelation. For John the image of the second death connects symbolically with a number of themes important for fundamentalists. In the text, of course, it represents a critical moment in the final judgment when all sinners are raised from the dead after the first biological end of their existence and are condemned to ultimate punishment and everlasting damnation in their second death in the lake of fire, into which is also thrown death itself. Death, in other words, dies its own death, which can only be the second time around in the mystical imagery of Revelation. In another sense the idea of a second death connects significantly with another important dimension of fundamentalism, namely, that in the fundamentalist world important things have to happen twice. To be redeemed one must be born again, and to be adequately saved *all* of one's enemies must not only die but must suffer an awful eternal second death in the lake of fire. The dynamic relationship between one's personal redemption and the suffering of sinners is not accidental. In fact one suspects that in terms of the revenge motif in the book the totality of the suffering of sinners plays an important psychological role in the salvation of the faithful.

The violence of the revenge motif in Revelation is ethically masked for the individual believer because of the reversal of agency. It is not the believer who wishes all sinners, idolaters, fornicators, and homosexuals to suffer. The reader who enters into the spirit of the text need not own in a psychological or ethical sense the violence that is inflicted on his or her enemies. It is only God who is wrathful. It is he who carries out the judgment, rains down violence, turns the rivers red, and carries out the final judgment. God is the agent, which furthermore makes the violence not simply necessary but inevitable and worthy. It is easy and actually quite common for otherwise gentle and believing fundamentalists to revel in this world of violent and radical revenge against nonbelievers without owning to any significant degree the implications of such violence.

One can only maintain such separation, however, by a systematic disowning of one's own feelings. Splitting and dissociation lie at the center of the fundamentalist self, which is inevitably broken and divided to allow for such easy separation of thoughts and feelings. Fundamentalists' personal stories, as in Revelation, are discontinuous and full of trauma. Only the experience of being reborn through faith heals them. That trauma in the lives of fundamentalists enters into their deepest experiences and then finds meaningful expression in the rhetoric of Revelation. That rhetoric in turn builds on the divisions within the fundamentalist self and reflects in the violent revenge motif the evil and pained past that has been discarded in the experience of being reborn. These dualisms are further reflected in the text: Satan opposes God; only a remnant of the faithful survive the end times; violence pours out on the ungodly, and our bad, discarded, pre-Christian selves are washed clean in the suffering of those sinners at the hands of a wrathful God. The text of Revelation reflects these radical dualisms but also reinforces them in a powerful experience of ritualistic sacralization.

Four: Paranoia

Behind one of our seven seals lies the important theme of paranoia, which runs throughout the Book of Revelation. Reading the text in fact makes most decent people shiver with some fear of victimization, in part because the language and imagery are so powerfully evocative. It would be redundant, however, to dwell at this point on the paranoid theme in Revelation, which is discussed at length in my earlier chapter (chapter 6, "The Apocalyptic Other") and in the chapter by David Terman, "The Paranoid Gestalt" (chapter 5).

Five: Survivalism

A survivor is one who has been exposed to death and yet remained alive. Lifton notes that the central experience of the survivor is that of a *"jarring awareness of the fact of death."* That experience shatters any previous illusions of invulnerability and confronts the survivor with his or her own mortality and death anxiety. The survivor is left with a heightened vulnerability, a "breakdown of faith in the larger human matrix" and in the "general structure of existence." At the same time Lifton stresses that the survivor retains the opposite image within the self of having met death and conquered it, which can lead to a sense of *"reinforced invulnerability."* This experience or image gives the survivor a sense of having come back from the death experience with a deeper and more profound knowledge of having died and gone to the other side but then come back and been reborn. Lifton encountered these contrasting images in all of the survivors of Hiroshima, the *hibakusha*, he interviewed, but he notes that the same theme is evident in the literature of survivors of the Holocaust.[14]

Revelation is a narrative of survival that radicalizes it into a form of what I call *survivalism*. The saved suffer, remain pure, and are redeemed. They are arrayed against a host of evil forces, but God intervenes and saves them. They witness apocalyptic death and become themselves eternal. There is no sadness at the death of sinners, that is, no empathy, only gloating at their terrible suffering and demise. And so the fundamentalist world embraces evil. It confirms their persecution and certainty of redemption. Wishing for salvation, fundamentalists often therefore seek out evil and feed off it. "How long?" they cry, and John replies, "Soon." In the odd present that is merely a waiting period for the redeemed apocalyptic future, that certainty gives them a secret pleasure at sin that is far more than projected wish. Any visible proof of sin merits God's wrath and their salvation. Pornography, homosexuality, and abortion, for example, are abhorrent but also welcomed as living proof of the survival of the elect precisely because the text says so. It is all written down as the revealed future. It only needs to be lived out to be fulfilled.

Survivalism carries a violent undertow that remains a quiescent potential in most fundamentalists but can occasionally erupt on the margins. The visible presence of sin in the modern world as fundamentalists define it titillates those who live their spiritual lives in the active anticipation of watching idolaters, fornicators, and homosexuals suffer the brutality of God's wrath. They believe they know how the story ends. But it can be a bit too much for the more anxious and troubled to hold off waiting for God to act. Why not hurry it along? The rhetoric of a genocide of aborted babies assures the faithful of their salvation but can encourage extremists to act on God's behalf and murder the doctors who carry out the abominable procedures.[15] Sometimes during historical crisis such impulses can coalesce into vast apocalyptic movements of great destructiveness, as with the Nazis. The radical embrace of violence by the Nazis was quite telling, and it led to making war against all enemies and an attempt to wipe out the great evil other. The final Götterdämmerung realized that original impulse toward survival out of death. In this apocalyptic world survivalism is the twin of destruction.

Six: The Elect

The surviving elect who are saved from God's wrath in Revelation and are ultimately redeemed as his chosen few share some rather curious characteristics that have important meanings for the fundamentalist movement. In the text it is made clear that the surviving remnant will be definitely few in number. Those who huddle under the altar are so limited in number that they can be easily counted. Such counting of those who count becomes an important, if baffling, issue in the sealing of the 144,000 chosen from the tribes of Israel. The spiritual issue is not so much the exact meaning of the 144,000 but that any number would be so clearly demarcated for redemption. There is also no question that the elect will suffer significant persecution in this lifetime for which they will be rewarded in the hereafter. Besides the huddling martyrs, these 144,000 seem to be virgins and "not defiled with women" (14:4). In their purity the elect are deemed worthy to be protected by a tender God. The same Almighty who destroys the earth and fills it with blood reaches down with a gentle hand to nurture the elect and ensure their ultimate salvation: "For the Lamb who is in the midst of the throne shall feed them, and shall lead them unto living fountains of waters; and God shall wipe away all tears from their eyes" (7:17). This carefully constructed dichotomy between the split God who wreaks vengeance on the one hand and on the other wipes tears from those who suffer breaks down in the final judgment, when it seems part of the glee at salvation lies in the total destruction of one's enemies.

This dualism surrounding the images of the elect carries over into the actual fundamentalist world, which thrives on evil without and the certainty of salvation for the elect within. Such a rigid dualism often incurs the consequence of fragmenting churches into small totalistic communities in which the sense of persecution and victimization by an outside evil world can push some groups into cults. This process of isolation and rising paranoia tends to sanctify cultists own victimization, which can allow for an easy switch into violence. At Waco, for example, David Koresh and his followers were in fact the victims of persecution by authorities who believed that illegal activities were going on in the community (including legitimate concerns about child abuse). Koresh and his key aides gathered together weapons, food, and other instruments of survival in a way that sought protection against an evil world but also anticipated and even welcomed an attack. When the authorities then bungled their own approach and in fact unnecessarily assaulted the compound, the small group of faithful were prepared for full-scale battle and fired back, killing four ATF agents. What ensued was a travesty of government power but one in which the cult itself cocreated the violence. Another, equally tragic potential outcome of this process of radical concentration and simplification is Jonestown. There collective suicide was the response to the persecution, even if largely imagined, from without.

Seven: Redemption

There is much that is hopeful in the Book of Revelation: "He that overcometh, the same shall be clothed in white raiment: and I will not blot his name out of the book of life" (3:5). There is no question it is a text that has inspired positive social change. A Marxist analysis, which has been important for many in the developing world, especially in Latin America, interprets the dichotomous images of good and evil in class terms. It is the evil bourgeoisie who ultimately incur the wrath of God, while the all-suffering proletariat are redeemed in the New Jerusalem. The poor and oppressed will inherit the earth in Marx's transformative and definitely apocalyptic vision of a classless utopia. Revelation also inspired the abolitionist movement in the United States. Once abolitionism got under way in the 1830s it drew on Revelation imagery to assure the hopeful of the doom awaiting those truly evil masters for all the cruelty inflicted on the slaves, whose suffering from the bloody whip, the brutality of broken families, the abuses, and the legitimized violence fit precisely the story line.[16]

But it is frankly disturbing to witness the current uses of the text by privileged white Americans. There is great potential for violence when the ruling class feels victimized. There are certainly those who suffer in America, especially in communities of color and whose lives are suffused in violence, who draw hope from the firm belief that they may now be huddling beneath the altar but will eventually be called forth by a loving God to ease their pain on those golden streets of the New Jerusalem. But fundamentalism in America is basically a white phenomenon and one that is moving up the social scale. It huddles now behind gated communities. There is something malevolent in those with the most privilege embracing this particular text of violent retribution, paranoia, and revenge to define the contours of their spiritual landscape. It feeds their prejudices and in political terms puts a brake on implementing the equality for all so easily within our reach. The violence can spin out of control in completely unpredictable ways.

Revelation is a dangerous and ugly book. We need to read it closely to contain its violence on the page. It must not break out.

11

The Unsettling of the Fundamentalist Mindset

Shifts in Apocalyptic Belief in Contemporary Conservative Christianity

Lee Quinby

To say that the fundamentalist mindset is becoming unset or at least unsettled in the United States is not to deny the unquestionable upsurge of right-wing Christian political organizing and sentiment during the past quarter-century. The entrenchment of fundamentalist values in the late twentieth century was most notably marked by the establishment of the Moral Majority and groups like the Promise Keepers, the growth and power of institutions such as Liberty University, and the rise of Christian home schooling. Nevertheless deep-rooted fundamentalist beliefs and practices—especially around gender, sexuality, and related issues of social justice—are showing marked signs of instability that go much deeper than the sphere of political organizing associated with the religious right. While some of this alteration is due to the stunning failures of George W. Bush during his eight years in office and the corresponding disappointment of his conservative Christian supporters, disaffection is not the only factor. The unsettling of the fundamentalist mindset also results from over half a century of activist struggles for civil and human rights.

Because of the latter influence in particular, some scholars are quite sanguine about these changes. Walter Russell Mead, for example, argues that religious movements in the United States are "following a path toward pluralism and moderation."[1] Alan Wolfe describes this tendency as worldwide.[2] Yet the change is neither so uniform and simple nor so directly progressive. Christian fundamentalism these days exhibits much more volatility than such assessments would have it. Some members are decisively moving forward toward democratic Christianity, yet others are defensively stepping backward toward patriarchal fundamentalism, embracing isolation, moral rigidity, and militant authoritarianism; many are content with an increasingly diluted form of fundamentalist belief. In each case the third crucial factor propelling shifts that are taking place is the momentous effect of media-saturated commodity capitalism. This is also the factor that is most unpredictable both in nature and consequence.

What I am calling the unsettling of the fundamentalist mindset is visible in expressions of apocalyptic belief, which has long been prevalent in American culture generally and is a mainstay of Christian fundamentalism. The old apocalyptic frame of mind is still clearly delineated in the most doctrinaire religious denominations and is continually reinforced by institutionalized power structures of end-time Christian family, church, and school. At the same time, however, a dilution of apocalyptic values is gaining cultural acceptance, partly through the rise of megachurches that preach prosperity and positive thinking and particularly through media momentum, which often partakes of satire and sensationalism regarding end-time belief. In this chapter I explore shifts within contemporary apocalypticism to gauge a sense of their effects on American fundamentalism and evangelicalism in the twenty-first century.[3]

There are, of course, many important distinctions to be made between fundamentalism and evangelicalism, as well as among denominations within each camp. Nevertheless they—and even many secular Americans—have long exhibited a tendency to see the world and its inhabitants through an apocalyptic lens. As Charles Strozier explained in his pathbreaking discussions of the psychology of Christian fundamentalism in America, this includes a disposition toward moral absolutism, a sense of self propelled toward future salvation, literalist rather than metaphorical thinking, and strict divisions between good and evil.[4] Such views are integral to those who adhere to end-time religions, but they are also influential in the wider sphere of American society. American patriotism, for example, is rife with a sense that the United States is a chosen nation; anxieties over climate change and pandemics often take their drama and urgency from rhetoric and images associated with the Book of Revelation; and the acceptance of gender oppositions that divide women into virgins and Jezebels continues to be felt in a wide variety of everyday practices, from family to fashion. Yet it is precisely these patterns that are undergoing the shift that is worthy of our attention, especially if it is possible to encourage those changes to embrace more democratic values.

Changing patterns of the religious mindset are borne out in surveys conducted in the past few years by the Copernicus Marketing Firm and the Pew Forum on Religion and Public Life. Drawing on data from the University of Chicago's National Opinion Research Center, the Copernicus survey looked at whether Americans consider themselves to be religious liberals, moderates, or fundamentalists, and found that the number designating themselves liberal increased from 18 percent in 1972 to 29 percent in 2002, while the number of those who call themselves fundamentalists increased only from 27 to 30 percent in the same period. The number of moderates, by contrast, decreased from 52 to 36 percent.[5] While this shows fundamentalism holding steady in terms of self-designation, liberalism is clearly expanding, apparently drawing from moderates. I want to show that even the group that identifies itself as fundamentalist is far more diverse within that category than in previous decades. The Pew findings show a great deal of fluidity within religious affiliation, indicating that 28 percent of Americans "have left the faith in which they were raised in favor of another religion—or no religion at all" and that the biggest gain was among the unaffiliated, at 16.1 percent.[6]

Both of these surveys demonstrate that American religion functions within a competitive marketplace. Which religion one belongs to is increasingly perceived as a question of choice, placing the onus of attraction largely on pastors who must appeal to followers. Apocalyptic belief circulates within this theological bazaar at a time when it is also being decisively altered by media representation. In the first part of this chapter I describe the old apocalyptic way of thinking, particularly in light of its gender and sexual premises and the psychological strife it creates. In the second part I look at gradual shifts in the patriarchal legacy that reflect the impact of social justice movements and social change generally, and in the third part I consider the ramifications of current, rapid-fire modifications in American apocalypticism due to the propulsions of media- and commodity-influenced portrayals.

THE APOCALYPTIC LEGACY: FUNDAMENTALLY GENDERED AND SUBJECT TO SUBMISSION

It has long been my contention that American society is apocalyptic in a loose sense, stemming largely from the considerable impact of the Christian New Testament's Apocalypse, or Book of Revelation, on the culture at large.[7] My argument is basically that for the most part the Book of Revelation has had a detrimental effect, instilling a sense of fatalism that envisions the world as a battlefield between cosmic forces of good and evil and diminishes a sense of human agency necessary for democratic justice. When disasters such as Hurricane Katrina occur, when wars are waged, or when economies slump, the apocalyptic mindset generates an impulse to regard the crisis as inevitable and justified, as if the sufferers deserved punishment. Thus a sense of divine determinism seeps in, human fault is ignored, and human aid is neglected.

It is particularly useful to explore the gender dualism of the Book of Revelation because it is so intertwined with, and partly responsible for, the apocalyptic tendencies of American culture.[8] The stark relief of gender dynamics in Revelation makes clear why it is important to ease gender division rather than shore it up in the way fundamentalist groups would have it. This is no easy task. Modernizing gender and sexual relations alters the family itself and deeply threatens fundamentalist values. In the face of those alterations the fundamentalist inclination is to shore up patriarchal values. Of course to characterize the Book of Revelation as patriarchal is hardly novel, since it came out of a culture in which God is described as the supreme and fearsome Father and earthly patriarchs held power and authority over their group and hence over other men, whose obedience was mandated. Those men in turn ruled over the members of their family, so that women were subordinated to men in general. It is not surprising that the text echoes that belief system and the relations of power out of which it emerged.[9] What is at stake for us is to see how and why these patterns of thought and distribution of power remain operative in the contemporary world, how and why they continue to channel social expectation, and, crucial to this chapter, how and why certain changes in that pattern are under way.

Apocalyptic gender patterns unfold as a series of dualisms, with retribution waged against iniquity. Revelation's basic dualisms line up as a cosmic conflict between Good and Evil, Truth and Deception, and the Faithful and the Unfaithful. These seem to be gender-free, but it turns out that they are underwritten by sexual purity and sanctioned male messianic violence, a conflict between Spiritual Purity and Bodily Impurity, 144,000 Virginal Men and Jezebel and her followers, New Jerusalem and the Whore of Babylon, and Warrior Jesus and Warrior Satan. The unsurpassable drama of Revelation results from the rigidity of these opposing forces. Any gray areas would dilute the moral force of the argument. This dualistic system insists on an authoritarian morality that condemns any other view of morality as an evil force.

The naturalization of these dualisms and the power relations they support are foundational to the apocalyptic mindset as manifest in American society. But how did American society come to be so apocalyptic in its orientation? Three main avenues of explanation—history, discourse analysis, and analysis of subjectivity—show how apocalypticism became entrenched in American culture. Historically, apocalyptic belief was most forcefully imported with the Puritans, whose theocratic government used the Old Testament as a guide for their laws and the Book of Revelation as prophecy of what was to come. The providential history worldview of the Puritans was thoroughly saturated with images and concepts from the Book of Revelation, and clearly the governors and magistrates found it a useful tool to maintain strict order and hierarchy within their colonies. Furthermore, in accordance with its moral vision, violence was used as a direct means of control. Puritan plans for colonization justified displacing and at times annihilating their perceived enemies. This included the indigenous population, whom they cast as Satan's pawns. Dissenters from within their own community were tortured, executed, or exiled, which usually meant death. The Puritans saw themselves as fulfilling God's preordained vision of creating a "city on a hill," a New Jerusalem. This readiness to destroy the perceived enemy of one's ideals may be understood as a function of what David Terman identifies as the "paranoid gestalt." As he argues, "It is often a moral imperative, indeed a moral virtue to eradicate, kill, those who want to prevent or destroy the establishment of the ideal condition; in fact that destruction itself is often seen to lead to the ideal state."[10] In other words they thought of themselves as the Chosen, those whom God favored, and Revelation provided justification to deploy their earthly power while awaiting divinely wrought fulfillment.

I call this abiding sense of being chosen *electism* and see it as an ongoing element of American exceptionalism today.[11] Electism ordains the Faithful versus the Unfaithful or We versus They dualism that apocalyptic belief is built on. In this system of thought there is always an unredeemable enemy. During the Revolutionary War England was the ungodly threat, and the moral righteousness and urgency characteristic of apocalyptic belief was marshaled on behalf of the divinely ordained nation. As Strozier has demonstrated, in the Civil War both sides saw themselves as doing God's bidding.[12] Over many subsequent wars U.S. nationalism has been infused with electism and its justification for defeating a demonized enemy.

A more recent example of electism can be seen in President Bush's "Remarks on the War on Terror" from October 2005. Here the president twice appeals to a concept of evil and a call to total victory that is saturated with apocalyptic zeal:

> The evil that came to our shores on September 11th has reappeared on other days and in other places. In cities across the world, we have seen images of destruction and suffering that can seem like random acts of madness but are part of a larger terrorist threat. To combat this evil, we must remember the calling of September 11th—we will confront this mortal danger to all humanity and not tire or rest until the war on terror is won.[13]

This passage shows how deftly historically imported apocalyptic discourse can be expanded to include new arenas and justify violence. That this distinctive discourse has been stretched around so many new events over two millennia is due to the unique elasticity of the concepts and languag Revelation. Because Revelation is intensely symbolic and nonlinear it can readily be attached to a given cause, demonize an enemy, and apply to one's own time. This has been done in American culture time and time again. Even when God as the prime authority falls out of the picture, the categories of transcendent moral authority, inevitability, and urgency remain. So too do the book's images of destruction and its promises of triumph for the deserving. As a discourse apocalypticism has been one of the handiest tools for religious and political leaders ever devised. It marshals solidarity against a perceived enemy, catalyzes a sense of urgency, and promises believers that the truth is on their side. At a personal level fathers as leaders of their families have been able to draw on these same principles to buttress their authority.

But apocalypticism also has to be renewed constantly since it is incongruous with experience. This is not to deny very real threats to humanity, whether from nuclear catastrophe or the ruination of the earth and its resources from global warming. It is rather to question the certainty that accompanies claims for ultimate destruction, to bring a bit of skepticism to prophetic warnings. First of all, the promise of the end time happening soon has been wrong for more than two thousand years—and many times over. And its absolutism flies in the face of all kinds of ambiguity. This is where subjectivity, and more precisely subject formation, comes into the analysis. Drawing on the insight of Michel Foucault, we can see how apocalyptic power/knowledge relations produce apocalyptic subjects, both within families and as members of the nation.[14] Combining Foucault's insight with Freudian psychology, Judith Butler points out, "Power is not simply what we oppose but also, in a strong sense, what we depend on for our existence and what we harbor and preserve in the beings that we are."[15] Understanding power in this way means that an inner life is produced in the very process of subject formation. Although the psyche is inscribed with many prohibitions, it is not simply repressive. Rather it is the effect of incorporated training, as found in family structures, schools, religious institutions, clinics, dance classes, popular culture, and so on. It thus makes sense to talk about an apocalyptic subjectivity to designate a psychology subjected to the teachings and values found in the Book of Revelation. Gender dualism, messianic rescue, and obedience to authority are foundational to that psychology.

Crucial to the link with Freud, Butler argues, is that cultural processes of subjection produce a radical ambivalence in which the subject emerges through "passionate attachment" to his or her own subordination.[16] This formulation helps clarify why members of even a democratic society are so susceptible to compliance with power relations that subordinate them, and it is clearly integral to a fundamentalist mindset. The traditional family structure in which fathers are seen as the final authority, which held sway until only recently and still does in strict fundamentalist circles, reauthorizes for every generation a sense of obedience to higher authority as a profound virtue. The inevitable tensions that surround obedience versus the desire to throw it off are accentuated in a culture that also espouses freedom from submission.

These tensions are exacerbated by the gender dualism of apocalyptic belief. Its patriarchal legacy hardens ambivalence about women. An infant's extreme dependency on his or her mother as a far more powerful being inevitably produces conflicting bonds of love, hatred, fear, and rage since we come into being as subjects filled with desire for those who have power to both sustain and annihilate us. This may well be inexorable, although it can be eased by shared child rearing. But in apocalyptic belief, because women are deemed subordinate to men yet are also exclusively responsible for childcare, this desire becomes a source of sharper psychic conflict for both men and women, though this conflict is differentiated for each. What does it mean to desire a woman, a subordinate being? What does it mean to be one? What does it mean to identify with one's mother if one is male and is not supposed to? Such questions prompt reflection about the kinds of turmoil and possible violence that the apocalyptic mindset ferments within the psyche.

Traditional forms of violence associated with patriarchal cultures are currently subdued in American fundamentalism. Punitive physical violence against transgressive women—"Jezebels"—is less often sanctioned. In fact if we take the long view, which incorporates outright torture of such women, apocalyptic vengeance has steadily softened over the past few centuries. These days dissenters are subjected to therapeutic treatment as a means to promote normative conduct. Violence thus takes the form of psychic violation that accentuates tendencies toward self-abasement. The difficulty a Christian fundamentalist woman faces is in learning to love the father and later the husband who renounces her desire for life beyond the domestic sphere but also idealizes the spiritualized feminine principle she represents but can never be. As a mother she is called upon to control her children and keep them from sin, one reason that home schools have become one of the duties of many fundamentalist mothers. The resolution she is offered involves learning to experience an intensity of love for a masculine God who encourages expression of her inherent worthlessness and is ready to bestow eternal punishment on her if she fails to fully submit to his authority. Her reward is the possibility of being reborn into the spirit, that is, without the burden of her gender. In this light feminist espousals of freedom and liberal democracy's insistence on the equality of women are perceived as threats, stirring fear and anger toward such groups. Outright violence against them is unlikely. Instead women are urged to channel their energy toward political and legal suppression of their sexual and reproductive freedom.

For fundamentalist men violence and psychic violation come through a different struggle. There is an intertwined obligation to do violence in the name of love. This is cultivated through coercive emulation of the masculine God who enacts sacred violence on behalf of the Chosen. There is also an inward violence against any features associated with femininity. Men's difficulty comes in renouncing within themselves that which they initially identify with and depend on. The fear they experience in relation to the mother figure may aid this process of self-renunciation, but it makes the mandate of heterosexuality more difficult. As men they must love what they fear and renounce as a threat to their salvation. Further they are under obligation to renounce desire for other men while at the same time intensely desiring a masculine God. Significantly homophobia is one area in which rhetorical violence and legal denial of rights remains most pronounced in Christian fundamentalism.

The maintenance of a patriarchal gender/sexual dualism is why Christian (and not just fundamentalist) men are more likely than women to become involved in physical violence against others. As Ruth Stein has explained, a "'vertical' homoerotic quest for God's love" takes its most extreme form in fundamentalism, and when manifest in socially extreme circumstances can lead to violence against those perceived as an obstacle to desire for God's love.[17] Mark Juergensmeyer points to the problem of sexuality for those, again mostly men, who become terrorists on behalf of religious fundamentalism. Sex "out of place," as homosexuality is perceived to be, or "out of control," as with women who determine their own sexual freedom via abortion or birth control, is seen as a threat to morally rigid men.[18] In some instances such threats have resulted in drastic actions, such as bombing abortion clinics and killing doctors who perform abortions. Domestic violence against women and homophobic violence remain a problem in the United States but cut across all religious denominations. They are the result of Americans' patriarchal apocalyptic morality in general rather than that within fundamentalism specifically.

In contemporary American culture, when patriarchal apocalyptic principles and psychic turmoil show up in the extreme, they are easy enough to spot. Take, for example, *The Turner Diaries*, the blatantly sexist and racist book that Timothy McVeigh carried in his car when he bombed the Oklahoma City Federal Building in 1995. It is said to have served as his handbook for carrying out divine retribution for the U.S. government's actions at Waco against the Branch Davidians.[19] At one point in *The Turner Diaries* the narrator, Earl Turner, records the following telling commentary: "Liberalism is an essentially feminine, submissive world view. Perhaps a better adjective han feminine is infantile. It is the world view of men who do not have the moral toughness, the spiritual strength to stand up and do single combat with life, who cannot adjust to the reality that the world is not a huge, pink and blue, padded nursery in which the lions lie down with the lambs and everyone lives happily ever after."[20] Thankfully in the United States today there aren't that many Earl Turners around. But when they do appear on the scene—as with McVeigh, or Rev. Paul Hill, who killed Dr. John Britton and his bodyguard James Barrett outside Britton's abortion clinic—they put the danger of the apocalyptic mindset into sharp focus.[21]

For the most part, however, Christian fundamentalists in the United States today would be fairly characterized as nonviolent, even if many are highly conflicted at a psychic level. Thus we don't see many Earl Turners in action, though we hear echoes of his antiliberalism and misogyny. Although certain conditions could presumably lead to eruptions of large-scale violence, in the United States we have not had such recent outbreaks of the kind that occur against women, homosexuals, and other avowed enemies in stridently patriarchal cultures around the world. The eruptions here are more likely to be found in headline scandals about fundamentalist preachers and politicians caught with male or female prostitutes. Their atonement usually involves getting psychological therapy.

There is one exception I would like to note, however. Fundamentalists, but also other apocalyptic-minded Americans, remain dangerously susceptible to the patriarchal mandates of higher authority, in particular of the president and military leaders. If we take into account the kind of violence that is sanctioned by war in American nationalism we witness justifications of killing proclaimed in blatant apocalyptic terms. As we saw after 9/11, the Bush administration drew on Revelation's dualisms full force, proclaiming America as God's chosen nation, mandated to take revenge on its designated enemy. Long-standing gender dualisms place the United States in a masculine messianic role and the enemy as abjectly feminine. This was brought sharply into focus with the instances of feminizing and humiliating of male prisoners at Abu Ghraib, where the imprisoned men were made to be seen as women and degraded as such. It is also noteworthy that women participated in the feminization of the men, seeing themselves as part of the vengeful "good guys." Interestingly, once the scandal broke the press tried to make sense of Lyndie England as an Appalachian Jezebel.[22]

War is thus the primary cultural arena in the United States in which patriarchal fear and hatred endemic to apocalyptic belief continue to be channeled. It is one way that the inner-directed aggression that stems from rigid gender dualisms turns outward and is manifest in those dualistic terms. Even so, the shocked and condemnatory responses to the tortures of Abu Ghraib make it clear that most Americans, regardless of religious denomination, no longer endorse such overt actions when it is brought to their attention as a national disgrace. And significant numbers of Christian fundamentalists have become openly opposed to the war against Iraq. Does this signal an end time to the patriarchal apocalyptic mindset? Such an assessment is better left to historical analysis than prophecy.

History does show that the patriarchal foundation began cracking some time ago from a number of disparate sources. Nineteenth-century feminism's claim for women's moral authority is just one factor that began to upend confidence in a patriarchal vision. Industrialization and urbanization liberalized social practices ranging from reproduction to wage earning. Throughout the twentieth century the rise in divorce and practices of remarriage and blended families have radically changed family hierarchy and with it psychic pressures. In this sense the establishment of the term *fundamentalism* in the early twentieth century and an insistence on the authority of the fundamentals of biblical values are clearly a reaction formation to changes in the culture at large. Even though fundamentalism has worked for a century to isolate and fortify believers against these changes, the steady encroachment of individualism, pluralism, and commodity values has continued to undermine traditional apocalypticism for many. One of the new edifices being put into place is far more open to democratic possibility, but that effect is also far from inevitable, as I show in the next section.

DEEP SHIFTS IN APOCALYPTIC BELIEF

If I had to choose one contemporary individual whose views epitomize the shifts that have taken place within fundamentalism, it would be Leah Daughtry, an African American Pentecostal preacher on Sundays, whose weekday job at the time of this writing (2008) is chief of staff for Howard Dean, chairman of the Democratic National Committee. Daughtry certainly defies Revelation's gendered stereotype of Jezebel, whose authority as an unconventional female preacher was viewed a supreme threat.[23] She has ample authority, both in the pulpit and in politics, while advocating views that are, at best, unconventional to both camps. As Daniel Berger, writing a profile of her for the *New York Times Magazine,* states, "Though she is a biblical literalist who sees no problem with teaching creation theory side by side with evolution—'For me, the Bible is history'—she, following the teaching of her father's church, is also pro-choice. 'God allows us to choose in the biggest matter,' she said, 'whether to accept Him in our lives. How then can we take away choice on other profound issues? We don't believe the government should interfere.'"[24]

Such logic is simply incomprehensible within the frame of the patriarchal apocalyptic mindset, with its rigid gender and sexual hierarchy and oppositions. Yet this unsettling of the apocalyptic mindset is not unique to Daughtry. The loosening of patriarchal morality is reflected in the rising divorce rate among evangelicals, currently "as high or higher than the national average"; so too it is reported that "57% of 'born-again' Christians age 16–29 criticize their own church for being 'anti-homosexual.'"[25] Such views are characteristic of "new evangelicals," leaders of megachurches and faith-based activists who have declared their disagreement with the traditional religious right views that dominated American conservative politics since the Reagan era. In fact they are not as new as that designation would have it. Joel C. Hunter is a case in point. Senior pastor of an Orlando, Florida, congregation that numbers in the tens of thousands and board member of the National Association of Evangelicals, Hunter, now in his sixties, has been a critic of the religious right since it came to prominence in the 1980s. Weary of the polarization that the older generation of fundamentalist leaders like Jerry Falwell and Pat Robertson fueled, he and other like-minded pluralistic evangelicals seek a place at the democratic table, trying to set it with fundamentalist principles only. Though they might not agree with Daughtry's view of abortion, they do adhere to the idea that government should not interfere with issues of personal morality, and they tend to see poverty and health care as issues that democratic government should take responsibility for. In other words, they do not fit within Republican religious right categories, and, more to the point, their views no longer fit within the traditional apocalypticism that once held the religious right together.[26]

Fault lines in the foundation of traditional apocalypticism may be seen in the work of even the most traditional fundamentalist leaders. Indeed these may be more telling in regard to the changes taking place than those who don't cling as fiercely to that "old time religion." Take, for example, James Dobson, a licensed psychologist and the founder and leader of Focus on the Family, whose radio programs are heard by more than two hundred million people daily, according to his publications. As Dobson himself says on his website, he is not a trained theologian. For that, he guides his readers to the theological work of Billy Graham and Charles Swindoll, both of whom follow fundamentalist teachings about scripture as God's revelation and the coming end time. As Swindoll describes the final end, "It's probably going to be more like star wars. The good news is this: I have no plans to be around at the premier showing."[27] The cinematic metaphor notwithstanding, this image is in keeping with Revelation's emphasis on spectacle.

Dobson laments the diminution of the religious right within which he came to wield power. He is also concerned about the psychological well-being of his day-to-day listeners and readers. His 2001 book *Bringing Up Boys* provides a clear instance of the way patriarchal dualisms are maintained within a contemporary Christian fundamentalism that has absorbed some of the principal challenges to patriarchal views from feminism and the human sciences. This absorption can be seen in the way he accords women an equal but different status, akin to the arguments of early feminists. In a more contemporary vein he supports such measures as Title IX funding for girls' sports and is sensitive to the personal agonies of homosexual desire in a culture that penalizes it. Every bit as much as Freud, Dobson accords sexual desire a foremost, disruptive role in the psyche. But for Dobson desire's disruptive force can and must be put back in "order" and lived in accordance with divine principles. This clearly follows the patriarchal law of gender dualism, but that traditional view has been modified to accommodate psychological conflict and therapeutic healing.

Dobson's descriptions of divinely mandated gender differences employ the softer rhetoric of psychological cures rather than the punitive declarations of Genesis, in which painful childbirth is women's curse and hard labor men's: "Because it is the privilege and blessing of women to bear children, they are inclined toward predictability, stability, security, caution, and steadiness." In contrast to women, men "value change, opportunity, risk, speculation, and adventure. They are designed to provide for their families physically and to protect them from harm and danger."[28] In keeping with the dualistic notion of gender, he argues that stay-at-home mothers and breadwinner fathers are the only way to bring up healthy boys, defined pretty much as rambunctious heterosexuals. But also in keeping with the shifts I am pointing to, in which secularism softens apocalyptic values, Dobson administers a big dose of psychological healing with his theological stance in an effort to remain relevant in a changed culture.

The kinds of shifts in process from Dobson to Daughtry do have democratic promise, especially in comparison with conservative fundamentalism, which clings to the moral authority of patriarchal apocalypticism, but that promise is often thwarted in today's cultural and economic arena.

APOCALYPSE: THAT'S ENTERTAINMENT

Although shifts in apocalyptic belief toward social justice and psychological treatment less abusive than corporal punishment (although in Dobson's case, still coercive) are heartening, it is not so clear to say, as does Walter Russell Mead, that the "evangelical movement in the United States looks as if it is maturing."[29] That view ignores the magnitude of two intertwined arenas of intense impact: the media and commodity capitalism. Here there are three main effects to explore that work against democratization even as they signal disruptions in the traditional apocalyptic narrative that has held sway in the United States for so long. First, most popular culture depictions of apocalypse dilute and confuse apocalyptic doctrine. This is the case even in fundamentalist versions, such as the *Left Behind* series, in which entertainment values often trump doctrine. Although these depictions may dislodge orthodoxy, they don't necessarily reduce patriarchal values. Second, a great deal of media apocalypse is sexist and violent with impunity. The masculine bravado of films like *Terminator* and *X-Men* and a whole array of world-destroying video games glorify the patriarchal legacy of apocalypse. Third, some appropriations satirize apocalypse in the vein that Jon Stewart and Steven Colbert have made popular. This is the form that offers the most decisive break from the patriarchal apocalyptic mindset in the name of liberal democracy. Yet here the danger of replacing apocalyptic dogmatism with apathetic cynicism remains a concern.

Apocalypse has always been geared toward the popular. It is, after all, a proselytizing belief. But that is not the same thing as being geared toward entertainment, as it is increasingly these days. Given the secular—or more precisely, the media-driven commodity capitalist—pull of contemporary life, some Christian pastors try to meet congregations on today's cultural playground. Frances Fitzgerald has documented the debate about megachurches within the conservative Christian community, noting that "some evangelical pastors and scholars—typically from fundamentalist or Calvinist denominations—have attacked [certain megachurches] as market-driven churches that cater to entertainment," referring to the preaching as "Christianity lite" that offers "me-centered" teaching.[30]

Of course they are right. Giant video screens transport the concept of the ever watchful eye of God onto the audience itself, who now watch themselves being broadcast for television audiences, as if the service were a reality show. A correlation between large audiences and watered-down doctrine accompanies this drift toward apocalypse as entertainment. The large interdenominational tent that megachurches pitch—and require for financial support—dilutes the traditional doomsday end-time message, replacing it with a full-service, creatively branded good-time scene. The move toward entertainment is especially pronounced in regard to youth, with Christian rock concerts, for instance. These trends may encourage the kind of social justice activism that Joel Hunter emphasizes for his congregation. Or they may simply promote the kind of me-centered, prosperity-seeking capitalist worship of many of the new megachurches.

More problematically, going with the flow of popular culture can mean absorbing sensationalized patriarchal values. A case in point: some Protestant evangelical churches tapped into Microsoft's wildly popular video game, "Halo 3." Following the success of "Halo" and "Halo 2," the release of "Halo 3" in September 2007 shattered all previous first-day sales records of electronic media by grossing $170 million in the United States in the first twenty-four hours of availability.[31] It is clear what the appeal is for gamers, regardless of their religious orientation. "Halo 3" launches a full-throttle killing spree in which players battle it out between the heavily armed good guy, known as "Master Chief," and his powerful enemy combatants, rather confusingly called the Prophet of Truth, the Flood, and the Covenant. As one evangelical player quoted in the *New York Times* put it, "It's just fun blowing people up." Church youth directors cite the game as an effective way to bring in youth—in this case, primarily boys—for the fun and then have them stay on for a religious lesson. In the words of Pastor Ken Kenerly of Atlanta, "With gamers, how else can you get into their lives?"[32]

The use of the "Halo" series was challenged by some parents and pastors worried that it could have "a corroding influence." Recognizing that the violence of the game is what gets the gamers' adrenalin pumping, they worry that it sends the wrong message before the right one kicks in.[33] Some parents also voiced dismay that game night is specifically targeting twelve- to fourteen-year-olds, who by law are not able to buy "Halo 3" because its M rating limits it to buyers who are at least seventeen. Yet when parents expressed concern about the violence in "Halo 3," as, for example, at Colorado Community Church, the youth minister convinced them and the pastor that it was "a crucial recruiting tool." As the *New York Times* reports, "In one letter to parents, Mr. Barbour wrote that God calls ministers to be 'fishers of men.' 'Teens are our 'fish,' he wrote. 'So we've become creative in baiting our hooks.'"[34]

That debate did in fact occur around this particular youth group practice is evidence of some dynamism within conservative Christian communities. But the terms in which the reported discussion occurred actually sidestepped the more complex and crucial issue of the gender blueprint of Christian apocalypse, in which male violence is accentuated in ways that give "Halo 3" a run for its money. Perhaps this is not surprising, even for conscientious parents like the ones who objected to "Halo 3." As likely readers of the *Left Behind* books, they are accustomed to passages like the following on Armageddon: "And with those very first words, tens of thousands of Unity Army soldiers fell dead, simply dropping where they stood, their bodies ripped open, blood pooling in great masses." And this one: "With every word, more and more enemies of God dropped dead, torn to pieces. Horses panicked and bolted. The living screamed in terror and ran about like madmen—some escaping for a time, others falling at the words of the Lord Jesus Christ."[35] This is media-magnified patriarchal violence of the sort that Revelation revels in.

The fact that "Halo 3" was retained as a recruiting tool is evidence of how patriarchal views squelch dissension and incite submission to existing authority.

Such hyperbolic imagery has become the meat and potatoes of contemporary fundamentalism, but it is also typical fare for immensely popular television comedy these days. Both the *Daily Show* and the *Colbert Report* regularly draw on apocalyptic themes, not only as satire of politics gone amok but also as outright ridicule of end-time belief. *South Park* brazenly mocks apocalyptic belief and believers. Acceptance of such irreverent humor on a wider than ever scale is a pretty clear sign of changing attitudes about apocalypticism in American society in general and is part of what the Copernicus study characterized as the liberalization of American culture. Yet changing attitudes do not necessarily mean a rise in democratic values. For radically conservative Christians such views most likely reinforce suspicions of cultural decadence, further isolating them from mainstream American citizenry. The response so far has been a hardening of their apocalyptic arteries. Less orthodox fundamentalists and evangelicals tend to compete with media mavens like Stewart and Colbert. As with "Halo 3" and the *Left Behind* books, they too reach for the popular in an effort to attract followers. The danger here is that what is left behind is the residue of patriarchal principles and the thrill of vengeance.

What, then, given the dramatic social changes currently under way, better cultivates the democratic without fueling the demagogic? Responses run along the religious-political spectrum from fundamentalist to unaffiliated, to use the Pew Foundation's categories. Megachurches with the approach that Joel Hunter brings to his congregation are vital advocates for social equality, strengthening both religious freedom and democratic deliberation. Far more pluralistic than the traditional religious right, they make social justice a priority toward which to work. Ironically their goals may be undercut by more politically moderate competing megachurches that elevate personal prosperity over eradicating poverty as a preeminent concern rather than by orthodox antichoice fundamentalists. Even though apocalyptic satire risks alienating hardcore fundamentalists, it can be effective in promoting skepticism about moral absolutism. When it shades too far into its own form of absolutism and cynical certitude, it too suffers from demagoguery and furthers polarization. That is also why it is important for traditionally secular leftists to acknowledge these avenues of social change within fundamentalism while continuing to advocate their own agendas. As Jodi Dean has argued, socialist feminism provides a model for this kind of political struggle, combining as it does a critique of patriarchy and of capitalism.[36]

What these disparate forms of social, cultural, and political activism have in common is a collective effort to further unsettle the fundamentalist mindset. Clearly this is no easy task, and as the historical reflections in the last part of this volume indicate, traumatic cultural events such as economic crisis or a future terrorist attack will tend to galvanize the moral rigidity and sense of paranoia that are so foundational to the fundamentalist mindset.

Part IV

GLOBAL AND HISTORICAL CONTEXTS

12

The Psychology of the Global Jihadists

Farhad Khosrokhavar

THE AMBIVALENCE OF FUNDAMENTALISM

Fundamentalism is an issue that is historically related to Protestantism, as much as *integrism* is related to Catholicism in the French-speaking world. To apply fundamentalism to the jihadists needs explanation.[1] In Islam at least three features distinguish so-called Islamic fundamentalism from its Christian equivalent. The first one is the relation to politics and the use of violence. Aside from a few cases, such as the so-called Reconstructionists, Christian fundamentalists do not contest the global political framework of the societies in which they operate. They believe that the democratic systems leave them much leverage to deliver their own message, and therefore the bulk of their action is deployed within the society from the bottom up rather than from the top down. Civil society, not the state (or the government), is the main target.[2] In Muslim societies many so-called fundamentalist groups (the Muslim Brotherhood and those inspired by their model) profess peaceful transition to an Islamic government and reject the use of violence to achieve that end. They aim at legally conquering the power at the top in order to establish the rule of God on earth. In many cases this official position is contested by people who consider it a ruse to seize power rather than a sincere democratic declaration of faith. Other groups have broken their ties to fundamentalist groups and constituted new circles officially advocating the use of violence to achieve their Islamic aims. This is particularly true of the Groupe Islamique Armé (GIA), a violent offshoot of the Algerian Front Islamique de Salut (FIS) that was overthrown by the military in 1992 after it won the national elections in Algeria. The transformation of FIS into GIA entailed ten years of civil war in Algeria and the killing of more than a hundred thousand civilians in guerrilla warfare against the army.[3]

In other cases radicalized groups have been the result of splits among fundamentalists. Consider, for example, the Egyptian group Takfir wal Hijra, which began in the 1960s as a splinter group of the Muslim Brotherhood but gained international fame in 1981 with the assassination of Egyptian president Anwar al Sadat. Whether by splinter groups (Takfir wal Hijra) or direct offshoots of political parties inspired by the Muslim Brotherhood (GIA), imposing a theocracy in the name of Islam is the goal of many fundamentalist parties within Muslim societies. More generally fundamentalist groups in Islam can aim at the political structure at the highest level (the government) and become extremely violent in their different offshoots.

Another feature differentiating fundamentalism in Islam from its Christian counterpart is that fundamentalism in the Christian world is, politically speaking, a minority phenomenon, whereas if free elections were held in Muslim countries, the probability is high that the fundamentalist groups inspired by the Muslim Brotherhood would win the majority of the votes (in Egypt, Algeria, Morocco, and Jordan for sure, and probably in other countries as well). We have two distinct categories of fundamentalist Muslims, one with ambiguous claims of nonviolence and the other openly advocating violence to gain political power. Jihadists are among the group of hyperfundamentalists that militate for the establishment of Islamic power worldwide through the explicit use of violence. But among jihadists are two further categories with different psychological features. Islamic nationalists use violence against an enemy who occupies their land. Islam is simply a legitimizing means to their end of freeing their country from the yoke of foreigners. The Chechen, Kashmir, and Palestinian cases are of this kind. Islam for such groups serves as another name for nationalism. The second category is that of transnational jihadists. In this case the fight against the enemy is vague and the violence the more intense. The enemy is the West, epitomized by the United States, the absolute other with whom no compromise is possible and whose existence is illegitimate as such. The only way to cope with this enemy is to eliminate it.

The new generations of global jihadists, particularly after September 11, are modernized, Internet-oriented, and electronically savvy youth (less than thirty years old in most cases). They look for revenge in a world where America and its allies are oppressing the Muslims in Afghanistan, Iraq, Pakistan, Palestine, Lebanon, and elsewhere. The revenge element in jihadism is extemely important. This revenge is based on a psychology of resentment that is similar to the notion developed by Nietzsche; it is a reaction rather than an action, based on a feeling of hatred that distorts reality and sees the enemy as depraved. The self-imageis in turn defined by this resentment and loathing. But part of this resentment follows another logic: it is the resentment made exhibitionist through the media. A new lust for being important, a fascination with the "star system," becomes a new psychology of Westernized fetishism turned against the West by virtue of antagonistic Westernization. In this respect jihadism is not a clash of civilizations but an antagonistic Westernization, mostly within Western culture (the case of the converts to the radical version of Islam and the second or third generation of Europeans of Pakistani, Bangladeshi, Algerian, Moroccan, Tunisian, or Syrian origin) or by those who have been deeply Westernized in their attitudes in the Muslim world (most of the jihadists are from the new middle classes and have scientific backgrounds: physicists, physicians, engineers, etc.).

Jihadists belong to two different worlds, the Islamic world and the Western, with major differences. In Europe (most of the Western Jihadists are Europeans, either converts or belonging to the Islamic communities there) they are mostly either downtrodden and poor or in the lower middle classes, close to the bottom, or they are educated but unable to secure a job that matches their diploma. They are deeply imbued with a sense that they are denied citizenship in European societies. They feel rejected and stigmatized. In the Muslim world most jihadists are from the newly emerging modernized middle classes; in a minority of cases they come from the traditional classes.

The psychological features of the global jihadists can be briefly summarized. First is the internalized humiliation and the attempt at reversing the sense of humiliation in a disproportionate manner.[4] Second is victimization. Third is the will to narcissistic recognition through the world media. Jihadists are the products of the global communication system; their recognition process, unlike that of the national jihadists, is based on the ubiquity of their images in media worldwide.

VICTIMIZATION

The strong feeling of being robbed of one's dignity due to the illegitimate actions of the Western world is a shared feature among nationalist and global jihadists. Even those in the Muslim world who are successful and belong to the middle classes share this deep feeling of mental despondency in regard to the West. In the Muslim world the trauma of the establishment of the state of Israel and the perception of Israel as solely the creation of the West, particularly the United States, enhances Muslims' opposition to the West and its main representative, the United States. Victimization is a psychological process that operates in a dichotomous way: one is either victim or oppressor. This feeling of victimization is deeply shared by many Muslims who not only deplore the unbalanced American policy in the Middle East but sincerely believe that oppression has been a constant feature of the Christian West from the beginning. Islam is the absolute victim of the intolerance of the West. This total victimization, and the Manichaean thinking that results, has its counterpart in the West among those who believe that Muslims are the absolute other, the bad guy against the good guy, namely Western civilization. But in the Muslim world, due to its major political, social, and cultural crises, this feeling is far more deeply entrenched in the minds of radical minorities than in the West. Victimization builds on historical and contemporary facts; the result is the deep sentiment of hopelessness and the inability to act positively to resolve the situation. There is no other way to fight against the arrogant West than through generalized violence.

The way victimization works is noteworthy. In our interviews many young Muslims in French prisons said that they were mistreated by the French police, administration, and more generally the society in much the same manner as Palestinian youth are mistreated by the Israeli army and institutions.[5] Among the disaffected youth in England the feeling prevails that British Muslims are mistreated in the same fashion as the Kashmiris by the Indian army.

These views about the self and the other, conceptualized in absolute terms (i.e., Muslims are "totally" rejected in France and Britain), are sociologically wrong according to prevailing objective data. A sizable minority of Muslims in both countries have achieved middle-class status. Still, many Muslims remain either downtrodden or reduced to the status of petty middle classes (even though the latter attain a university education) due to racism or social prejudices. Among most of the downtrodden Muslims the feelings of total hopelessness and absolute victimization are paramount. The colonial background in both of these countries reinforces this hopelessness and despair. Again the fact that there is a sizable middle class of North African origin in France and of Pakistani origin in England contradicts this sentiment of absolute victimization. But disenfranchised young people deeply believe in it, and as such, this perception of the self as being an absolute victim of an inhospitable society in which Muslims are at best unwelcome and at worst repressed is widespread among many young Muslims of the second or third generation in poor districts and suburbs in Europe.

Absolute victimization in turn legitimizes the use of absolute violence against "godless" societies that reject their Muslim citizens simply because they are Muslims. The shift from private violence (violence against racism and the stigma of deviance) to collective violence (in the name of the Islamic *umma*, the Islamic community) is facilitated through an extremist version of Islam, namely jihadism.[6] In the same fashion passive victimization is transformed into action through this radicalized version of Islam. In Europe, where a large proportion of Muslims, mainly second- or third-generation migrants, are economically excluded and culturally stigmatized, jihadism is part of a narrative to demand recognition for those who believe they are denied recognition, as much in the Muslim world as in European societies. It is the inversion of the quest for recognition. Since Muslims are not recognized as full-fledged citizens, they opt for a jihadist identity that pushes them to the zenith of violence by which they will be recognized as villains and dreaded instead of despised. Inspiring fear is ersatz for the lack of recognition as respected citizens, mainly in Europe where radicalized Muslims believe that they are unwelcome, even more, rejected and scorned. In the Muslim world it is the lack of recognition as political citizens with a say in social and political matters that pushes some to become jihadists.

The values of the society are thus turned into countervalues: "lax morals" are denounced, and restrictive, hyperpuritanical, and instransigent "Islamic values" are proposed as a substitute. The depravation of Western societies is denounced; homosexuality, women's public nudity, and consumption of alcohol and narcotics are signs of the decadence of godless societies that destroy themselves and others through their perversion and their denial of God. A culture of inverted Westernism is promoted that is inspired by the rancor against the West as much as by traditional Islamic values that are being rigidified and ossified in a characteristic manner.

HUMILIATION

In traditional societies humiliation is mainly based on a "loss of face" in regard to the people of the same group, clan, or class. The individual dimension of humiliation is not paramount, and there is no egalitarian view underlying the notion of humiliation. Subservience toward the higher classes is therefore not necessarily "humiliating," whereas the same attitude toward one's own class will be experienced as entailing a loss of face and be abasing. In other words, humiliation is resented when the differential social code of honor is broken, and this code is not universal and restricted to the group. In this sense the whole idea of humiliation is based on inequality and different types of dignity. Modernization in the world means principally the introduction of the ideology of egalitarianism and the notion that all human beings have the same dignity, independent of race, religion, birth, clan, or tribe. What was merely perceived as the result of the differential dignities of different groups has become a unique and universal exigency of human dignity. That is why humiliation has become one of the leading categories driving human conflicts to paroxysms of violence in modern societies and those that are being modernized. Still, in spite of this universalism, each culture interprets humiliation in its own fashion.

Russian, Israeli, and American forms of degrading Muslims (in Chechnia, in the territories occupied by Israel, in Iraq and Afghanistan) stir humiliation in the modern sense. But another sense is present as well, one that is specifically culture-bound.[7] Non-Islamic Western mores such as consumption of alcohol, the "nudity" of women (i.e., women who are not veiled), financial relations based on "usury" (interest), gender relations in which sexual intercourse is practiced outside of marriage, and particularly Western cultural industries are seen as fundamentally perverse and humiliating for Muslims because they call into question a way of life based on gender segregation, veiled or "modest" women, the banning of alcohol, and the rejection of interest.

Fundamentalism is usually defined as a reaction against secularization. This definition is at best incomplete. In the Muslim world both the reaction against Western mores and the egalitarian feeling resulting from secularization are jointly present. The globalized communication system (particularly the Arab Al Jazeera) shows Muslims vivid pictures of humiliation in Gaza, Iraq, Afghanistan, Pakistan (the bombing of Pakistani villages by American drones). The major difference between Islamic fundamentalism and Western fundamentalism rests in the different manner the two movements are articulated. In the Muslim world the secularization process creates an overwhelming feeling of dispossession, in addition to domination by an alien civilization (the West). In the West fundamentalists reject many Western values, but they operate within the Western cultural framework in which there is no domineering alien. In the Muslim world such a Western framework is loaded with a feeling of domination and violence against Islamic norms in a humiliating manner in which both components are omnipresent. This is why many jihadists are modernized Muslims who reject not only Western values (secularization) but also the insidious Western domination through these values. In this understanding of history the West has always played an anti-Islamic role.

GLOBAL JIHADISM AND HUMILIATION

Global jihadism is a reaction against humiliation. It is based on a vision of the self as humiliated by the dominant West,[8] and the reaction is to humiliate the humiliator.

There are at least three types of humiliation. The first is physical, transcultural humiliation: Russian soldiers perform full body searches of Chechens; Israeli soldiers stop and search Palestinians at checkpoints; Indian soldiers search Kashmiri civilians. This type of humiliation aims at the body of the other; one can surmise that it is universal in that everyone feels its pinch. This type is felt only in war zones or in situations of acute crisis.

The second type of humiliation, the most universal in the Muslim world, is humiliation by proxy. The French Muslim who believes that he is humiliated in the same way as the Palestinian by the Israelis, or the English Muslim who feels humiliated in the same fashion as the Kashmiris by the Indian army, is imagining a humiliation that is only palpable through a projection. He feels downgraded in the same manner as the Palestinian or Kashmiri he imagines, without any concrete basis other than images on the TV. (Most do not precisely know the social, historical, or cultural context in which the Palestinians' or Kashmiris' claim for recognition evolved.) This imaginary humiliation sometimes has a real substrate: the racist attitude of police or the contemptuous behavior of civil servants. But the extent of this humiliation has nothing to do with what people in war zones experience. In this respect humiliation by proxy is a product of the media and the intense victimization process undergone by the young "Arabs" (Frenchmen of North African origin), the "Pakis" (Englishmen of South Asian origin), or the "Perkers" (Danes of Middle Eastern origin) in Europe. The chasm between the direct humiliation and its imaginary dimension is deep. It can be understood only by contextualizing the humiliation in a situation in which there is no promising future.

Such humiliation arises especially keenly among second- and third-generation stigmatized Muslims. Sometimes, as the young disaffected youth of the poor suburbs recount, a glance from a white person perceived as derogatory can spark an aggressive reaction that can go as far as killing. Hyperaggressivity results from the cumulative feeling of humiliation. The young "Pakis" or "Arabs" sincerely feel a relentless colonialism in the guise of stigmatization, and they can misinterpret the most harmless remark as an insult, setting off a disproportionate aggressivity against the presumed culprit.

Cumulative humiliation by proxy results in a disproportionate aggressivity toward the "white men" by the "gray" (*les gris*, that is, the "Arabs," who are neither white nor black but in between) or the "Pakis" who feel deeply vilified by a harmless remark or the slightest allusion with a disagreeable undertone, intentional or not. The violence in this sense is private, personal, and directed against the "culprit." The feeling of humiliation and victimization induces a hyperaggressive attitude toward society and an attitude of defiance that justifies deviance and criminality without the slightest guilt. Toward a society perceived as "totally" racist and stigmatizing, cynicism and lack of a balanced ethics (that would not condemn the other in a holistic manner) is regarded as legitimate.[9] If a young man joins a peaceful fundamentalist group, he becomes more temperate in his attitude toward society, looking for peace in a close-knit group and developing detachment toward a society in which he feels at best marginal. Fundamentalism transforms "marginality with malaise" into an "assumed marginality." But if the young man joins a jihadist group, his anger and hatred (*haine* in French, the expression having won wide currency in the social sciences dealing with the poor suburbs in France) mutate into an all-out war with society. From private and personal, humiliation shifts into a global posture through jihadism.

This third kind of humiliation is based on its ideological justification through reference to the sacred register of jihad. Through this process, aggressivity shifts from individual and personal to general and holistic. The target of aggressivity in humiliation by proxy is individualized and directed against specific persons who dare despise the humiliated Arab or Paki. Through jihad aggressivity can target with impunity the entire society. Before adhesion to jihad it could point to society at large through criminality. But this attitude has no ideological content. It simply declares legitimate any felony against a society that stigmatizes its immigrants' sons and grandsons. Cynicism serves as a reaction to stigma. The third type of humiliation transforms stigma into absolute enmity toward the society. The aim is to destroy a society that is impious and godless and hates Muslims because of their faith.

Such a Manichaean fundamentalist view blends with an apocalyptic vision that allows for total violence against an enemy who is dehumanized because he is a staunch heretic, who shows no mercy toward Muslims and endeavors to destroy their faith. In the second type of humiliation, religion plays no role at all. Criminality becomes at the same time revenge and a means to ascend the social ladder to achieve the status of the middle classes. But in this third type humiliation is transformed into an absolute antagonism toward society as such. The others are godless and therefore unworthy of living. Death becomes the central act that transforms humiliation into pride at taking the life of the other. There is no longer a question of personal revenge and the ascension by illegal means to the status of the middle classes. The major question is henceforth how to inflict the gravest damage on the other, in an undifferentiated manner, simply for the sake of putting them all to death. Counterhumiliation merges with a politics of death, and thanatos becomes the focal point. The reasons are as much psychological as instrumental. The West is militarily, technologically, and economically far superior to the Muslims and their radical spearheads. It cannot be vanquished in a normal way, by military confrontation or by classical means. For the jihadists, the only way to defeat the West is symbolically, through deep humiliation. Muslims do not dread death. They wish it for the sake of Islam.

Martyrdom in this respect is an ardent desire of theirs, unlike the coward Westerners who fear death and wish to live even under the predicament of dire indignity. In this idealized, deeply narcissistic picture of the self, Muslims long for heroic death at the service of Islam; by dying they achieve a symbolic superiority for Muslims over the miscreant Westerners who cravenly aspire to live for life's own sake, devoid of any sacred ideal. The image of the Westerner is that of illegitimate supeiority in material terms with a real inferiority in the existential field. In this perspective, the mere fact of being fond of life is a humiliation, and the Muslim who dies for his religion as a martyr, putting to death the gutless Westerners by bombing or blowing up crowds in public places, shows not only the power of his group and religion but also the helplessness of the arrogant Westerner, thus transforming humiliation into glory and the humiliator into the pitiful humiliated. Jihadism turns private action into collective action in the name of a radical version of Islam; aggressivity becomes boundless, confined by no frontier, its only limit the physical capacity of inflicting death through "human bombs" who die in the name of a radical version of religion.

SYMBOLIC RECOGNITION THROUGH GLOBALIZED MEDIA

Global jihadism is the product of a globalized world, particularly its media. Before September 11 many jihadists looked for recognition through the media: symbolic recognition in the absence of real recognition. They believe the world is dominated by the globalized West, and only resistance is global counterdomination by transnational jihadism. This can be achieved through the world media. Before joining the jihadist ranks many young people in the poor suburbs of France and poor districts of England, among other places, dreamed of achieving fame through infamous means. Many deviant youngters in the poor French suburbs told me that they had achieved higher fame than their neighbors because they had access to the main French TV channel (TF1), while their neighbors had access only to the second best channel (France 2).[10] Disenfranchised youth compete to become "someone" through the media, and since they cannot perform the fame in a positive way (that is, by acts recognized as positive by the majority in the society), they choose negative fame. Becoming infamous is considered far better than being an underdog, or at best an inferior nobody. The narcissistic dimension of meanness is a major component in the attitude of these young men, who for the most part see no bright prospect for their future. Beyond their national boundaries, achieving fame in the globalized world means joining the world scene, going beyond the predicament of insignificance, which is the lot of most of the young disenfranchised people in the European ghettoes and in the Muslim world, those who aimlessly pace up and down the Algerian streets (the so-called Trabendists who hug the walls) or in spite of their university diploma are denied a decent job in the Muslim world, in Algeria, Egypt, Morocco, or Pakistan. Even modernized young people of the middle classes in the Muslim world join the ranks of the global jihadists because they are dissatisfied with their lot: corrupt and authoritarian elites do not give them the opportunity to participate in public life. Frustration, lack of real opportunity, social stigma and prejudice in Europe, combined with the deep sense of alienation in the Muslim world push these young men toward a radicalization that is reinforced by world media coverage of indiscriminate violence.

In this way the narcissistic desire to be admired is satisfied, although this admiration is negative and based on fear and repulsion. In the absence of real acceptance and positive fame jihadists long for negative fame and achieve it through global media. At the same time they satisfy their need for revenge against a hostile world where an arrogant West keeps on humiliating them by denying them justice. (Palestinian, Iraqi, Afghan, and Chechnian mistreatment is shown on TV.)

But the jihadists achieve more than mere ill fame. Not only do they achieve notoriety in the West that denies them justice and equality, but they also gain fame from their imagined Muslim *umma* for their heroic deeds. Jihadists thus blend a logic of revenge against the mean West and a logic of hope based on veneration by the imagined Muslims who approve of their epic acts. The negativity attached to the ill fame is compensated by the act of becoming a new Islamic Prometheus. The quest for fame radically alters the moral categories of good and evil. Since they are seen as evil by the Westerners, they necessarily are good according to jihadist moral standards. The category of jihadists who look for fame are thus satisfied in their own way (being famous or infamous is seen as desirable to the utmost, the first out of reach, the second highly valued), and the category of jihadists who are ideologically convinced of the wickedness of the West also settle their account: wicked Westerners have to be punished in the eyes of the world.

The world media are thus the magic ingredient of the jihadist self-Image. Media confer on them the status of negative heroes and invert the vector of humiliation. Media display the powerlessness of the West (in particular America) in the face of a paroxysmal violence; they give prominence to world jihad and they heighten the intensity of the violence through the repetition of the striking images that multiply by the thousands the effects of the destruction. To cite but one case, the September 11 attacks killed around three thousand people, but their symbolic effect was that of millions. In the same way the endless repetition of the sequences on TV for weeks on end boosted the effects of the violence beyond any common measure. The shift from humiliation to counterhumiliation, from passivity to activity, from inferiority to superiority is less the product of the jihadists' activity than the effect of the media. September 11 opened the way to the symbolic kingdom of the horrifying images of violence. Their actors achieved fame and momentarily dethroned the West by suffusing the disgruntled Muslims with a sense of reconquered dignity through new means, unimaginable a few years earlier. Under the crude light of the world media indiscriminate violence is perpetrated not only against the enemy, but also against the bystanders (that is, all those, Muslim or Christian or otherwise, who constitute the anonymous crowd that does not take the side of the global jihadists), who die not only for the sake of a sacred cause but in order to give violence the status of apocalypse. Exhibited on TV screens the world over, superlative violence becomes a symbolic apocalypse, although, in real terms, it is at most on the scale of a small war (the September 11 attacks killed far fewer than those killed in the war in Iraq, with its wounded and psychologically destabilized cohorts of soldiers). Violence is perpetrated not only against the enemy, but also to bring before the eyes of the world the spectacle of the new jihadist symbolic power.

Even though highly critical of Al Qaeda and its blind violence, many Muslims in the Middle East, and more generally in the Muslim world, found solace in the September 11 attacks. Bin Laden became an Islamic Robin Hood in a world where violence was, up to then, the exclusive monopoly of the West against the Muslims. Bin Laden symbolically restored the balance by exerting violence against America, whose policies in the Muslim world are interpreted as intent on humiliating Muslims.

Thus generalized violence fulfills a double function. On the one hand it is revenge, a counterhumiliating posture, a reaction to violence whose main actor has been the United States as the paragon of the Occident. On the other hand generalized violence is synonymous with generalized fame, in an inverted register. Since September 11 inspired awe and apprehension in the West by occupying the screens of the world's TVs for months it has been synonymous with the recognition of Al Qaeda as the major global actor in the world. The exposure, even more, the exhibitionism of September 11 on the world scale by TV has transformed the predicament of the victim (the Muslims) into the enviable position of the conquerer; it has made a radical turnabout in the story of victimhood and, from the viewpoint of the radicalized groups, granted Muslims the title of conquerors. This is the main topic on which one of the ideologues of Al Qaeda, Lewis Atiyat-ollah, finds solace in 9/11.[11] Henceforth Muslims are able to make history, to deny the end of the history, and to begin anew a history of their own, one in which they are active, not passive; dominant, not dominated; humiliators, not humiliated.

The major psychological problem facing the jihadists is that for them revenge must be violent, not peaceful. The Japanese and German postwar models of peaceful revenge through economic achievements are not considered credible by the jihadists because of their cultural and historical background (violence has to be met with more violence, not otherwise, according to their mindset) and because most Muslim governments are financially so corrupt and politically so blocked that any entrepreneurship is doomed to failure unless sanctioned by the authoritarian regimes within their clientelist cliques. The plight of the Muslims in Bosnia in the 1990s, the wars in Iraq and Afghanistan, and the unconditional American support during the presidency of George W. Bush for Israel's war in Lebanon in 2006 and Gaza in 2009 have caused a new sense of victimization among many Muslims worldwide. This in turn encourages global jihadism, whose main underpinning is the deep humiliation and victimization of Muslims in front of a self-righteous West, in particular America.

In democratic Europe long-entrenched prejudices and racism related to colonial times, resulting in a phobia of Islamic radicalism all over the world (the Islamic Revolution of 1979 in Iran, massive jihadist violence in Algeria between 1992 and 2005, suicide bombers in the last decade of the twentieth century, September 11 and European terrorist attacks in Spain and Britain), have prevented concrete solutions to the unrest among Muslims. Recourse to globalized violence corresponds to the ideals of a narcissistic fame suffused by the globalized media. The larger the scale of violence, the more spectacular it is and the more it mobilizes the world media by invoking awe, the major ingredient of attraction for the news.

Blind violence means total dehumanization of those who are subjected to it. This is rendered possible through the victimization process and subsequent dualistic thinking. Radical Muslims justify using generalized violence as a means of salvation because they believe they are the victims of a cruel anti-Islamic Crusader and Zionist conspiracy. From their viewpoint Western immoral acts are sanctioned by this conspiracy, without any ethical consideration. In a symmetrical way they refuse to adopt the ethical demeanor that the West refuses to apply to Muslims in spite of its human rights ideology. Blind violence against Westerners is justified in reaction to and retaliation against the blind violence exerted by the West against Muslims. Every time Israel disproportionately attacks its neighbors in the name of security, global jihadists find a new argument to stress Western cruelty and lack of moral categories.[12] In response they claim a right to violence that restores the balance and sets right the account with the West. Moral indignation gives way to a strategy of retaliation that is also the strategy adopted by many Western countries and Israel against the jihadists.

Lack of compassion characterizes the transnational jihadists in their attempts at blind violence against their enemies, whether or not they are

Muslims. Muslims suffer the most from their own acts, first through the sheer number of them killed in terrorist attacks, and then through the racism and Islamophobia as the result of the attacks. But insensitivity toward the other's suffering and lack of compassion are caused by the perspective of being absolute victims on the world stage and the necessity to break the siege of the Islamic world by the Crusaders. This would not have been possible without the secularization of the jihadists as a consequence of modernization during the past century. Without secularization the other (the Christian, the Jew) would have had rights within the Islamic framework (as "People of the Book," that is sharing Abrahamic roots), especially under the general heading of traditional hospitality. Secularization has washed away both of these restrictions. A cold, calculating attitude (similar to the West's ability to think in terms of "collatoral damage" by its armies) and a vision of retaliation based on lack of compassion toward the absolute enemy make for a formidable combination that allows total violence without remorse or any religious questioning. The logic of resentment and retaliation has substituted for that of traditional Islamic justice.

AMBIVALENT SECULARIZATION, LACK OF APOCALYPSE, AND THE MARGINALITY OF HELL

Secularization is the major underpinning of global jihadism. For the global jihadists (as distinct from national jihadists)[13] the entire world is populated by either heretics (that is non-Muslims) or heretics under the guise of Islam (the fake Muslims). Muslim governments are *taqut* (tyrannical non-Islamic governments), and Muslim societies are *jahiliya* (that is, godless, in the same manner as the pre-Islamic societies). Therefore, aside from the few marginal groups of devout Muslims who join the global jihad, the others are unworthy of being called Muslims. They are, in the same manner as real heretics (the believers of other faiths), outside the realm of authentic Islam. In this sense almost the entire world is "secular" (nonreligious in the genuine sense), Muslims included. Killing them for the sake of Islam does not induce any major guilt feeling. Killing innocent Muslims is vindicated in reference to the notion of "shielding" (*turus*), borrowed from the Middle Ages: if Muslims voluntarily or involuntarily shield the enemies of Islam, they can be put to death.

The distinction between non-jihadist Muslims and non-Muslims is at best blurred; all are, in a deep sense, non-Muslims, and therefore their death is justified through violence. Secularization is an avatar of religious change that goes beyond the traditional distinctions and introduces new ones based on a new global order: being a Muslim is not so much respecting rituals or following the traditional norms and rules of Islam, it is raising the standard of jihad against a ubiquitous enemy. The globalization of the enemy and the denial of Islam to the majority of nominal Muslims is the consequence of a secularization that redefines religion and the fight in its name in a global manner.

Another major ingredient of jihadism is its ambivalent opposition to the egalitarian modern view. Even the independence movements in the Muslim world were in awe before the superiority of the West and its capacity to dominate and rule. Leaders of independence movements were mostly secularized people, their educational background deeply influenced by their attendance in colonial schools or even universities, at home or in the colonial countries (in Paris and London, among other places). They felt equal to the colonizers, but still they were in awe of the latter's way of life and their systems of ruling. The global jihadists (as distinct from the national jihadists, who are very much influenced by the countries against which they fight) are no longer in awe of the West. Their attitude is influenced by the idea that the West is corrupt, morally and socially, and its educational, political, and economic systems are depraved. They do not refer, however, to historical Islam to replace it. Instead they refer to a utopian, idealized system, the so-called Medina period of the Prophet, who was at the same time the ruler and the religious leader, and they are intent on restoring it. The Shi'ite radicals refer to the rule of Ali (the fourth caliph among the "well-guided" ones) as the golden age of Islamic rule and are bent on reproducing it. For many Muslims, since these golden ages cannot be reproduced they have to accept the imperfection of the prevailing political systems, that is, the human imperfect governments that are not entirely religious and fail to attain the absolute flawlessness of the times of the origin.[14] Secularization is produced by the lack of perfection that pushes Muslims into the historical realm and its vicissitudes. Still, in the back of the minds of many Muslims, the perfect time of the Prophet can be attained through a renewed sense of religion. In modern times the Islamic revolution has been the combination of the modern idea of revolution and the return to the purity of the golden age. In this sense secularization is ambivalent in Muslim societies since the rupture with the golden age is not repaired, and this perfect age is not reconstituted. But the mere idea of revolution is an attempt at secularization, since humans are credited with a capacity to come close to the purity of the origins through collective action. In a sense an ambivalent secularization is at work in many Muslim societies with a revivalist vision of the return to the origins combined with a modern revolutionary view.

Another paradoxical secularization in global jihadism is the lack of apocalyptic vision and the substitution of "apocalypse now." The most notable jihadist thinkers—Maqdisi, Tartusi, Abu Qatada, Zawahiri, Al Suri, and many others—lack an apocalyptic vision.[15] The end of the world is not at hand, and there is no precise vision of the end of time other than in vague words.

In Islam the apocalyptic literature is abundant.[16] In global jihadist literature one finds some references to the end of time but in a rather marginal fashion. It is not apocalypse that entices the jihadists but the apocalyptic fight against *taqut*, that is, idolatry, embodied in Western governments and their Muslim lackeys. The world is dominated by *taqut*, and the violent opposition to it is of necessity the major calling for Muslims. They should declare holy war (jihad) against it in order to promote genuine Islam as against the Crusaders (Christians), the Zionists (Jews), and the protagonists of the "Sultan's *ulama*" (the corrupted Islam of the perverted *ulamas*, who are in the service of *taqut*).[17] In this fight, as shown above, boundless violence is susceptible to creating an apocalyptic situation that is made by the protagonists of global jihad with no apocalypse in sight. Apocalyptic violence is a secularized form of violence to establish the reign of genuine Islam here on earth, not to promote apocalypse.

In the same fashion the marginality of Hell is a distinctive feature in the literature of gobal jihad. Few of the major jihadist intellectuals refer to Hell as the abode of the "fake Muslims" or the Crusaders or Zionists or even the "worshippers of the cow" (mainly Brahmanic Hindus but also and by extension Buddhists and other religious protagonists). Hell is to be erected in this world. Non-Muslims and nongenuine Muslims have to be punished here, in this world, and not tolerated in the name of an otherworldly reckoning. Of course the presupposition of jihadism is that nongenuine Muslims (all those who do not join them in their ideology and acts) as well as the protagonists of other religions will go to Hell, but the motif of Hell is not a major topic of theirs. There is a secularization that makes global jihadism a this-worldly matter, in ideology as in attitude. The current jihadist movements would have been impossible had it not been for the secularization of the Muslim world that made the old quietism and fatalism impossible and their afterworld-oriented vision marginal.

We thus discern another characteristic of the jihadist movements: rejection of quietism and fatalism that singled out the Muslim societies before modernization. The idea of basically fatalist and quietist Muslim society has been strongly defended by Orientalism. Modernist studies, in part under the influence of Edward Said but also under the aegis of new Muslim reformists, contest many features of the so-called quietism. The history of the Muslim world is replete with protest movements against the powers that be. But these movements derived their vigor from their rejection of weakened governments and the reproduction of the latter's features once they succeeded in dislodging them from political power. The urban social movements showed the capacity for action (and therefore the antiquietist feature of the Muslim societies), but their action was mostly against the rulers, without calling into question the general style of the rule and the nature of the domination system. The Muslim world oscillated between chaos and quietism, and each had its limits, without infringing upon the nature of the power and with a weak capacity to open up the protest movements into a new type of rule wherein one could identify the nucleus of a civil society.

Modernization has induced paradoxical effects in the Islamic societies. On the one hand, we witness the formation of civil movements, religious and secular, with an attempt on the part of the religious ones to propose a democracy-friendly interpretation of Islam (the Islamic reformists). On the other hand, and opposed to this tendency, there is a radicalization of minority radical groups within the Muslim world, providing a bellicose vision of the world wherein the fight to the death becomes paramount in the name of global jihad. In this perception of Allah's religion, martyrdom and jihad find renewed meaning in the framework of a symbolic world war. One major consequence is the rejection of quietism in the sense of obedience to the power holders, governors, and the like. There is no more respect for them in the name of the sacredness of their office as representatives of the caliph, who is, theoretically, the lieutenant of the Prophet and therefore of God (the *ulul amr*, that is, the ruler as legitimized through its exercise, even if he is unjust). In the past the ruler was from time to time contested, but the nature of the power did not change through this contestation, even if it succeded in overthrowing the power holder and replacing him with another. Today jihadism rejects the power holders and intends to replace them with an Islamic ruler who would, in the name of Allah's religion, declare war against the entire world in a manner that has nothing to do with the *asabiya*, the traditional allegiance toward the rulers in terms of ethnic or tribal bonds. Universalism, the theoretical feature of Islam right from the beginning but never realized in terms of social movements or politics, finds here a debut of accomplishment: jihadist movements are mostly Arab-based, but they involve converts from all over the world and have adherents from all walks of life from among all Muslims in the world. Jihadist movements are genuinely universal. But contrary to the reformist movements that are universal through tolerance and separation of Islam and politics in order to accord power to the burgeoning civil society, they militate for a universalism based on the total hegemony of the power holder who represents Islam. It is a universalism that is not unlike communist movements, assigning to the leader the representation of the entire society. Global jihadism, in this respect, is the dark side of modernization in Muslim societies, in contrast to the bright side of Islamic reformism. Both represent the new tendencies within Muslim societies that go beyond the customary power structure, mainly based on clientelistic affinities.

Jihadism is more and more the ideology and the basis of conduct for those who are modernized and yet find modernity a calamity, led by the Occident against Islam and aiming at destroying Islam for the sake of total hegemony over them.[18] This vision makes the incompatibility between modernity and Islam total, the first one being a sinful attitude based on the rejection of Allah and the assertion of perverted Christian values that become, in the process, secular, democratic, and nonreligious, even antireligious. In this perspective Islam is the only bulwark against the perverted Christian faith. It is also the only legitimate way to fight against the godless world of secularism. From this viewpoint Islamic values are the only ones that can save the world from utter corruption through secularism, which is a man-made value system and as such heretical and sinful and a transgression of Allah's laws.

CONCLUSION

Global jihadism is an ideology and a pattern of action that is in an ambivalent relationship to Islamic fundamentalism. In many cases the same attitudes are prevalent in it, notably in regard to humilation and rejection of perverse Western values. But in regard to violence there is a large gap between the two major tendencies within the Islamic world. Fundamentalists consider a peaceful road to Islamic society one in which the political realm will be gradually Islamicized. Jihadists reject the peaceful, democracy-friendly fashion of attaining this goal and propose the recourse to jihad in the most violent manner so as to restore Islam to its former glory. Humiliation is not mastered in a way that might induce gradualism to achieve Islamic goals. On the contrary, it is put at the service of a violence that achieves worldwide focus through its hyperaggressive posturing. Total violence against globalized Western culture and domination is the major characteristic of global jihadism.

13

Ordering Chaos

Nazi Millennialism and the Quest for Meaning

David Redles

The conclusion of World War I left Germany in a profound state of political, social, and economic chaos. That the society was on the verge of civil war with the specter of a Soviet-style revolution omnipresent and with an economy in shambles left many Germans feeling lost and confused. These individuals were so troubled by the world they saw around them that many believed Germany was rushing toward a collapse of apocalyptic dimensions.[1] Many of these individuals began a quest for salvation, for themselves, their country, and even the world. In time they would convert to National Socialism, a movement that promised exactly such a salvation.[2]

Those who began their search for a new way, a new construction of order, most often began it feeling divided, confused, and hopeless. This period of crisis, the "dark night of the soul," as St. John on the Cross described it, is a common and perhaps necessary aspect of the preconversion mentality.[3] The crisis state is often experienced as a feeling of disorientation. This sensation was especially acute for German Front soldiers who returned home at the conclusion of World War I to find a world that seemed, and to a great extent was, quite different from the one they had left before the conflict. Adalbert Gimbel recalled, "As a veteran I came back from the World War and found before me a state where nothing corresponded with that which, as a volunteer, I had left behind." Similarly Otto Leinweber found, "When I came home after the war, everything was different than one had imagined it." Another veteran explained, "My brain could not grasp that everything should be different than it had been," and Gustav Bonn found, "The disorder was too great to comprehend, so that one interested oneself in what should happen to this knocked down and prone Fatherland." Karl Adinger stated, "With all these experiences it was incomprehensible to me why in our Fatherland such conditions dominated." A veteran and future Nazi explained,

"As a Front-fighter the collapse of the Fatherland in November 1918 was to me completely incomprehensible."[4] This sense of confusion and incomprehensibility reflected the inability these veterans, and many other Germans, had reconstructing a perception of ordered reality from one that had so totally collapsed.

Having a perception of order dissolve into disorder left many Germans feeling disconnected from the world around them, alienated and lost. A number of future Nazis referred to their condition after the war as "rootless."[5] Others felt hopeless, concluding that the disorder was simply too great to overcome. The story of one man demonstrates this experience. After the war he found, "A great hopelessness was in me." When the right-wing nationalist Wolfgang Kapp attempted to oust the left-wing government in Berlin in 1920 he saw a glimmer of hope. But when Kapp's putsch collapsed he noted, "Again came this dull hopelessness."[6] Perceptions of incomprehensibility, rootlessness, and hopelessness were psychic conditions that mirrored the chaos of Weimar Germany. One man who had "lost faith" in Weimar leadership and had been hit hard by the "inflation frenzy" remarked, "Inwardly I had lost my Fatherland and proceeded unsteadily through the bitter times of contemporary events."[7] The young soldier and future Nazi Emil Schlitz returned from the war and saw a Germany that made his perception of reality fall like the Tower of Babel: "I had believed adamantly in Germany's invincibility and now I only saw the country in its deepest humiliation—an entire world fell to the ground."[8] Reality, a sense of comprehensible order, collapsed into a psychic disorder so great that it was in turn projected onto a world now interpreted as approaching apocalypse. As Karl Hepp remarked, "The inner confusion, and, with it, the doubt in the dawn of the new, better age, was ever stronger."[9] The fear of apocalypse consequently elicited hope for the dawn of New Age: the Millennial Reich.[10]

One of the most significant factors that distressed these individuals was how divided postwar Germany was, both politically and socially. That the new democracy based in Weimar appeared so hopelessly divided and politically inept only intensified the connection of national division with the perceived impending apocalypse. The confusion and indecision that parliamentary democracy can create, particularly in a society unfamiliar with it, led to the perception of a "parliamentary quagmire" at exactly the time when a clear and decisive policy was sorely needed.[11] The proliferation of competing parties created what many termed pejoratively the "Parteisystem." This "system" became a symbol of the disunity and chaos that was bringing Germany to the verge of apocalypse. It was a common complaint that "party quarrels and squabbles splintered the Volk."[12] Hans Otto observed that parties "grew like a fungus upon the earth."[13] Another Nazi agreed:

> One government alternated with another. Marxist mass gatherings! The citizenry was splintered into smaller and smaller parties. Program upon program swirled through the air. A completely uniform and clear direction was lacking. It appeared impossible in this witch's temple to find one's way from one slogan or another. The Volk was fissured in interests and opinions, in classes and estates—a plaything of enemy powers and nations.[14]

The metaphors of filth, depravity, and decomposition are associated with the disunity that was bringing Germany to the abyss. What they called for were purity and a regeneration of society, something the Nazis would make a fundamental tenet of their beliefs. The apocalyptic chaos was interpreted as reflecting a sudden decrease in morality. A return to morality therefore could cleanse Germany of its degeneracy.

The disunity of Germans divided by class was especially troublesome to returning veterans, as it was contrasted with the perceived unity of the trenches, where being German was more important than one's occupation or class. The Nazi emphasis on community, conceived as racial unity, as being crucial for salvation appears to have been the key metaphor for eliciting the conversion experience for many of the Old Guard. This was especially true for war veterans who longed for the lost camaraderie of the Front, part of what the historian George Mosse called "the myth of the war experience."[15] The war itself was in many ways a transcendent experience, which the individual self was surrendered to the needs of the collective. Selfishness was replaced by sacrifice. Words such as *fissure, fragmentation,* and *splintering* occur throughout the testimonies of Old Guard Nazis, reflecting their perception that society was breaking apart at the seams. Although this social disintegration was never as real as these Nazis believed it to be, it was real enough to be believed. And once again this sense of fragmentation in society reflected, at least in part, a projection of the psychic fragmentation that occurs when a perception of order is destroyed by rapid and radical change. The desire for social unity through racial homogeneity in turn reflects the need to reconstruct reality into an ordered and meaningful worldview.

This is not to say that German society was not, in many real ways, profoundly divided.[16] But the real social schisms were intensified in the shattered psyches of many Germans. In this way social division was seen as reflecting moral decline, which in turn generated a search for a messianic leader who would create the unity necessary to achieve national salvation.[17] The Nazi reaction to the profound changes of the Weimar period was obviously extreme. Many who became Nazis interpreted this period as not simply hard times, but, in apocalyptic fashion, as a total collapse of German civilization. The apocalyptic construction of reality reflects in part the collapse of an inner perception of order. Not consciously aware of this, these individuals projected their inner chaos onto a world that was in extreme disarray, though by no means approaching apocalypse. Viewing the world through apocalyptic lenses, many early Nazis believed that Germany was at best threatened by "enslavement," and more frequently "annihilation." One early Nazi supporter said of the times that "Germany seemed doomed" in a "struggle against an overwhelming fate," where "the world was turned upside down" and the "the suffering and despair of the people, subjected to foreign occupation and a number of communistic uprisings, was terrible. . . . There was a constant tension in the air. . . . There was no unity of purpose anywhere."[18]

This sense of imminent annihilation was common; as another early Nazi noted, "Germany staggered more and more towards the abyss."[19] That Weimar was generally described by such words as *disorder, confusion, abyss,* and, most often, *chaos* points to a psychological inability to structure a perception of reality into a coherent and meaningful pattern. Gustav Bonn felt "the disorder was too great to comprehend"; Albert Barnscheidt believed, "It was a spiritual and corporeal struggle—the disorder nearly overpowered me—no party, nor person, could help me."[20]

The perception of a total collapse of Weimar society was extremely disorienting and caused great insecurity in those who eventually converted to Nazism. As with most millennial movements, and fundamentalist mentalities that often support them, the Nazis viewed these changes as resulting in part from a seeming loss of moral standards and the "relativization" of reality that this entailed. This view can be seen in the following statement by Gregor Strasser, an important leader of the Berlin Nazis:

> There is a terrible hopelessness in the souls of humanity, a dissolution of all firm values, an instability which looks in vain for stability which it does not find any more in religion and which it has lost in ethics! "Relativity"—that is the keynote of the culture of our times—relativity in all things, relativity in all knowledge, relativity in all feeling—and the numb anxiety of a bad conscience tries in vain to cover and excuse this inner instability with "psychoanalysis." The cure itself is eaten away and has to a great extent already been lost![21]

If social fragmentation was conceived as the key catalyst for apocalypse, then social unity was the only path to salvation. What many individuals searched for, then, was a movement that could both unify the Volk and vanquish its enemies, those perceived to be the demonic agents of fragmentation.

NATIONAL SOCIALISM AND THE POWER OF COMMUNITY

It was the Nazi worldview, what many Old Guard party members termed Hitler's "great idea," encapsulated in the concept of national socialism, that was to reshape the minds of those who converted to the movement. National Socialism replaced the perception of fragmentation with unity and community. As one Nazi from the aristocracy explained, "In the year 1928 I perceived that these paramilitary unions could achieve nothing so long as the German Volk was fissured into parties, interests and classes and that the liberation of the German people was possible only through a freedom movement that brought together all conscious German men from all social stratums and occupations."[22] The prime factor necessitating renewal in the minds of many Nazis was the division generated by party and class factionalism. What was termed *German* or *National* Socialism was interpreted by most party members, and many other Germans, as signifying a return to unity. The coming Millennial Reich would be a society wherein religious and class distinctions would no longer be relevant and therefore the political parties that represented them no longer necessary. What mattered according to the Nazi worldview was one's race, not one's occupation. The new German nation would be united by both biology and faith. To create the *Volksgemeinschaft* (community of people) it was deemed essential to create a *Glaubensgemeinschaft* (community of faith).[23]

Interpreting the divisiveness of Weimar as a sign of the apocalypse, many individuals searched for a movement that promised to unify Germany and thereby save it. One man believed that he had found this movement in the Nazis: "Finally a practical proposition for the renewal of the Volk—Destroy the parties! Away with the classes! True *Volksgenossen* [racial comrades]! These are aims . . . which I could totally support. Yet that same evening it was clear to me where I belonged: to the new movement. From them alone could I hope for the salvation of the German Fatherland."[24] According to true believer Otto Wagener, the communalism of Hitler's National Socialism was not so much that promoted in classical Marxism but the millennial communalism of the apostolic or gnostic Christians. Wagener recalled Hitler saying, "For almost two thousand years the Gospel of Christ has been preached, for two thousand years the sense of community has been taught." But according to Hitler that communalism had not been listened to but ignored: "We're to believe that we can restore the value of the word of God, the teaching of Christ, the truth of a holy religion, where generations upon generations, nations upon nations, the entire life span of a human cultural epoch, all were unable even to recognize the deep abyss in which they wandered or sojourned!"[25] National Socialism therefore was not inimical to Christianity as such but, in Hitler's mind, a return to the true racial socialism of Jesus of Nazareth.[26]

Those Germans who felt lost in the chaos of a divided Germany searched for a movement that could make sense of that chaos by reconstituting order. They began their search in a state of psychological turmoil, but with Nazism they found their world suddenly made sense again. And it was this sense of inner transformation that elicited so many Nazi conversions, experiences virtually indistinguishable from religious conversions.[27] According to one early Nazi this state of psychic conflict was necessary for an individual to find the right path: "He who searches for the right path must be inwardly in conflict." He is correct from a psychological perspective, for it is the resolution of conflict through the construction of a new perception of order that elicits the conversion experience, releasing enormous amounts of energy and giving the "reborn" new meaning and direction in life.[28] A detailed look at this man's conversion delineates typical elements of the Nazi conversion process. It begins with a feeling of inner or psychological conflict and unrest. Referring to his own problems in the early 1920s, he noted, "The struggle set in—a fervent, hard spiritual struggle." This spiritual conflict set him on his path for salvation. He searched from party to party, worldview to worldview, yet found no solace. He explained, "At this time I went through another inner struggle. Again and again I persuaded myself that it [one path or another] was, and must be, right. But always there was a voice there, very soft and scarcely audible, warning and again warning against it. . . . Inwardly dull, a scattered soul—I wandered about lost." After a seemingly fruitless intellectual quest, in Hitler's words he thought he might have finally found the right path. But, as is typical of many converts, there was a period of hesitation: "Inwardly, however, I was completely confused. Yet when I reconciled what I heard with contemporary events, I had to come to the conviction that the truth had been told." Listening to a speech by Joseph Goebbels pushed him further along this path. The gradual process of conversion then culminated in what he experienced as a sudden revelation:

> It was for me as if he [Goebbels] had spoken to me personally. The heart went out from me, the chest heaved, I felt as if something within was being put back together, bit by bit. . . . I plunged myself into some literature that was at hand, read Hitler's speeches, read the program of the N.S.D.A.P. and was gradually politically born again. . . . A totally pure joy came into my consciousness. . . . I was a National Socialist. No voice this time inwardly spoke against it, no mind worried about the thought of being a National Socialist. A joyful knowledge, a bright enthusiasm, a pure faith—Adolf Hitler and Germany.[29]

As Lewis Rambo has noted, a period of hesitation and inner conflict before surrendering the old self to a new self is a common stage in the conversion process.[30] The new life and new worldview or construction of reality that comes with it is tempting, but yielding control to some higher power or charismatic messiah or guru is a difficult step. It is the resolution of this conflict through surrendering control to an idea, movement, or individual, or some combination of all three, that elicits the conversion experience and he sense of liberation that comes with it. For the man just quoted, a period of confusion was resolved through the millennial rhetoric of Hitler and Goebbels, and the collapsed old order was replaced with a coherent and meaningful new order, the worldview of National Socialism. He had found his path to salvation.

In this way the perception of chaos propelled many Germans on a search for a new sense of order, what has been termed "the quest."[31] Karoline Leinweber went on this quest with her husband, Otto. Her account demonstrates the importance of familial networks for the spread of Nazism.[32] It also reflects the possessive quality of Hitler's "idea," as well as the religious nature of her subsequent conversion:

> When in the year 1922 I heard our Führer for the first time, I shifted my entire interest to the movement, if only because my husband was seized by the same idea. So we went jointly upon this uncertain path. However, a ray of light showed us the path. What the Führer willed, which was holy to us, we surrendered blood and everything that we had. Insults, knocks and taunts we let make us even harder. So we went side by side through bitter deprivation, yet ever wider triumphed the truth. What the Führer did and said was right.[33]

Eduard Hohbein, discussing the difficulties of the struggle years, claimed, "In spite of all this, and every dark happening, I will never in my life let myself be led astray from the good path. I feel myself to be accountable only to our Lord God and my Führer."[34] Hohbein was convinced he had found the righteous road to salvation. Nothing could lead him astray, not violence, not hunger, not poverty. What made the Nazi conversion experience seem so powerful, and so right?

The Nazi conversion experience was most often referred to as an "inner" or "inwardly occurring" phenomenon, a description that points to its psychological basis. For many seekers the primary motivation leading to a conversion experience is a desire for transcendence, to search beyond themselves to find meaning and purpose.[35] This is true of many Nazi converts as well, especially those who rejected modernity and its perceived emphasis on materialism and "egoistic" selfishness.[36] They craved an experience that was spiritual and communal. Ludwig Heck said that he came to the Nazi movement through newspaper articles: "[There I] found inner contact with the spirit of National Socialism and it was my aspiration to work for this idea at my locality."[37] Similarly another man, speaking of the early 1920s, remarked, "At this time I studied several propaganda writings of the N.S.D.A.P. and felt myself intuitively drawn to the spirit which spoke from these writings."[38] This notion of being "inwardly" drawn to the Nazi worldview is fairly common. That the written word could carry such magical power for so many Germans points to the powerful attraction of millennial rhetoric.[39] It was not simply the intellectual force of the Nazi argument, but something ineffable. One man stated that if someone had asked him why he placed all his faith in the Nazis, he would have responded, "To tell the truth, I would not have been in a position to answer. I only know that I followed an inner voice, an impulse, which I was not in a position to withstand."[40] The belief that one is following a higher power or truth is a common and powerful aspect of the postconversion personality, and fundamentalist mentalities in general. For the convert, doubt and confusion are replaced with certainty and clarity as the world suddenly makes sense again.

The spoken word was especially noted for its ability to draw individuals to Nazism. For some converts that attraction seemed almost supernatural. Peter Weber attended a gathering and found, "Instantly I came to a decision, and I said to myself, that only this party can save Germany. From this time on I attended every gathering—it drew me to it, so to speak, with magical power, and on March 1, 1928, I became a member."[41] Franz Madre first came into contact with the movement when he was fourteen years old: "While I could not as yet understand everything completely, still something inside me said that here exists something to which I belong."[42] In other words, the Nazi use of millennial symbols and metaphors deeply touched this man. It was the "awakening" or bringing to light (consciousness) of the new worldview (the new construction of order) that led to the Nazi conversion experience. The remarks of another man elucidates this psychological process: "Through National Socialist propaganda I became aware of the movement and visited several gatherings. Without at first being clear about its goals, I felt instinctively the spiritual transformation that [occurred] inside me [through] the liberating idea. . . . Later I read the Führer's book, then heard him in person and . . . believed."[43]

Often these converts believed that they had always been Nazis but simply had not been aware of it. This is in accordance with their conviction that Nazi propaganda was simply awakening or bringing to the surface something lying dormant within the soul or blood of all true Aryans. From a psychological standpoint, this is in fact a more accurate description of the conversion process then perhaps the Nazis themselves were aware. Hitler's "great idea," filled with symbols of annihilation and salvation, messianism and demonism, helped them simultaneously reconstruct a sense of order and create a new life. This process is evident in the following account by Martha von Reuss. Here she relates her first encounter with a Nazi proselytizer:

> I could have listened to this man all night. Inside a voice would often say: "Yes, entirely correct, as I have always believed." In this hour I knew finally, after many searches and headaches, where I belonged. Then it was very easy for me to see that I was really always there [a Nazi] without knowing it. There Adolf

> Hitler's people were willing as fighters to stand up against Marxism, and were willing to bleed and to die for this holy idea of our beloved Führer. It was clear to me that my goal and wish was attained. It kindled in me a fire for this movement, and I perceived that one does not learn National Socialism, rather one must experience it. And for the second time in my life, exactly like with the war, I regretted that I was not a man.[44]

This search for salvation was in the words of many seekers for "clarity" and "light." One man, impressed by his son's willingness to die for Nazism, recalled, "That was the crucial hour for me. For a long time I pondered how it was possible that my only son would be willing to let himself be killed for an idea. It struck me that there must be something about the idea other than what I had heard about it. In all secrecy I bought myself a copy of *Mein Kampf.* Then I went to some National Socialist meetings, and I began to see the light."[45] The common conversion metaphors of moving from confusion to clarity, from darkness to light, reflect the psychological process of having a perception of order collapse into disorder, then having it reconstructed through a millennial worldview. The sense of order generated by Nazi apocalyptic cosmology was experienced as a revelation of simple but profound truths. An excerpt from the life of one seeker highlights this process. Poor and hungry, tempted to steal yet holding fast to his values, this man struggled through the Weimar period—until National Socialism came into his life:

> I had held, up until then, many illusions and had to experience them gradually turn to dust. . . . Then came the economic misery—one experienced its hunger and saw full stores, saw the splendor of the streets of the capital, saw the luxuriant department stores. And yet I held myself straight. And when I alas often had not a bite to eat for three days I lived by the strongly held conviction to pass them by, not to become wicked, but to live in misery, to go into the earth without sin. And then the light came into my life.[46]

One convert recalled that after his first Nazi speech he had no doubt "that this movement must be accepted if the German Volk is not to lose its faith in itself and in the Fatherland. This faith in itself, therefore, only slumbers in the German Volk and only requires a piercing voice to be wide awake."[47]

The message of that "piercing voice" was of impending apocalypse, with salvation possible only through Nazism. Nazi rhetoric struck a chord with the millenarian longings of many hopeless and frustrated Germans. Elisabeth Kranz recalled that the speaker at her first meeting entered the room like an apocalyptic prophet, saying, "Give room, you people, give room. We are the last messenger! Thus we are the last—the last contingent, the last bulwark against communism. Behind us comes nothing more, behind us comes chaos—destruction."[48] The first time Elisabeth heard Hitler speak, during the Party Days in Nuremberg in 1927, convinced her that salvation was indeed forthcoming: "All my hopes, wishes, and yearnings went to this city, where the Führer came, the man who God sent us to save our poor tormented Fatherland, to save us from shame and disgrace, from sorrow and despair, from external enemies, and from frightful internal decay—the Führer whose magnificent words and speeches I had read!"[49]

The story of the Nazi storm trooper Johannes Christ demonstrates the life-changing capability of a conversion experience, in which the old self dies and a new self is born. He remarked that while attending a speech by Gregor Strasser he came to the sudden realization, "[My] inner confusion [simply marked] the end of one world. I was slowly ruled by a different spirit."[50] It was the Nazi explanation of the cause of Weimar chaos that was the catalyst for Hans Grün. Once again Nazism structured the chaos he perceived around him by placing the German collapse within an eschatological framework, thus transforming what appeared meaningless into something meaningful. In other words, the chaos was no longer perceived as random and meaningless but reflective of the historic turning point wherein Germans could choose annihilation through Weimar politics or salvation through National Socialism. According to Grün:

> The gathering made an incredible impression upon me. Why? I had never yet experienced such a thing. The speaker resolved in me what had until then been unclear with an account of the recklessness of the men of the government system and its institutions, as well as all its spawn. This, as well as the entire course of the rally was for me a life experience. I could not wait until the next gathering was announced.[51]

The Nazi emphasis on community and unity as being crucial for salvation appears to have been the key metaphor for eliciting the conversion experience for many of the Old Guard. This was especially true for World War I veterans. Through Nazism, especially when experienced in a mass gathering, whether a speech gathering or a Party Day ritual, the lost unity of the trench experience celebrated a rebirth. One veteran described his conversion this way:

> The speaker spoke: naturally and unpolished flowed the words. Every sentence preached unvarnished truths. The heart intuitively demolished the barriers of my narrow-minded inhibitions. I felt myself suddenly in a community. I had, after a long while, a cessation of an inner experience. The company community of the field [war camaraderie], . . . which I once subscribed to with life and soul, celebrated a resurrection. From this day on I completely supported the idea-world of National Socialism. . . . From day to day I perceived ever clearer that Adolf Hitler clothed it in understandable words for my dull senses to lead me to community. The unknown soldier Adolf Hitler formed the unequivocal demands of National Socialism. I was again filled with the spirit of community and could no longer escape it.[52]

The reference to the restoration of "community" as being essential for the salvation of Germany is a common theme found throughout the testimonials of minor Nazis. As the politics and social fragmentation of the Weimar period imparted an apocalyptic sense of division within many German psyches, the Nazi millennial worldview in turn conferred a sense of oneness via its racial concept of a unified Volk, a community of blood.[53] Hitler exclaimed that politicians who turn workers against employers are turning racial brother against racial brother, a "sin against the blood." He countered, "We must release these misled people from foreign allurements! These people who feel abandoned by the Volk even though they themselves are the Volk—we must reunite them with the other racial comrades! A united Volk must come into being! One faith! One will!"[54] As division creates chaos, unity generates order. This type of reasoning can be seen in the following testimonial:

> The struggle of a few SA [Sturmabteilung (Storm Section)] men, workers, white-collar workers and peasants—almost entirely unemployed for a lengthy period—was almost desperate. Each and every one of them was a hero. More and more, however, through the indefatigable canvassing of the Führer and his faithful, knowledge of the correctness and purity of the Idea, and above all, the single most possibility of a turning away from communistic chaos, penetrated the masses.[55]

The experience of Karl Schworm also points to the importance of national unity for converting some Germans to Hitler and Nazism. Schworm called his conversion experience "the most significant milestone in [his] life."[56] He had already read about Hitler in the *Deutsche Zeitung*, and on May 6, 1921, he went to hear Hitler speak for the first time at the Festsaal of the Hofbrauhaus in Munich. Hitler spoke that night against the Jewish-led "world revolution" that pitted worker against bourgeoisie, and instead called for German unity through National Socialism. He concluded, "In its deepest misery beat the new German people's hour of birth!"[57] Hearing that Germany would be reborn through Nazism, Schworm recalled the audience's, and his, response:

> There, to the thunderous applause of thousands who surged again and again to the man at the speaker's tribune, I perceived with joyous and complete certainty: this simple son of the people will be Germany's savior, as he preached the only true gospel that will save us from every misery in the Fatherland. This evening was an unforgettable hour of revelation for me, and as I returned home to the Pfalz, I was a National Socialist.[58]

Hitler became the very symbol of unity and consequently salvation. The story of Heinz Hermann Horn's first encounter with Hitler portrays his charismatic effect as an orator. Horn, overwhelmed by hearing Hitler speak, wrote, "I no longer knew what he spoke about, I only knew that I was so taken by the spell of the Führer that I scarcely dared to breathe. And then, as he finished, again this jubilation, this enthusiasm like no one was ever acquainted with. This was fanatical veneration, like the will of complete devotion." After Hitler ended his speech, the Horst Wessel song was sung. As Hitler made his way to his coat, which was lying nearby, Horn "lunged toward him, seized the coat and helped him put it on." According to Horn, "My comrades were considerably envious of me for my good luck to have put on the Führer's coat. Perhaps one might laugh about it today, but for me it was a great joy that I was able to shake his hand for the first time. He looked around, observed me and gave me a light smile." Horn was enchanted: "I was simply lost and could no longer rest as I observed his eyes. My comrades chided me later that I did not wash my hand for fourteen days, but they were envious of me. Thus I saw the Führer for the first time."[59]

As is typical of conversion experiences, converted Nazis acquired a new sense of faith, one that replaced the preconversion sense of hopelessness. With the sudden realization or intensification of faith, listlessness and depression disappeared and they subsequently felt an infusion of power or energy.[60] Faith was an essential aspect of the new worldview and the new life of the converts.[61] One Nazi described himself during the struggle in this way: "Unwavering in faith in the mission of the National Socialist worldview I fought this struggle. . . . In spite of all my injuries and my sickness, I struggled unshakably further in the faith in the victory of the National Socialist worldview." Recalling the final years before the assumption of power, when the "terror" was at its peak, another individual explained that "there one saw, and profoundly experienced, the struggle for German humanity, for its soul." Struggle itself, in the minds of some Nazis, generated the needed faith. Karl Dörr explained, "As the Führer was what he was through his war experience, I was through the war made a faithful fighter for the Führer's holy idea."[62]

Faith in Hitler and his "great idea" called Old Guard Nazis to the movement like a spell; as one man explained, "We acted as if under a compulsion. Even had we wished to, we could not have been untrue to the movement without having our hearts turn out of our breasts. Unshakeable faith and unselfish devotion to the hallowed cause were our weapons against apparently invincible opponents."[63] This faith was based on the certainty of belief that underscores fundamentalist mentalities. Converts are utterly convinced that their new worldview, to which they are now attached through life and death, is entirely and solely correct. All contrary worldviews must as a consequence be wrong, perhaps dangerous, and even demonic.

APOCALYPTIC ANTI-SEMITISM AND THE JEW AS EVIL OTHER

The notion of one faith, one will, and one people was based on both racial and ideological exclusivity. National Socialists dreamed of a Third Reich that was biologically and intellectually unified. Consequently, like many fundamentalist mentalities, National Socialism accepted no deviance of thought. To achieve the Third Reich the *tausendjährige Reich* (millennial kingdom), which was conceived as a Volk (people or race) unified by a common *Glaube* (faith or belief) and race, any difference in belief or blood was unacceptable and intolerable. Those of mixed blood were to be removed from the nation's body, either through sterilization, euthanasia, or exportation. This included those deemed "life unworthy of life," such as African Germans, the Sinti-Roma (Gypsies), the physically and mentally handicapped, and of course the Jews. The Nazi millennial kingdom was envisioned as a world cleansed of all impurity, whether biological or spiritual (intellectual) in nature. And this cleansing process could only be violent in nature, as the reconstituted and purified caliphate or a Christian millennial kingdom that is prophesied to come with the deaths of billions of nonbelievers.[64]

Significantly the Nazis believed that demonic forces had caused the apocalyptic chaos of postwar Germany. In particular they believed a conspiracy of international forces, led by a secret coalition of Jews, Freemasons, and Jesuits, was behind the approaching apocalypse.[65] The need to unify German Catholics and Protestants led the Nazis to rather quickly back off from anti-Jesuit accusations, and anti-Freemasonry, a leftover of nineteenth-century conspiracy theories born as a result of the French Revolution and the social changes it wrought, found little resonance with most twentieth-century Germans. However, Nazi anti-Jewish accusations, especially when linked with anti-Bolshevism, found a much more responsive audience.

The successful Communist Revolution in Russia in 1917 and the German loss in World War I the following year led Hitler's intellectual mentor, Dietrich Eckart, to the conviction that the Jews were to blame for both. His worldview, and that of other Nazis, reflected a dualism found in many fundamentalist mentalities. Writing in 1919 Eckart interpreted World War I as a component of a larger epic battle that was not over: "This war was a religious war, that one finally sees clearly! A war between light and darkness, truth and lies, Christ and Antichrist." He concluded, "When light clashes with darkness, there is no coming to terms! Indeed there is only struggle for life and death, till the annihilation of one or the other. Consequently the World War has only apparently come to an end."[66] Eckart believed not only that the struggle between good and evil was to continue, but that it had reached an eschatological moment: "The hour of decision has come: between existence and non-existence, between Germany and Jewry, between all and nothing, between truth and lies, between inner and outer, between justice and caprice, between sense and madness, between goodness and murder—and humanity once again has the choice."[67]

Joseph Goebbels had much the same interpretation of contemporary history, writing in his diary in the early 1920s, "Evil forces are today still at work. Yet for how long? The thought lives and marches before us in the future. Salvation and victory! For a new humanity!" Salvation was a possibility, but what or who was behind the evil? For Goebbels the answer was simple: "Money is the force of evil and the Jew its protector. Aryan, Semite, positive, negative, building up, tearing down. The Jew has his fateful mission to bring the sick Aryan race back to itself. Our salvation or our ruin—it depends on us." The Nazis therefore had a countermission to save the world from the evils of Jewry: "We are the will of the future. We want Germany to save the world and not the world to save Germany." And just how would Germany save the world? According to Goebbels, by creating a Third Reich that was conceived as a community of racial Germans fully conscious of their salvation mission: "We want to stamp German conceptions into a new form, the form of the Third Reich. We want this Third Reich with the last fervency of our heart; the Third Reich of a Greater Germany; the Third Reich of a socialistic common destiny." If Germany was to save the world, the world's enemy, Jewry, needed to be vanquished: "We want to take up the fight against the world enemy. We want Germany to be [the] state that will make the German people into a nation. This people should be made ready to stab its enemy in the middle of its heart."[68]

Like Eckart, Goebbels conceived of this struggle in apocalyptic terms: "Thus the last gigantic battle was enflamed, a battle, which will bring us victory or collapse."[69] Such a linkage of a coming final battle against Jewry with the subsequent extermination of the Jews also can be seen in the early speeches and writings of Adolf Hitler. From the early 1920s Hitler conceived of the Nazi movement as one day creating a millennial Reich envisaged as a New World Order led by the Nazis themselves. It was a world that could not be fully realized until a final battle against the demonic force of Jewish Bolshevism had been won, once and for all. The loss of the war and the chaos that followed was seemingly explained in 1919 with the appearance of the German edition of *The Protocols of the Elders of Zion*.[70] This notorious hoax purported that the Jews were using a demonic combination of capitalism, communism, mass media, and world conflict to ultimately take control of the planet. *The Protocols*, and the conspiracy myth it seemingly legitimated, was received by the Nazis as a revelation that the Jews were indeed making a final push for world domination in fulfillment of the covenant. This prophesied Jewish millennial kingdom was interpreted as a countermillennium to the Third Reich that the Nazis hoped to realize. The Nazis believed that if the Jews were successful the end result would not be peace on earth, but the extermination of humanity.[71]

It was this apocalyptic worldview that led the Nazis to conclude that humanity had reached a historic turning point that could lead only to salvation, envisioned as the millennial third and final Reich, or apocalypse, conceived as the extermination of Aryans at the hands of the Jews. The Aryan-Jewish conflict was interpreted quite literally as an eschatological war. Hitler defined Marxism as a "poison" deliberately produced by the Jewish "prophet" Karl Marx "in the service of his race" to bring about the "swifter annihilation of the independent existence of free nations on this earth."[72] The final battle would come in a fight to the death with Jewish Bolsheviks. In his first important speech after leaving Landsberg prison in 1925, Hitler explained the Nazi aim: "Clear and simple: Fight against the satanic power which has collapsed Germany into this misery; Fight Marxism, as well as the spiritual carrier of this world pest and epidemic, the Jews. . . . As we join ranks then in this new movement, we are clear to ourselves, that in this arena there are two possibilities; either the enemy walks over our corpse or we over theirs."[73] A year later he reiterated in another speech, "There is going to be a final confrontation, and that will not come in the *Reichstag* but in an overall showdown which will result in the destruction of either Marxism or ourselves." It was the Nazis' mission to prepare Germany for this impending final conflict. He continued, using imagery taken from Revelation 12 and thereby transforming Satan into the Jewish Bolshevik:

> It is our mission to forge a strong weapon—will and energy—so that when the hour strikes, and the Red dragon raises itself to strike, at least some of our people will not surrender to despair. I myself represent the same principles that I stood for a year ago.
>
> We are convinced that there will be a final showdown in this struggle against Marxism. We are fighting one another and there can be only one outcome. One will be destroyed and the other be victorious.
>
> It is the great mission of the National Socialist movement to give our times a new faith and to see to it that millions will stand by this faith, then, when the hour comes for the showdown, the German people will not be completely unarmed when they meet the international murderers.[74]

The battle lines were thus drawn. Two opposing forces faced one another: the forces of good and evil, creation and destruction, order and chaos, form and formlessness, God and Satan. Only one force could prevail. It was the mission of Nazism to ensure that Aryan humanity was victorious.[75]

Most Old Guard Nazis, and most Germans for that matter, knew little of the Nazi inner circle's gnostic worldview that envisioned an imminent eschatological battle between the forces of light and dark, good and evil, Aryan and Jew. And perhaps they would have cared little as well. However, this does not mean that the racial salvationism of the Nazi elites, and the apocalyptic anti-Semitism that underscored it, was meaningless for the average party member. As a construction of the Evil Other, and the conspiratorial mentality that elaborates it, gives form and meaning to chaos by explaining away chance, so too for many Old Guard Nazis blaming the Jew provided an explanatory and therefore an ordering function. Though their reasoning usually did not include interpreting Jews as an evil occult power, it nonetheless was an important element of their personal millennial worldview. For some the seemingly inexplicably lost war and subsequent postwar revolutionary atmosphere could be explained only as the dark work of "the Jew." As one veteran and later Nazi explained, using typical apocalyptic metaphors:

> Barely 18 years old, I went to the field [the Front] to defend our homeland against a world of instigating enemies. Twice I was wounded. Then in November 1918 the Marxist revolution broke out—dark thunderclouds descended over Germany that for fifteen years allowed no rays of light and no sunshine upon the earth. In Germany everything went upside down. The Spartacists, clothed in sailor's uniforms, devastated and destroyed everything they could lay a finger on. The Jew rose to the pinnacle.[76]

In this way the war, the postwar social divisions, and the much hated Versailles Treaty that wrought both national shame and near economic collapse were reinterpreted as an apocalypse-inducing conspiracy of the Jews. Confusion was transformed into a coherent worldview by blaming the Evil Other. This is seen in the testimony of Emil Hofmann:

> It was clear to me what had brought the war and the revolt of 1918, namely a class state: here peasant, here city person, there worker and the laughing third, the Jew. Each party believed itself to be right. They went after, however, the final goal which was not the welfare of the Volk, rather each was concerned solely for itself. No wonder the German Volk had lost the faith and will to live. In its place tread shame, disgrace and baseness. The Versailles Dictate robbed us of our colonies and we had to surrender entire districts to the enemies. Our beloved Fatherland appeared heading for its complete ruin. Jews governed with their helpers, the Marxists and the bourgeoisie. Only one man understood these politics and that was Adolf Hitler, who opposed this madness.[77]

As with other fundamentalist mentalities, the seeming cultural decay of modernity, as traditional forms of beauty and order devolved into a formless and morally degenerate Sodom and Gomorrah, also found meaning in a blaming of the Jewish Evil Other. One Nazi who rejected the stark modernism of Weimar culture described the scene in the following way:

> Meanwhile Germany further decayed. In unpleasant ways an entire Volk was alienated from itself. A new society spread out which only recognized the

> majesty of one's own ego. Sinister poison gushed forth into the brains and blood of German men in theaters and cinemas, in varieties and in dance halls. German youth, often still children carried in one's arms, moved about this hideous depravity, as all that was great and holy in our Volk drifted away. An unbelievable sensual orgy had seized Germany and a Volk danced a death dance to the rhythm of foreign music—and the Jew held the baton.[78]

This Nazi's story clearly demonstrates the explanatory power of the elusive, albeit imaginary, "international Jew." A civil servant, he claimed to have become an anti-Semite through his job experience. He wrote:

> In the year 1924 I changed my official function. I was entrusted with the protection of the administration of justice in the political division of the Office of the District Attorney. This activity gave me a frightening image of the correct comprehension of a form of government that had gained its power through lies, deceit, and perjury. From year to year I understood more, that justice allowed itself to be debased as a prostitute to politics. However, I perceived especially the ways in which the German press worked, and thereby my eyes opened and I saw the enemy of our Volk; the international Jew.

This man clearly associated the trauma of Weimar with its government, which he then associated with the symbolic Evil Other, the "international Jew." It was his "experience" with Jews that he alleged led him to become a vocal anti-Semite. He explained that although he had previously had "an aversion for Jews," he had not been an "outspoken anti-Semite": "[But] now I was one, and I began more and more to hate with all my soul this race well-known as the eternal trouble-maker in the world." In his mind Weimar chaos had found its causal agent: the Jew as trickster figure, an Evil Other pulling the strings of German misfortune. Consequently this man used his position within the justice department to battle the Jews. He also became an ardent Nazi.[79]

Still other Old Guard Nazis claimed to have been "awakened" to the "reality" of the so-called Jewish Question in Volkish youth groups. In 1922 Willi Altenbrandt was a member of such a group, and it was there that he heard for the first time certain "Aryan paragraphs." Through this encounter the random nature of Weimar chaos was transformed by the totalistic and conspiratorial knowledge of its true nature: "The initial knowledge about the Jewish Question was conveyed to me here. Now I began to understand that events in this November-Germany, from all areas, whether political, economic or cultural, resulted not from pure chance or fate, but rather it had been prepared for a long time and had been systematically carried out through actions, to the shame of Germany."[80] Young Willi learned his lesson well. He grew up to be an SS Storm leader in Frankfurt.

Hubert Schummel, who developed a "natural sense" for anti-Semitism from his father, came to accept the Nazi apocalyptic version of the Jew as

Evil Other out to destroy the world. He argued that the "last goal of this world Jewry" was "the final annihilation of individual classes and thereby the German Volk altogether." This was achieved by driving "worker against peasant, peasant against worker or civil servant, artisan against salesman . . . parties against parties." Echoing *The Protocols of the Elders of Zion,* he explained that this was the "final goal of world Jewry and its footmen":

> They wanted the complete annihilation of the German people from all districts, whether it was upon racial, economic, socialistic, cultural or moral relationships. They wanted to bring about the eternal decline of Germany and therewith annihilate the greatest, most heroic and spiritually high standing and industrious people on earth, the German, the Teutonic. With the realization of this goal world history certainly lost its meaning.[81]

Schummel admitted that as a young boy he knew nothing of this: "All these demonic machinations as a young German I did not understand." Later he explained, "The party erected new fundamental ideas and endeavored to actualize the millennial dream of all Germans—a single German Volk under a single great Führer."[82]

Another man reacted to the divisiveness of the Weimar "party system" in much the same way, interpreting the factions not as a natural byproduct of parliamentary democracy, but rather as a deliberate destructive technique of the Jews: "Party quarrels seized men ever more. The Jews had achieved a foundation of a kind, and they understood how to bring about, behind the scenes, the inner attrition. Wherever one looked out, wherever one called out, one found above all the controlling Jews." Having decided that the Jews were behind the civil chaos, this man felt "a kind of hatred":

> So that it occurred to me one time in 1922, since I led a local branch of war-wounded, to struggle against the Jews entirely in the open, without being able to judge the significance in my inner self to where this group should be led. I searched for something to grasp onto; I bought a book that illuminated Jewry concerning its kind of life and its conscious goals. I studied Freemasonry and found out that this dreadful war was in fact deliberately caused. If one wanted to persuade us that we were to blame for this war, so what had awakened within me with this understanding, was that it was all but an unparalleled play of intrigue, a net of lies, that in world history had yet been produced.[83]

For this man the belief that the Jews were to blame for the postwar political chaos intensified his preexisting yet formless anti-Semitism. *The Protocols,* or a similar work, gave his anti-Semitism a new myth, the apocalyptic Evil Other, which in turn explained the war and the postwar chaos as part of a larger international conspiracy of Jews. Some historians argue that Nazi anti-Semitism was not a particularly important part of the movement's success in recruiting members, stressing instead the economic and political chaos of the Weimar years; they miss the central point that the two are inextricably linked, with the former providing a causal agent for the latter and thus also providing a solution: remove the instigator, and there will be peace on earth. In this way racial salvation and racial extermination can be seen as linked conceptions. From the Nazi perspective, the eternal struggle between the Aryans and Jews reached an eschatological turning point. Nazi success would ensure salvation in the millennial Third Reich. Failure could only bring apocalypse. As one Old Guard Nazi concluded, paraphrasing a leading party anti-Semite, Julius Streicher, "Without a solution to the Jewish Question, there is no salvation for the German people."[84]

Following an inexplicably lost war and witnessing a Germany in a state of perpetual collapse, some Germans were left confused and feeling hopeless. The chaos of modernity was interpreted as a sign of approaching apocalypse. For those Germans who converted to Nazism this new worldview gave them a sense of hope and meaning. The fear of apocalyptic collapse was replaced with hope of a dawning millennial Reich of peace and prosperity, with all *Volksgenossen* (racial comrades) united for the betterment of all. National Socialism helped these individuals reconstruct a collapsed world into an ordered and consequently meaningful worldview. Perceptions of social divisions were replaced by dreams of communal (racial) unity. But significantly the divisions that so plagued postwar Germany were blamed on an Evil Other, the imaginary but fervently believed in "Eternal Jew." This shadowy phantom, or so *The Protocols of the Elders of Zion* appeared to reveal, was involved in a conspiracy to take over Germany and the world through war and communist revolution. Removing this figure from the folk community became essential for salvation. This apocalyptic dualism removed any gray areas and replaced them with a black-and-white world of good and evil, light and dark. The attempt to exterminate the Jews of Europe was a logical, albeit horrid, consequence of this mentality.

14

Rumor, Fear, and Paranoia in the French Revolution

David P. Jordan

Rumor was the firstborn of the French Revolution's offspring. The child was robust from birth, more than mischievous, and although not as precocious and creative as later children, especially the extraparliamentary political clubs—the Jacobins and Cordeliers particularly—drove events relentlessly. Rumor was not invented by the Revolution. It had been the bane of court life during the ancien régime. Spiteful and venomous, it was the idiom of Versailles. But at court rumor was the institutionalization of gossip, focused on human foibles, shortcomings, and gaffes as well as the intricacies of preferment, seduction, and intrigue. These uses of rumor continued in the Revolution, but only as a trickle, another banal reminder of the perniciousness of the ancien régime, now finally toppled. Revolutionary rumor was, as so much else about the Revolution, different, novel, unique. It was about plots and conspiracies, both political and public, and sometimes paranoid: not whispered in the corridors or the boudoirs of nobility, but openly proclaimed. Rumor had become democratic. It still was spread to explain hidden motives and actions, gloss speeches, make observed behavior the evidence of a sinister subtext (which became increasingly a plot to overthrow the Revolution), but now even misbehavior and misdemeanors were considered counterrevolutionary. Politics had become all-encompassing and Manichaean.[1]

Rumor thrived on ignorance and gullibility, but stirred new passions, touched new fears, and often manifested itself in revolutionary action. From the earliest days of the Revolution the world was turned upside down. The French lost their bearings, not just institutionally but emotionally. The long-smoldering hatred for the aristocracy now took on political significance. The Revolution made aristocracy illegal (on June 19, 1790), and along with it went the code by which the privileged had lived for centuries. No new code, no new mores, were yet in place, hence the enormous appeal of the Jacobins and other revolutionary fanatics in insisting on new, revolutionary kinds of behavior and ideas. The Jacobins did not invent revolutionary rectitude, a kind of revolutionary Puritanism, but they benefited from it. Traditional symbols of monarchical authority collapsed within days. The royal government itself imploded as functionaries fled their posts and were lynched. The king's writ ceased to run, and the new parliamentary regime stumbled its way toward governing. The Church, once the Civil Constitutions of the Clergy were promulgated (in 1790), lost its traditional authority, especially over morals, as it lost any influence over the public sphere. Ecclesiastical land was confiscated by the state and clergy were required to swear an oath to uphold the secular constitution. At the same time the cloistered orders were dissolved and church schools closed. No one knew what might fall next.

Immanuel Kant, one of the early supporters of the Revolution even though living in far-off East Prussia, literally at the end of the Germanic world, had defined Enlightenment as man's liberation from the spiritual and moral tutelage of dogma and authority. Minds were now set free. Revolution set man's entire self free, adrift from traditional moorings, cut off from the social and institutional supports and habits that had prevailed for hundreds of year. There were now no barriers to rumor, no familiar channels in which it might run or be diverted. The public spaces where rumor of plots and conspiracies now spread went unpoliced in the first years of revolution; dozens and dozens of newspapers, newly created, printed what they pleased; and there were more and more extravagant rumors flying, for history had exploded and accelerated. Increasingly the Revolution saw enemies everywhere, even (and increasingly) in its own bosom.

The fall of the Bastille was rumor's first conquest and became the weld that bound together disparate bits of information, imagined and real, into a master plot. At Versailles, some eighteen miles west of Paris, where the Estates General, the French parliament, was meeting for the first time in 175 years, the king momentarily shook off his lethargy and overcame the deep sorrow and depression into which the death of his son had cast him, and sacked Jacques Necker.[2] Necker, the Crown's first minister, was a Swiss banker and a Calvinist. He was thought sympathetic to the demands of the Third Estate, which he endorsed cautiously and vaguely. Louis sacked him on Saturday, July 11, 1789. In some embarrassment Necker excused himself from a dinner party where he had learned of his dismissal, went home, packed his bags, and departed the kingdom. The curt dismissal was doubtless meant to humiliate the discharged first minister and publicly assert the power and triumph of the reactionaries at court, especially the king's two younger brothers. The time chosen, a weekend when the Third Estate, which had seized the initiative from the two privileged orders and on June

17 renamed itself the National Assembly, was not in session, was deliberate. The deputies would not officially learn of Necker's disgrace as a fait accompli until Monday. The court, in its arrogance and ignorance, had unwittingly chosen an impolitic moment for its political coup. The Third Estate would not assemble until Monday, but Sunday was the traditional market day in France (and so it remains). Rumors of Necker's sacking reached marketing Paris on Sunday morning and set the city in revolutionary motion.

Paris had no formal confirmation of Necker's firing, but rumor has no need of evidence. The hitherto dispersed pieces of information and hearsay about what was thought to be going on at Versailles were now collected into a court conspiracy against the Revolution. Fear, uncertainty, and the instinctive distrust of the court put the pieces together into a vast plot. On June 23, 1789, Mirabeau, the first great parliamentary leader of the Revolution, told the king's messenger, Dreux-Brézé, that the Third Estate would not disperse except at bayonet point. A few days earlier the Third Estate had declared itself the National Assembly (June 17), and on June 20 swore an oath in the Tennis Court at Versailles that it would not disperse until France had a constitution. The proclaimed independence of the Third Estate had been set in motion by the king's wooden and obstinate charge to the Estates-General not to touch the foundations of the old privileged state (May 23, 1789). To this was added the unexplained troop movements at Versailles and outside Paris as the king assembled loyal soldiers, and along with much else, all contributed. The roused city began arming itself.

The first victims of revolutionary rumor (and violence) were Joseph-François Foullon and his son-in-law, Bertier de Sauvigny, who were lynched and decapitated (July 12, 1789).[3] Gun shops and armorers in Paris were looted, ad hoc neighborhood vigilante bands were formed, and the fifty-four tax booths surrounding the city, walled in by the detested Tax Farmers in 1785 to tariff everything that came into Paris, were attacked, the officials roughed up, and a few booths set on fire. All this took place on Sunday, July 12. On Monday a huge mob marched on Les Invalides, the military hospital in Paris, where it was rumored that muskets and ammunition were stored. The nervous governor of the place temporized with the crowd, assuring them he could not act without first consulting his royal master. The crowd drifted off and continued to prepare Paris for the momentarily expected attack being plotted by the treacherous king, or rather his reactionary brothers and advisors, for Louis XVI still had the public trust.

The crowd returned to Les Invalides the next day, July 14, and were having none of the governor's excuses. They forced their way into the great building and seized thirty-two thousand muskets, but there was neither shot nor powder. A new rumor swept the mob that shot and powder were stored at the Bastille, the hated royal prison (lately reserved for writers and journalists who had committed lèse majesté). The mob crossed Paris, heading for the eastern gate, growing as it wound through the tangle of medieval streets. At the Bastille, with its walls ninety feet high and thirty feet thick at the base, they began to parlay with the governor of the place, the Marquis de Launay. There was no way a miserably armed mob, whatever its numbers, could capture the fortress without siege weapons and the knowledge to use them. Both soon arrived when soldiers were sent by the still loyal city government to disperse the mob. Instead they joined their now fellow citizens and turned their artillery against the fortress. When a seven-year-old boy (the youngest *vainqueur* of the Bastille) cut the ropes of the drawbridge the mob rushed into the inner court. Someone fired, and despite the hundreds of eyewitness accounts we do not know if the first shot came from the battlements or the courtyard. The now enraged mob stormed the Bastille. The seven prisoners held there, none of them political and, ironically, none of them victims of royal arbitrariness, were liberated and Governor de Launay was lynched on his way to city hall, his head severed and stuck on a pike, a macabre foreshadowing of what was to come. The rumored royal attack on Paris never came, but on July 17 the king performed a symbolic surrender to the city and in doing so acknowledged that Paris, and within months much of France, was in the hands of the revolutionaries.

Exactly what Louis and his advisors were planning between the sacking of Necker and the attack on the Bastille we do not know. If he wanted to destroy the Revolution in his capital the plan was bungled. It is true that the king, in his personal sorrow and political ineptitude, had turned increasingly to his wife, Marie-Antoinette, for support (and the advice that came with it). Not only did she side with the reactionaries at court, but her own advice was uniformly bad, her political instincts nil. This inquiry into motive, however, is academic. It was the rumor sweeping Paris that mattered, not the truth, which could not be known. Thenceforth, with increasing intensity, rumor, now broadcast by the new revolutionary press, wall placards, and the political clubs, all original creations of the Revolution, played a significant role. Increasingly Paris, populace as well as politicians, fearful and apprehensive in the Manichaean world of the Revolution, was willing to believe almost anything wicked about the court, a place of plots and conspiracies, which became synonymous with the counterrevolution.

It soon became clear that the peasantry too was driven by rumor, their detestation of the nobility, and the perennial nervousness that enveloped the countryside in the weeks before the harvest would begin. Soon after the surprising collapse of the Bastille, a heavily laden symbol of royal whim and injustice, rumor captured the countryside. A peasant rebellion broke out in mid-July 1789; it would grow to the largest such revolt in France up to that time. Within this massive uprising was a smaller and very distinct peasant rebellion, which soon was absorbed into the huge *jacquerie*. Known as the Great Fear it remains the most bizarre of peasant uprisings in a country where violent peasant protest was familiar. Georges Lefebvre has written the still unsurpassed history of the Great Fear.[4] He was able to track its spread as well as its timetable as it moved along the roads of rural France, especially the military road system, from town to town, in a series of ever-expanding concentric circles, although its origin is unknown. As the Fear reached one important provincial city after another it then spread from these urban centers ever farther inland, again along the royal roads. The peasants rose in rebellion as soon as news of the "brigands" reached them. The Great Fear, announced by riders from a nearby town, was that brigands, hired by the nobility, were coming to destroy the crop about to be harvested, starve the peasants, and thus subdue the countryside and destroy the Revolution. July, just before the harvest, was always a tense time in rural France, and the news of the Bastille's fall, as well as the earlier agitation surrounding elections to the Estates-General, added to the willingness to believe almost anything of the wicked and conspiratorial nobility. The usual form of the rumor was not only that the brigands were coming—some swore they had seen these murderous bands—but that resisting them was doing the king's bidding. A few imaginative rumormongers produced dubious but official-looking documents for their illiterate auditors that, they insisted, deputized the peasants to fight the brigands. No brigands ever appeared, but the countryside rose in rebellion anyway. Because the royal authority had collapsed and the still emerging revolutionary authority was in chaos, and anyhow had no interest in stopping a rebellion directed against noble landlords even if they could have done so, the Great Fear spread unchecked, petering out only when it encountered some natural barrier. (The Alpine provinces were untouched, as was the impenetrable *bocage* country of western France.) Within a few weeks rumor had set off the greatest urban insurrection and peasant rebellion of the Revolution, which together destroyed the authority of the monarchy, successfully destroyed the financial foundations of the privileged orders, saved the National Assembly from dispersal, and, for better or worse, made Paris the epicenter of the Revolution. The Great Fear, however, is distinct from the rumors of an impending royal attack on Paris. In the countryside the brigands were a figment of peasant imagination or folk mythology. As Lefebvre explains it, centuries of hatred for the nobility; the timing—the fragile weeks before the harvest, when last year's food was nearly exhausted and the new crop not yet gathered, when a sudden thunderstorm could spoil part of the crop—and the seasonal tramping of strangers looking for day labor during the harvest put the jittery population on edge. These timeless patterns and passions were now infected by news and rumors of the fall of the Bastille.

Lefebvre's study of the Great Fear rests largely on Gustav Le Bon's work on mass psychology. Once Lefebvre, one of the great historians (especially economic and social historians) of the Revolution, had counted all the separate rebellions under the umbrella of the Great Fear and examined all the traditional sources used by historians, he invoked Le Bon's theories to explain the collective paranoia that gripped the countryside. We now have more sophisticated tools to work with, but Lefebvre's is a pioneering work that recognizes the need to generalize individual psychology (or even pathology) and observe the changes it undergoes when applied to the group.[5]

The reign of rumor was just begun. The war, declared on April 20, 1792, was in part instigated by rumor. The attack on the Tuileries palace that overthrew the monarchy on August 10, 1792, was sparked by a rumor that the king, now a virtual prisoner in Paris, was again preparing to capture the capital. The ghastly prison massacres in the first week of September 1792, which killed about fourteen hundred prisoners and went on for seven days, was fired by rumor-provoked fear that the prisoners might escape and murder the defenseless Parisians, whose menfolk were leaving for the front to defend the Revolution against the invading Prussians.

Fear and rumor also produced the legislation that made the Terror possible, a response to reports of a brewing military coup d'état and the belief that the recent food riots (this is in the spring of 1793 and was a thesis argued by Maximilien Robespierre) were the work of aristocratic provocateurs and politically ambitious schemers. The Terror was the locus classicus of rumor and fear, the time when the Manichaean universe of good and bad, revolutionary and counterrevolutionary, patriots and traitors, was almost daily described in the press, the clubs, and the National Assembly. As the Terror became bureaucratized and seemingly insatiable, conspirators and traitors were unmasked and denunciations were common. On October 10, 1793, Terror was declared the order of the day. As revolutionary law it had an administration, law courts, juries, and a public prosecutor, the feared and sadistic Antoine Fouquier-Tinville. By the winter of 1794 the Terror reached into the ranks of the political elite. Everyone was potentially a counterrevolutionary and/or a patriotic delator.

In the first years of the Revolution the violence was sporadic, but from these beginnings it grew gradually into a systematic and bureaucratized revolutionary enterprise. Lynchings announced the beginning of the Revolution in Paris, and at the Champ de Mars Massacre (July 17, 1791) the revolutionary government of Paris, headed by the mayor Bailly, ran up the red flag of martial law and General Lafayette's National Guard shot and sabered hundreds of unarmed Parisians. Still, although more often than not set in motion by fears carried by rumor, these outbursts were improvised. The Terror was of another order. It was the law of the land, with special legal procedures and courts, with a new set of crimes against the Revolution, of which conspiracy was the most important, and with only one penalty: death. The Terror did not go after individuals for their transgressions so much as it went after groups, conspiracies. It was assumed by all that counterrevolutionaries acted together, that they plotted and conspired to destroy the Revolution, that they were part of a *queue*, a group, even though the Revolutionary Tribunal was rarely able to establish any convincing evidence of this. Plot after plot, conspiratorial group after conspiratorial group, hitherto considered patriotic, was discovered, exposed, judged, and guillotined. The Girondins, the Hébertists, the Dantonists, among other constructed, invented, or imagined plotters and conspirators, died on the scaffold. Conspiracy, it should be noted, accounted for the largest percentage of convictions.[6] There is not much doubt that the juries who sent men and women to the guillotine as conspirators believed the Revolution was riddled with plots. Fouquier-Tinville was more cynical. As a legal category conspiracy has the advantages of convicting groups without having to prove a crime was committed. It was (and is) a favorite legal weapon for beleaguered governments possessed by fear.

Even the end of the Terror was infected by rumor. Robespierre's fall, which effectively ended the official Terror—revolutionary violence then reverted to lynching and massacre, especially in the rural backlash to the year of Jacobin domination—was triggered by rumor. Some days before he was overthrown by a parliamentary conspiracy (this one quite genuine) of those who had abundant reason to fear for their lives, it was bruited about and believed that he was planning to marry the dead king's daughter—the future Duchesse d'Angoulême, the only surviving member of the royal family who remained in France—and declare himself king.[7]

From early September 1793 to Robespierre's fall on July 26, 1794, the year of the Terror in the French Revolution, politics was in no small part about discovering and exposing plots imagined and real. Men made careers out of denunciation; practically every branch of government had its secret police to ferret out conspirators (again both real and imagined); and some seventeen thousand men, women, and children went to the guillotine. More than double that number are usually counted as victims of the Terror, not on the scaffold but in the verminous, disease-ridden, and deadly prisons of the day or killed by local vigilantes, massacred en route to prison, or done to death without coming before the notorious revolutionary tribunals centralized in Paris.[8] The politics of fear dominated. Plotters and the citizenry were both terrorized, and the line between reality and fantasy was blurred and porous. France had her back to the wall, the Revolution was endangered, there was civil war and foreign war, and a substantial part of the country was not controlled by the government. Was it paranoia to see plots, imagine destruction, and see conspiracies at home and abroad, or was this a not unfamiliar response of populations to war, especially one that is going badly? It was both.

Political extremists in the neighborhoods, or forty-eight sections of Paris (similar to our political wards), could get almost anyone arrested, and by the last months of the Terror, when the hideous laws of 22 Prairial year II (in the Revolutionary calendar; June 10, 1794, in the Gregorian calendar) were in effect, streamlined legal procedures that led inexorably to the scaffold.[9] For a time there were entrepreneurial terrorists in the provinces who set themselves up as the enforcers of revolutionary rectitude (from which they excused themselves). The struggle for political power, intensified by the ongoing war, was murderous, and it was widely believed that conspirators and traitors were everywhere.[10] During the year of the Terror France had an emergency government, the twelve members of the Committee of Public Safety, who wielded almost limitless power and are credited with saving the Revolution from destruction abroad while governing at home through Terror.

I have deliberately chosen an episode other than the Terror as a case study in the politics of fear. The war, which lasted off and on for the entire Revolution, from 1792 until Napoleon's fall (1815), exacerbated all the crises that beset France and simplified politics: you were either for the Revolution or against it, for the war or a counterrevolutionary. France was at war and dissent gave aid and comfort to the enemy. It was treason, deliberate or unwitting. The idea, let alone the reality, of a loyal opposition disappeared. Factional struggle turned fatal. But all this lay in the future in the winter of 1791 and spring of 1792, when the Revolution debated whether or not to go to war. The declaration of war, I think, is the truer measure of the significance of rumor, fear, and paranoia, precisely because the decision was publicly debated, was proclaimed when the Revolution did not have its back to the wall, and because the growing hysteria was only loosely tied to the realities of foreign and domestic politics in the Revolution. The months of debate reveal the formation of the rhetoric of fear. In the course of this public debate, both in the National Assembly and in the Paris Jacobin Club—this latter not yet the all-powerful organization that mediated between the pressures and politics of the Paris streets and the National Assembly—ideas were not so much clarified as proclaimed with increasing intensity, urgency, and hyperbole. The debate on the advisability of war split the republican Left of the Revolution, which for the moment fought out their differences only in words.

The nightly gatherings and speechifying at the Jacobins soon became more important than the debates in the National Assembly. The war debates were the strategic dimension of the earlier constitutional debate over who could declare war, the king or the National Assembly. That debate had been a searching exploration of the place and nature of war in the Revolution and in the new Constitution.[11] For some the debate turned on which of its former absolutist powers the new constitutional monarchy would retain. More interesting, however, were those who probed war itself as a part of the Revolution. The deputies, among their early acts, had declared that the Revolution would not make war unless attacked. War, as so much else that confronted the revolutionaries, was a hated remnant of the ancien régime. The kings and nobles had made war almost incessantly; it was what they did in the former society, where military glory and the codes that set it at the apex of society determined social importance and worth. The new world no longer needed war, many argued, as it no longer needed a military caste to pursue the dynastic and territorial ambitions of the old monarchy. The Revolution proclaimed it had neither dynastic nor territorial greed. It desired only the liberation of humankind. The question of war and revolution was never answered, but the solution hit upon by the National Assembly, that it alone could declare war, was thought to have removed monarchical and noble values from society. Now, in early 1792, war reasserted itself.

I am concerned here only with the immediate causes of the war. The Legislative Assembly, the first French assembly elected under a constitution, was not only deeply divided politically—there was a sizable monarchical faction, for example—but it was filled with new men. Robespierre had been instrumental in having a self-denying ordinance passed in the first National Assembly: no member of the Constituent Assembly could serve in the Legislative Assembly. It was, ironically, the only one of his proposals that garnered the support of a majority. None of the leaders who had emerged in the Constituent, none of the combinations and cliques that had wielded influence, could be returned to the new assembly. In their place were men with no legislative experience, many of whom had a name to make for themselves. It is arguably this second revolutionary assembly rather than the first that deserves the accusation of Edmund Burke:

> Nothing which they afterwards did could appear astonishing. Among them, indeed, I saw some of known rank, some of shining talents; but of any practical experience in the state, not one man was to be found. The best were only men of theory. But whatever the distinguished few may have been, it is the substance and mass of the body which constitutes its character and must finally determine its direction.[12]

In addition these new men were hampered by a constitution that set up a clumsy relationship between the Court and the National Assembly. The king had only a suspensive veto, which would delay but not ultimately prevent legislation. The ministers were appointed by the monarchy and beyond the control of the Assembly. No politician, no would-be parliamentary leader, no faction could hope to succeed unless it had the support of the Court. In the course of the Legislative Assembly's short life—it lasted less than a year—all those who sought to lead were compromised by having to deal with a duplicitous Court. The king despised the constitution as a curb to his God-given authority to do good; the reactionary party at Court, including the queen, played on Louis's opinion and instincts; and a host of nobles conspired—again a quite real plot—to get rid of or hamstring the Revolution. As a consequence of all these tensions (and many more) the Legislative Assembly got very little business done. It was hopelessly divided, a condition welcomed by the Court.

The immediate spur to the war debates was Louis's veto of some laws dear to the left wing of the Legislative Assembly.[13] The priests who had not sworn the oath to uphold the constitution (the Civil Constitutions of the Clergy) as well as the nobles who had voluntarily gone into exile (the king's immediate family was the first to flee) were thought, correctly, to be fomenting counterrevolution, an invasion of France by the armies of monarchical Europe, which they would spearhead. The old monarchy would be reestablished and the Revolution would be destroyed. Louis vetoed the new laws directed against the émigrés and the nonjuring priests. In addition he stonewalled all attempts of the Legislative Assembly to have him demand that his fellow monarchs expel the renegade nobility and priests from their lands. Koblenz, in the part of the Rhineland belonging to the Holy Roman Empire, whose emperor was Marie-Antoinette's brother, was the gathering place for this opposition. Like a catch in a rhyme, or better yet like Cato the Elder reiterating "Carthage must be destroyed" in every speech, the war party in the Legislative Assembly hammered away at the plotters in Koblenz.

Those clamoring for war were well served by their orators. Pierre Vergniaud, a brilliant lawyer from Bordeaux, was the most eloquent; Jacques-Pierre Brissot, a hack writer of impeccable personal morality, the most passionate and exaggerated. Their rhetorical interventions were long prepared by several more obscure deputies in the Legislative Assembly. M. Depère, a deputy from southwestern France, made the general arguments for war on January 14, 1792. France is the object of a vast foreign plot, he began. The monarchs of Europe "have become the driving force of a league that they intend to organize against the French nation." The French have responded heroically to the plot; France "has seen the various powers conspiring against her and she has shown them the countenance of a lion who, at his awakening, sees the inhabitants of the woods all united against him."[14] Gensonné, closely identified with Brissot, Vergnaiud, and Roland—who with a few others would come to be known as the Brissotins, the Rolandists, or more familiarly the Girondins, the major foes of the Jacobins—added the domestic dimension of the international crisis: "When a great conspiracy menaces us from without . . . when the malevolence of the false friends of the Constitution are busy sowing the seeds of discord in France . . . when you are called upon for the first time to deliberate on war and to exercise one of the most important articles of your newly born constitution, [the nation must] give all of Europe the most striking example of the harmony which ought to regenerate [France]."[15] The war, it was consistently argued, would solve both the foreign and the domestic crises confronting France. Vergniaud added the priests to the plot, both those still in France and those who had emigrated. "The seditious priests prepared," he argued, "in the secret realm of conscience and publicly from their pulpits, an uprising against the Constitution. They lit the last torches of fanaticism against the laws that were destroying their power."[16] The conspiracy of all Europe—renegade priests and aristocrats, the kings and their counselors, the British Parliament, the pope and his acolytes—conspiring against the Revolution was now complete. A few details would be added, but mostly the debates were reiterations of this international conspiracy. Maximilien Robespierre was the most notable opponent of the war.

More often than not Robespierre is dismissed as a suspicious fanatic whose revolutionary career is a gradual unfolding of his narrow, shallow, suspicious, even paranoid and treacherous personality.[17] In the war debates at the Jacobin Club in Paris, however, he was the voice of practical and political reason, for which he was increasingly isolated as war fever rose. At the outset of the debates he cautioned against exaggeration, which went unheeded as the rhetoric became increasingly wild and bellicose. The monarchies have indeed adopted a belligerent stance, he insisted, but they were more likely to threaten than to attack.[18] He thought war "the greatest flail that can menace liberty in the circumstances where we find ourselves."[19] The Revolution was not yet secure. Treading carefully through the thickets of passionate patriotism, he argued that he too wanted war, "but only to the extent that the nation needs war," and the proposed war in 1792 was not necessary for the state or the Revolution's security or survival. The Revolution should deal with its internal enemies before marching "against . . . foreign enemies."[20] Robespierre in 1791 cautions restraint, a careful examination of the evidence being presented as theorems by the war party speakers, and he warns against the seduction of rumor: "Recall the false rumors that have been spread; recall the very orators who have been introduced with affection at the bar of the Assembly, and who are now suspect."[21] Prudence was no match for passion. Brissot's wild proclamations were immune to reasonable criticism. On December 29 and 30 he gave his two most incendiary speeches. "War is necessary for France," he insisted on the 29th, "[for] her honor, external security, internal tranquility, to reestablish our finances and public credit, to put an end to fears, treason, and anarchy. This war is a national benefit." The following day he famously proposed his homeopathic prescription: "We have need of great treasons, our safety lies there because there are still deadly doses of poison in the very breast of France. It will take powerful explosions to purge them."[22] Here is the full-blown politics of fear fueled by rumor.

Robespierre responded on January 2, 1792: "The most extravagant idea that can be born in the mind of a political leader is to believe that it is enough for a people to invade a foreign country, sword in hand, in order for them to adopt his laws and his constitution." He drove the idea home with an aphorism: "No one loves armed missionaries."[23] Besides its inherent absurdity, he continued, Brissot's war would divert attention from the Revolution's true enemies. "The true Koblentz is in France," he continued, where there is a "profound conspiracy against liberty . . . whose chiefs are in our midst."[24] This conspiracy is not merely metaphorical. It is true that the speaker was naturally suspicious, but it is equally true that the Court was fecund with plots, although Robespierre had no specific evidence. These domestic plotters, he insisted, must first be destroyed before embarking on foreign adventures. He proposed his own conspiratorial theory to trump Brissot's.

These are practical, expedient arguments, but Robespierre's attacks on the war party would not be complete and uniquely his without the moral dimension that marked all his political thinking. What set him apart from so many of his contemporaries was not a more intense playing on fear, not some kind of virtuosity in maneuvering in the world of fear, danger, even paranoia, but his ability to give his clear and rigorous analysis of contemporary politics a moral meaning. This he invariably did by invoking his own revolutionary self, in the manner of Rousseau's long public confessional, arguably the most influential philosophical and moral critique of politics available to the revolutionaries. Robespierre, in the manner of Marat, presented to the people his transparent self. Let each look into his soul and see the motor of his politics: "The love of justice, of humanity, of liberty is a passion like any other. When it is dominant one sacrifices all. Once one has opened one's soul to these passions of another species than the usual—the lust for gold or honors—one immolates everything else for the glory, the justice, the humanity, the people and the motherland. This is the secret of the human heart."[25]

This identity of political ideas with a personal passion for morality was not unique to Robespierre; although it is most highly developed in him it was characteristic of Jacobin discourse.[26] Jacobin politics was not the Bismarckian formula of the art of the possible. It was the art of the morally necessary. It is useful here to compare what Robespierre has to say about the war with the remarks of Jean-Paul Marat, the most radical and inflammatory of the revolutionary journalists.

Through the early months of the war debates Marat was in hiding. After the Champ de Mars massacre the Paris government hunted down the republicans. Many, including Robespierre, changed lodgings because they feared for their lives. A few never slept in the same bed two nights in a row. Marat hid out in the sewers, where he is thought to have contracted the horrible skin disease for which he found relief only in a bath, which is where Charlotte Corday found and stabbed him. His political career was launched by his newspaper, *l'Ami du Peuple*, which specialized in exposing conspiracies, publishing denunciations, and calling for heads to roll (long before the Terror). Bitterly resentful of having had his scientific theories—he was a medical doctor—ignored by the Académie, Marat discovered his unique gift for incendiary journalism in the Revolution. In the early years of the Revolution, when newspapers spawned overnight—there were at least a hundred such in Paris alone—it stood out. *L'Ami du Peuple* was not only the name of a newspaper, it was also Marat's revolutionary persona.

Even more than Robespierre, Marat was suspicious by nature, and suspicion was central to his politics. The nobility, the *académiciens*, the court generally, indeed the whole elite of the ancien régime was guilty until proven innocent. He too infused his ideas with his self, as he once lectured Robespierre: "Learn that my reputation with the people rests, not on my ideas, but upon my boldness, upon the impetuous outbursts of my soul, upon my cries of rage, of despair, and of fury against the rascals who impede the action of the Revolution. I am the anger, the just anger, of the people, and that is why they listen to me and believe in me."[27]

On April 12, 1792, after a hiatus of nearly four months, Marat began publishing *l'Ami du Peuple* again. His was another antiwar voice, in the same register as Robespierre's. "Led astray by the overwrought speeches of Brissot, Lemontey, Girardin, Lacroix, Gouvion, Buvras, and other scoundrels who sold themselves to the court," he thundered, "seduced by a false picture of our armed forces; drunk on the fumes of Gallic vanity, the people appear no less anxious for war than their implacable enemies. For three years I have warned that war is the last resource of counterrevolutionaries, and I have not ceased to work against the various plots of the cabinet to start a war."[28] In his extravagant way he proposed that rather than shed the "precious blood" of patriots the Revolution should hold Louis XVI, his wife, his son, his daughter, and his sisters as hostages and "make them responsible for whatever happens."[29] "Let us look at the men who will lead our armies," he argued a few days later, expressing the same fear Robespierre had ignited. General Luckner is "a soldier of fortune, a creature of the court." Rochambeau, who fought in America with Lafayette, is "a vile courtesan," and

Lafayette himself is "less known for his scandalous machinations against public liberty than for his abject prostitution to the court." "Gouvon is Lafayette's stooge," and Lameth is a "despicable courtesan who has covered himself with shame and opprobrium by his hypocrisy and his treasons." Narbonne, "a child of the court, [was] driven from the ministry by public pressure, as the most audacious of the conspirators."[30]

These accusations, no more than Robespierre's, neither delayed nor prevented the declaration of war on April 20, 1792. Marat and Robespierre temporarily lost their following. They were outcast prophets; their conspiracies were rejected in favor of those of the Brissotins. When both men were later elected to the Convention Assembly (in September 1792), which succeeded the defunct Legislative Assembly, they carried on the war they had once opposed with undiluted intensity. There were no sour reminders of their earlier antiwar stance.

Looking back from a safe historical distance, long after revolutionary warfare had run its bloody course, the war of 1792 has seemed to virtually all students of the Revolution, whatever their politics, a tragic mistake. After 1792 the Revolution lived under a war economy, eventually set up an emergency government, imposed price controls, sacrificed countless men's lives, created the circumstances for a military coup d'état, and simplified politics into those who fought the enemy and those who, for a multitude of reasons and circumstances, did not and were considered traitors. Revolutionary politics became brutally reductionist, and once the Terror was in place—it was always seen as the domestic dimension of the war—all the remaining opposition was choked off. Most important of all the war changed the nature of the Revolution every bit as much as did the fall of the Bastille. The former attached Paris, with its unique problems, population, and power, to the Revolution, which it then dominated. The war put the people in arms. In the words of Marcel Reinhard, the war "revolutionized the Revolution." It eventually brought the army and the generals to power in the person of Napoleon. In less dramatic fashion it redefined patriotism, created an armed citizenry that sometimes was more politically radical than the civilian politicians, and it made the Revolution both militant and crusading.

The war debates present a curious spectacle. All the parties involved preach and practice the politics of fear. All imagine circumstances, more or less accurate or lurid, that best support their view. And all are equally devoted to conspiracy as an explanatory mode that itself needs no explanation. Robespierre and Marat, the more and the less measured republican opponents of the war, are almost alone in their opposition. But in the midst of practical arguments—the generals and the court will be returned to power, the army is unprepared for war, if the court seeks war it must be for its own benefit, the counterrevolutionaries at home will use the war to destroy the

Revolution—are a series of near paranoid assumptions they share with the war party: the kings are conspiring against the Revolution, the court is in cahoots with the émigrés and the nonjuring priests, the ministers are purposefully lying, and the counterrevolutionaries are lurking everywhere, biding their time. These are the elements of the plot against revolutionary France.

There are, I think, paranoid aspects in the French Revolution, but even these have nuances that do not fit the pathology. The rumors that fueled the Great Fear as well as the rumors of Robespierre's intended marriage to the king's daughter and the proclamation of a monarchy are not true, but they played an important role in the Revolution. They could, at least in the popular understanding of paranoia, be so designated.

When we move to the war and the Terror the case for collective paranoia becomes more fragile, even tenuous. The war may have been unnecessary, a drastic and risky tactic by a political group to gain power and destroy the monarchy, but there was enough truth in the group's assertions, however exaggerated, to convince reasonable men that the Revolution was threatened. There were émigrés and nonjuring priests conspiring against France. They did have the ear of some of the monarchs, and the monarchical conspiracy against revolutionary France was real enough. Although not well organized or coordinated, the monarchies of Europe were anxious to destroy the Revolution by any means. By 1792 the kings had sufficiently realized the revolutionary threat to contemplate war themselves. Indeed the Austrians were on the verge of declaring war against France, and the French king had unsuccessfully tried to flee France and join the counterrevolution in the Holy Roman Empire.[31] Still, the frenzy of approaching war—we saw it as recently as the debate and then the invasion of Iraq—is familiar, and to call it paranoid implies that at some point, exceptionally difficult to identify, fear has crossed the line and become pathology.

The Terror presents a similar though even more tangled skein of fear, rumor, and paranoia. The Terror did indeed kill many innocent people, although we have no accurate way of separating the guilty from the innocent. It did indeed cause many to spin fantastic yarns about plots,[32] and it did become an instrument by which the Committee of Public Safety kept itself in power long after it had lost popular support and the Revolution was not militarily threatened. The emergency government of the Revolution ruled by terror from the winter of 1794 until its fall in July. In addition the Committee played upon and encouraged popular paranoia to keep up the fever of unmasking plots and executing the conspirators. The Terror became a juggernaut whose wheels crushed all who tried to stop it. The Terror was murderous, cruel, and terrible, spreading fear everywhere. But it was popular with some segments of revolutionary society and did not rest on pure fantasy, delation, personal persecution, or some precocious kind of totalitarian pathology. There were plots aplenty; there were spies. There were counterrevolutionaries; the English were dumping counterfeit paper money; the Revolution was at war with most of Europe and had three civil wars simultaneously aflame; and France had been anathematized by the papacy. The juries who convicted hundreds and hundreds of conspiracy doubtless believed they had the evidence to send them to the guillotine. Whether imagined or not conspiracies were fundamental to the Revolution, sometimes as a description of a perceived reality, sometimes as a reflex of a dangerous world, sometimes cynically played on by those wanting to save their own skins by sending their enemies to their death, sometimes manipulated by a government that had steadily lost its popular support. Still, the Jacobins and the Committee of Public Safety, using the weapon of Terror, did get the French Revolution through the most desperate months of its existence.

Where does this leave us? To my mind somewhat short of being able to present the French Revolution as an example of the paranoid perceptions of a bunch of fanatics. I would like to offer a historian's explanation for the war and the Terror that attempts to explain the same phenomenon but stops just short of proposing a kind of pathological template that would fit the French Revolution, or any revolution. Here I must backtrack a bit.

Rhetorically, political arguments are over what is the will of the people in the French Revolution (and in democracies generally) that must be pursued at all cost. Part of this argument is whether or not there is a vast conspiracy against the Revolution, whether or not there are counterrevolutionaries in the very bosom of the Revolution (and what to do about them), whether or not violence is necessary to save the Revolution from those who would destroy it, whether or not there are only revolutionaries and counterrevolutionaries, patriots and traitors, aristocrats and the people. These assumptions and the words and actions they engendered were accepted by all. The differences in the broad spectrum of revolutionary politics were about how the Revolution was envisioned, the meaning of conspiracy and political infighting, who truly represented the will of the people, whether the Terror should be slowed or accelerated, how a nation creates citizens, and in some cases abstract principles of virtue and republicanism. While all these profoundly important issues were being debated or defended everyone accepted that they lived in a dangerous world, that there were counterrevolutionaries, that conspiracies did exist. François Furet, arguably the most imaginative historian of the Revolution in recent generations, goes at these questions and assumptions without using the language of psychological categories.

Furet was offering an alternative explanation for the Terror, which I'll get to in a moment, in opposition to what contemporaries and their later followers regularly explained as the outcome of external circumstance, of which the war was central. Terror, said the Jacobins, and many have subsequently adopted the same explanation, was forced upon the Revolution by a concatenation of dangerous and potentially fatal circumstances: foreign war, civil war, food riots, inflation, the murderous struggles for political dominance, treacherous generals, unruly Paris mobs. A perfect storm for political catastrophe. Terror was inaugurated and conducted by reluctant terrorists. There were excesses, some of them grim and barbaric, which the more reasonable Jacobins acknowledged. But the Terror saved the Revolution from destruction.[33]

Furet rejects this thesis. For him the causes of the Terror were not external to the Revolution, they were innate, embedded in the ideology of the Revolution (and by implication, all revolutions). The external circumstances that impinged upon the Revolution were, in fact, the result of an opportunistic Revolution seeking and creating these circumstances, sometimes as diversions, sometimes as dangerous political gambles, sometimes as ideological imperatives. The war, he argues, is an excellent example of this dynamic. War was declared with the zeal typical of a crusade. It was expected not only to spread the Revolution abroad by defeating its foreign enemies, but to force a reluctant king to reveal himself as either for or against the Revolution and flush out all those counterrevolutionary conspirators who hitherto had hidden behind the screen of parliamentary politics.

Furet traces the origins of the Terror (and the war) back to the philosophical societies of the French Enlightenment. The argument is subtle and complex and can only be simplified here.[34] The philosophical societies—provincial and metropolitan academies of science or philosophy that met regularly, published their proceedings, sponsored essay contests, and tended to attract the most talented and ambitious commoners as well as liberal aristocrats—were one of the few places where debate on political issues could be practiced under the ancien régime. These societies were the forerunners of the political clubs of the Revolution. They assumed truth was to be discovered through the dialectic of discussion and debate. Once found, deviations would be treated as perverse, for there could be only a single truth. This is a model of an association that demands all its members be in accord and follows Rousseau's ideas about democracy, which were most perfectly expressed by what he called the General Will. Those who did not conform to the General Will, he insists in *The Social Contract*, would be "forced to be free." I don't want to argue this here, but rather to track these ideas into the French Revolution.[35]

The philosophical debates of the ancien régime burst their narrow confines and became public and political with the Revolution. Their monistic assumptions would undergo a transformation when they left the closed world of ideas and entered an especially brutal political arena. The intolerance of diverse views, the Rousseauian model for a democratic society that insisted upon unanimity and was intolerant of dissension, meant that some were excluded from the Revolution. During the Terror this meant that those groups—the Revolution detested the word *faction*, preferring *queue*—where not just ostracized, they were destroyed by the victors. Furet found this exclusiveness first articulated in 1788, in the great political pamphlets of Abbé Siéyès, especially *What Is the Third Estate?* Siéyès not only set forth the ideology of the Revolution as the will of the people, but he simultaneously (and logically) excluded the privileged orders, the clergy and the nobility, from the body politic. Liberty and the nation could not be created until the privileged orders were eliminated. Inherent in the Revolution was a Manichaean mentality that divided the world into *them* and *us*, and which demanded the expulsion of *them* as a precondition to liberation. Siéyès does not propose killing the privileged, but he does insist that the nation has no need of them. They are parasites.

For Furet the French Revolution was ideologically suspicious. It is one of the reasons Robespierre and Marat, themselves deeply suspicious, are so successful. This cast of mind readily finds an external world fraught with danger, threat, and conspiracy and is driven to destroy *them*. In the early years of the Revolution, before the extreme crisis of the summer of 1793, which the Revolution confronted with an emergency government and Terror, exclusion from this or that club, ostracism from this or that faction was sufficient. After 1793 exclusion became the prelude to death.

The counterrevolution is born with the Revolution and is fundamental to the dynamic of the Revolution. This is a commonplace. Furet's originality is to propose that the Manichaean ideology of the French Revolution was not created by circumstances but was itself born with the Revolution. Revolutionary politics allowed of no middle way, no gradualism, no compromises. In the assemblies of the Revolution those who sat in the Center, neither on the Right nor the Left, were contemptuously referred to as the *Marais* (swamp), or more scornfully the *crapauds* (toads) of the Marais. Moderates had no secure place in the Revolution. As the Revolution evolved it became increasingly dangerous for the uncommitted, and those who had once suffered only exclusion were now forced to pay a much higher price for their opinions.

It is always potentially treacherous to generalize from one historical moment to another. Furet would probably argue (although he has not directly done so in print) that all revolutions share a Manichaean view of the universe—whether it be the bourgeoisie versus the proletariat or the bourgeoisie versus the aristocracy or the landowners versus the peasantry—and their ideological underpinnings thus provide the philosophical, moral, historical, or religious justification for exclusion and ultimately forcible exclusion, that is, terror. What he does specifically say in his magisterial history of the Revolution (*La Révolution française*) is that the "secret" of the French Revolution was hatred of the nobility, which is not precisely class war in the Marxist sense, but rather the profound clash of two societies, two cultures, two social structures. Determining whether or not Furet is correct would require a careful examination of the evidence of the modern revolutions (Russia, China, Cuba, et al.), which is beyond my competence. What is worth pointing out here is that historians as well as psychologists are looking for some fundamental explanatory thesis to account for the wild variety of historical experience, to explain the violence of revolutions and the seeming need for terror as an instrument of revolution.

There is tension between psychohistory and the more conventional narrative variety that I practice. It is not an ideological question but a technical one: the nature of the evidence. Once history shifted from being an essentially contemporary activity, writing the history of one's own time—Herodotus and Thucydides are the fathers of this genre, with many, many distinguished practitioners over the centuries—to writing the history of the past from documents (overwhelmingly literary documents), generally accepted criteria for evidence and the constraints imposed by the surviving evidence have pertained. There also developed a prejudice, beginning with Leopold von Ranke (1795–1886), for archival sources, documents whose original purpose was not historical writing or interpretation but doing the mundane (or not so mundane) business of government and society. The bias remains: archival materials are closer to what they treat, are not mediated by being filtered through other minds in other times, and have no philosophical, ideological, nationalistic, or religious purpose directly in mind. They are not intended for the general public.

The tension arises over the question of motive. Fundamental to any historical writing is why this or that was done in the way it was done. History is about human actions, albeit in a world where the great forces that move men and events are not always apparent and operate over long stretches of time and space. Nevertheless what men think they are doing and are able to do is the concern of the historian. To get at motive we make psychological assumptions about human behavior. History cannot be written without these assumptions. They may be derived from personal experience, from the evidence at hand, or from the disciplines of psychology and social psychology. Our assumptions organize the evidence into meaningful patterns. We necessarily impose order on what the past has left us.

The past, however, is notoriously inconsiderate about the needs of historians. The surviving record, in its many forms—verbal, visual, artifacts, natural phenomena—is messy, an accumulation rather than a collection. In matters touching on human motive and behavior the evidentiary record is often maddeningly thin, incomplete, tainted, fragmentary, even irrelevant. Public documents as opposed to archival materials don't often concern themselves with motive. Relatively few men and women have left verbal or visual records, and of these few indeed are psychologically revealing. Even those who leave personal records (diaries, letters, autobiographies) often hide their true motives by artifice or ignorance, and we have no way to corroborate their stories. These are difficult and sometimes treacherous materials to handle. More troubling is the fact that the vast majority of mankind is historically mute; they leave nothing behind but a fingerprint here and there in the official records of the state. We have to get at the masses indirectly, mostly through the eyes and ears and biases of others: their governors, their masters, their enemies.

I think there is a fundamentalist mindset, and in the politics of the French Revolution it is an ideologically driven mindset, although that mindset is secular rather than religious. But we simply do not know the motives of Robespierre and his opponents in the war debates, although we do know what they said. I think there was paranoia in the thinking of the revolutionaries, both individually and collectively, but I use the term in a popular sense, with the imprecision of a layman. Paranoia in the French Revolution was an extreme form of fear during a time of exceptional crisis and genuine danger. This is perhaps not the most satisfactory conclusion to a deeply important problem, but it is as close, I think, as the documents let us come.

15

Hindu Victimhood and India's Muslim Minority

John R. McLane

In this chapter I attempt to answer these questions: Why have many Indians become much more receptive to the Hindutva (Hinduness) movement's anti-Muslim teachings in recent decades? What is the connection between the spread of anti-Muslim sentiment, the rise in Hindu-Muslim violence, and the emergence of the Bharatiya Janata Party (BJP) as one of the two largest political parties in India? Why have so many people responded to the alternating messages of Hindu victimhood and impotence, on the one hand, and Hindu grandeur and virility, on the other?[1] Why do Hindu extremists act as if the Indian nation is dirty and incomplete as long as Muslims are not removed? Are acts of revenge against innocent Muslims giving rise to violent Islamist movements inside India? In short, what has the Hindutva movement gained by scapegoating Muslims as a grave danger to India?

India's vibrant form of militant nationalism is more accurately referred to as Hindu nationalism, extremism, or militancy than as Hindu fundamentalism. Although the Hindutva movement does see the Vedic age and its religion as the golden age of Indian harmony and spirituality and incorporates religious practices from many Indian sects, it rarely focuses on a return to religious scripture or fundamentals. Instead it teaches that without self-strengthening and unification of Hindus, Hindu civilization is threatened by non-Hindu forces, including the anglicized ways of some leaders of the Congress Party, the party of the Nehru family. Hindu nationalism emerges and gains strength from the cultivation of a sense of collective anxiety about Hindu powerlessness, the presence of non-Hindu others, and the penetration of alien customs and thought. Colonialism's displacement of Indians from power induced anxiety and critical self-reflection, which grew more intense as independence approached. And since the 1947 Partition of colonial India into the separate states of India and Pakistan, apprehension about Islamic Pakistan and the secession movement among Muslims in Indian-held Kashmir has allowed Hindu nationalists in India to focus that anxiety more exclusively on Muslims inside India. In the process they have popularized the myth that Indian history over the past thousand years or so is the history of war between Hindus and Muslims.[2] For the minority of Hindus who identify with Hindu nationalism, Muslims have come to represent the source of national humiliation, and their marginalization will restore Hindu pride and make the nation whole.

The first part of this chapter concerns the half-century or so leading up to World War I, when Indian intellectuals asked the question, What gave Muslims and then Christians the political and social strength to invade India and conquer Hindus? They often concluded that caste and sectarian divisions impeded Hindu social cohesion and that a preference for tolerance and nonviolence left Hindus poorly prepared to resist invaders. They also concluded that Hindu weaknesses made Hindus vulnerable to victimization by resident foreigners. Hindu reformers searched for ways to strengthen Hindu society and restore India to the golden age that they imagined had existed before the Muslim and Western invasions. Often this strengthening led Hindus to emulate Muslim and Christian practices.[3] Reformers advocated egalitarian behavior and congregational worship, martial arts, and the honoring of Hindu heroes who had resisted invaders. They worked to expand the social boundaries of Hindu society by experimenting with famine relief for the poor and reconverting low-caste converts from Islam and Christianity. They labored to compensate for what Hinduism seemed to lack and Islam and Christianity had: social solidarity, monotheism, a founder prophet, a single revered text, a sense of being a chosen or at least a superior people, and a countrywide ecclesiastical organization.

The second section examines the period from World War I to the 1980s, the period before militant Hinduism transformed itself into a mass movement. In 1925 Hindu nationalists founded the Rashtriya Swayamsevak Sangh (the National Volunteer Society), known familiarly as the RSS, to execute that agenda. The RSS, ostensibly apolitical, sought to create a monolithic, patriotic Hindu community inspired by the warrior god Ram (or Rama) and the Hindu general Shivaji, who rebelled against Mughal rule in the seventeenth century. The exile of Ram and Sita in the epic *Ramayana* evoked the sense of loss felt by Hindu nationalists in an India dominated by foreigners and anglicized Indians who had assimilated non-Hindu values, while recalling Ram's defeat of the demon Ravanna and Shivaji's victories stoked hopes for a return to Hindu supremacy and national harmony. As Hindu militants worked to arouse animosity toward Muslims they preached, with no apparent sense of irony, the superiority of Hindu civilization because it embodies the values of tolerance and multicultural inclusiveness.[4]

Since the 1920s the Hindutva movement, under RSS guidance, has been recruiting Hindus into a broad array of cultural and political organizations to strengthen and protect Hindu society and instill patriotic pride in India's Hindu culture. The thrust of the Hindutva movement's message is that India is a Hindu country. Its majoritarian attitude toward non-Hindus is perhaps best captured in V. D. Savarkar's well-known formulation: a Hindu (i.e., an Indian) is someone for whom India is his *pitribhumi* (fatherland) and his *punyabhumi* (holy land). This formulation defined Hindus, Sikhs, and Buddhists as Indians but relegated Muslims and Christians to the status of second-class citizens or foreigners. It also implied that secular nationalists, such as the Nehru family, whose tastes were said to be shaped by foreign influences, were not truly national.[5]

The final section examines the campaign to build a Hindu temple on Ram's birthplace and the spread of Hindu militancy and violence to new groups of the population. I conclude with a brief summary of Muslim responses to Hindu militancy, responses that suggest a violent future.

Until the late 1970s the Hindu nationalist political parties were no match for the Congress movement, which maintained its electoral dominance under the leadership of members of the Nehru family. Founded in 1885 to unite all Indians behind demands for increased self-rule, the Indian National Congress Party claimed to be secular, it took pride in India's composite culture, and it actively recruited Muslim and lower-caste supporters. While the British ruled India, vastly more Indians supported the Congress in its anticolonialism. By the 1980s, though, Hindu nationalists were challenging the Congress for electoral supremacy, charging the party with favoritism toward Muslims as well as failures in economic development. The BJP, the political party of Hindu nationalism after 1980, grew rapidly in the 1980s and 1990s, establishing a broad base outside its high-caste leadership. Beginning in the 1990s it competed with the Congress Party to lead coalition governments at the national level. The BJP also defeated the Congress Party and led governments in various states in north and central India. Thus the 1980s and 1990s saw a major transformation of Indian cultural and electoral politics as the Hindutva movement capitalized on the Congress Party's unpopularity and a fear of Muslims in its campaign to build a temple to Lord Ram on the site occupied by the sixteenth-century Mughal mosque, the Babri *masjid* at Ayodhya, considered to be Ram's birthplace. By destroying that mosque in 1992 Hindutva followers seemed to seek revenge and erase the humiliation for the alleged Muslim destruction of a Hindu temple centuries earlier. In the process they spread the message that Islam was a violent and alien civilization and that a revived Hindu nation was such a mighty force that the state's police and armed forces were helpless to protect the mosque.

MAKING THE MUSLIM THE "OTHER"

Hindu-Muslim violence has risen with the growth of the Hindutva campaign to make Hindu civilization dominant once again. Fear and resentment of Muslims have been central to the extraordinary successes of Hindutva cultural and political movements in post-Independence India. Literate Hindus knew from the start of British rule, and even earlier, that Muslims from Central Asia had conquered and then governed India for over five centuries. Almost two centuries of British colonial rule led many Hindus and Muslims to strengthen and consolidate separate identities. British textbooks and Hindu and Muslim chauvinists made more Indians than ever aware of past Muslim domination, including examples of destruction of Hindu temples and forced conversions to Islam. After the Congress Party was founded in 1885 to unify nationalist Indians, most of its leaders stressed the history of Hindu-Muslim accommodation and coexistence, not communal discord. Jawaharlal Nehru anticipated that the partition of colonial India into the new states of India and Pakistan in 1947 would give Muslim separatists their own arena for cultural and political self-expression and would thus diminish Hindu-Muslim friction. As it turned out, the Partition brought trauma beyond imagination. It forced uprootings and migrations for millions, ethnic cleansing, rape, and kidnapping.[6] Partition was also followed by an inconclusive war over possession of Kashmir in 1947–48. The new state of Pakistan now held most of South Asia's Muslims, while India's Muslim population had shrunk to 12 to 13 percent of the population (but still the third or fourth largest in the world), leaving India with a Hindu population of over 80 percent.

In the first century of sporadic British colonial expansion over India's independent territories (1757–1857) there is slight evidence that most Hindus and Muslims saw each other as homogeneous groups. Hindu society was relatively inchoate; boundaries and identities were loose; the very category "Hindu" was far from universal. Hindus had served in high positions in the civilian and military branches of the Mughal government (1526–ca. 1707) and in the successor states governed by Muslims in the eighteenth century. Although intermarriage was not common, an important minority among elites showed mutual curiosity about each other's music, literature, and religion. Brahmins seeking employment under Muslim rulers learned Persian and studied Islamic law. In peasant communities cultural syncretism was widespread. Historians assume that most nonelite Indian Muslims were descended from converts to Islam rather than foreign immigrants from Central Asia, and they further see the integration of minorities into land-based and religiously mixed social hierarchies as having been eased by the indigenous origin of so many Muslims. Before the Indian Mutiny of

1857, a major revolt that affected about a third of India, there were not many recorded instances of broad-based Hindu-Muslim violence. During the Mutiny Hindu and Muslim rebels allied and fought against the British-Indian colonial army. In short, violent communalism is largely a recent phenomenon, a product of modernization and colonialism.

From the middle decades of the nineteenth century on, more Europeans, Hindus, and Muslims were likely to attribute pejorative characteristics to caste, regional, and religious groups (e.g., wily Brahmins, stingy Banias, fanatical Pathans, effeminate Bengalis). Many factors contributed to this trend, including the "Orientalist" conventions of European scholarship, which stereotype population groups in order to demonstrate Hindu and Muslim difference and backwardness. Administrative practices of enumerating the population in the decennial census strengthened consciousness of religious and caste identities, as did selecting representatives from religious communities to advise colonial officials and serve in the colonial administrative and military services. As the government introduced embryonic, local forms of representative institutions, political leaders grew increasingly sensitive to demographic statistics about religious categories. Before the census began in the 1870s most Bengali and Punjabi Hindus living in urban communities probably imagined that Hindus outnumbered Muslims, given Hindu wealth and literacy in many towns. The census findings taught Hindus in both the Punjab and Bengal that they were a minority, a concept that mattered more and more as the ideal of representative and majority rule spread, along with consciousness of the violence of early Muslim invasions.[7] A major appeal of the Hindutva movement has been the claim that Hindus are in some sense like a minority, that they are victims: victims of the pre-Partition Muslim majorities in Bengal and the Punjab, victims of the pseudo-secular favoritism toward Muslims attributed to Congress governments, and victims of Pakistan, which three times invaded India and which has supported cross-border terrorism in Kashmir and elsewhere.

THE ORIGINS OF A SENSE OF HINDUS AS VICTIMS

The practice of portraying Hindus as victims of Muslim violence and oppression thus reaches far back into the colonial period. The preoccupations of early Hindu reformers differed from region to region, depending on factors such as demography and the timing and experience of colonial conquest and domination. But a narrative of Muslim brutality and tyranny was shared among chauvinist writers from Bengal in the east, up the Ganges, through the United Provinces (now Uttar Pradesh) to the Punjab, and southward through Gujarat and Maharashtra.

Bengal was the first area the British conquered. In a region long under British administrative and commercial domination, Bengali Hindu intellectuals were among the first and most insistent in complaining about humiliations under both Muslim and British governments. Even though Hindu-Muslim friction in nineteenth-century Bengal was not acute, Hindu intellectuals often wrote about past Muslim tyranny with what Nirad C. Chaudhuri called "a retrospective hostility . . . for their one-time domination of us."[8] Nowhere was the Hindu discourse about effeminacy and cowardice more widespread than in Bengal, whose military and cultural conquest was said to have been lightly resisted. A common self-deprecating Bengali tradition said that thirteen Muslim horsemen from northern India conquered Bengal.[9] British writers such as Thomas Babington Macauley stigmatized Bengalis as effeminate and cowardly, and Bengali vernacular writers picked up the refrain. The greatest Bengali novelist of the nineteenth century, Bankimchandra Chatterji (1838–94), was unsparing in describing the Bengali *babu*, a generic term for a clerk working for the British but extended to high-caste, English-speaking Bengalis in general. Bankimchandra described the ironic self-contempt of the colonized Bengali subject: "He whose strength is one-time in his hands, ten-times in his mouth, a hundred times behind the back and absent at the time of action is a *babu*. . . . One who drinks water at home, alcohol at his friend's, receives abuse from the prostitute and kicks from his boss is a *babu*."[10] Swami Vivekananda was presumably thinking of his fellow Bengalis when he said they are "a race of women" and when he wrote, "O thou Mother of Strength, take away my weakness, take away my unmanliness and MAKE ME A MAN!"[11]

Bankimchandra's famous novel, *Ananda Math* (Monastery of Bliss), told the story of a band of Hindu ascetics who rebelled again their Muslim rulers. Their patriotic song, "Bande Mataram" (Hail to the Mother or Mother-goddess), has been adopted as one of India's two national anthems. When high-caste Hindus formed secret societies to commit acts of violence against the British beginning in 1907–8, some of them modeled themselves on the heroes of *Ananda Math*, as if they were trying to overcome the stigmas that Bengali Hindus were compliant, weak, and cowardly. Bankimchandra was just one example among many Bengal novelists and dramatists who wrote about Bengali Hindus who resisted tyrannical Muslim rulers. The Hinduization of Bengali politics in the early twentieth century set back prospects that Bengali Muslims might join Bengali Hindus in resisting British rule. The British contributed to the Hindu-Muslim divide by splitting Bengal into two provinces in 1905, one with a Hindu majority and the other with a Muslim majority. An explicit motive was to set Muslims against Hindus and weaken the anticolonial movement.[12] The 1905 partition of Bengal may have deepened a sense of collective Hindu ineffectiveness.

Nationalist politics reached the United Provinces (the UP) and the central Gangetic plain later than it did Bengal. But polemics about Muslims as an aggressive people were not far behind. The UP had a larger class of educated Muslims, many from families who had served the imperial Mughals. Hindu-Muslim rivalry for government employment and over the use of Devanagri and Urdu or Arabic scripts for administrative purposes stimulated communal identity formation. Well-known Hindi writers, including Bharatendu Harishchandra (1850–85), wrote about Muslim rule as the story of "rape and abduction of Hindu women, the slaughter of sacred cows, and the defilement of temples."[13] Such stereotyping of Muslims made it more difficult for Hindus trying to make common cause with Muslims against British colonialism.

After the Indian National Congress Party was founded in 1885 with the goal of obtaining representative institutions for India, it tried to recruit Hindu and Muslim followers in the United Provinces. In 1887 Sayyid Ahmad Khan, the head of the Mohammedan Anglo Oriental College at Aligarh, ridiculed the Congress Party and its demands in words that reflected familiar aristocratic, regional, and communal prejudices of privileged Muslim and Hindu landowners of north India. He stated his view that the Congress was the organ of cowardly Bengali Hindus who would flee at the mere sight of a table knife and whose interest in democracy was laughably out of touch with Indian traditions and realities of his own upper India. He went further and suggested that contrary to the Congress platform, India was not one nation but two.[14] Sayyid Ahmad's ridicule echoed a British assumption that India contained "masculine" races, such as the British and immigrant Muslims, and "feminine" races such as Bengalis.[15] His ridicule of democratic aspirations reflected the budding anxieties of minorities, such as landed elites, Muslims in a Hindu-majority province, and Hindus in a Muslim-majority province. Educated and landowning Muslims from upper India stayed away from the early Congress Party and then in 1906 came together to found the All-India Muslim League. In 1906 a Muslim League delegation asked the British government to pay particular attention to Muslim interests because Muslims were the former imperial rulers and were numerically a minority in India. Sayyid Ahmad Khan's two-nation theory seemed to be spreading.

No other part of late nineteenth-century India matched the Punjab in anxiety about the future and in the rawness of communal rhetoric. No other province equaled the Punjab in communal migrations and violence in the months before and after the 1947 Partition. Punjabi Hindus who joined the Arya Samaj, a Hindu revivalist group founded by Swami Dayananda in 1876, were especially concerned about their future in a Muslim-majority area. Concerns about demographic balance among Hindus, Muslims,

Christians, and Sikhs underlay a broad array of Hindu concerns about diet, physical strength, fertility, sexuality, education, and conversion. Dayananda attacked Islam as unmodern and intolerant and claimed that Muslims made a practice of killing innocent people for no other reason than their failure to embrace Islam.[16] He and his followers were especially afraid the Christian missionaries were draining away lower castes from Hinduism. The programs sponsored by the Arya Samaj may be viewed as a response to perceived threats from Muslims and Christians; each program could be viewed as implying distrust and fear of Christians and Muslims. Programs included famine relief for the poor (famines were often the occasion for Christian religious conversion), the *shuddhi* (purification and reconversion) movement, schools to prepare Hindus to love their Hindu culture and compete in the new competitive world of literacy and science, and the cow protection movement to protect both a source of Hindu nutrition and a sacred symbol of Hindu culture. The Samaj's cow protection movement in the Punjab, UP, and Bihar brought Hindus trying to rescue cattle into violent conflict with Muslim cattle traders and butchers in 1893. Petitions to the British Parliament requesting a legislative ban on cattle slaughter correctly anticipated actions of Hindu legislative majorities in an independent India.[17]

Bombay Province, containing present-day Maharashtra and Gujarat, is the last of these regional examples of Hindu hostility to Muslims. Maharashtra has been the nursery for Hindutva leaders. Although Muslims are a small minority in Maharashtra, historical memories of Maharashtrian rebellion and expansion against the Mughals in the seventeenth and eighteenth centuries remained strong. Both Bal Gangadhar Tilak and Vishnu Damodar Savarkar, Brahmins from Poona, were inspired by Maharashtrian heroism and stand out as architects of the Hindutva movement. Tilak, who was active in the Indian National Congress, pioneered mass mobilization and vernacular journalism in the 1880s and 1890s. He started a public festival in which devotees carried an image of the elephant-headed god Ganesh, son of Lord Shiva, through the streets. He did so at a time when at least a few other Congress leaders with Western education were embarrassed by "idol worship" and were distancing themselves from the popular forms of "temple Hinduism." By employing a popular deity to stand for the nation, as Bengalis had done with the mother goddess, Tilak was mobilizing political support for the anticolonial movement in a manner that made it difficult for colonial authority. After the experience of the Mutiny of 1857 government officials were reluctant to appear to interfere with religion.[18]

More controversially Tilak also started a festival celebrating the Maharashtrian general, Shivaji, who rebelled against the Mughals. Tilak helped make Shivaji into a patriotic hero who rose up against the alien, Muslim oppressor and who acted to protect what was seen as the Hindu way of life.

Tilak was sentenced to jail in 1899 on British sedition charges growing out of his justification for Shivaji's assassination of a Mughal general, Afzhal Khan, indicating that Hindu violence against foreign tyrants was both traditional and morally legitimate.[19] High-caste Hindus in Maharashtra were more intensely divided than in other provinces about questions of social reform concerning the age of marriage, the right of widows to remarry, and the education of females.

Tilak also led the section of Brahmins who were determined to protect Hindu custom from Western and Indian reformers. The resistance to a British-Indian legislative measure that raised the age of consent for sexual intercourse to twelve was especially bitter. Nationalists of many kinds suspected that the colonial investigation into the sexual practices in early marriages was motivated by a desire to humiliate Indian males. The powerful opposition to the Age of Consent Bill in Maharashtra and Bengal was another sign that some Hindu males were determined to reassert their role as the traditional guardians and protectors of Indian womanhood.[20] The growing popularity of traditional games such as wrestling and *lathi* (stick) play and gymnasiums (*akharas*) also indicated a move toward "muscular Hinduism," toward readiness to protect Hindu women should it become necessary.

THE RSS AND THE GROWTH OF HINDU-MUSLIM VIOLENCE

While Tilak merged politics and religion in innovative ways, justified patriotic violent resistance, and popularized a Hindu hero who fought for independence from Muslim rulers, Vinayak Damodar Savarkar provided a more comprehensive rationale for a more belligerent and populist nationalism. In a prison colony in the Andaman Islands, serving a life sentence beginning in 1910 for participating in a terrorist conspiracy, he found it humiliating that his fellow Hindu prisoners showed so little aggressiveness and social solidarity in responding to Muslim bullying and efforts to convert Untouchables to Islam. He taught his fellow prisoners to fight back against Muslim bullies and to welcome low-caste people back into the community of Hindus, even if they had become more deeply impure through their contact with Muslims. He was especially critical of a preoccupation among Indian Muslims with contemporary events in the Middle East, with the Muslim angst over European efforts to dismantle the Ottoman Empire that undermined the Turkish khalif in his guardianship of the sacred Islamic sites at Mecca, Medina, and Jerusalem. Savarkar questioned the patriotism of Muslims who looked outside India for their spiritual history and guidance.[21]

European encroachments on the Ottoman territories of the khalif stirred Muslim anger in many parts of India. The khilafat movement was one of the stimuli of an agrarian rebellion in 1921 in what is now the state of Kerala. Moplah (Mapilla) Muslims, descendants of early Arab settlers, attacked their Hindu landlords and also Europeans in what they called a jihad. It took the colonial army months to restore order. This communal violence was almost unprecedented, but it reinforced the idea that Hindus should be better prepared to defend themselves from Muslim attack. The 1920s saw an increase in communal riots in other parts of India. Gandhi and the Congress Party tried to stem this worrisome trend by electing Muslims as president of the party five times in ten years. They also supported Muslim demands backing the khalif until Ataturk's revolution abolished the office.[22]

In 1923 Savarkar published *Hindutva: Who Is a Hindu?* and elaborated the history of and need for Hindu self-defense. This book shaped the Hindutva movement more than any other single book. It reviewed the historical solidarity of Hindus (and Buddhists and Sikhs) and celebrated their martial exploits. Then in 1925, with the lessons of the 1921 Moplah rebellion in mind, Savarkar's admirers from Maharashtra organized the Rashtriya Swayamsevak Sangh. Ever since, the RSS has been the backbone of the Hindutva movement and the source of most Hindutva leaders, including the leaders of the BJP, the current Hindutva political party.

The RSS is a bottom-up effort to strengthen Hindu society by instilling pride in Hindu culture and building character among Hindu youth. A major activity is training young Hindus to be prepared to fight Muslims when they attack. The RSS was directly inspired by the perception that in the rising number of Hindu-Muslim riots of the 1920s, Hindus were not as organized or effective as the Muslim rioters. The RSS began with a program of paramilitary and body-strengthening exercises for Hindu youth, organized through branches called *shakas*. Savarkar and the RSS *shakas* offered a clear alternative to Gandhi's tactics of allying with Muslims and using nonviolent (*ahimsa*) resistance against the British, both recently adopted by the Indian National Congress. The RSS intended to Hindu-ize or Saffron-ize India. They seemed to want to convince Hindus that violence was just as Hindu as Gandhi's *ahimsa*. And they clearly viewed Muslims as a greater threat to Hindu security, at least in the long run, than the colonial British. For example, the RSS conducts six annual festivals (*utsav*). In most there are references to heroes who are famed for resisting Muslims (Shivaji, Rana Pratap, Guru Govind Singh) and reminders of the need for Hindu self-sacrifice, solidarity, and self-protection.[23]

From 1925 to 1945 the RSS and its openly political Hindutva allies failed seriously to challenge the Congress Party in electoral politics. The RSS described itself as nonpolitical and did not organize for elections. The

Congress, with its emphasis on popular education, moderate agrarian reform, and Hindu-Muslim amity, was a far stronger vehicle for electoral victory and gaining independence than Hindutva parties such as the Hindu Mahasabha. Before 1940 many nationalists tolerated the Gandhian goal of Hindu-Muslim unity because Muslim separatism was not yet explicit. Before 1940 not even the Muslim League had demanded the partition of India and the creation of a separate Islamic country. The Muslim League, with its incipient separatism, was less popular with Muslim voters in the Muslim-majority provinces of Bengal and the Punjab than Muslim or multicommunity regional parties willing to cooperate with the Congress. Before the Muslim League demanded partition in 1940 and began to attract mass Muslim support, the Congress remained a possible party for Hindu nationalist voters to support. Gandhi's emphasis on courage and Indian spirituality resembled Hindutva teachings.

Although the RSS was founded in the context of the communal riots during the khilafat movement, in response to the belief that Muslims threatened Hindus, and although the daily meetings of the *shakas* included paramilitary exercises, vigorous games, and celebration of Hindu warriors who fought Muslim armies, the primary focus of RSS activities was inward-looking and character- and community-building. The RSS sought to weld Hinduism's castes and sects into a homogeneous Hindu nation, not primarily to create hatred and fear of Muslims. The analyses of the RSS by Walter Andersen and Shridhar Damle, Christophe Jaffrelot, Thomas Hansen, and others make it evident that the major thrust of the *shakhas*, at least until the 1980s, was to integrate Hindus into a composite upper-caste, Sanskritic Hindu culture so that Hindus would resist Islamic, Western, Christian, communist, and materialist influences that were represented as antithetical to the superior values of spiritual Hinduism. During the Partition-era riots, *shakas* emerged as active protectors of Hindus. Andersen and Damle provide testimony that at the time of Partition, *shakas* in the Punjab and Delhi region served as militias to defend Hindus.[24]

The popularity of RSS defense efforts is reflected in the estimates that between 1943 and 1948 the number of *swayamsevaks* (volunteer members in the RSS) swelled from 76,000 to 600,000. But the assassination of Gandhi in 1948 was a huge setback for the RSS. Naturam Godse, the Maharashtrian Brahmin killer, had been associated with the RSS, and this brought the weight of government and public opinion down on the organization. The government arrested twenty thousand *swayamsevaks* and banned the organization. But the setback was temporary. The ban was lifted and membership climbed back to 600,000 by 1951, the year of independent India's first parliamentary elections. RSS leaders formed a party, the Bharatiya Jan Sangh (Indian People's Party), to contest the elections.[25]

The founding of the Jan Sangh was part of a new RSS strategy to reach out beyond its base in the urban upper castes. RSS leaders realized that the Congress, the Communists, the Socialists, and others were mobilizing interest groups for the new politics with universal voting rights under free India's first constitution. The RSS responded by creating its own front groups or "wings." Starting in 1948 the RSS established organizations of students, tribes, labor unions, peasants, and, in 1964 for the first time, religious leaders. The multiplication of Hindutva organizations, called the Sangh Parivar (the family of associations), expanded support for the movement. Several of the organizations in the 1980s exceeded the RSS in the intensity of their contempt for Muslims. These included the Vishwa Hindu Parishad (VHP; World Hindu Society, founded in 1964) and its youth affiliate, the Bajrang Dal (the Army of Hanuman's Monkeys; Hanuman was Ram's loyal monkey-helper and general).

THE VHP AND THE NEW MILITANCY IN THE 1980S

The emergence of the VHP in the 1980s as the most aggressive and innovative Hindutva organization marks a new phase in the movement of Hindu militancy. The VHP conducted reconversion and welfare activities among tribal Christians, Muslims, and low castes. It reached out to Hindu diaspora communities around the world. It brought together religious leaders from different Hindu and Sikh sects to stress what they had in common. And it started a spectacular, multiyear mass campaign to build a temple to mark the place where Lord Ram was born. The VHP and allied organizations were creating a parallel universe of organizations whose goal was to make their version of a newly homogenized Hindu culture both ubiquitous and dominant. In the late 1980s, largely because of the VHP, the message of Hindu pride and Muslim threat gained real traction, in large part through the temple campaign.[26] The BJP, the main Hindutva political party since replacing the Jan Sangh in 1980, increased its seats in Parliament from two in 1984 (out of a total of 545) to eighty-six in 1989. In 1991 the BJP won 119 seats, with 23.2 percent of the vote. In the 1990s the BJP became the largest political party in the Indian Parliament. And the Sangh Parivar controlled the largest student and labor unions in India.[27]

As they proliferated, Hindutva groups pulled in opposite directions. The closer BJP leaders came to gaining real elective power, the greater was the pressure for them to moderate their aggressive anti-Muslim stance in order to keep alive the possibility of alliances with other parties that disapproved of Muslim bashing. The BJP benefited in elections at least as much from popular disillusionment with the Congress Party in the 1980s as from anti-Muslim sentiment. Mediocre economic performance and corruption sapped the popularity of the Congress. However, BJP election prospects were threatened by the new assertiveness and political independence of lower- and middle-caste parties in northern India. Especially worrisome were the recommendations of the Congress-appointed Mandal Commission (1980) for a major expansion of "reservations" (reserved places in schools and government service) for the Other Backward Castes (OBCs). Expanded reservations meant fewer opportunities for high-caste families. In 1990 Prime Minister V. P. Singh decided to implement the Mandal recommendations. This seemed to intensify the desire of Hindutva leaders to use the Ram temple campaign to deflect attention away from upper-caste opposition to reservations. Opposition to affirmative action was counterproductive in efforts to attract votes from the lowest castes and the OBCs.

Distrust of Muslims remained a potent source of votes in some regions. Some hard-line Hindus, in the VHP especially, objected to softening the anti-Muslim thrust. Poverty fed the envy of Hindus, who saw Muslim guest workers return from the Gulf states with new wealth and who saw the construction of new mosques. Some Hindus believed Muslims prospered from the favoritism of the pseudo-secularist Congress governments. However, this was largely a myth. The reality was that Muslims, who constituted 13.4 percent of the population, made up only 3.4 percent of college graduates in India and 3.2 percent of officers in the civil services in 2004–5.[28]

In 1989 Hindu militants gained a new argument against Muslims when the Kashmiri Muslim secessionist movement turned violent for the first time after decades of New Delhi's manipulation of Kashmiri politics. Kashmir had been the exception to the general Partition of 1947, when Muslim-majority areas shifted to Pakistan. The status of Kashmir, with its Muslim majority, had not been resolved in 1947 because the British Partition plan allowed Kashmir's Hindu maharaja to accede to India. India and Pakistan went to war over Kashmir in 1947–48 and again in 1965, and the territory has been divided and under dispute ever since. When the secessionists took up arms in 1989 they drove several hundred thousand Hindus out of the main valley of Kashmir. The Hindutva movement has used the Kashmir rebellion to support its message that Muslim separatists forced the Partition of 1947 and continued to threaten India. Partition was the great failure of the Congress-led freedom movement; the Kashmir conflict keeps awareness of that failure alive. Hindus refer to the Partition of their *Bharatmata* (Mother India) with emotionally loaded terms, such as *vivisection, rape,* and *amputation.* Hindutva schools and societies display the map of *Akhand Bharat* (undivided India), promoting a fantasy that somehow the Partition might be reversed. Many Indians attribute violence by Kashmiri Muslims to Pakistani cross-border terrorism rather than to Kashmiri Muslim discontent with Indian rule.

Thus several developments came together in the late 1980s and early 1990s that provided urgency and opportunities for Hindu militants. Kashmiri Muslim separatists took up arms; the Congress Party was losing popularity because of corruption and economic failures and a perception that it pandered to Muslims and slighted Hindu culture; the prime minister in 1990 announced an expansion of reservations for the newly assertive OBCs, which would squeeze opportunities for the upper castes who were the main support for the Sangh Parivar; and the BJP was finally in a position to challenge the Congress electorally after decades of RSS efforts to persuade Hindus to think "We are Hindus and Hindusthan is our country."

THE ANGRY HINDU AND THE TEMPLE CAMPAIGN

In the 1980s the militant VHP and its allied organizations discovered a potent new way to stir up anti-Muslim sentiment as a means to mobilize Hindus. It was a campaign to rebuild Hindu temples that Muslims were alleged to have destroyed centuries earlier. Hindutva supporters had called attention to Muslim iconoclasm long before Independence. Muslim chronicles, made available in published British translations, provided evidence about Muslim destruction of Hindu temples. Temple building had often been simultaneously an act of piety and an act of political self-assertion. The great Shiva temple at Somnath, Gujarat, which had been destroyed by Mahmud of Ghazni in 1024 in a notable event in the history of Muslim global expansion, was rebuilt by Hindu nationalists and government officials in the 1940s and then dedicated by the president of independent India. In that case controversy was not great because the mosque that stood on the site was moved rather than destroyed.

The site of the destroyed temple at Ayodhya, which supposedly had marked the place where Ram was born, was altogether different. The Hindutva movement had transformed Ram into a symbol of Hindu militancy and virility, the Babri Masjid stood on Ram's supposed birth site, and the mosque theoretically was under state and court protection. Shortly after Independence Hindu extremists had installed images of Ram in the Ayodhya mosque in the middle of the night, claiming that Ram had miraculously returned to India now that it was free.[29] *Ram Rajya* (the rule of Ram) had returned. In both Gandhi's and the Hindutva movement's teachings, *Ram Rajya* means the rule of righteousness and harmony. Doordarshan, the government of India's television network, helped popularize the *Ramayana* as a national myth by broadcasting a serialization of the story that was watched by millions over seventy-eight weeks in 1987 and 1988.

In 1983 the militant VHP announced its intention to "liberate" Ramjanmabhumi, the birthplace of the god Ram in Ayodhya. The VHP was said to have a list of three thousand mosques built on the ruins of destroyed Hindu temples. Because Ram's supposed birthplace was occupied by the mosque the Babri *masjid*, built in 1528 by an officer of Babur (occasionally spelled Babar or Barbar), the Mughal conqueror and dynasty founder, this movement ingeniously tapped into the anxiety about Muslims that Hindutva teachings and Pakistan's hostility had been fueling. Until the Hindu extremists destroyed the Babri *masjid* on December 6, 1992, leaders of the Hindutva movement maintained that their goal was to build the Ram *mandir*. They denied that they intended to destroy the mosque, although Hindutva rhetoric often suggested otherwise. Zafah Agha, an Indian Muslim who had regularly watched performances of the Ram *lila* (a performance about Ram's adventures) with family and friends, visited the Babri *masjid* for the first time in 1986 to witness the Hindutva campaign. "Suddenly, the Indian Muslim was being turned into Barbar's *santaan* (descendants)," he said. "It was no longer enough that I was an Indian. I kept hearing speeches reminding Hindus that the Muslims had destroyed Hindu temples. I kept hearing the exhortation: make up your mind—either go to Pakistan or hand over the masjid to the Hindus."[30]

The Ramjanmabhumi movement proved highly useful for the Hindu nationalists in the short run. Thousands participating in each stage of the campaign seemed to feel an energizing pride in being Hindu and in avenging centuries of foreign tyranny. Just as useful, the movement provoked the very Muslim violence about which Hindu nationalists had been warning. The temple movement began in 1984, when the VHP organized its first procession to Ayodhya, demanding the liberation of Ram's birthplace.[31] In 1986 Congress Prime Minister Rajiv Gandhi, worried about losing the Hindu vote, allowed a local court to remove the lock from the *masjid*, thus opening it to Hindu prayers to Ram. This was only one of the Congress's acts appeasing Hindu extremists. In the summer and fall of 1989 the VHP organized a provocative procession across India, carrying specially consecrated bricks to Ayodhya for construction of the new Ram *mandir*. The Congress government, fearing that the young men of the Bajrang Dal might storm the mosque, agreed to let the organizers carry out a Hindu ritual on disputed land near the mosque, in a *shilanyas*, or foundation-laying ceremony. Muslims protested in a numerous towns, and this led to riots between Hindus and Muslims.[32] In September 1990 L. K. Advani, the BJP leader, began his provocative thousand-kilometer procession (*Rathyatra*) to Ayodhya, riding in a motorized chariot (*rath*) in Ram's iconic pose, with his arm drawn back ready to fire an arrow. Images of Ram now showed him less often as the benevolent, tranquil *raja* and more often as the "*ugra*, angry, exercised" warrior.[33]

When the 1990 procession reached Ayodhya Hindu *karsevas* (volunteers) tried to reach the mosque again, and more than twenty died when government soldiers fired. The movement now had its martyrs, whose photos began to appear on the walls of some of the thousands of Hindutva schools. Hindu activists cremated the bodies and then carried the ashes back to the towns and villages of India.[34] The movement now referred to the OBC chief minister of the UP who ordered the police firing as Mullah Muyalam Singh Yadav, equating mullahs (Muslim religious leaders) with tyranny.[35]

The leaders of the Ram *mandir* movement, who included the top leaders of the BJP, were riding a movement they could barely control. They had tapped into social groups containing people ready to risk arrest, who were willing to fight the police under the pretext that they were executing a just vengeance and protecting their society and who were hoping to be considered heroes by their communities. Religious mendicants (*sadhus* and *sadhvis*), professional wrestlers, lower-middle-class urban shopkeepers, and artisans joined the processions.

Women, some of them lower caste, played a striking and unfamiliar role in the several-year buildup to the final, successful 1992 assault on the Babri *masjid*. The patriarchal leaders of the RSS, like the leaders of the Congress Party, had created an ancillary movement for women before Independence that seemed no threat to male dominance. The Rashtrasevika Samiti's training of females in self-defense would not only enable them to protect themselves in the workplace as more women worked outside the home, but the training might also suggest that Hindu women were endangered by would-be Muslim rapists. The paramilitary training camps for females produced a number of leaders for the Ram *mandir* campaign.

A fiery, celibate Punjabi leader, Sadhvi Rithambara, was particularly popular in both her numerous appearances and in the thousands of audiocassettes that sold all over India. Sudhir Kakar has analyzed her standard speech, showing that she activated a sense of Hindu communal loss and humiliation at the hands of Muslim, British, and Congress secularist rulers. She helped to create a "persecutory fantasy" in which lustful Muslims ("the sons of Babur") tyrannized Hindus, destroyed their temples, forced India's dismemberment in 1947, and now enjoyed the special and privileged treatment by Congress governments while they bred "like mosquitoes and flies," thus threatening to dominate Hindus despite their economic inferiority and despite being outnumbered by Hindus in India by an 8 to 1 margin.[36] Kakar wishes to persuade his readers that far more is at work than the instrumental task of winning elections or diverting attention from the new reservations for OBCs.[37] He believes that "nonrational processes" rooted in attachments to traditional culture and the threats of dislocation caused by common experiences of modernization, migration, and globalization subject people to the anxieties on which the Hindutva movement feeds. He explains the persecutory fantasy in these words:

> As in individuals, where persecution anxiety often manifests itself in threats to the integrity of the body, especially during psychotic episodes, Rithambara's speech becomes rich in the imagery of a mutilated body. Eloquently, she conjures up an India—the motherland—with its arms cut off, Hindu chests cut open like those of frogs, rabbits, and cats, the thighs of young Hindu women burnt with red-hot iron rods; in short, the body amputated, slashed, raped.[38]

Rithambara implied that Hindus had been like Sita, who in the *Ramayana* was abducted by a Muslim-like Ravanna, and now Hindus needed to become like Ram and rescue Sita, the mother or the motherland. The bad Muslim, "the son of Babar," was like lemon in a glass of milk, causing it to curdle: "The world knows the fate of the lemon. It is cut, squeezed dry and then thrown on the garbage heap."[39] In egging on Hindu men to confront Muslims and the government security personnel guarding the mosque, Rithambara was inverting the usual role of Hindu women, as Tanika Sarkar has pointed out. In suggesting that Hindu men were cowards and not really men unless they fought, a woman was asking males to come to the rescue of Ram, instead of Ram rescuing Sita.[40] Rithambara was telling men how they could recuperate their helpless, depleted selves and restore Hinduism to its former greatness. She dehumanized the Muslim enemy by suggesting that Muslims were the opposite of Hindus in every way: Hindus were inclusive while Muslims were exclusive; Hindus worshipped the cow while Muslims went to heaven by killing it; Hindus ate with their right hand while Muslims ate with their (polluted) left; and because Hindus ate with their mouth Muslims should "do the opposite," that is, they should eat with their anuses.[41]

In the destroyed Hindu temple Hindu nationalists had found a symbol of "Islamic intolerance and violence" that could stand in for what Hindu extremists were often not allowed by Indian law to say in public: that Islamic civilization was tyrannical, cruel, and destructive. Indian law and practice came down hard on persons convicted of stirring up enmity between religious groups. A campaign to rebuild a sacred temple was not so obviously anti-Muslim. The destroyed Hindu temple became Hindu nationalism's "chosen trauma," as Sudhir Kakar has argued, using Vamik Volkan's term. When a group felt threatened it could summon up the memory of a collective humiliation, a "chosen trauma," in order to reactivate group solidarity and the identity of victimhood.[42]

The instrumental consequences of the Ram *mandir* campaign were mixed. Although the mosque was demolished, Indian Muslims still lived under Islamic family law, with polygamy permitted, long after the Congress government had passed the Hindu Code Bills that outlawed polygamy for Hindus and enhanced inheritance rights for Hindu females. Non-Kashmiris were still not allowed to purchase land in Kashmir, to the chagrin of militant Hindus. The Ram temple had not been built and perhaps will not be unless Hindu extremists agree to a different site or Muslims relinquish their legal title to the land on which the mosque stood. The BJP pragmatically dropped the *mandir* from its platform after the destruction of the mosque, to the disgust of many Hindu extremists. The BJP understood the proposal to build the Ram *mandir* damaged their electoral and coalition prospects in most parts of India because it had resulted in communal violence and widespread destruction and criticism. But transformation of Hindu culture rather than winning political control of the state had been the primary goal of the Hindutva movement. It sought to unify Hindus through the threat of Muslim and other "foreigners" and convince Hindus of the superiority of Hindu culture.

If a goal of the Ram *mandir* campaign was to provoke Muslim violence in order to demonstrate that Muslims endangered Hindus and give the police and Hindu vigilantes the chance to retaliate disproportionately, the campaign fulfilled that goal. Some three thousand people died when Muslims rioted across India following the abortive attempt to tear down the Ayodhya mosque in 1990. Most were Muslims.[43] After the mosque was demolished on December 6, 1992, thousands more died when Muslims protested. In both Bombay and Ahmedabad the police watched as Hindu rioters looted and burned Muslim shops and homes and the police shot and killed Muslims. In Bombay (called Mumbai since 1995) alone 620 people, mostly Muslims, were killed. Muslims retaliated in 1993 by setting off bombs in the Bombay stock exchange and other buildings.[44]

In 2002 ethnic violence in Gujarat, which for decades has had the highest level of ethnic violence, reached Partition-level proportions. It began when people, assumed by most commentators to be Muslims, torched a rail carriage carrying Hindu activists from Ayodhya back to Gujarat, killing fifty-eight people. In retaliation Hindu mobs attacked innocent Muslims over a wide area of Gujarat, killing more than a thousand, sometimes in a manner that suggested they were motivated by fantasies of Muslims as fast-breeding and lustful rapists. Rioters displaced as many as 150,000 Muslims, and the BJP-led state government abetted the ethnic cleansing by remaining passive for days. Rioters destroyed "roughly twenty mosques" in Ahmedabad, they raped "scores of Muslim girls and women," and they cut the fetuses out of some pregnant women before murdering them.[45] A reliable eyewitness reported that rioters flooded a house with water and then electrocuted the nineteen occupants "with high-tension electricity." Ashis Nandy has written with exceptional insight, passion, and pessimism about the 2002 Gujarat riots, which were videotaped and seen throughout India. Years of rioting in Gujarat had led to the "ghettoisation of the Muslims" and the realization that Muslims could not expect protection from state agencies. This in turn led to "the growth in the power of Mafia-like bodies in both (Hindu and Muslim) communities, always itching for a fight and acting like protectors of the Hindus and the Muslims at times of rioting." In Nandy's prescient view, the systematic killing and displacement of Muslims in 2002 "produced the sense of desperation that precedes the breakout of terrorism."[46]

Gujarat was not alone in being a place where Muslims experienced persistent violence at the hands of Hindus. In Kashmir Indian security forces countered years of Muslim separatist violence with broad human rights abuses, including the summary execution of Muslim detainees, disappearances, and tens of thousands of deaths.[47]

Had the myth of centuries of Muslim violence become the mother of reality? That is unclear. Before 2000, in spite of Hindutva rhetoric, Indian Muslims other than Kashmiris were rarely accused of bombings inside India. But since then there have been signs that Indian Muslims, stirred by pan-Islamic sentiments for well over a century, increasingly identified with Muslim militants in Palestine, Iraq, Iran, Afghanistan, Pakistan, and perhaps most of all Kashmir. Indian authorities have implicated Indian Muslims working with Muslim extremists in Pakistan in a large number of attacks within India, beginning with attacks in 2001 on the legislative assembly building of Jammu and Kashmir and on the Indian Parliament. The year 2008 saw a heightened number of terrorist attacks, presumably by Muslims, with hundreds of people killed in Jaipur, Bangalore, Lucknow, Varanasi, Faizabad, Bangalore, Ahmedabad, Delhi, and, most spectacularly, Mumbai on November 26. Commentators wondered if Muslim extremists were trying to incite Hindu-Muslim violence in order to radicalize the Muslim population.[48] A small number of Indian and Pakistani Muslim extremists seemed to be gripped by an alternating mix of apocalyptic fear and myths of grandiosity, similar to the lethal combination of "persecutory" and "grandiose" fantasies promoted by the extremists in Sudhir Kakar's analysis of the Hindutva movement.[49]

The irony is that while the Hindutva movement's hate-mongering and violence stimulated Muslim extremists, bombings by Muslims had increased at the same time that the appeal of Hindu hyperpatriotism seemed to have peaked. We might expect that India's significant growth in prosperity, international stature, and self-confidence would undercut the myths of Indian impotence on which Hindu extremism has fed. Will Indian pride in the country's new roles in globalization and in the society's traditions of inclusiveness prevail over the toxic, circular, self-destructive processes of communal hatred and violence? Possibly it will. Hindu reactions to the wave of

Muslim attacks in India in 2008 were notably restrained, compared to Hindu communal violence in New Delhi in 1984 following Indira Gandhi's assassination by her Sikh bodyguards, in Bombay in 1993 following the destruction of the mosque at Ayodhya, and in Gujarat in 2002 following the attack on the train carrying Hindu pilgrims from Ayodhya.

Extremist Hindu nationalism resembles other so-called fundamentalist movements in postcolonial societies in being inspired less by an urge to return to the basic sources of a religious tradition than by political and social anxieties coming out of the unsettled conditions of state formation, modernism, and globalization. Hindutva leaders mostly belong to the small minority of high castes whose traditional economic and political privileges are directly challenged by the social-leveling effects of state patronage and reverse discrimination in favor of the low-caste majorities and by the self-assertion of formerly dependent classes and minorities in mass-based education and democratic politics. In claiming leadership of a movement to reconnect modern Hindus more closely with Hindu traditions, by seeking to substitute a harmonious Hindu community in place of multiethnic competition and strife, Hindu nationalists exaggerate the basic differences between Indian Muslims and Hindus. They use the supposed threat of the weak Muslim minority to divert attention from the gross inequalities and tensions within the Hindu social order. With motives that seem as much instrumental as traditional, they produce the totalizing and polarizing worldview of David Terman's "paranoid gestalt" common to other fundamentalist movements. Hindu nationalists construct a paranoid-sounding view of the history of Hindu-Muslim relations in which Hindus have been the victims of Muslim violence and aggression. The selective and stigmatizing emphasis on past Muslim violence is made more plausible by current threats from Muslim extremism, which have served as a goad for the Hindu nationalist violence and intolerance of the recent past.

How else does Hindu extremism fit into the fundamentalist mindset? Charles Strozier has pointed to the important connection between the rise of fundamentalism and apocalyptic thinking in the United States and the fear of nuclear catastrophe. Yet in India it is less clear that consciousness of the dangers of nuclear destruction is widespread. Moreover Hindu traditions lack a concept of the apocalypse, an end of time. Instead time is cyclical, with gradual degeneration followed by renewal and rebirth. But in the *Ramayana* and elsewhere tradition does hold out the promise of a great war between absolute good and evil, between Ram and Ravanna. And that war ends in total victory and a return to *Ram Rajya*, harmony and righteousness. To that degree also Hindu nationalism belongs in the fundamentalist family.

To date Hindu nationalists have not rallied anything close to a majority of Hindus behind their chauvinism and sense of victimhood. The future credibility of their claims that a minority, poor and backward and constituting 13 percent of the population, seriously threatens the huge Hindu majority might fade if India were able to find a mutually acceptable solution to the Kashmir problem and if Pakistan succeeded in checking Islamic militancy.

Conclusion

A Fundamentalist Mindset?

James W. Jones

A discernable constellation of beliefs, emotions, and schemas of self and world characterize fundamentalism wherever it exists—in Nazism, in the terror of the French Revolution, in the jihadis, in the Hindu nationalists, and in certain segments of American Christianity. This fundamentalist mindset is exemplified by (in the words of the book's first chapter) traits such as dualistic thinking, "paranoia and rage within a group," apocalypticism, and a "totalized conversion experience." Fundamentalism is not, in this context, synonymous with orthodox belief and practice, or any particular beliefs or practices, but is rather a particular way of holding and believing the tenets of any particular religion, philosophy, or political theory. Fundamentalism is not a religion but a way of being religious. The existence of such a mindset ties together this diverse collection of theoretical analyses and historical examples.

This book has two trajectories: theoretical interpretations, all of which are psychological in some sense, and illustrative examples that serve to support the claim that such a mindset exists. Despite this disciplinary diversity, these broadly psychological interpretations converge on many points. Many of them seek to answer the question of why some people resonate with and feel attracted to the narratives of apocalypticism and paranoia that we have seen constitute the fundamentalist mindset. Others seek to account for the transition to violence often found there. The theme of humiliation is found in virtually all of these accounts and is certainly aptly illustrated by stories from Germany after Versailles as described by Redles, jihadis in the European Muslim diaspora described by Khosrokhavar, and Christians described by Quinby and myself. They are drawn to a singularly apocalyptic version of their religion. Strozier's and Terman's chapters delineate the many pathways by which humiliation gives rise to paranoia and apocalyptic fantasies in individuals and in groups. Humiliation represents the collapse of an idealization (for example, the defeat and collapse of a supposedly invincible Germany) that evokes a search for someone to blame and punish for this loss. Such "paranoia" in this sense is not a psychosis or other mental disorder but a way of experiencing the self and the world characterized by hostility and feelings of victimization that are blamed on an out-group. Psychologically a very short distance separates constellating a despised other from fomenting a violent apocalyptic crusade against him. Individuals who see the world in this way (returning World War I German veterans, those drawn to apocalyptic Christianity in America, members of the Muslim diaspora in Europe, Hindu nationalists in India) find that the proclamations of a fundamentalist group make sense to them.

Another theme analyzed theoretically and illustrated in detail throughout the book is the dichotomizing of the world into totally opposed camps of the completely pure and righteous against demonic and evil enemies. The world of the fundamentalist is a world at war, a war of good against evil. Apocalypticism inevitably constitutes an evil other who carries the evil that rules the world until history's climactic battle. Paranoia requires an out-group who is responsible for the suffering the subject is experiencing. Redles traces how Hitler tried pointing the finger of paranoid responsibility at several groups and finally settled on the Jews. In Jordan's essay the Terror of the French Revolution, fueled by rumor, seeks out party after party until none is safe from the scaffold. McLane describes how the Hindu majority in India envisions itself as victimized by the Muslim minority and so constructs the Muslims as an evil other. Apocalyptic Christians yearn for bloody Armageddon, when non-Christians will burn forever in a lake of fire and the earth will be transformed into a pure and sterile state.

These and other themes are theorized in a variety of ways here. These various theoretical interpretations do not constitute a linear argument. Rather they surround the topic of a fundamentalist mindset and approach it from many different angles. Strozier emphasizes the significance of the apocalyptic in understanding the fundamentalist mindset. Terman employs frameworks from contemporary psychoanalysis to explicate the "paranoid gestalt" that he sees as the psychological foundation of fundamentalism. These chapters perform a psychoanalytic reflection on the possible roots of the furious drive for purification and the elimination of the impure found in many fanatically violent religious movements. Muenster and Lotto use the theoretical resources of cognitive social psychology to discuss some of the psychological processes implicated in the fundamentalist mindset. Hill brings to bear the findings of attachment theory and its connection to the processes of affect regulation to account for some of the qualities associated with the "fundamentalist faith state." Readers coming to this topic with a particular theoretical orientation have seen how their orientation might be applied to fundamentalism. However, readers need not (and should not) think they must choose from among these different paradigms. Rather a multidisciplinary pluralism has invited the reader to examine the fundamentalist mindset from a variety of perspectives and to see how different theoretical lenses clarify its different aspects, for the fundamentalist mindset contains cognitions, affects, behaviors, unconscious processes, group dynamics, and all the elements of human experience.

Many different movements, religious and nonreligious, have been found to support the claim of a fundamentalist mindset. The powerful psychological motifs and motivations that make up the fundamentalist mindset predispose fundamentalism toward violence. Put another way, the turn toward violence on the part of fundamentalist movements requires reference to the fundamentalist mindset in order to be fully understood. Social, economic, and political considerations alone are not sufficient to account for the violence of the French Revolution, the paranoia of the Nazis, or the appeal of the bloody language of the Book of Revelation. The fundamentalist mindset not only dichotomizes the world into opposing camps; it also constructs the opposing other as evil, abject, subhuman, and so worthy of elimination. Thus religion's virtually universal struggle for purification is ultimately transformed into a drive to eliminate the other by violence. Apocalyptic religion historicizes an inner spiritual struggle with the wickedness in every human heart into a battle that must take place in real time and in history. So jihad comes to mean eliminating the *kifur* (the impious and unrighteous) from the face of the earth, and Paul's image of "spiritual warfare" in the New Testament is rewritten in American apocalyptic Christianity into a violent war narrative of cosmic proportions. The Nazis, the Committee of Terror in the French Revolution, the jihadis, the devotees of the Book of Revelation all witness that apocalypticism is inherently prone to violence.

Psychological examinations, especially the clinical theorizing that is the basis of many of the chapters here, begin from work with individuals. Yet fundamentalism is a group phenomenon. The fundamentalist mindset is not simply an individual psychology; it is also a group ideology. How can psychological categories shed light on group processes? Terman addresses this question directly in chapters 2 and 5, where he lays out many different paths between the individual and the group. Terman's own analysis illustrates how one can move constructively between these paths and use clinically derived categories to understand group behavior. Strozier also demonstrates this dialectic in his discussion of the "apocalyptic other." In different ways the chapters on American apocalyptic Christianity, Nazism, the French Revolution, the Hindu nationalists, and others display sensitivity to the issue of theorizing the connections back and forth between group processes and individual psychologies.

The argument of this book thus simultaneously narrows and broadens some common terms. *Fundamentalism* is not simply the orthodox or traditional form of a religion, as it is often portrayed in popular discourse. Rather it represents a *mindset* that can be found in both religious and secular movements. *Paranoia* is not here a psychiatric diagnosis or a synonym for insanity but a sensibility or way of experiencing the self and the world that can coexist with technical and literary skill. Fundamentalists are not crazy or psychopathological; they can fly planes, author powerfully rhetorical speeches and tracts, design websites, and make complex tactical plans. However much those outside these groups may tend to regard them in psychopathological terms, the authors here are committed to not pathologizing them. But not regarding them as sick does not mean that common psychological traits cannot be discerned across groups. Nor does this refusal of pathologizing keep the authors from recognizing the disturbing potential within the fundamentalist mindset for violence and destructiveness. Quite the reverse. And in this volume the *apocalyptic* is not primarily a theological category but a state of mind that dichotomizes the world in black-and-white terms and seeks a total, almost always violent purification of the world.

None of the editors or authors of this volume claims that this psychologically oriented approach is the only approach to take to understanding fundamentalism. We do, however, maintain that it is an important approach and one that has been neglected. That neglect has been detrimental to our understanding of these movements. For this psychologically oriented approach brings with it significant insights into fundamentalism.

What are the heuristic gains in thinking in terms of such a fundamentalist mindset? First, it becomes clear that the fundamentalist mindset is a discernable and coherent psychological constellation. The traits that make up the fundamentalist mindset are not random or accidental but fit together in an interrelated pattern. It is not coincidence that fundamentalists idealize their religion, tribe, or nation, constellate an evil other, split the world into opposing camps of the pure against the impure, and anticipate a bloody apocalypse. Several chapters here explicate the psychological ties among these differing themes.

Second, seeing some of the psychological processes underlying the fundamentalist mentality helps to make understandable the appeal of fundamentalism to those inclined to split the world into opposing camps, to look for someone to blame for their troubles, to demand absolute certainty, and to seek a totalistic purification of self and world and the establishment of a perfect state. Attachment patterns, unconscious dynamics, and social learning predispose some to embrace this sensibility.

Third, fundamentalism's slide into violence and terror becomes a much more complicated issue than is often portrayed in contemporary analyses. Although all these factors may play a role, fundamentalist violence is not simply the result of social marginalization, economic deprivation, modernization, or political grievance. The turn to violence is also rooted in the personal, internal psychological dynamics that constitute the fundamentalist mindset, with its totalistic mentality, splitting, creation of an abjected other, and drive for purification through bloodshed. These dynamics get shaped and reinforced by a group ideology that sets itself up as pure and holy and opposed to evil others, that makes totalizing demands on its members, and that also provides the tactical planning and methods of violence that enable individuals to carry out murderous deeds. The Terror of the French Revolution, the Nazi Holocaust, and the 9/11 attacks would not have happened without the various revolutionary parties and assemblies, or the Nazi movement, or Al Qaeda. Terman's chapter demonstrates the fruitfulness of Kohut's notion of a "group self" by arguing that fundamentalist ideology arises from the psychology of the group; this group psychology results from the humiliation of the group and from threats to the group's identity and core values.

These are some of the crucial elements in fundamentalist movements, both religious and secular, that must be grasped if we are to fully understand fundamentalism's appeal and its links to violence. This mindset is a form of psychological organization that has probably existed throughout the history of *Homo sapiens*. It is not a modern phenomenon but has probably been around as long as human beings have lived in organized social groups. This mindset has been responsible for some of the worst and most savage acts in human history. It may also have given rise to some of our most revered institutions. For example, the ideals of the French Revolution have inspired many groups, even if the Revolution itself was a nasty and brutish episode from which it took France a century to recover. And the Book of Revelation has inspired powerful social reform movements as well as dreams and plots of horrific apocalyptic bloodletting. We must accept this ambiguity. The fundamentalist mindset can probably not be completely eliminated. We can only live with it and guard against its potential to disrupt the creation of a humane and civilized world. We must refrain from demonizing it while seeking to contain it. We hope the light we shine on the fundamentalist mindset in this volume will contribute to our understanding of it and our ability to restrain its violent and destructive potentials.

Notes

FOREWORD

1. Martin Marty and R. Scott Appleby, eds., *Fundamentalisms Observed*, vol. 1 (Chicago: University of Chicago Press, 1991); *Fundamentalisms and Society*, vol. 2 (Chicago: University of Chicago Press, 1993); *Fundamentalisms and the State*, vol. 3 (Chicago: University of Chicago Press, 1993); *Accounting for Fundamentalisms*, vol. 4 (Chicago: University of Chicago Press, 1994); and *Fundamentalism Comprehended*, vol. 5 (Chicago: University of Chicago Press, 1995). See also Martin Marty, R. Scott Appleby, and Emmanuel Sivan, *Strong Religion: The Rise of Fundamentalisms around the World* (Chicago: University of Chicago Press, 2003).

INTRODUCTION

1. Garry Wills, *Under God: Religion in American Politics* (New York: Simon and Schuster, 1990), 15.
2. See chapter 10.
3. Martin Marty and R. Scott Appleby, eds., *Fundamentalisms Observed*, vol. 1 (Chicago: University of Chicago Press, 1991); *Fundamentalisms and Society*, vol. 2 (Chicago: University of Chicago Press, 1993); *Fundamentalisms and the State*, vol. 3 (Chicago: University of Chicago Press, 1993); *Accounting for Fundamentalisms*, vol. 4 (Chicago: University of Chicago Press, 1994); and *Fundamentalism Comprehended*, vol. 5 (Chicago: University of Chicago Press, 1995).
4. In Strozier's fieldwork among Christian fundamentalists in the late 1980s and early 1990s over five years, he never encountered anyone whom he would describe as violent. Charles B. Strozier, *Apocalypse: On the Psychology of Fundamentalism in America* (Boston: Beacon Press, 1994).
5. Even a discussion of violence was skirted in the Marty project. The closest one comes to our concerns was David C. Rapoport's discussion of "militancy" in "Comparing Militant Fundamentalist Movements and Groups," in *Fundamentalism and the State: Remaking Politics, Economics, and Militance* (Chicago: University of Chicago Press, 1993), 429–61. Rapoport began to sing a different tune after 9/11; see "Modern Terror: The Four Waves," in *Attacking Terrorism: Elements of a Grand Strategy*, ed. Audrey Cronin and James M. Ludes (Washington, DC: Georgetown University Press, 2004), 46–73.
6. See the discussion of the work of Bernard McGinn in this regard in chapter 3.

7. "And whosoever was not found written in the book of life was cast into the lake of fire" (Revelation 20:15).

CHAPTER 1

1. Nancy T. Ammerman, "North American Protestant Fundamentalism," in *Fundamentalisms Observed,* vol. 1, ed. Martin Marty and R. Scott Appleby (Chicago: University of Chicago Press, 1991), 2.

2. Martin Marty and R. Scott Appleby, eds., *Fundamentalisms Observed,* vol. 1 (Chicago: University of Chicago Press, 1991), viii.

3. Michael Barkun, "Racist Apocalypse: Millennialism on the Far Right," in *The Year 2000,* ed. Charles B. Strozier and Michael Flynn (New York: New York University Press, 1997), 201. Manichaeanism was a Gnostic religion that flourished between the third and seventh centuries. It is characterized by dualistic theology positioning good and evil as two equal yet opposing powers.

4. Stanley Schneider, "Fundamentalism and Paranoia in Groups and Society," *Group* 26, no. 1 (2002): 17–27.

5. Eric Hoffer, *The True Believer: Thoughts on the Nature of Mass Movements* (New York: Perennial Classics, 1951), 124.

6. Robert Jay Lifton and Eric Markusen, *The Genocidal Mentality: Nazi Holocaust and Nuclear Threat* (New York: Basic Books, 1990), 84–85.

7. Bernard McGinn, *Visions of the End: Apocalyptic Traditions in the Middle Ages* (New York: Columbia University Press, 1979), 4. McGinn says that both apocalypticism and eschatology propose that the present is the last age; however, apocalypticism anticipates the last age is about to end. Both believe in evil; however, apocalypticists believe it can be identified and that they know who the evil are. Both perceive that one's life is occurring in the end of times as opposed to believing one's life events are the end of times. Although McGinn warns that there is no single unifying apocalyptic belief, he argues that apocalyptic groups from different times and places and of different faiths "display family resemblances" (10). These include a "structure of history conceived as a divinely predetermined totality," belief in the imminent end, and "belief in the proximate judgment of evil and triumph of the good" (10).

8. Thomas L. Long, "Utopia," in *Encyclopedia of Millennialism and Millennial Movements,* ed. Richard Landes (New York: Routledge, 2000), 420–24.

9. Charles B. Strozier, *Apocalypse: On the Psychology of Fundamentalism in America* (Boston: Beacon Press, 1994), 1.

10. Robert Jay Lifton, *Destroying the World to Save It* (New York: Metropolitan Books, 1999); Robert Jay Lifton, "Reflections on Aum Shinrikyo," in Strozier and Flynn, *The Year 2000.* See also Charles B. Strozier, "The Apocalyptic Guru," in *Psychological Undercurrents of History,* ed. Jerry S. Piven and Henry W. Lawton (San Jose, CA: Authors Choice Press, 2001).

11. Strozier, *Apocalypse.*

12. Bob Altemeyer and Bruce Hunsberger, "A Revised Religious Fundamentalism Scale: The Short and Sweet of It," *International Journal for the Psychology of Religion* 14, no. 1 (2004): 47–54. Altemeyer and Hunsberger define religious fundamentalism as belief in an inerrant truth about man, thereby implying totalistic thinking as a crucial element. In "Fundamentalism, Father and Son, and Vertical

Desire," *PsyART* 8 (2004), available at www.clas.ufl.edu/ipsa/journal/2004_stein01.shtml (accessed Dec. 31, 2004). Ruth Stein describes the fundamentalist mindset as "binary oppositions" (good and bad, etc.) that simplify complexities to generate feelings of certainty and feeling that one is right. In "Fundamentalism and Forgiveness," *Personality and Individual Differences* 43, no. 6 (2007): 1437–47, Ryan P. Brown, Collin D. Barnes, and Nicole Judice Campbell write that fundamentalism is a "rigid cognitive orientation" in relation to strong convictions. In "Fundamentalism and Paranoia in Groups and Society," *Group* 26, no. 1 (2002): 17–27, Stanley Schneider describes fundamentalism as "a rigid, dogmatic, skewed view that dismisses other competing and conflicting viewpoints" (19). This implicates a perverted perception of the world such that things are categorically interpreted as supporting one's ideology or being against it. Bernard McGinn, in "Apocalyptic Spirituality: Approaching the 3rd Millennium," in Strozier and Flynn, *The Year 2000*, focuses on apocalyptic concerns; he writes that fearing the imminent end "has often led to black and white judgments about *what* is right and wrong and (more tragically) *who* is right and wrong" (78). Apocalyptic literature, according to Mortimer Ostow in "Mood Regulation: Spontaneous and Pharmacologically Assisted," *Neuro-Psychoanalysis* 6 (2004): 77–86, is characterized by dualistic thinking differentiating the good from the bad and by "alterations" or the shift in power between good and evil in cyclical form, in which the good ultimately succeeds (82). In "Protocols to the Left, Protocols to the Right: Conspiracism in American Political Discourse at the Turn of the Second Millennium," paper presented at the conference *Reconsidering The Protocols of the Elders of Zion*: 100 Years after the Forgery, The Elie Wiesel Center for Judaic Studies, Boston University, October 30–31, 2005, Chip Berlet describes how *The Protocols of the Elders of Zion* establishes a dualistic narrative that demonizes Jews. However, see also Chip Berlet, "When Alienation Turns Right: Populist Conspiracism, the Apocalyptic Style, and Neofascist Movements," in *Evolution of Alienation: Trauma, Promise, and the Millennium*, ed. Lauren Langman and Devorah Kalekin-Fishman (Lanham, MD: Rowman & Littlefield, 2006), 115–44. In this essay Berlet argues, "Not all forms of apocalyptic belief are necessarily dualistic or demonizing in a political or social context" (121).

13. Robert M. Young, "Fundamentalism and Terrorism," in *Terror and Apocalypse: Psychological Undercurrents of History*, vol. 2, ed. Jerry S. Piven, Paul Ziolo, and Henry W. Lawton (San Jose, CA: Writer's Showcase, 2002), 210, 211. Young suggests that fundamentalists are often the poor, disenfranchised, and displaced people; however, he clearly indicates that fundamentalists do not have to come from an economically poor background.

14. Robert Jay Lifton, *Thought Reform and the Psychology of Totalism: A Study of "Brainwashing" in China* (Chapel Hill: University of North Carolina Press, 1989).

15. Hoffer, *The True Believer*, 80, 156. When discussing the fanatic, Hoffer states, "The blindness [of absolute conviction] . . . is a source of strength (he sees no obstacles), but it is the cause of intellectual sterility and emotional monotony" (156).

16. Lois Ann Lorentzen, "Phallic Millennialism and Radical Environmentalism: The Apocalyptic Vision of Earth First!" in Strozier and Flynn, *The Year 2000*, 146.

17. Lee Quinby, "Coercive Purity: The Dangerous Promise of Apocalyptic Masculinity," in Strozier and Flynn, *The Year 2000*, 155.

18. Berlet, "Protocols," 36–37.

19. Dick Anthony and Thomas Robbins, "Religious Totalism, Exemplary Dualism, and the Waco Tragedy," in *Millennium, Messiahs, and Mayhem: Contemporary Apocalyptic Movements*, ed. Thomas Robbins and Susan J. Palmer (New York: Routledge, 1997), 267.

20. Barkun, "Racist Apocalypse," 201. Barkun discusses the concept of *appropriative millennialism*, which he defines as "claiming as one's own the special status claimed by another group." He suggests that this type of thinking, which incorporates paranoid tendencies, "exaggerates the Manichaeanism present in all apocalyptic groups" such that they "view the world as a battleground between pure good and pure evil" (201). See also Berlet, "Alienation Turns Right," and Berlet, "Protocols." Berlet acknowledges the paranoid nature of the apocalyptic, which he believes underlies many conspiracy theories. He suggests that the paranoid style that describes conspiracism that distinctly identifies a scapegoat is related to the dualistic thinking promoted in the apocalyptic narrative. Dualistic thinking that is associated with an apocalyptic narrative "creates a dynamic that encourages the construction of conspiracy theories that blame a demonized and scapegoated 'other'" (121). Note also in this regard the discussion by Strozier of the "apocalyptic other" in chapter 6.

CHAPTER 2

1. Eric R. Marcus, "Paranoid Symbol Formation in Social Organizations," in *Paranoia: New Psychoanalytic Perspectives*, ed. John M. Oldham and Stanley Bone (Madison, WI: International Universities Press, 1994), 81–96. Marcus is quite clear about the differences between individuals and groups and the pitfalls in applying psychoanalytic theory to groups without sufficient awareness of those differences: "We must be careful, however, in applying individual psychoanalytic psychology to groups, especially psychoanalytic metapsychology. The problems of definition, of semantics, and of relationship to observation, all are magnified if one directly applies metapsychology to groups. This is especially so if one considers the group a hypothetical person. A group does not have an inborn instinctual nature, nor a psychological structure except as it is a collection of individuals. However, groups do not act as merely a collection of individuals, but, rather, with certain responses that are only seen when the individuals form a group. In this sense, the group is like a new and unique single individual rather than a collection of individuals. But this does not mean that metapsychology of the individual can be automatically applied. 'Group' and 'individual' are different conceptualizations" (84).

2. Kurt Lewin, "Problems of Research in the Social Sciences" (1943), in *Resolving Social Conflicts and Field Theory in Social Science* (Washington, DC: American Psychological Association, 1997), 283. See also Kurt Lewin, "Experiments in Social Space," in *Resolving Social Conflicts*: "The properties of a social group, such as its organization, its stability, its goals, are something different from the organization, the stability, and the goals of the individual" (60).

3. Heinz Kohut, "Some Thoughts on Narcissism and Narcissistic Rage," in *Psychoanalytic Study of the Child*, vol. 27 (New York: Quadrangle New York Times Books, 1972), 360–400. In this essay Kohut introduces the concept of narcissistic rage in the individual. It is the most unbounded and intense anger of which humans are capable, and is characterized by the relentless, insatiable wish for revenge. Kohut links

its arousal to threats or damage to the central configurations of the nuclear self. These qualities of relentlessness and need for revenge fit much of the psychology of the group when it has experienced damage to the central constituents of the group self. These are further discussed in chapter 5. Their position as formations in the group that are *analogous* to those in the individual must be kept in mind.

4. See Terman, chapter 5.

5. Jeff Victoroff, "The Mind of the Terrorist: A Review and Critique of Psychological Approaches," *Journal of Conflict Resolution* 49, no. 3 (2005), 3–42.

6. Sigmund Freud, "Group Psychology and the Analysis of the Ego," in *Standard Edition of the Complete Psychological Works of Sigmund Freud*, vol. 18, ed. James Strachey (London: Hogarth Press, 1955), 67–143.

7. Melanie Klein, *Contributions to Psychoanalysis, 1921–1945* (London: Hogarth Press, 1948). See also Melanie Klein, *Love, Guilt, and Reparation, 1921–1945* (London: Hogarth Press, 1948).

8. For a good summary of Bion's theory of groups, see Leon Grinberg et al., *Introduction to the Work of Wilfred Bion* (New York: Jason Aronson, 1977).

9. Didier Anzieu, *The Group and the Unconscious* (London: Routledge and Kegan Paul, 1984), 127, translation of *Le Groupe et L'Inconscient* (Paris: Bordas, 1975). Expanding on Bion's contention that the group grows out of conflict between the individual and the group, Anzieu states, "The only way a group can protect itself and make use of external stimulation and the wishes and drives with which it is cathected by its members is to fabricate an overarching group psychical apparatus on top of those of the individuals composing it" (100). He later states, "To exist at all the group needs an overarching agency that envelops it. Thus the group is organized around the same agencies as the individuals composing it. The unconscious and conscious functioning of the group will differ depending upon the agency that serves as envelope to the group psychical apparatus" (101).

10. René Kaes, "Processus et Fonctions de l'Ideologie dans les Groupes," *Perspectives Psychiatriques* vol. 33 (1971): 27–48. One of the functions of ideology is to deny reality, especially the reality of castration. So for Kaes ideology is structured like a perversion: it denies the reality by substituting idealized objects. The individual who cannot tolerate the idea of a person without a penis denies that there are people without penises (i.e., women), so he puts penises on women. This mechanism is then applied to the organization of group psychology.

11. Anzieu, *The Group and the Unconscious*, 127.

12. Otto Kernberg, *Ideology, Conflict, and Leadership in Groups and Organizations* (New Haven, CT: Yale University Press, 1998), 40. In this volume Kernberg spells out many of his ideas about the nature of organizational structure and especially the role of leaders and the relationships between the leaders and the group. See his interesting, nuanced discussion of the tensions in the politics of a democratic society. Kernberg certainly notes the ubiquity of paranoid organizations in many groups.

13. Ibid. The reader is referred to chapter 7, "The Moral Dimension of Leadership," 104–21, for the full discussion of the nature of the interaction between the members of the group and the leader that explores the many dynamic issues that may arise.

14. This kind of thinking is very cogently critiqued in Celia Brickman's work on notions of primitivity in psychoanalytic theory. Brickman traces its origins to the

colonial experience of native populations. Celia Brickman, *Aboriginal Populations in the Mind* (New York: Columbia University Press, 2003).

15. Marcus, "Paranoid Symbol Formation," 83.

16. For an excellent discussion of the function of ideology, see Clifford Geertz, "Ideology as a Cultural System," in *The Interpretation of Cultures* (New York: Basic Books, 1973). Geertz summarized much of the psychological analysis of ideology as belonging to what he termed "strain theory," which considers it a kind of sickness (as the formulations of regression, unconscious conflict, and psychotic anxiety all suggest): "It is through the construction of ideologies, the schematic images of social order, that man makes himself for better or worse a political animal. . . . The function of ideology is to make an autonomous politics possible by providing the authoritative concepts that render it meaningful, the suasive images by means of which it can be sensibly grasped" (218).

17. See Heinz Kohut, *Self Psychology and the Humanities*, ed. Charles B. Strozier (New York: Norton, 1985), 206–7, 227. There is an extended discussion with Strozier about the nature of a group self, which Kohut sees as analogous to the individual. I differ with his ideas only in his evocation of unconscious elements of the group self.

18. Vamik Volkan has coined two felicitous terms to characterize this aspect of what I would call the group's self: *chosen trauma* and *chosen glory*. Vamik Volkan, *Bloodlines* (Boulder, CO: Westview Press, 1997).

19. Some documents, for example, become quite central for the beliefs and values of political and social groups. The Declaration of Independence and the Constitution strongly define the values and character of Americans and are accessible and conscious to all in the nation. The works of Marx and Lenin occupied a similar place in the former Soviet Union, and the texts of the Qur'an as interpreted by writers such as Sayyid Qutb have been essential elements of the Islamic fundamentalist upsurge.

20. Kernberg, *Ideology*, 42.

21. For an excellent discussion of the history of the concept of paranoia, see Ian Dowbiggen, "Delusional Diagnosis? The History of Paranoia as a Disease Concept in the Modern Era," *History of Psychiatry* 11 (2000): 37–69.

22. See David Swanson et al., *The Paranoid* (Boston: Little, Brown, 1970); William W. Meissner, *The Paranoid Process* (New York: Jason Aronson, 1978); Oldham and Bone, *Paranoia*.

23. Sigmund Freud, "Psychoanalytic Notes on an Autobiographical Account of a Case of Paranoia" (1911), in *The Standard Edition*, vol. 12 (1958), 3–82.

24. For an interesting follow-up on the reality of Schreber's childhood, see William Niederland, *The Schreber Case: Psychoanalytic Profile of a Paranoid Personality* (New York: Quadrangle, New York Times Book, 1974).

25. Melanie Klein, "Notes on Some Schizoid Mechanisms," in *Envy and Gratitude and Other Works, 1946–1963*, ed. M. Masud R. Khan (London: International Psycho-Analytical Library, 1975).

26. Freud, "Psychoanalytic Notes on an Autobiographical Account of a Case of Paranoia," 71.

27. Harry Stack Sullivan, "The Paranoid Dynamism," in *The Collected Works of Harry Stack Sullivan*, vol. 2, ed. Helen Swick Perry et al. (New York: Norton, 1956), 146.

28. John Frosch, "The Role of Unconscious Homosexuality in the Paranoid Constellation," in *The Psychotic Process* (New York: International Universities Press, 1983), 12. This essay is an excellent, succinct history of the psychoanalytic thinking about paranoia.

29. Meissner, *The Paranoid Process*, 114–21.

30. John M. Oldham and Stanley Bone, "Paranoia: Historical Considerations," in Oldham and Bone, *Paranoia*, 12.

31. David Shapiro, "Paranoia from a Characterological Standpoint," in Oldham and Bone, *Paranoia*, 53, 54 (emphasis added).

32. Shapiro, "Paranoia from a Characterological Standpoint," 55.

33. See Terman, chapter 5.

34. Sigmund Freud, "Beyond the Pleasure Principle," in *The Standard Edition*, vol. 18 (1920).

35. Sigmund Freud, "Civilization and Its Discontents," in *The Standard Edition*, vol. 21 (1930).

36. Sigmund Freud, "Why War," in *The Standard Edition*, vol. 22 (1932).

37. Erich Fromm, *The Anatomy of Human Destructiveness* (New York: Holt, Rinehart and Winston, 1973), 271.

38. Anthony Storr, *Human Destructiveness* (New York: Basic Books, 1972), 108.

39. See Terman, chapter 5, for an extended discussion of the nature of such damage and its sequelae.

40. Jerome Frank, "Psychological Aspects of Violence," in *Dynamics of Violence*, ed. Jan Fawcett (Chicago: American Medical Association, 1971), 34.

41. Again, the reader is referred to Victoroff, "The Mind of the Terrorist," for a comprehensive review of the theories of the psychology of terrorism. Though he is also quite critical of many of the proposals for understanding the group, Victoroff sees that approach as having the most promise.

42. Nehemia Friedland, "Becoming a Terrorist: Social and Individual Antecedents," in *Terrorism: Roots, Impact, Responses*, ed. Lawrence Howard (New York: Praeger, 1992), 81–93.

43. Mark Juergensmeyer, *Terror in the Mind of God* (Berkeley: University of California Press, 2000).

44. Martha Crenshaw, "How Terrorists Think," in Howard, *Terrorism*, 71–80.

45. Jerrold M. Post, *The Mind of the Terrorist* (New York: Palgrave Macmillan, 2007), 8. He provides many detailed portraits of the leaders of these movements and their operations.

46. Marc Sageman, *Leaderless Jihad* (Philadelphia: University of Pennsylvania Press, 2008). Sageman disputes that such reactions also evoke humiliations, and he questions the importance of humiliation in motivating revenge. In fact, part of the psychological constellation in moral outrage is intense narcissistic injury, which does lead to narcissistic rage, the relentless and boundless need to right the wrong.

47. Volkan, *Bloodlines*.

48. George De Vos, "Ethnic Pluralism: Conflict and Accommodation," in *Ethnic Identity*, ed. George De Vos and Lola Romanucci-Ross (Palo Alto, CA: Mayfield, 1975), 5–41. De Vos defines the ethnic group as "those who hold in common a set of traditions not shared by the others with whom they are in contact." Such traditions typically include "folk religious beliefs and practices, language, a sense of historical

continuity, a common ancestry, place of origin and shared history" (9). He makes the further point that ethnic groups need to feel unique and special and differentiate themselves from others, often their neighbors. He also notes, "Defining oneself in social terms is one basic answer to the human need to belong and to survive" (17).

49. Volkan, *Bloodlines*, 48: "I use the term *chosen trauma* to describe the collective memory of a calamity that once befell a group's ancestors. It is, of course, more than a simple recollection; it is a shared mental representation of the event, which includes realistic information, fantasized expectations, intense feelings, and defenses against unacceptable thoughts. . . . I maintain that the word *chosen* fittingly reflects a large group's unconsciously defining its identity by the transgenerational transmission of injured selves infused with the memory of the ancestor's trauma." I would qualify this interesting and important idea by emending the concept of unconscious transmission of such a schema. Instead I would call its continuation implicit. There is no established record of a fact in a previous generation that is accessible to the majority of members of a later generation, so there is no actual awareness of a given fact. The *attitudes, stories, myths,* and so on that are developed in relation to the fact can indeed be transmitted and can powerfully influence the group, but the historical "reality" is usually unknown and hence cannot be said to be repressed or unconscious. "The mental representation of a historical event that induces feelings of success and triumph, what I call a 'chosen glory,' can bring members of a large group together. Usually such triumphs are deserved victories over another group" (81–82).

CHAPTER 3

1. An interesting variation of such destruction is the "green apocalypse" of the Hopi Indians in which most (but not all) humans die and the earth is preserved. See Charles B. Strozier, *Apocalypse: On the Psychology of Fundamentalism in America* (Boston: Beacon Press, 1994), chapter 8.

2. Bernard McGinn, "Apocalyptic Spirituality: Approaching the 3rd Millennium," in *The Year 2000*, ed. Charles B. Strozier and Michael Flynn (New York: New York University Press, 1997), 76.

3. Strozier, *Apocalypse*.

4. Bernard McGinn, *Visions of the End: Apocalyptic Traditions in the Middle Ages* (New York: Columbia University Press, 1979), 30.

5. McGinn, "Apocalyptic Spirituality," 76.

6. See David Mann, "The Infantile Origins of the Creation and Apocalyptic Myths," *International Review of Psycho-Analysis* 19 (1992): 471–82. Like McGinn, Mann describes cultures that experience time in a cyclical manner. See also Catherine Keller, "The Breast, the Apocalypse, and the Colonial Journey," in Strozier and Flynn, *The Year 2000*. Keller describes Christopher Columbus's apocalyptic narrative and how he saw himself as "the indispensable agent" for spreading Christianity (52). She describes his seeking to acquire and conquer paradise in his exploration such that "he must find himself at the center of biblical prophecy about time . . . [and] he will bend time backward, making of it a commodifiable place" (52).

7. Stephen O'Leary, *Arguing the Apocalypse: A Theory of Millennial Rhetoric* (New York: Oxford University Press, 1994), 6.

8. Charles B. Strozier, "The Global War on Terror, Sliced Four Ways," *World Policy Journal* 24, no. 4 (2008): 90–98. See also Strozier, chapter 6; Carol Mason, *Killing for Life: The Apocalyptic Narrative of Pro-Life Politics* (Ithaca, NY: Cornell University Press, 2002). Philip Rieff used the two words in Greek to distinguish time, *chronos* and *kairos*. He argued that in trauma the individual experiences time in a kairotic fashion. See his *Freud: The Mind of the Moralist* (Chicago: University of Chicago Press, 1979). See also Richard Hofstadter, *The Paranoid Style in American Politics and Other Essays* (Chicago: University of Chicago Press, 1979).

9. Richard Landes, "Millennialism," in *The Oxford Handbook of New Religious Movements*, ed. James R. Lewis (New York: Oxford University Press, 2003), 335, 345.

10. Jean Baudrillard, "Hysteresis of the Millennium," in Strozier and Flynn, *The Year 2000*, 250–62. See also Landes, "Millennialism," 334. Landes describes how millennialists are "driven by a sense of imminence" such that "believers can become disruptive, even engaging in revolutionary efforts to overthrow sociopolitical order in an attempt to bring about the kingdom of 'peace'" (334).

11. There is a distinction, reflected in most religious traditions, between millennialists who want to force the end and millennialists content with waiting patiently for the end. Among many discussions of the issue, see Nancy Ammerman, "North American Protestant Fundamentalism," in *Fundamentalisms Observed*, ed. Martin E. Marty and R. Scott Appleby (Chicago: University of Chicago Press, 1991), 1–65.

12. Benjamin Beit-Hallahmi, "Death, Fantasy, and Religious Transformations," in *The Psychology of Death in Fantasy and History*, ed. Jerry S. Piven (London: Greenwood, 2004), 87–114.

13. Charles B. Strozier and Michael Flynn, eds., *The Year 2000: Essays on the End* (New York: New York University Press, 1997). The thinker who first clarified this relation between the psychology of individual death and the group is Robert Jay Lifton in *The Broken Connection: On Death and the Continuity of Life* (New York: Simon and Schuster, 1979).

14. McGinn, "Apocalyptic Spirituality," 78. McGinn writes, "Promised in apocalyptic texts was more than just the immortality of the soul that pagan philosophers had taught; it centered on the resurrection of the body—a belief difficult, even absurd, to human reason" (78). See also McGinn, *Visions of the End*.

15. Richard Landes, "The Apocalyptic Year 1000: Millennial Fever and the Origins of the Modern West," in Strozier and Flynn, *The Year 2000*, 17.

16. Eric Hoffer, *The True Believer: Thoughts on the Nature of Mass Movements* (New York: Perennial Classics, 1951), 66.

17. Mortimer Ostow, "Apocalyptic Thinking in Mental Illness and Social Disorder," *Psychoanalysis and Contemporary Thought* 11 (1988): 290. See also Keller, "The Breast," 53, who describes the patriarchal militancy of apocalyptic tradition; Samuel Heilman and Menachem Friedman, "Religious Fundamentalism and Religious Jews: The Case of the Haredim," in Marty and Appleby, *Fundamentalisms Observed*; Bryan Wilson, "Millennialism in Comparative Perspective (Review Article)," *Comparative Studies in Society and History* 6, no. 1 (1963): 97–98. Wilson distinguishes between the types of actions millennial groups partake in: those who only warn others about the end, those who conduct individual activities to ensure they are prepared for the end, those who perform symbolic collective activities, and those who perform activities that "imitate rational steps toward the establishment of a new

dispensation, and which bring the movement into conflict with authorities" (97–98).

18. Strozier, *Apocalypse*; Mason, *Killing for Life*.

19. Mortimer Ostow, "Mood Regulation: Spontaneous and Pharmacologically Assisted," *Neuro-Psychoanalysis* 6 (2004): 77–86. See also Charles B. Strozier, introduction to Strozier and Flynn, *The Year 2000*, 2; Jerry Piven, "The Psychosis (Religion) of Terrorists and the Ecstasy of Violence," in *Terrorism, Jihad, and Sacred Vengeance*, ed. Jerry Piven, Chris Boyd, and Henry Lawton (Haland, Norway: Psychosozial-Verlag, 2004). Piven discusses how a holy war needs an established evil enemy.

20. Lee Quinby, "Coercive Purity: The Dangerous Promise of Apocalyptic Masculinity," in Strozier and Flynn, *The Year 2000*, 156.

21. Ostow, "Apocalyptic Thinking," 278. See also Sara Diamond, "Political Millennialism within the Evangelical Subculture," in Strozier and Flynn, *The Year 2000*, 207–9. Diamond claims that "hard millennialism, linking a timetable for Christ's return to current events in world politics . . . [has] tended to promote a sort of siege mentality" (207–9).

22. Strozier, *Apocalypse*. Jesus says in Matthew 25:13 (King James Version), "Watch therefore, for ye know neither the day nor the hour wherein the Son of man cometh." See also McGinn, "Apocalyptic Spirituality," 73, where he describes Augustine and Thomas Aquinas as opposing Christian apocalyptic groups that are inclined to setting the date for Jesus' return.

23. Diamond, "Political Millennialism," 214.

24. Beit-Hallahmi, "Death, Fantasy, and Religious Transformations." Beit-Hallahmi warns that an apocalyptic group that perceives itself to be on the defense against outside forces may become violent, particularly if it is a relatively small group with an authoritarian leader in the possession of weapons.

25. Robert Jay Lifton, *Destroying the World to Save It* (New York: Metropolitan Books, 1999). See also Robert Jay Lifton, "Anger, Rage, and Violence," in *Terror and Apocalypse: Psychological Undercurrents of History*, vol. 2, ed. Jerry S. Piven, Paul Ziolo, and Henry W. Lawton (San Jose, CA: Writer's Showcase, 2002), 87. Lifton acknowledges the feelings of guilt, responsibility, and self-blame that a human associates with the imagery of killing another person, thereby making such action a difficult undertaking. He suggests, "The anger-rage-violence constellation provides a means of assigning responsibility and blaming others for that same death imagery" (Lifton, 2002, 87). This process of cognitive reorientation contributes to aggressive numbing.

26. Strozier, introduction, 5. See also Robert Jay Lifton, "Reflections on Aum Shinrikyo," in Strozier and Flynn, *The Year 2000*, 116. Lifton writes, "The nuclear culture in which we all grow up creates an Armageddon-like expectation or set of images in all of us that can be seized upon by a person with the right 'words'" (116). See also Lifton, *The Broken Connection*; Robert Jay Lifton and Richard Falk, *Indefensible Weapons: The Political and Psychological Case against Nuclearism* (New York: Basic Books, 1982); Margaret Thaler Singer, "On the Image of 2000 in Contemporary Cults," in Strozier and Flynn, *The Year 2000*, 142. Singer writes, "Nuclear threat has made us all 'end timers,' as the means of destruction are now scientific and real" (142).

27. Catherine Keller, *Apocalypse Now and Then* (Boston: Beacon Press, 1996), 5. Keller says that premillennialists anticipate the apocalypse "probably in nuclear

exchange with 'the evil empire'" (5). See also Michael Barkun, "Racist Apocalypse: Millennialism on the Far Right," in Strozier and Flynn, *The Year 2000*. Barkun says that the nuclear threat and environmental concerns have generated secular apocalyptic scenarios.

28. O'Leary, *Arguing the Apocalypse*, 7, 209.

29. Landes, "Millennialism," 338.

30. See Strozier, *Apocalypse*, 2; Charles B. Strozier, "The Apocalyptic Guru," in *Psychological Undercurrents of History*, vol. 1, ed. Jerry S. Piven and Henry W. Lawton (San Jose, CA: Authors Choice Press, 2001); Strozier, "The Global War on Terror," 94–95; Charles B. Strozier, "The World Trade Center Disaster and the Apocalyptic," in Piven, Boyd, and Lawton, *Terrorism, Jihad, and Sacred Vengeance*, 20; Strozier and Flynn, *The Year 2000*, 5. The apocalyptic fervor in the world is heightened by the existence of nuclear weapons. Osama bin Laden attempted to acquire ultimate weapons and called for a fatwa that would allow him to use such weapons against the United States. Aum Shinrikyo also sought such weapons and was able to acquire and use sarin gas in the Tokyo subway, killing eleven and injuring up to five thousand people.

31. Amos Funkenstein, "A Schedule for the End of the World: The Origins and Persistence of the Apocalyptic Mentality," in *Visions of Apocalypse: End or Rebirth?*, ed. Saul Friedlander, Gerald Holton, Leo Marx, and Eugene Skolnikoff (New York: Holmes and Meier, 1985), 44–60. Only Funkenstein articulates his belief that apocalyptic groups defined by the unique "balance of myth, method and way of life existed only for 200 years" among the Jewish and early Christian populations (57). He believes history has witnessed the continuous decline in apocalypticism since that time period.

32. Frank Kermode, "Apocalypse and the Modern," in Friedlander et al., *Visions of Apocalypse*, 86. See also David Miller, "Chiliasm: Apocalyptic with a Thousand Faces," in Piven and Lawton, *Psychological Undercurrents of History*, vol. 1, 30. Miller thinks Kermode's description is too narrow. He sees the "apocalypse not as vision and scripture, not as myth and dream, but as acting-out, literally lived, imminent 'sense of an ending;' really and not merely literary trope, explained by Frank Kermode" (30).

33. Wilson, "Millennialism," 103–4. Wilson's recommendation is important to dissuade people from focusing on what they consider abnormal psychological behavior in groups that may not be considered as such in the cultural context.

34. O'Leary, *Arguing the Apocalypse*, 6, 197, 93. O'Leary suggests two types of rhetoric, the tragic and the comic. He argues that the "internal tensions in the discourse and external social pressures" due to the inability to end slavery and institute temperance "combined to make the comic optimism of postmillennialism unsustainable. With the collapse of the comic frame of acceptance, Millerism offered a tragic interpretation of history as predestined and moving toward its catastrophic close, an interpretation that was distinctly pessimistic about the utility of political and social reform" (93).

35. Mortimer Ostow, "Myth and Madness: A Report of a Psychoanalytic Study of Antisemitism," *International Journal of Psycho-Analysis* 77 (1996): 15–31.

36. Norman Cohn, *Pursuit of the Millennium: Revolutionary Millenarians and Mystical Anarchists of the Middle Ages* (New York: Oxford University Press, 1961), 37.

Cohn states, "The tradition of apocalyptic prophecy was only one of several preconditions of the movements of which this book is concerned." He acknowledges the "sociological import" of the information he provides in the foreword he contributed to the latest version of the book in 1970 (12).

37. See also Dan Liechty, "Hasten the Apocalypse! Historical and Psychological Perspectives on the American Militia Movement," in Piven and Lawton, *Psychological Undercurrents of History*, vol. 1, 75. Liechty explains how a social transition, such as the contemporary shift from a "manufacturing-based economy to [an] information-based economy . . . results in deep-seated fears" (75). The "conquering evil" ideology can have a pertinent appeal, particularly to youth and those experiencing a midlife crisis, suffering through the turmoil of socializing in times of change.

38. Norman Cohn, "Medieval Millenarianism: Its Bearing on the Comparative Study of Millenarian Movements," in Strozier and Flynn, *The Year 2000*, 40.

39. Ostow, "Mood Regulation." Others have called this process a form of projection, including Strozier, *Apocalypse*; McGinn, "Apocalyptic Spirituality." McGinn writes, "Apocalyptic spirituality often appears as a projection of the least noble aspects of human hopes and fears onto history" (75–76).

40. Mortimer Ostow, "The Psychodynamics of Apocalyptic: Discussion of Papers on Identification and the Nazi Phenomenon," *International Journal of Psycho-Analysis* 67 (1986): 283.

41. Ostow, "Myth and Madness."

42. Martin Buber, "Prophesy, Apocalyptic, and the Historical Hour," in *Pointing the Way*, ed. Maurice Friedman (1954; New York: Books for Libraries, 1957), 192–207. See also Harvey Cox, "Christianity and the Apocalypse," paper presented at the second Conference on the Apocalypse, Providence, Rhode Island, June 14–17, 1990, comments summarized by Michael Perlman; Paul D. Hanson, *The Dawn of the Apocalyptic: The Historical and Sociological Roots of Jewish Apocalyptic Eschatology* (Philadelphia: Fortress Press, 1979).

43. Strozier, *Apocalypse*. The Grady House fundamentalists, a group of privileged believers in New York City, described in Strozier's *Apocalypse* are examples of upper-class individuals who are attracted to the appeal of hope offered in the apocalyptic narrative. For this book Strozier also studied a multicultural congregation of fundamentalists at Abiding Light and a predominantly black congregation at Calvary in Harlem. See also O'Leary, *Arguing the Apocalypse*: "Apocalyptic discourse shows that its appeal has historically cut across class lines" (9).

44. Ostow, "Apocalyptic Thinking," 294. See also Christopher Lasch, *Culture of Narcissism: American Life in an Age of Diminishing Expectations* (New York: Norton, 1991).

45. Strozier, *Apocalypse*. This book discusses the upper-class fundamentalists at Grady House, as well as lower-class fundamentalist groups at other churches in New York City in the early 1990s.

46. Cohn, *Pursuit of the Millennium*. The Free Spirit heresy consisted of small groups of Christian heretics living mostly in East Central Europe, during the fourteenth and fifteenth centuries. The heretics believed that it was possible to reach perfection on earth by following a life of asceticism and spiritualism. They believed that the Christian church was not needed for intercession, but that they could communicate directly with God.

47. Lois Ann Lorentzen, "Phallic Millennialism and Radical Environmentalism: The Apocalyptic Vision of Earth First!," in Strozier and Flynn, *The Year 2000*, 149. O'Leary criticizes theories that claim the apocalyptic appeal is based on economic distress because these theories "fail to account for [the] wide variety of class and education in apocalyptic audiences" (*Arguing the Apocalypse*, 9).

48. Singer, "On the Image of 2000," 137. Speaking specifically of cults, Singer writes, "Education is no vaccine against being led to join a cult" (137). Similarly O'Leary warns, "It is unfair and dangerous to dismiss these arguments as irrational and the audiences persuaded by them as ignorant fools" (*Arguing the Apocalypse*, 4).

49. Philip Charles Lucas, "Shifting Millennial Visions in New Religious Movements: The Case of the Holy order of MANS," in Strozier and Flynn, *The Year 2000*, 121.

50. O'Leary, *Arguing the Apocalypse*, 61. See also Mann, "Infantile Origins." Mann uses the psychodynamic paradigm to suggest that apocalyptic myth derives from traumatic birth experience. He suggests that the hope of rebirth is similar to the longing for a return to the womb, where all needs were satisfied.

51. Lifton notes "an ultimate level of universal need for human connectedness, for a sense of being part of a great chain of being that long preceded, and will continue endlessly after, one's own life span" (*Destroying the World*, 13). Wilson writes that both Cohn and Muhlmann suggest that all mankind is generally receptive to salvation, "but it is an idea always subject to re-interpretation, to new associations with other cultural elements and aspirations" ("Millennialism," 97). See also Heinz Kohut, in *The Search for the Self: Selected Writings of Heinz Kohut*, ed. Paul Ornstein, 2 vols. (New York: International Universities Press, 1978), 1:427–60.

52. Marc Sageman, *Leaderless Jihad* (Philadelphia: University of Pennsylvania Press, 2008); Christopher Dickey, "'Jihadi Cool': Comic Book Action Heroes May Be Better Weapons against Terror Than Bullets or Bombs," *Newsweek*, April 15, 2008. Dickey's article refers to Scott Atran's work, finding that people who join the jihad often do so because family members, friends, or teammates are also involved in the movement, rather than for the sake of the ideological cause.

53. Beit-Hallahmi, "Death, Fantasy, and Religious Transformations."

54. Mann, "Infantile Origins." Mann suggests that the desire for the future period of salvation represents the desire to return to the womb, where all physical needs were met.

55. Ostow, "Apocalyptic Thinking," 291.

56. Leon Festinger, Henry W. Riecken, and Stanley Schachter, *When Prophecy Fails: A Social and Psychological Study of a Modern Group That Predicted the Destruction of the World* (New York: Harper & Row, 1956).

57. Wilson claims that one cannot assume that millennial movements are "moving towards a genuinely realistic appraisal of social circumstances." Though they may desire change or adjustment, it may be "in a way analogous to a neurosis in the individual, the adjustment is at a false level—and it is difficult to see how it can be otherwise" ("Millennialism," 106).

58. Chip Berlet, "When Alienation Turns Right: Populist Conspiracism, the Apocalyptic Style, and Neofascist Movements," in *Evolution of Alienation: Trauma, Promise, and the Millennium*, ed. Lauren Langman and Devorah Kalekin-Fishman (Lanham, MD: Rowman & Littlefield, 2006), 115–44. Berlet discusses how the dualistic apocalyptic narrative is found in right-wing populism, which appeals to people

in multiple socioeconomic classes. Successful middle- and upper-middle-class Americans join the Christian Right, while the gun-wielding militia men often feel that they have or will soon suffer economic hardship.

59. O'Leary, *Arguing the Apocalypse*, 9, 13, 195. O'Leary says that scholarship that exclusively analyzes texts and doctrine is limited. Ultimately, he believes, studying the rhetoric of apocalyptic discourse utilizes the insights offered by other fields of studying "without being bound by the limitations of [those] fields" (195).

60. Ostow, "Mood Regulation."

61. Robert M. Young, "Fundamentalism and Terrorism," in Piven, Ziolo, and Lawton, *Terror and Apocalypse*, 209–10. See the earlier discussion of Didier Anzieu in chapter 2.

62. Funkenstein, "Schedule for the End of the World."

63. Hoffer writes, "Fear of the future causes us to lean against and cling to the present, while faith in the future renders us receptive to change." He argues that "no faith is potent unless it is also faith in the future; unless it has a millennial component," suggesting that the hopeful nature of millennialism is not dependent on achievement in an earthly, human future (*The True Believer*, 9). He stresses the paradox between hope and millennial-inspired actions: "There is often a monstrous incongruity between the hopes, however noble and tender, and the action which follows them. It is as if ivied maidens and garlanded youths were to herald the four horsemen of the apocalypse" (11).

64. Lucas, "Shifting Millennial Visions," 121–30. Lucas does acknowledge that the new religious movements he studied did not follow canonized scripture, which made changing the ideology an easier task.

65. Robert Jay Lifton, "The Image of 'The End of the World,'" in Friedlander et al., *Visions of Apocalypse*, 151–67. See also Mason, *Killing for Life*, 131.

66. See Strozier, introduction, 2. Strozier discusses the role of Charles Hodge, Archibald Alexander Hodge, and Benjamin Warfield in the development of textual literalness and inerrancy in American Christian history. Miller emphasizes that the "literal and metaphoric belong together, [however] the proper dialectic of this paradox involves a movement from literal to mythic, not the reverse" ("Chiliasm," 34). He suggests that a believer should sense the end by experiencing the ills of life and then put that sense into a mythical scenario "knowing that fantasies of the end are transpersonal, archetypal, [and] fundamentally religious" (34).

67. Mason, *Killing for Life*, 131.

CHAPTER 4

1. Marc Sageman, *The Leaderless Jihad: Terror Networks in the Twenty-first Century* (Philadelphia: University of Pennsylvania Press, 2008). Sageman describes how the most recent wave of terrorist attacks were conducted by individuals and small groups without a leader or centralized authority. On the other hand, in *The True Believer: Thoughts on the Nature of Mass Movements* (New York: Perennial Classics, 1951), Eric Hoffer argues, "Without [the leader] there will be no movement" (113). It can be assumed that Hoffer did not anticipate the advent of the modern computer age and the new forms of interaction and relationships that exist in cyberspace; however, although the leaderless jihad movement does not have a leader dictating

direction from above, the movement does have Osama bin Laden as a leader-like figurehead. See also Norman Cohn, "Medieval Millenarianism: Its Bearing on the Comparative Study of Millenarian Movements," in *The Year 2000*, ed. Charles B. Strozier and Michael Flynn (New York: New York University Press, 1997): "A millennial revolt never formed except around a prophet" (36). See also Bryan Wilson, "Millennialism in Comparative Perspective (Review Article)," *Comparative Studies in Society and History* 6, no.1 (1963): "At some level there must be agents to promulgate and transmit ideas and visions, even if they do not claim these as their own. Social action is not simply a matter of response—it is also summoned forth" (101). In *The Mind of the Terrorist* (New York: Palgrave Macmillan, 2007), 8, Jerrold M. Post lays particular stress on the role of the leader in the formation of these groups. He provides many detailed portraits of the leaders of these movements and their operations.

2. Hoffer, *True Believer*, 80, 116. Hoffer states that "the effectiveness of a doctrine does not come from its meaning but from its certitude. . . . [It will not] be effective unless it is presented as the embodiment of the one and only truth" (80). Hoffer also argues, "It was not the intellectual crudity . . . which won and held their following but the boundless self-confidence which prompted these leaders to give full rein to their preposterous ideas. . . . The quality of ideas seems to play a minor role in mass movement leadership. What counts is the arrogant gesture, the complete disregard of opinion of others, the singlehanded defiance of the world" (116).

3. Anthony Storr, *Feet of Clay: Saints, Sinners, and Madmen, a Study of Gurus* (New York: Free Press, 1997).

4. Stephen O'Leary, *Arguing the Apocalypse: A Theory of Millennial Rhetoric* (New York: Oxford University Press, 1994), 53.

5. Charles B. Strozier, "The Apocalyptic Guru," in *Psychological Undercurrents of History*, ed. Jerry S. Piven and Henry W. Lawton (San Jose, CA: Authors Choice Press, 2001), 4. See also Robert Jay Lifton, *Destroying the World to Save It* (New York: Metropolitan Books, 1999). Lifton argues that "intense personal conviction is essential to the guru's success. But that conviction can be helped considerably by grandiose ambitions and manipulative inclinations" (19).

6. Heinz Kohut, "Thoughts on Narcissism and Narcissistic Rage," in *Psychoanalytic Study of the Child* 27 (1972): 360–400. See also his "On Leadership," in *Self Psychology and the Humanities: Reflections on a New Psychoanalytic Approach*, ed. Charles B. Strozier (New York: Norton, 1985), 51–72.

7. Wilson, "Millennialism," 102.

8. Cohn, "Medieval Millenarianism," 40.

9. Lifton, *Destroying the World*, 14.

10. Hoffer, *True Believer*, 66–67.

11. Chip Berlet, "Protocols to the Left, Protocols to the Right: Conspiracism in American Political Discourse at the Turn of the Second Millennium," paper presented at the conference Reconsidering *The Protocols of the Elders of Zion*: 100 Years after the Forgery, The Elie Wiesel Center for Judaic Studies, Boston University, October 30–31, 2005. See also Charles B. Strozier, *Apocalypse: On the Psychology of Fundamentalism in America* (Boston: Beacon Press, 1994); Norman Cohn, *Pursuit of the Millennium: Revolutionary Millenarians and Mystical Anarchists of the Middle Ages* (New York: Oxford University Press, 1961).

12. Margaret Thaler Singer, "On the Image of 2000 in Contemporary Cults," in Strozier and Flynn, *The Year 2000*, 137.

13. Cohn, *Pursuit of the Millennium.*

14. Robert Jay Lifton, "Reflections on Aum Shinrikyo," in Strozier and Flynn, *The Year 2000*, 116–17.

15. Erik H. Erikson, *Identity: Youth and Crisis* (New York: Norton, 1968), 80–81. Lifton also uses the term *totalism.* See Lifton, *Destroying the World;* Robert Jay Lifton, *Thought Reform and the Psychology of Totalism* (Chapel Hill: University of North Carolina Press, 1989).

16. Ralph W. Hood Jr., Bernard Spilka, Bruce Hunsberger, and Richard Gorsuch, *The Psychology of Religion: An Empirical Approach* (New York: Guilford, 1996), 268.

17. Lewis L. Rambo, *Understanding Religious Conversion* (New Haven, CT: Yale University Press, 1993). See also Eugene V. Gallagher, "Conversion," in *Encyclopedia of Millennialism and Millennial Movements*, ed. Richard Landes (New York: Routledge, 2000), 109.

18. Hood et al., *Psychology of Religion.* See also Rambo, *Understanding Religious Conversion.*

19. Brian J. Zinnbauer and Kenneth I. Pargament, "Spiritual Conversion: A Study of Religious Change among College Students," *Journal for the Scientific Study of Religion* 31, no. 1 (1998): 162.

20. Willem Kox, Wim Meeus, and Harm't Hart, "Religious Conversion of Adolescents," *Sociological Analysis* 52, no. 3 (1991): 227–40. A study comparing adolescent converts to a Pentecostal group with matched controls found that 67 percent of converts reported having problems within three to five years before converting, as compared to 20 percent of the nonconverts. More converts also told of a major life stress before their conversion. Compare to *Cults: Faith, Healing and Coercion* (New York: Oxford University Press, 1999) Marc Galanter found significantly higher levels of emotional distress just prior to conversion in those joining the Unification Church.

21. Raymond F. Paloutzian, "Religious Conversion and Spiritual Transformation," in *Handbook of Psychology of Religion and Spirituality*, ed. Raymond F. Paloutzian and Crystal L. Park (New York: Guilford Press, 2005), 336.

22. Rambo, *Understanding Religious Conversion.* See also A. Mahoney and K. Pargament, "Sacred Changes: Spiritual Conversion and Transformation," *Journal of Clinical Psychology* 60, no. 5 (2004): 481–92; and K. Pargament, *The Psychology of Religious Coping* (New York: Guilford Press, 1997). However, see also David G. Bromley and Anson D. Shupe, "Just a Few Years Seem Like a Lifetime," in *Research in Social Movements, Conflicts, and Change*, vol. 2, ed. Lewis Kriesberg (Greenwich, CT: JAI Press, 1979), 159–85; and H. Gooren, "Reassessing Conventional Approaches to Conversion: Toward a New Synthesis," *Journal for the Scientific Study of Religion* 46, no. 3 (2007): 337–53.

23. Allen E. Bergin, "Values and Religious Issues in Psychotherapy and Mental Health," *American Psychologist* 46, no. 4 (1991): 401.

24. Benjamin Beit-Hallahmi, "Death, Fantasy, and Religious Transformations," in *The Psychology of Death in Fantasy and History*, ed. Jerry S. Piven (London: Greenwood, 2004), 87–114.

25. Carol Mason, *Killing for Life: The Apocalyptic Narrative of Pro-Life Politics* (Ithaca, NY: Cornell University Press, 2002).

26. Strozier, *Apocalypse*, 76, 81. Strozier describes Monroe's vision of the millennium as "a kind of Christian Wall Street," where productivity will be optimal and the GNP will be "astounding" (75). He remarks that "the concept of the millennium . . . lends itself to highly subjective constructions, since it is not literally biblical . . . [meaning it] is nowhere explicitly described in the Bible" (75).

27. Ibid., 46, 55, 23.

28. Lifton, *Destroying the Earth*, 78, 72, 73.

CHAPTER 5

1. See Terman, chapter 2.

2. In *Empire of Conspiracy* (Ithaca, NY: Cornell University Press, 2000) Timothy Melley, although questioning who has the right to categorize whom, notes that the psychology of seeing oneself the victim of malevolent forces beyond one's control is a common cognitive organization spanning the political and social spectrum in the United States in the past half-century. He attributes the prevalence of this way of thinking to the real challenges to the liberal conception of humans as autonomous individuals who can determine their own destiny. The experience of social and technological change has been perceived as a lethal threat to this central and highly valued self-concept, and this has given rise to the feeling of malevolent manipulation. This is certainly consistent with the idea that the paranoid gestalt is stimulated by the perception of threats to one's psychological existence, for such forces do threaten the death of the self as we have known it. Melley writes, "Together, these studies suggest that the rise of conspiracy and paranoia as major themes in late-twentieth-century American culture is connected to changing social and technological conditions and to new conceptions of human subjectivity. The numerous narratives that grapple with these challenges are often conflicted in their attempts to represent social control while defending a fantasy of individual autonomy and distinctness. With their intimations of conspiracy, their interpretive uncertainties, and their curious expressions of paranoia, these texts register serious cultural concerns about the power and autonomy of persons" (44).

3. The earliest example of the paranoid gestalt in an organized social and political group may be found in the reign of Akhenaten, the eighteenth-dynasty pharaoh of Egypt. Akhenaten has been the subject of many interpretations. For a thorough and nuanced discussion of the way he has been understood at various points in modern history, see Dominic Montserrat, *Akhenaten, History, Fantasy and Ancient Egypt* (London: Routledge, 2000). His utopian perfection was a new religion of one god, the sun. Though researchers in the late nineteenth century and early twentieth considered it the earliest form of monotheism, subsequent scholarship has shown that it was the further deification of the pharaoh himself. The work of Donald Redford, *Akhenaten: The Heretic King* (Princeton, NJ: Princeton University Press, 1984) and others emphasize the self-deification of the Aten revolution. An integral part of the process of establishing the sun and himself as the central gods of Egypt was the erasure of all the images of Amun (the prevailing cult with its multiple gods, Amun chief among them) from every building and monument in Egypt. The task was so vast that armies had to be withdrawn from the borders of the empire, a move that greatly weakened the country. The completion of the paranoid gestalt paradigm

would require that Amun was regarded as the evil other. We know of the actions of Akhenaten and his court, and their actions are certainly suggestive of a paranoid gestalt, but we do not know the attitude with which they struck out those images. However, Egyptians did believe that striking out the image-name was the same as murdering the person. The zeal with which the hieroglyphs were effaced and the thoroughness of the effacement (the soldiers searched out all private as well as public monuments) suggest enormous animus that was likely equivalent to the status of evil other. If Amun were indeed the evil other to them, this would be the first such instance of a universal human tendency that is not confined to the twentieth century or even to modernity. Since the paranoid gestalt did clearly appear in 95 with the writing of the Book of Revelation (see the discussion below and in chapter 10), it seems to be a universal way that human beings and human societies organize in the face of challenges to their essential group self. We may be able to infer that the Manichaean dichotomy was part of the Egyptian group self *of Akhenaten and his court if not of the population in general*. The confinement of the movement to the court was likely responsible for the fact that it did not outlive Akhenaten. For further discussion of the effect of Akhenaten's revolution, see Robert Ritner, *The Mechanics of Ancient Egyptian Magical Practice* (Chicago: Oriental Institute, 1993). We do not know what challenges would have led to the creation of such a gestalt by the eighteenth-dynasty pharaoh.

4. See Jordan, chapter 14 for an extensive description and discussion of the French Revolution. Jordan is reluctant to label either the Terror or the decision to go to war as an outcome of the paranoid gestalt because of the presence of real enemies of the Revolution. However, the presence or absence of real threats does not determine whether the gestalt is the guiding cognitive structure of the group. The rumor at the beginning of the Revolution (and indeed all through it), the Great Fear, and the Terror fully demonstrate all the characteristics that I have described here.

5. See Redles, chapter 13 for a discussion of the millennialism of the Third Reich.

6. Norman Cohn, *The Pursuit of the Millennium* (New York: Harper and Row, 1961).

7. David Terman, "Anti-Semitism: A Study in Group Vulnerability and the Vicissitudes of Group Ideals," *Psychohistory Review* 12 (1984): 18–24.

8. Rosemary Ruether, *Faith and Fratricide* (New York: Seabury Press, 1974). Ruether's discussion of the origins of Christian anti-Semitism extensively chronicles the attitudes and writings of the early Church fathers in the milieu of the competition between Judaism and early Christianity in the Roman Empire.

9. Richard Hofstadter, *The Paranoid Style in American Politics* (Cambridge, MA: Harvard University Press, 1965).

10. See Jones, chapter 9 for a discussion of an important aspect of contemporary American Christian fundamentalism.

11. Jones, chapter 9.

12. See Terman, chapter 2 for an extended discussion of the history of psychoanalytic hypotheses about paranoia.

13. Heinz Kohut, "Thoughts on Narcissism and Narcissistic Rage," in *Psychoanalytic Study of the Child*, vol. 27, New York: Quadrangle New York Times Books, 1972), 360–400.

14. For an additional discussion of narcissistic rage, see David Terman, "Aggression and Narcissistic Rage: A Clinical Elaboration," *Annual of Psychoanalysis* 3 (1975): 239–55.

15. Kohut, "Thoughts on Narcissism," 396.

16. Ernest Wolf, *Treating the Self* (New York: Guilford Press, 1988).

17. See Heinz Kohut, *The Analysis of the Self* (New York: International Universities Press, 1971).

18. For additional evidence of the role of conspicuous and public humiliation in the genesis of extreme violence in individuals, see Muenster and Lotto, chapter 7, in which they cite studies that show the importance and ubiquity of such experience in the histories of mass murderers. Muenster and Lotto also discuss the importance of humiliation in general in the social context. The parameters of social humiliation are virtually isomorphic with the factors involved in individual humiliation. The greater power of the group in relation to the individual member is analogous to the psychological position of the parent in development, for example. They too note the importance of the helplessness of the individual to effect a response to the exposure of weakness as a factor that engenders the experience of humiliation.

19. *Negative selfobject* refers to the seamless molding of the self by responses of the caretaker that are angry, judgmental, and demeaning that become an intrinsic part of the way one experiences oneself. Because of the way the child is made by the affective responses of the caretaker in which there is no choosing the affect of the responder, the child is involuntarily molded and knows that about himself or herself with certainty.

20. The power of narcissistic injury is impressively documented in Jack Katz, *Seductions of Crime* (New York: Basic Books, 1988). There he describes one result of narcissistic injury and narcissistic rage: murder. In a section titled "Righteous Slaughter" he describes three elements that are present in such a situation: "1. The would-be killer . . . must understand not only that the victim is attacking what he, the killer, regards as an *eternal human value*, but that the situation requires a last stand in defense of his *basic worth* [my emphasis]. 2. He must transform *an eternally humiliating situation* into a rage. In rage, the killer can blind himself to his future, forging a momentary sense of eternal unity with the Good. 3. . . . The project is the honoring of the offense that he suffered through a marking violently drawn into the body of the victim" (18–19). Katz notes that this kind of murder mostly occurs in the working and lower classes, where there is "a convergent disrespect in a person's occupation and intimate life" (45). The narcissistic vulnerability and injury, in a word, the humiliation the killer experiences in so many areas of his life leaves him no escape, and with his basic sense of dignity and self-respect damaged he kills in the name of his values to reestablish his dignity, which is also his righteousness. He wipes out the offense to his pride. Katz also notes, "The situations from which righteous slaughters emerge are either conventionally humiliating or involve the victim's self-conscious efforts to ridicule or degrade, or include the assailant's perception that the victim's actions are defiant and disrespectful" (22).

21. See Terman, chapter 2 for a review of psychoanalytic theories of paranoia. Sullivan's seminal idea of the centrality of inferiority and defect is further elaborated by David Shapiro, "Paranoia from a Characterological Standpoint," *Paranoia: New Psychoanalytic Perspectives*, ed. John M. Oldham and Stanley Bose (Madison, CT:

International Universities Press, 1994), who also emphasizes the centrality of issues of self-esteem and the secondary place of projection in the genesis of paranoia.

22. Heinz Kohut, "Creativeness, Charisma, Group Psychology: Reflections on the Self-Analysis of Freud," in *Self Psychology and the Humanities*, ed. Charles Strozier (New York: Norton, 1985). See also the discussion of the group self in Terman, chapter 2.

23. I am aware that there are various kinds of large groups: social, political, ethnic, national, religious, and so on. Though there are particular differences that define each kind of group, I believe they share the structure of a group self in order to be a group at all, either to its members or to those outside it. George De Vos in "Ethnic Pluralism: Conflict and Accommodation," in *Ethnic Identity*, ed. George De Vos and Lola Romanucci-Ross (Palo Alto, CA: Mayfield, 1975), describes ethnicity as "a feeling of continuity with the past": "Ethnicity is also intimately related to the individual need for a collective continuity" (17). Ethnicity is also a sense of sharing a particular ancestry, origin, and religion or customs. All these qualities of ethnicity are central aspects of the nature of groups. Nations, on the other hand, are often collections of ethnic groups, but as they have group selves they too share histories, goals, and ideals. In *Fantasy and Reality in History* (New York: Oxford University Press, 1995) Peter Loewenberg discusses the dynamics of nationalism and points to the factors of shared history, culture, and fate.

24. For a discussion of the work of Nehemia Friedland, see Terman, chapter 2.

25. Jack Katz, *Seductions of Crime* (New York: Basic Books, 1988). A full discussion of Katz is in note 20.

26. Heinz Kohut, "Forms and Transformations of Narcissism," *Journal of the American Psychoanalytic Association* 14 (April 1966): 243–72.

27. Volkan, *Bloodlines* (Boulder, CO: Westview Press, 1997). Volkan underlines the importance of what he calls the "ethnic tents," large group identities, in conflicts between groups and stresses the importance of maintaining the difference between groups and the pride they engender in their members.

28. Redles, chapter 13, eloquently describes the psychological state of many of the members of the military who later became Nazis. One referred to the "knocked down and prone Fatherland"; Another said, "As a Front-fighter the collapse of the Fatherland in November, 1918 was to me completely incomprehensible"; still another said, "I had believed adamantly in Germany's invincibility and now I only saw the country in its deepest humiliation—an entire world fell to the ground."

29. See Bernard Lewis, *The Crisis of Islam* (New York: Random House, 2004), and *What Went Wrong? Western Impact and Middle Eastern Response* (New York: Oxford University Press, 2002).

30. Jordan, chapter 14, discusses these phenomena as they apply to the French Revolution. An analogous collapse of guiding ideals is documented by Redles, chapter 13. He describes many German veterans of World War I having the feeling that the ideals that guided them and in which they believed were destroyed by the war and the chaos of the Weimar Republic.

31. Farhad Khosrokhavar, *Quand Al-Qaida Parle: Temoignages derriere les barreaux* (Paris: Bernard Grasset, 2006): "La chute du communism et la desparition d'un ennemi interne ont fait naître chez certains un profound sentiment d'oppression dû à l'absence d'alternative dans un univers où les individues se sentient démunis et

livrés à eux-mêmes. Ils décovrent dans l'islam un principe de dignité, d'opposition à l'Occident et dépassement de la peur face à la duplicité occidentale et à son incapacité à apporter une solution aux problemes soulevés en son sein" (326). ("The fall of communism and the disappearance of an internal enemy caused a deep feeling of oppression among some people due to the absence of an alternative in a universe where they feel deprived and left to themselves. They discover in Islam a principle of dignity, of opposition to the West, and an overcoming of their fear in the face of Western dishonesty and their own inability to find a solution to problems stirred up in their own beings" [my translation].)

32. Thomas Frank, *What's the Matter with Kansas: How Conservatives Won the Heart of America* (New York: Henry Holt, 2005); Kevin Phillips, *American Theocracy: The Peril and Politics of Radical Religion, Oil and Borrowed Money in the 21st Century* (New York: Viking Adult, 2006).

33. Khosrokhavar, *Quand Al-Qaida Parle*, and see Khosrokhavar's extensive discussion in chapter 12 of the transmutation of personal experience of humiliation into the identification with the humiliation and revenge embodied in the jihadi movement.

34. Eric Hoffer, in his classic and prescient work, *The True Believer: Thoughts on the Nature of Mass Movements* (New York: Perennial Classics, 1951), outlined many of these issues.

35. Raphael Ezekial, *The Racist Mind* (New York: Viking Press, 1993).

36. See McLane, chapter 15, for detailed discussions of V. D. Savarkar and the Hindutva movement in India.

37. See Strozier, chapter 10.

38. Ruether, *Faith and Fratricide.*

39. Charles Strozier, *Apocalypse: On the Psychology of Fundamentalism in America* (Boston: Beacon Press, 1994).

CHAPTER 6

1. Richard Hofstadter, "The Paranoid Style in American Politics," in *The Paranoid Style, and Other Essays* (Chicago: University of Chicago Press, 1964), 3–40.

2. Sigmund Freud, "Psycho-analytic Notes on an Autobiographical Account of a Case of Paranoia (Dementia Paranoides)," in *The Standard Edition of the Complete Psychoanalytical Works of Sigmund Freud*, vol. 12, ed. James Strachey, 23 vols. (London: Hogarth Press, 1958), 3–84.

3. Jerrold M. Post, ed., *The Psychological Evaluation of Political Leaders: With Profiles of Saddam Hussein and Bill Clinton* (Lansing: University of Michigan Press, 2003); Jerrold M. Post, *Leaders and Their Followers in a Dangerous World: The Psychology of Political Behavior* (Ithaca, NY: Cornell University Press, 2004); Barry R. Schneider and Jerrold M. Post, eds., *Know Thy Enemy: Profiles of Adversary Leaders and Their Strategic Cultures* (Maxwell Airforce Base, AL: USAF Counterproliferation Center, 2003). Vamik Volkan, *Bloodlines: From Ethnic Pride to Ethnic Terrorism* (Boulder, CO: Westview Press, 1999); Vamik Volkan, *Killing in the Name of Identity: A Study of Bloody Conflicts* (Baltimore: Pitchstone Publishing, 2006). Joseph H. Berke, Stella Pierides, Andrea Sabbadini, and Stanley Schneider, *Even Paranoids Have Enemies: New Perspectives on Paranoia and Persecution* (New York: Routledge, 1998). Note as

well some interesting materials in Robert S. Robbins and Jerrold M. Post, *Political Paranoia: The Psychopolitics of Hatred* (New Haven, CT: Yale University Press, 1997). Robert Jay Lifton, *The Broken Connection: On Death and the Continuity of Life* (New York: Basic Books, 1979). This is Lifton's most theoretical book, but there is much of great interest on fundamentalism, violence, and paranoia in the twenty-six volumes he has written or edited thus far. Strozier, *Apocalypse: On the Psychology of Fundamentalism in America* (Eugene, OR: Wipf and Stock, 1994); Strozier and Flynn, *Trauma and Self* (Lanham, MD: Roman and Littlefield, 1996); Strozier and Flynn, *The Year 2000* (New York: New York University Press, 1997); Strozier and Flynn, *Genocide, War, and Human Survival* (Lanham, MD: Roman and Littlefield, 1997).

4. Heinz Kohut, "Forms and Transformations of Narcissism," in *The Search for the Self: Selected Writings of Heinz Kohut: 1950–1978*, vol. 1, ed. Paul H. Ornstein, 4 vols. (New York: International Universities Press, 1978), 427–60. See also my biography of Kohut, *Heinz Kohut: The Making of a Psychoanalyst* (New York: Farrar, Straus and Giroux, 2001).

5. Hofstadter, "The Paranoid Style," 35–37.

6. Charles B. Strozier, "Apocalyptic Violence and the Politics of Waco," in Strozier and Flynn, *The Year 2000*, 97–111.

7. Robert Jay Lifton, *The Nazi Doctors: Medical Killing and the Psychology of Genocide* (New York: Basic Books, 1985); Robert Jay Lifton, *Destroying the World to Save It: Aum Shinrikyo, Apocalyptic Violence, and the New Global Terrorism* (New York: Metropolitan Books, 1999).

8. Tim LaHaye and Jerry B. Jenkins, *Left Behind: A Novel of the Earth's Last Days* (1996); *Tribulation Force: The Continuing Force of Those Left Behind* (1997); *Nicolae: The Rise of Antichrist* (1998); *Soul Harvest: The World Takes Sides* (1999); *Apollyon: The Destroyer Is Released* (2000); *Assassins: Assignment: Jerusalem, Target* (2000); *Antichrist* (2001); *The Indwelling: The Beast Takes Possession* (2001); *The Mark: The Beast Rules the World; Desecration* (2001); *Antichrist Takes the Throne* (2001); *Glorious Appearing: The End of Days* (2004); *Armageddon* (2004). All from Carol Stream, IL: Tyndale House. See also Glenn Shuck, *Marks of the Beast: The Left Behind Novels and the Struggle for Evangelical Identity* (New York: New York University Press, 2004). James W. Jones is writing a psychological study of the series; see "The Divine Terrorist," paper presented at the Psychology of Fundamentalism conference, Chicago Institute for Psychoanalysis, February 24, 2006.

9. Jacques Derrida, Pascale-Anne Brault, and Michael Naas, *The Work of Mourning* (Chicago: University of Chicago Press, 2003); Paul Virilio and Chris Turner, *Ground Zero* (London: Verso, 2005); Giovanni Borradori, *Philosophy in a Time of Terror: Dialogues with Jürgen Habermas and Jacques Derrida* (Chicago: University of Chicago Press, 2004).

10. See my chapter, "The History of American Endism," in Strozier, *Apocalypse*, 167–93.

11. Catherine Keller, *Apocalypse Now and Then* (Boston: Beacon Press, 1997), xi–xiv.

12. Lois Ann Lorentzen, "Phallic Millennialism and Radical Environmentalism: The Apocalyptic Vision of Earth First!," in Strozier and Flynn, *The Year 2000*, 144–53. See also Bron Taylor, "Green Apocalypticism: Understanding Disaster in the Radical Environmental Worldview," *Society and Natural Resources* 12, no. 4 (1999): 377–86;

Bron Taylor, "The Tributaries of Radical Environmentalism," *Journal for the Study of Radicalism* 2, no. 1 (2008): 27–61.

13. John Mack, *Abduction: Human Encounters with Aliens* (New York: Ballantine Books, 1995).

14. Jürgen Moltmann, *Theology of Hope* (New York: Harper and Row, 1967); Keller, *Apocalypse Now and Then.*

15. Robert Jay Lifton, *Home from the War: Learning from Vietnam Veterans* (Boston: Beacon Press, 1973), 65.

16. Robert Jay Lifton, *Thought Reform and the Psychology of Totalism: A Study of "Brainwashing" in China* (New York: Norton, 1961), 433–37. Here Lifton writes of the "dispensing of existence" as central to what he calls "thought reform."

17. Lifton, *The Broken Connection*, 369.

18. Michael Scheuer, the author of *Imperial Hubris: Why the West Is Losing the War on Terrorism* (Dulles, VA: Potomac Books, 2004), revealed later in the year that he published his book the quite remarkable fatwa that bin Laden sought from a radical Saudi sheik after the September 11 attacks. Scheuer was the senior intelligence analyst at the CIA in the latter part of the 1990s. He headed the secret group of analysts following bin Laden then and for several years after September 11, 2001. Shortly after his resignation from the CIA he appeared on *60 Minutes*, the CBS news program (November 14, 2004), where he said two things about bin Laden and nuclear weapons. He confirmed how serious had been the efforts of bin Laden before the September 11 attacks to acquire weapons of mass destruction. And he reported that in the period after the attacks, in part responding to criticism from some in the Muslim world regarding the killing of Muslim civilians, bin Laden sought and secured a fatwa from Hamid bin Fahd in May 2003 that specifically allowed for the use of nuclear weapons against Americans.

CHAPTER 7

1. N. R. Kleinfield, "Before Deadly Rage, a Life Consumed by a Troubling Silence," *New York Times*, April 22, 2007.

2. Interview with Osama bin Laden, *Frontline*, PBS, May 1998, p. 5, retrieved August 30, 2008 from www.pbs.org/wgbh/pages/frontline/shows/binladen/who/interview.html.

3. Mark R. Leary, Robin M. Kowalski, Laura Smith, and Stephen Phillips, "Teasing, Rejection, and Violence: Case Studies of the School Shootings," *Aggressive Behavior* 29 (2003): 213. Even though a history of depression was cited as a factor in many school shootings, it is doubtful that any shooter acted out during a depressive episode. In light of these and other data clearly showing males as having a predominant role in perpetrating violence, we refer to victims and perpetrators as male. In doing so we by no means intend to claim that females do not commit violent acts.

4. Bert R. Brown, "The Effects of Need to Maintain Face on Interpersonal Bargaining," *Journal of Experimental Social Psychology* 4 (1968): 107–22.

5. Roy F. Baumeister, *Evil: Inside Human Violence and Cruelty* (New York: W. H. Freeman, 1996).

6. Avishai Margalit, *The Decent Society* (Cambridge, MA: Harvard University Press, 1996), 85.

7. Mark Danner, *Torture and Truth: America, Abu Ghraib, and the War on Terror* (New York: New York Review of Books, 2004); James Gilligan, *Violence: Reflections on a National Epidemic* (New York: Vintage Books, 1997); Linda M. Hartling and Tracy Luchetta, "Humiliation: Assessing the Impact of Derision, Degradation, and Debasement," *Journal of Primary Prevention* 19, no. 4 (1999): 259–78; William I. Miller, *Humiliation and Other Essays on Honor, Social Discomfort, and Violence* (Ithaca, NY: Cornell University Press, 1993).

8. Gilligan, *Violence*, 110, 96.

9. Donald C. Klein, "Managing Humiliation," *Journal of Primary Prevention* 12, no. 3 (1992): 255–68; Miller, *Humiliation*; Margalit, *The Decent Society*; Jean T. Griffin, "Racism and Humiliation in the African-American Community," *Journal of Primary Prevention* 12, no. 2 (1991): 149–67.

10. Mark A. Jackson, "Distinguishing Shame and Humiliation," *Dissertation Abstracts International: Section B: The Sciences and Engineering* 61, no. 4-B (2000): 2

11. Paul Gilbert, "Shame and Humiliation in the Treatment of Complex Cases," in *Treating Complex Cases: The Cognitive Behavioral Therapy Approach*, ed. N. Tarrier (New York: Wiley, 1998), 241–71; Heinz Kohut, "Thoughts on Narcissism and Narcissistic Rage," *Psychoanalytic Study of the Child* 27 (1972): 360–400.

12. Maury Silver, Rosario Conte, Maria Miceli, and Isabella Poggi, "Humiliation: Feeling, Social Control and the Construction of Identity," *Journal for the Theory of Social Behavior* 16, no. 3 (1986): 269–83.

13. Carolyn F. Swift, "Some Issues in Inter-gender Humiliation," *Journal of Primary Prevention* 12, no. 2 (1991): 123–47; Thomas J. Scheff, *Bloody Revenge: Emotions, Nationalism, and War* (Boulder, CO: Westview Press, 1994).

14. Miller, *Humiliation*.

15. Gilbert, "Shame and Humiliation," 262.

16. Baumeister, *Evil*

17. Jeanne S. Zechmeister, Sofia Garcia, Catherine Romero, and Shona N. Vas, "Don't Apologize Unless You Mean It: A Laboratory Investigation of Forgiveness and Retaliation," *Journal of Social and Clinical Psychology* 23, no. 4 (2004): 532–64.

18. Brian M. Quigley and James T. Tedeschi, "Mediating Effects of Blame Attributions on Feelings of Anger," *Personality and Social Psychology Bulletin* 22, no. 12 (1996): 1281.

19. Jennifer R. Dunn and Maurice E. Schweitzer, "Feeling and Believing: The Influence of Emotion on Trust," *Journal of Personality and Social Psychology* 88, no. 5 (2005): 736–48.

20. Gilbert, "Shame and Humiliation," 260. This type of reasoning also provides a logical explanation for the adaptive value of both shame and guilt if they are acknowledged either privately or openly. It becomes evident that the exclusionary purpose of humiliation cannot possibly have any adaptive value for the victim since chances of survival are contingent on social inclusion.

21. Mark R. Leary, Jean M. Twenge, and Erin Quinlivan, "Interpersonal Rejection as a Determinant of Anger and Aggression," *Personality and Social Psychology Review* 10, no. 2 (2006): 111.

22. Wendi L. Gardner, Cynthia L. Pickett, and Marilynn B. Brewer, "Social Exclusion and Selective Memory: How the Need to Belong Influences Memory for Social Events," *Personality and Social Psychology Bulletin* 26, no. 4 (2000): 486–96.

23. Geoff MacDonald and Mark R. Leary, "Why Does Social Exclusion Hurt? The Relationship between Social and Physical Pain," *Psychological Bulletin* 131, no. 2 (2005): 214.

24. C. Nathan DeWall and Roy F. Baumeister, "Alone but Feeling No Pain: Effects of Social Exclusion on Physical Pain Tolerance and Pain Threshold, Affective Forecasting, and Interpersonal Empathy," *Journal of Personality and Social Psychology* 91, no. 1 (2006): 11.

25. MacDonald and Leary, "Why Does Social Exclusion Hurt?" 214; Daniel M. Heiser, "A Study of Fundamentalism and Cognitive Complexity among Undergraduate Studies at a Fundamentalist College," *Dissertation Abstracts International: Section B: The Sciences and Engineering* 66, no. 2-B (2005): 1172.

26. DeWall and Baumeister, "Alone but Feeling No Pain."

27. Stanley Budner, "Intolerance of Ambiguity as a Personal Variable," *Journal of Personality* 30, no. 1 (1962): 2, 16.

28. Albert Bandura, Claudio Barbaranelli, Gian Vittorio Caprara, and Concetta Pastorelli, "Mechanisms of Moral Disengagement in the Exercise of Moral Agency," *Journal of Personality and Social Psychology* 71, no. 2 (1996): 364. Not surprisingly males were shown to exhibit higher levels of moral disengagement than females.

29. Jean M. Twenge, Liqing Zhang, Kathleen R. Catanese, Brenda Dolan-Pascoe, Leif F. Lyche, and Roy F. Baumeister, "Reminders of Social Activity Reduce Aggression after Social Exclusion," *British Journal of Social Psychology* 46 (2007): 205–24.

30. Kohut, "Thoughts on Narcissism and Narcissistic Rage," 380.

31. Heinz Kohut, *Self Psychology and the Humanities: Reflections on a New Psychoanalytic Approach*, ed. Charles B. Strozier (New York: Norton, 1985).

32. See Terman, chapter 5, for his elaboration of these ideas.

33. Karl Aquino, Robert J. Bies, and Thomas M. Tripp, "Getting Even or Moving On? Power, Procedural Justice, and Types of Offense as Predictors of Revenge, Forgiveness, Reconciliation, and Avoidance in Organizations," *Journal of Applied Psychology* 91, no. 3 (2006): 653–68.

34. Zechmeister et al., "Don't Apologize Unless You Mean It."

35. Ibid.

CHAPTER 8

1. Charles B. Strozier, *Apocalypse: On the Psychology of Fundamentalism in America* (Boston: Beacon Press, 1994).

2. James W. Jones, *Terror and Transformation* (New York: Taylor and Francis, 2002).

3. See Allan N. Schore, *Affect Regulation and the Origin of the Self: The Neurobiology of Emotional Development* (Hillsdale, NJ: Lawrence Erlbaum, 1994); Daniel J. Siegel, *The Developing Mind* (New York: Guilford Press, 1999); Peter Fonagy, Gyorgy Gergely, Elliot Jurist, and Mary Target, *Affect Regulation, Mentalization, and the Development of the Self* (New York: Other Press, 2002).

4. See L. Allan Sroufe, *Emotional Development: The Organization of Emotional Life in the Early Years* (New York: Cambridge University Press, 1996); Schore, *Affect Regulation*.

5. Schore, *Affect Regulation*; Siegel, *Developing Mind*.

6. John Bowlby, *Attachment and Loss*, vol. 1: *Attachment* (New York: Basic Books, 1969); John Bowlby, *A Secure Base*, 2nd ed. (New York: Basic Books, 1988).

7. Myron A. Hofer, "Hidden Regulators: Implications for a New Understanding of Attachment, Separation and Loss," in *Attachment Theory: Social, Developmental and Clinical Perspectives*, ed. Susan Goldberg, Roy Muir, and John Kerr (Hillsdale, NJ: Analytic Press, 1995), 203–30; Sroufe, *Emotional Development*; L. Allan Sroufe and Everett Waters, "Attachment as an Organizational Construct," *Child Development* 48 (1977): 1184–99; Judith R. Schore and Allan N. Schore, "Modern Attachment Theory: The Central Role of Affect Regulation in Development and Treatment," *Clinical Social Work Journal* 36 (2008): 9–20.

8. Fonagy et al., *Affect Regulation*; John G. Allen, Peter Fonagy, and Anthony Bateman, *Mentalizing in Clinical Practice* (Washington, DC: American Psychiatric Press, 2008).

9. Peter Fonagy, *Attachment and Psychoanalysis* (New York: Other Press, 2007), 169.

10. Schore, *Affect Regulation and the Origin of the Self.*

11. Fonagy, *Attachment and Psychoanalysis*, 85.

12. Mario Mikulincer and Philip R. Shaver, *Attachment in Adulthood* (New York: Guilford Press, 2007); Andrew Stevens, *Archetypes: A Natural History of the Self* (New York: Braziller, 1982); Michael J. Garanzini, *The Attachment Cycle: An Object Relations Approach to the Healing Ministries* (Mahwah, NJ: Paulist Press, 1988); Lee A. Kirkpatrick, "An Attachment Theory Approach to the Psychology of Religion," *International Journal for the Psychology of Religion* 2 (1992): 1–31; Lee A. Kirkpatrick, "Attachment Theory and Religions Experience," in *Handbook of Religious Experience*, ed. R. W. Hood Jr. (Birmingham, AL: Religion Education Press, 1995), 446–75; Antti Oksanen, *Religious Conversion: A Meta-Analytical Study* (Lund, Sweden: Lund University Press, 1994); Bruce D. Reed, *The Dynamics of Religion: Process and Movement in Christian Churches* (London: Darton, Longman and Todd, 1978); Brant Wenegrat, *The Divine Archetype: The Sociobiology and the Psychology of Religion* (Lexington, KY: Lexington Books, 1990); Lee A. Kirkpatrick, *Attachment, Evolution, and the Psychology of Religion* (New York: Guilford Press, 2005), 56; Mary Ainsworth, "Attachments across the Life Span," *Bulletin of the New York Academy of Medicine* 61(1985): 792–812.

13. Peter Benson and Bernard Spilka, "God Image as a Function of Self-esteem and Locus of Control," *Journal for the Scientific Study of Religion* 12 (1973): 297–310.

CHAPTER 9

Sections of this chapter are taken from James W. Jones, *Blood That Cries Out from the Earth: The Psychology of Religious Terrorism* (New York: Oxford University Press, 2008) and are here used with permission.

1. Christopher Filley et al., "Toward an Understanding of Violence: Neurobiological Aspects of Unwarranted Physical Aggression: Aspen Neurobehavioral Conference Consensus Statement," *Neuropsychiatry, Neuropsychology, and Behavioral Neurology* 14, no. 1 (2001):1–14.

2. Terry Levy and Michael Orlans, "Kids Who Kill: Attachment Disorder, Antisocial Personality, and Violence," *Forensic Examiner* 8, nos. 3–4 (1999): 19–24; Andrew Hill-Smith, Pippa Hugo, Patricia Hughes, Peter Fonagy, and David Hartman,

"Adolescent Murderers: Abuse and Adversity in Childhood," *Journal of Adolescence* 25, no. 2 (2002): 221–30.

3. Herbert Thomas, "Experiencing a Shame Response as a Precursor to Violence," *Bulletin of the American Academy of Psychiatry and the Law* 23, no. 4 (1995): 587–93; James Gilligan, *Violence: Reflections on a National Epidemic* (New York: Random House, 1997).

4. Brad Bushman and Roy Baumeister, "Does Self-love or Self-hate Lead to Violence?," *Journal of Research in Personality* 36, no. 6 (2002): 543–45.

5. James Waller, *Becoming Evil* (New York: Oxford University Press, 2002).

6. Kevin Browne and Catherine Hamilton-Giachritsis, "The Influence of Violent Media on Children and Adolescents: A Public-Health Approach," *The Lancet* 365, no. 9460 (2005): 702–10; Cecillie Gaziano, "Toward a Broader Conceptual Framework for Research on Social Stratification, Childrearing Patterns, and Media Effects," *Mass Communication and Society* 4, no. 2 (2001): 219–44; Christine Kiewitz and James Weaver, "Trait Aggressiveness, Media Violence, and Perceptions of Interpersonal Conflict," *Personality and Individual Differences* 31, no. 6 (2001): 821–35; Brad Bushman and Craig Anderson, "Media Violence and the American Public: Scientific Facts versus Media Misinformation," *American Psychologist* 56, nos. 6–7 (2001): 477–89.

7. Bushman and Anderson, "Media Violence," 477.

8. Bruce Bartholow, Marc Sestir, and Edward Davis, "Correlates and Consequences of Exposure to Video Game Violence: Hostile Personality, Empathy, and Aggressive Behavior," *Personality and Social Psychology Bulletin* 31, no. 11 (2005): 1573–86; Nicholas L. Carnagey and Craig A. Anderson, "Violent Video Game Exposure and Aggression: A Literature Review," *Minerva Psichiatrica* 45, no. 1 (2004): 1–18. Craig Anderson, "An Update on the Effects of Playing Violent Video Games," *Journal of Adolescence* 27 (2004): 113–22. On the other side Gee and others argue that video games can provide a positive learning experience. See James Paul Gee, *Why Video Games Are Good for Your Soul: Pleasure and Learning* (New York: Common Ground, 2005); Lawrence Kutner and Cheryl Olson, *Grand Theft Childhood* (New York: Simon and Schuster, 2008); Cheryl Olson, Lawrence Kutner, and Eugene Beresin, "Children and Video Games: How Much Do We Know?," *Psychiatric Times* 24, no. 12 (2007): 1–2; Cheryl Olson, "Media Violence Research and Youth Violence Data: Why Do They Conflict?," *Academic Psychiatry* 28, no. 2 (2004): 144–50; C. J. Ferguson, "The Good, the Bad and the Ugly: A Meta-analytic Review of Positive and Negative Effects of Violent Video Games," *Psychiatric Quarterly* 78, no. 4 (2007): 309–16. See also H. Polman, B. O. de Castro, and M. A. van Aken, "Experimental Study of the Differential Effects of Playing versus Watching Violent Video Games on Children's Aggressive Behavior," *Aggressive Behavior* 34, no. 3 (2008): 256–64, which argues that "after the active participation of actually playing the violent video game, boys behaved more aggressively" than those who only watched the game (256).

9. C. Anderson, "An Update," 113.

10. I have heard this claim stated in public several times but I have not found any reliable sources for it, so I repeat it with some hesitation. But there is no question that the military uses video games for training and recruitment. See http://archives.cnn.com/2001/TECH/ptech/11/22/war.games/index.html; www.wired.com/gaming/gamingreviews/news/2003/10/60688. Examples are games titled "Full Spectrum

Warrior" and "America's Army"; the latter is a first-person shooter game developed by the U.S. Army and marketed to both military personal and civilians. For a review, see http://dspace.mit.edu/handle/1721.1/39162. This review reports that the game is especially popular among American evangelicals and is used to recruit and train the military. See also http://blog.wired.com/defense/2008/07/army-wants-firs.html.

11. Quoted in Joyce M. Davis, *Martyrs: Innocence, Vengeance and Despair in the Middle East* (New York: Palgrave Macmillan, 2003), 154.

12. Gilligan, *Violence*; William Miller, *Humiliation and Other Essays on Honor, Social Discomfort, and Violence* (Ithaca, NY: Cornell University Press, 1993). See also Terman, chapter 5.

13. Nancy Ammerman, "Accounting for Christian Fundamentalism," in *Accounting for Fundamentalisms*, ed. Martin Marty and R. Scott Appleby (Chicago: University of Chicago Press, 1994), 153.

14. Quoted in Fathali Moghaddam, "The Staircase to Terrorism: A Psychological Exploration," *American Psychologist* 60, no. 2 (2005):165.

15. Robert J. Lifton, *Destroying the World to Save It* (New York: Henry Holt, 2000), 56, 60.

16. Paul Hill, "Mix My Blood with Blood of the Unborn," www.armyofgod.com, 8 (accessed April 17, 2006).

17. Mark Juergensmeyer, *Terror in the Mind of God* (Berkeley: University of California Press, 2000), 151. This is one of the ways religiously motivated terrorists fit Terman's model of the "paranoid gestalt" (chapter 5) and Strozier's image of the "apocalyptic other" (chapter 6).

18. Beth Brokaw and Keith Edwards, "There Is a Relationship of God Image to Level of Object Relations Development," *Journal of Psychology and Theology* 22, no. 4 (1994): 352–71; Kathleen Spear, "Conscious and Pre-Conscious God Representations: An Object Relations Perspective" (PhD diss., Fuller Theological Seminary, 1994); Theresa Tisdale, "A Comparison of Jewish, Muslim, and Protestant Faith Groups on the Relationship between Level of Object Relations Development and Experience of God and Self" (PhD diss., Rosemead Graduate School, 1997).

19. Ivan Strenski, "Sacrifice, Gift, and the Social Logic of Muslim 'Human Bombers,'" *Terrorism and Political Violence* 15, no. 3 (2003): 1–34.

20. Nasra Hassan, "An Arsenal of Believers," *New Yorker*, November 19, 2001, 39.

21. Jones, *Blood That Cries.*

22. Jerrold Post, Ehud Sprinzak, and Laurita M. Denny, "The Terrorists in Their Own Words: Interviews with 35 Incarcerated Middle Eastern Terrorists," *Terrorism and Political Violence* 15, no. 1 (2003): 175, 179, 178, 179.

23. Photo in Scott Atran, "Genesis of Suicide Terrorism," *Science* 229, no. 5612 (2003): 1536.

24. Quoted in Bruce Hoffman, *Inside Terrorism* (New York: Columbia University Press, 2006), 240.

25. Kenneth Grossman, "View of God Can Predict Values and Politics," *USA Today*, www.usatoday.com/news/religion/2006–09–11-religion-survey_x.htm (accessed September 11, 2006).

26. "America's Evangelicals," *Religion and Ethics Newsweekly*, PBS episode 733, April 16, 2004. Text available at www.pbs.org/wnet/religionandethics/week733/

release.html. For a broader understanding of American evangelicalism, see Quinby, chapter 11.

27. Jon Pahl, "What's Behind Left Behind?," unpublished lecture, 2005, used with permission of the author.

28. Tim LaHaye and Jerry Jenkins, *Left Behind* (Wheaton, IL: Tyndale House, 1995), 29, 126, 207. This is the first book in the *Left Behind* series. For a broader discussion of this apocalyptic theology, see Strozier, chapters 6, 10.

29. Charles Strozier, *Apocalypse: On the Psychology of Fundamentalism in America* (Boston: Beacon Press, 1994), 147–48, 147.

30. Tim LaHaye and Jerry Jenkins, *Glorious Appearing* (Wheaton, IL: Tyndale House, 2004), 204. This is the final book in the *Left Behind* series. Subsequent quotations are cited parenthetically in the text. I include many quotations from that novel so that readers do not think I am selecting one or two particularly violent passages out of context simply to make a point, and I quote them without comment so readers can experience their full impact.

31. Strozier, *Apocalypse*, 165. See also chapters 6, 10.

32. Zack Pelta-Heller, "Kids Kill in Violent Christian Videogame," *AlterNet*, July 21, 2006, www.alternet.org/story/38873./%20%20%20Last (accessed July 1, 2008).

33. Ibid.

34. Left Behind Games website, *Left Behind Games Inc.*, www.leftbehindgames.com/pages/the_games.htm (accessed July 1, 2008).

35. Full disclosure requires that I note that both my wife and I have children living in SoHo, Uptown, and elsewhere in New York City, and the thought that Christian adolescents are practicing killing them, or their friends and neighbors—for many of the game's scenes show civilians, not just armed soldiers, being killed—is more than disgusting to me.

36. I could not find any psychological research that used "Eternal Forces" in a study of the effects of video violence, so I have no specific research proving the effects of this particular game. But given that it is designed to compete with and mimic other violent games, there is every reason to think the general research on this topic also applies here. There was a plan by an evangelical organization to send copies of "Eternal Forces" to soldiers serving in Iraq, but this was canceled when pressure was put on the Pentagon by several groups. See Schecter, Anna (2007–08–15), "DOD Stops Plan to Send Christian Video Game to Troops in Iraq" at http://blogs.abcnews.com/theblotter/2007/08/dod-stops-plan-.html (accessed 10/15/09). Given that it is being marketed through evangelical megachurches, I want to suggest a potentiated effect from playing this game in a religious context, where such violence is defended theologically.

37. Strozier, *Apocalypse*; Strozier, chapters 6, 10. See also Michael Barkum, *Disaster and the Millennium* (New Haven, CT: Yale University Press, 1974); Amy J. Frykholm, *Rapture Culture: Left Behind in Evangelical America* (New York: Oxford University Press, 2004); Terman, chapter 5.

38. Strozier, *Apocalypse*, 90.

39. Brokaw and Edwards "Relationship of God Image"; Jones, *Blood That Cries*; Tisdale, "A Comparison of Jewish, Muslim, and Protestant Faith."

40. Jones, *Blood That Cries*; James W. Jones, *Terror and Transformation: The Ambiguity of Religion in Psychoanalytic Perspective* (London: Routledge, 2002).

41. For further discussion of that possibility, see Jones, *Blood That Cries*; Strozier, *Apocalypse*.

CHAPTER 10

1. I witnessed this repeatedly in my fieldwork in churches in the late 1980s and early 1990s; see my *Apocalypse: On the Psychology of Fundamentalism in America* (Boston: Beacon Press, 1994).

2. All citations to the Book of Revelation are from the New Scofield Reference Bible of the King James Version, edited by C. I. Scofield, first published in 1909 and kept in print by Oxford University Press. The King James text is the one most commonly cited by fundamentalists themselves. The 1909 Scofield version broke the taboo of joining commentary directly to the text in the form of elaborate footnotes. These notes incorporated what was then some three-quarters of a century of fundamentalist theological thought about premillennial dispensationalism and the theory of inerrancy. The Scofield glosses on the text of Revelation, including the way John structured the headings and subheadings of the text itself, have influenced countless popularizers. It could well have been the most influential book in the twentieth century. U.S. Religious Landscapes Survey, *The Pew Forum on Religion and Public Life* (2007), http://religions.pewforum.org/affiliations (accessed 11/1/2009).

3. By the time of the collective suicide Bonnie Lu Nettles had died of cancer.

4. The one contradiction in this unrelieved tale of destruction is a very curious reference in chapter 11 to those who "fear [God's] name small and great," that they "shouldest destroy them who destroy the earth" (11:18), though of course even this "green" passage is exterminatory.

5. In my interview study, *Apocalypse*, one of my respondents, Otto, calculated precisely the rolling waves of death in Revelation: "It [Revelation] talks about one place where He sends out judgment over one quarter of the earth to kill. That means to kill one quarter of the earth. At another place it talks about . . . killing over one third of the earth, so if you take one quarter, you have three quarters left, and if you take one third of three quarters you have half the population gone" (70). I was struck with the numbness with which he explained his calculations.

6. Garry Wills, review of Jimmy Carter, *Our Endangered Values: America's Moral Crisis* (New York: Simon and Schuster, 2005), *New York Review of Books*, February 9, 2006.

7. Natalie Angier, "Making Sense of Time, Earthbound and Otherwise," *New York Times*, January 23, 2007, section F1, pp. 1, 3.

8. Philip Rieff, *Freud: The Mind of a Moralist* (Chicago: University of Chicago Press, 1959); Sigmund Freud and Joseph Breuer, *Studies on Hysteria*, in *The Standard Edition of the Complete Psychological Works of Sigmund Freud*, vol. 2, ed. James Strachey, 23 vols. (London: Hogarth Press, 1955), 7.

9. See Strozier, *Apocalypse*, chapter 9, "Jews, Israel, and the Paradox of the Ingathering," 194–208.

10. Bruce Lawrence, ed., *Messages to the World: The Statements of Osama bin Laden* (London: Verso, 2005).

11. Cited in Strozier, *Apocalypse*, 5.

12. Personal communication, March 10, 2003.

13. Jan Assmann, *Death and Salvation in Ancient Egypt*, trans. David Lorton (Ithaca, NY: Cornell University Press, 2006), 74–75.

14. Robert Jay Lifton, *Death in Life: Survivors of Hiroshima* (1967; Chapel Hill: University of North Carolina Press, 1991), 481–82; Robert Jay Lifton, "Perspective: Americans as Survivors," *New England Journal of Medicine* 352, no. 22 (2005): 2263–65.

15. Carol Mason, *Killing for Life: The Apocalyptic Narrative of Pro-Life Politics* (Ithaca, NY: Cornell University Press, 2002).

16. See Strozier, chapter 6, for further discussion of these alternative ways of understanding Revelation.

CHAPTER 11

1. Walter Russell Mead, "Born Again," *The Atlantic* (March 2008): 24.

2. Alan Wolfe, "The Coming Religious Peace: And the Winner Is," *The Atlantic* (March 2008): 56–63.

3. These effects no doubt have an impact beyond the United States through both missionary and cultural export, but that is beyond the scope of this analysis.

4. Charles B. Strozier, *Apocalypse: On the Psychology of Fundamentalism in America* (Boston: Beacon Press, 1994).

5. Copernicus Marketing Consulting, "Religious Liberalism Rising Faster Than Fundamentalism in U.S. According to New Analysis From Copernicus," www.copernicusmarketing.com/about/docs/religion%20study.htm (accessed April 3, 2008).

6. Pew Forum on Religion and Public Life, "Reports," http://religions.pewforum/reports (accessed April 3, 2008).

7. Lee Quinby, *Anti-Apocalypse: Exercises in Genealogical Criticism* (Minneapolis: University of Minnesota Press, 1994).

8. Brenda Brasher and Lee Quinby, eds., *Gender and Apocalyptic Desire* (London: Equinox Press, 2006).

9. Jonathan Kirsch, *A History of the End of the World: How the Most Controversial Book in the Bible Changed the Course of Western Civilization* (New York: HarperOne, 2007).

10. See Terman, chapter 5.

11. Lee Quinby, *Millennial Seduction: A Skeptic Confronts Apocalyptic Culture* (Ithaca, NY: Cornell University Press, 1999), 3.

12. Strozier, *Apocalypse*, chapter 8.

13. George W. Bush, "Remarks on the War on Terror," fact sheet outline, www.whitehouse.gov/news/releases/2005/10/20051006–2.html (accessed October 6, 2005).

14. Michael Foucault, "Sexuality and Power" (1978), in *Religion and Culture: Michel Foucault*, ed. Jeremy R. Carette (New York: Routledge: 1999).

15. Judith Butler, *The Psychic Life of Power* (Stanford, CA: Stanford University Press, 1997), 2. As Butler goes on to point out, this is not simply a model of internalization. That notion presumes a kind of acceptance or choice made by a subject already formed. More in keeping with Althusser's notion of interpellation, the subject emerges at the moment he or she responds to the call of already existing Law. This is why it is so important to look to the power relations within a given social order if we are to grasp the psychology of those who live in it.

16. Ibid., 6–7.

17. Ruth Stein, "Fundamentalism, Father and Son, and Vertical Desire," *PsyART* 8 (2004). Available at www.clas.ufl.edu/ipsa/journal/2004_stein01.shtml. Dec. 31, 2004.

18. Mark Juergensmeyer, *Terror in the Mind of God: The Global Rise of Religious Violence* (Berkeley: University of California Press, 2003), 202.

19. Charles B. Strozier, "Apocalyptic Violence and the Politics of Waco," in *The Year 2000: Essays on the End*, ed. Charles B. Strozier and Michael Flynn (New York: New York University Press, 1997), 97–111.

20. Andrew MacDonald, *The Turner Diaries* (Fort Lee, NJ: Barricade Books, 1978).

21. For an insightful explanation of what motivates fundamentalist violence of this sort, see Matthias M. Beier, "On the Psychology of Violent Christian Fundamentalism: Fighting to Matter Ultimately," *Psychoanalytic Review* 93, no. 2 (2006): 301–27.

22. Carol Mason, "The Hillbilly Defense: Culturally Mediating U.S. Terror at Home and Abroad," *National Women's Studies Association Journal* 17, no. 3 (2005): 39–63.

23. Racist uses of the name Jezebel are also part of the history of white supremacy in the United States, which often used religious authority as its justification. As an African American religious leader, Daughtry also undermines the racism of that legacy.

24. Daniel Berger, "Can Leah Daughtry Bring Faith to the Party?," *New York Times Magazine*, July 20, 2008, www.nytimes.com/2008/07/20/magazine/20minister-t.html?pagewanted=all (accessed July 20, 2008).

25. David Van Biema, "An Evangelical Rethink on Divorce?," *Time*, November 15, 2007, www.time.com/time/printout/0,8816,1680709,00.html (accessed September 5, 2008).

26. Frances Fitzgerald, "The New Evangelicals" *New Yorker*, June 30, 2008, 28–34.

27. Charles R. Swindoll, "The Final War," www.insight.org/site/News2?page=NewsArticle&id=7787&news_iv_ctrl=1541 (accessed May 1, 2008).

28. James Dobson, *Bringing Up Boys: Practical Advice and Encouragement for Those Shaping the Next Generation of Men* (Wheaton, IL: Tyndale, 2001), 27.

29. Mead, "Born Again," 24.

30. Frances Fitzgerald, "Come One, Come All," *New Yorker*, December 3, 2007, 55.

31. Gamepro.com, www.gamepro.com/news.cfm?article_id=136548. (accessed October 8, 2007).

32. Matt Richtel, "Thou Shalt Not Kill, Except in a Popular Video Game at Church," *New York Times*, October 7, 2007.

33. Richtel says that Microsoft denies that its space epic has any "specific religious references." And that is true, depending on what one means by the word *specific*. Many of the names certainly seem drawn from a religious lexicon, but in contrast to Christian usage, in "Halo 3" the Covenant is a fanatical group that seeks the destruction of the earth, and the Prophet of Truth and the Flood are likewise enemies rather than proponents of good or a method of divine punishment. Thus Microsoft is off the hook in regard to one-to-one religious correlations. But my point is that this kind of popular culture influence is not only likely to muddle the

postgame theological lesson that the players have in store, but, more important, it tends to alter certain fundamentals of Christian fundamentalism.

34. Ibid.

35. Tim LaHaye and Jerry B. Jenkins, *Glorious Appearing* (Wheaton, IL: Tyndale House, 2004), 204, 205. See also Jones, chapter 9.

36. Jodi Dean, "Feminism, Communicative Capitalism, and the Inadequacies of Radical Democracy," in *Radical Democracy and the Internet*, ed. Lincoln Dahlberg and Eugenia Siapera (New York: Palgrave Macmillan, 2007), 243.

CHAPTER 12

1. I distinguish between global jihadists (such as those in Al Qaeda) and national jihadists (such as Hamas in Palestine, the Chechnian jihadists who oppose Russian occupation, and the Kashmiri jihadists who do not have the same type of ideology and legitimacy). The aim of the national jihadists is to oust the intruder and establish a national government, and all political and military acts are directed toward that goal. The global jihadists do not aim at establishing a national state. They intend to uproot "heresy" from the earth and harbor the utopia of a universal caliphate.

2. See David Zeidan, *The Resurgence of Religion: A Comparative Study of Selected Themes in Christian and Islamic Fundamentalist Discourses* (Leiden: Brill, 2003).

3. See Abderrahmane Moussaoui, *De la Violence en Algérie: Les Lois du Chaos* (Paris: Editions Actes Sud/MMSH, 2006); Farhad Khosrokhavar, *Inside Jihadism: Understanding Jihadi Movements Worldwide*, Yale Cultural Sociology Series (London: Paradigm, 2008).

4. The "disproportionate" dimension does not work in the case of national jihadists; on the contrary, Israeli and Russian military might kills and maims far more than do Hamas or the Chechnian jihadists.

5. See Farhad Khosrokhavar, *L'Islam dans les prisons (Broché)* (Paris: Balland, 2004).

6. Islamic Umma is the Islamic Community imagined by the Jihadists as having to be awakened through their heroic deeds. The reference is the idealized Umma of the times of the Prophet, mainly the small community who migrated in the year 622 from Mecca to the town of Medina where they settled, united under the political and religious leadership of the Prophet, before conquering the Mecca in 630.

7. Of course cultures are not monolithic, and there are subcultures within them. One subculture within Islam can be more affected than another by the adverse effects of modernization and Westernization. In the case of fundamentalists, the subculture of Islam is much more badly affected than other Muslims. In the case of global jihadists, their subculture is even more shaken than others. They develop a subculture of extreme violence in the Muslim world that is not shared by others.

8. The literature on humiliation is extensive. See James W. Jones, *Blood That Cries Out from the Earth: The Psychologiy of Religious Terrorism* (Oxford: Oxford University Press, 2008); Farhad Khosrokhavar, *Suicide Bombers: The New Martyrs of Allah* (London: Pluto Press, 2005). See also Muenster and Lotto, chapter 7; Terman, chapter 5.

9. To justify his demeanor, a young man in the French poor suburbs talked about how the French people treated him as an "insect" and how, to respond to them

adequately, he did not distinguish between "good" and "bad" Frenchmen. In prison a young man from the Dom-Tom (French former colonies that have become part of France) said that only one Frenchman out of a hundred was humane, and therefore his ruthless attitude toward them was completely justified. See Farhad Khosrokhavar, *L'islam des Jeunes* (Paris: Flammarion, 1997); Farhad Khosrokhavar, *Quand Al Qaeda Parle* (Paris: Grasset, 2006).

10. See Khosrokavar, *Islam des Jeunes.*

11. See the description of this ideology in my latest book, *Jihadism in the Two Worlds: Europe versus the Middle East,* Yale Cultural Sociological Series (London: Paradigm, 2008).

12. The 2006 war in Lebanon left more than twelve hundred dead and many more injured, with entire areas in major cities reduced to rubble because of the arrest by Hezbollah of two Israeli soldiers; the 2009 war in Gaza in reaction to the rocket attacks that killed in the course of many years fewer than twenty Israelis killed more than twelve hundred and injured many thousands, and many parts of Gaza city were destroyed. Israeli attacks against the Palestinians are by far more important symbolically than that of the Russians against the Chechens or the Indians against the Kashmiris, because of Jerusalem and the centrality of the Palestinian question in Arabs' eyes and the focus on Israel as an example of Western total support of its major ally in the region against the Muslims.

13. See note 3 for the explanation of the difference between the two.

14. See Olivier Carré, *L'Islam laïque ou le retour à la Grande Tradition* (Paris: Armand Colin, 1993).

15. For a general description of this literature, see Khosrokhavar, *Inside Jihadism*; David Cook, *Understanding Jihad* (Berkeley: University of California Press, 2005); Jean-Pierre Filiu, *Les Frontières du Jihad* (Paris: Fayard, 2006).

16. See David Cook, *Contemporary Muslim Apocalyptic Literature* (Syracuse, NY: Syracuse University Press, 2005), Jean-Pierre Filiu, *L'Apocalypse dans L'Islam* (Paris: Fayard, 2008).

17. The ulama are the religious authorities in Islam. By juxtaposing the two words "Sultan's Ulama" the Jihadists try to discredit the Islamic religious authorities that cooperate with those rulers they consider to be the illegitimate power holders in the Muslim world.

18. In the Muslim world a sizable number of jihadists are among the engineers, scientists, and related professions. In Europe jihadists are mostly recruited among the second- and third-generation Muslims who have been educated in modern schools. For the Muslim world, see Diego Gambetta and Steffen Hertog, *Engineers of Jihad,* Sociology Working Paper 2007–10, Department of Sociology, University of Oxford, www.sociology.ox.ac.uk/swp.htm/

CHAPTER 13

1. I discuss this at length in *Hitler's Millennial Reich: Apocalyptic Belief and the Search for Salvation* (New York: New York University Press, 2005). See also Klaus Vondung, *The Apocalypse in Germany,* trans. Stephen D. Ricks (Columbia: University of Missouri Press, 2000); James M. Rhodes, *The Hitler Movement: A Modern Millenarian Revolution* (Stanford: Hoover Institution Press, 1980).

2. Eric Voegelin, writing originally in the 1930s, saw in National Socialism, as well as fascism and communism, forms of political religion. He argued that modern totalitarian movements were essentially secular faiths that replaced traditional religious faiths weakened by the secularizing forces of modernity. See the essays collected in his *Hitler and the Germans* (Columbia: University of Missouri Press, 1999) and *Modernity without Restraint* (Columbia: University of Missouri Press, 2000). Voegelin's notion of political religion has seen a resurgence in the past decade. See Michael Ley, *Apokalypse und Moderne: Aufsätze zu politischen Religionen* (Vienna: Sonderzal, 1997); Michael Ley and Julius H. Schoeps, eds., *Der Nationalsozialismus als politische Religion* (Bodenheim b. Mainz: Philo Verlagsgesellschaft, 1997); Claus-Ekkehard Bärsch, *Die politische Religion des Nationalsozialismus: Die religiöse Dimension der NS-Ideologie in den Schriften von Dietrich Eckart, Joseph Goebbels, Alfred Rosenberg und Adolf Hitler* (Munich: W. Fink, 1998). Richard Steigmann-Gall questions whether National Socialism really is a political religion or simply a form of "religious politics." See his "Nazism and the Revival of Political Religion Theory," *Totalitarian Movements and Political Religion* 5 (2004): 376–96. Stanley Stowers essentially agrees with Steigmann-Gall that the Nazis saw themselves as inspired by traditional religious notions and not attempting to replace Christianity with a new secular faith. See Stowers, "The Concept of 'Religion,' 'Political Religion,' and the Study of Nazism," *Journal of Contemporary History* 42 (2007): 9–24.

3. As Lewis Rambo notes, a crisis, whether religious, political, cultural, or psychological, usually precedes the conversion process. See his *Understanding Religious Conversion* (New Haven, CT: Yale University Press, 1993), 44–55. See also William B. Bankson, H. Hugh Floyd Jr., and Craig J. Forsyth, "Toward a General Model of the Process of Radical Conversion: An Interactionist Perspective on the Transformation of Self-Identity," *Qualitative Sociology* 4 (1981): 279–97.

4. The Nazi Old Guard testimonials I cite primarily come from two separate archival sources. One is *Die alte Garde spricht* (The Old Guard Speaks), a four-volume collection of short biographies of early Nazis commissioned by Rudolf Hess in 1936. Two sets of this collection are housed at the Library of Congress (Washington, DC). Hereafter citations to this collection appear as *DAGS*, followed by volume number, author, and page number. The second set of testimonials is found in the Theodore Abel Collection at the Hoover Institution on War, Revolution and Peace (Stanford, CA). This collection contains 580 short autobiographical essays collected by Abel for his sociological study of Nazism, *Why Hitler Came to Power* (New York: Harvard University Press, 1938). I cite this collection as Abel, followed by the essay number and my own pagination. Used together, the autobiographical writings found in *Die alte Garde spricht* and the Abel collection provide an invaluable glimpse into the motivations and conceptions of those Germans who converted to Nazism. The quotations above come from *DAGS*, vol. 2, Adalbert Gimbel, 2; vol. 1, Otto Leinweber, 1; Abel #20, 1; *DAGS*, vol. 2, Gustav Bonn, 2; vol. 1, Karl Aldinger, 2–3; Abel #563, 1.

5. See, for instance, Abel #531, 1; Abel #245, 1.

6. Abel #579, 12.

7. Abel #50, 4.

8. *DAGS*, vol. 1, Emil Schlitz, 1.

9. *DAGS*, vol. 1, Karl Hepp, 2.

10. I discuss the Nazi conception of the coming millennial kingdom in "Nazi End Times: The Third Reich as Millennial Reich," in *End of Days: Essays on the Apocalypse from Antiquity to Modernity*, ed. Karolyn Kinane and Michael A. Ryan (Jefferson, NC: McFarland, 2009), 173–96. See also Thomas Flanagan, "The Third Reich: Origins of Millenarian Symbol," *History of European Ideas* 8 (1987): 283–95.

11. *DAGS*, vol. 3, Walter Gerwein, 1.

12. Abel #70, 2. Similarly, see Abel #4, 2; Abel #16, 3; Abel #2, 1; *DAGS*, vol. 3, Wilhelm Meder, 2; vol. 4, L. Eifert, 2. The German *Volk* can be translated as *folk, people, nation*, or *race*, with a romantic stress on conceptualizing an ethnic group as an organic entity that is bound by a collective spiritual connection that is mystical and ineffable.

13. *DAGS*, vol. 2, Hans Otto, 4.

14. Abel #24, 8.

15. See George L. Mosse, *Fallen Soldiers: Reshaping the Memory of the World Wars* (New York: Oxford University Press, 1990).

16. See the discussion of this social division in Detlev J. K. Peukert, *The Weimar Republic: The Crisis of Classical Modernity*, trans. Richard Deveson (New York: Hill and Wang, 1993).

17. Adolf Hitler certainly in time saw himself as this savior. See Michael Hesemann, *Hitlers Religion: Die fatale Heilslehre des Nationalsozialismus* (Munich: Pattloch Verlag, 2004); Friedrich Heer, *Der Glaube des Adolf Hitler: Anatomie einer politischen Religiosität* (Munich: Bechtle, 1998).

18. Abel, *Why Hitler*, 123–24. This sense that a social inversion had taken place, the "world turned upside down," is a common perception among millenarian movements throughout history and reflects the difficulty individuals have restructuring a coherent sense of an ordered reality.

19. Abel #3, 5.

20. *DAGS*, vol. 2, Gustav Bonn, 1; Albert Barnscheidt, 3.

21. Gregor Strasser, "Gedanken über Aufgaben der Zukunft," originally *NS-Briefe*, June 15, 1926, here as found in his collection *Kampf um Deutschland: Reden und Aufsätze eines Nationalsozialisten* (Munich: Eher, 1932), 137. Strasser, as with a number of the Berlin Nazis, interpreted the "socialism" of National Socialism in a more traditional economic way than Hitler ever intended. For Hitler socialism meant a racial communalism of a millennial sort. Strasser was later killed in the infamous Night of the Long Knives, accused of plotting a second revolution against Hitler.

22. *DAGS*, vol. 3, Philipp Balthaser Ripper zu Pfaffen-Beerfurth, 1.

23. Discussed in Klaus Vondung, "National Socialism as a Political Religion: Potentials and Limits of an Analytical Concept," *Totalitarian Movements and Political Religions* 6 (2005):87–95.

24. Abel #4, 2.

25. Otto Wagener, *Hitler: Memoirs of a Confidant*, trans. Ruth Hein (New Haven, CT: Yale University Press, 1985), 56–57.

26. Hitler was not the only Nazi, or German for that matter, who saw National Socialism as an expression of apostolic Christianity. This was especially true for so-called German Christians who hoped to expunge all "Jewish" elements from Christianity, often Aryanizing Jesus in the process. See Doris L. Bergen, *Twisted Cross: The German Christian Movement in the Third Reich* (Chapel Hill: University of North

Carolina Press, 1996); Richard Steigmann-Gall, *The Holy Reich: Nazi Conceptions of Christianity, 1919–1945* (Cambridge: Cambridge University Press, 2003); Karla Poewe, *New Religions and the Nazis* (New York: Routledge, 2006).

27. For more on Nazi conversion experiences, see Redles, *Hitler's Millennial Reich*, 77–107.

28. John Lofland and Rodney Stark, in "Becoming a World-Saver: A Theory of Conversion to a Deviant Perspective," *American Sociological Review* 30 (1965): 862–75, note that the stress and tension generated by crisis is an essential catalyst for conversion. Although this is a salient point, stress and tension are insufficient in themselves to cause such a dramatic transformation as found in a conversion experience. It is the rapid and radical change that brings about the crisis state, and conversion is the psyche's attempt to alleviate the crisis by constructing a new perception of order.

29. Abel #13, 6–9. N.S.D.A.P. refers to the National Socialist German Workers' Party or the German Nationalsozialistische Deutsche Arbeiterpartei. Note, the Nazis themselves were not consistent on how the party name was written, and sometimes it is Nationalsozialistische Deutsche Arbeiter-Partei.

30. Rambo, *Understanding Religious Conversion*, 133.

31. Ibid., 57–65.

32. In sociology this is referred to as network theory. The most influential study is Lofland and Stark, "Becoming a World Saver." See also John Lofland, "'Becoming a World Saver' Revisited," *American Behavioral Scientist* 20 (1977): 805–18; Rodney Stark and William Bainbridge, "Networks of Faith: Interpersonal Bonds and Recruitment to Cults and Sects," *American Journal of Sociology* 85 (1980): 1376–95; David A. Snow, Louis A. Zurcher Jr., and Sheldon Ekland-Olson, "Further Thoughts on Social Networks and Movement Recruitment," *Sociology* 17 (1983): 112–20.

33. *DAGS*, vol. 1, Karoline Leinweber, 3.

34. *DAGS*, vol. 2, Eduard Hohbein, 3.

35. Rambo, *Understanding Religious Conversion*, 50–51. According to Walter Conn, an expert on Christian conversion, the desire for self-transcendence is the primary motivational factor behind conversions. See his *Christian Conversion: A Developmental Interpretation of Autonomy and Surrender* (New York, Paulist Press, 1986) and "Pastoral Counseling for Self-Transcendence: The Integration of Psychology and Theology," *Pastoral Psychology* 36 (1987): 29–48.

36. Old Guard Nazis, like their Führer and other anti-Semites, almost uniformly blamed the Jews for the perceived materialism and egoism of modern life. Rejecting the materialism that seemed to define modernity was deemed essential to achieve the Nazi millennium and thwart the alleged conspiratorial machinations of the supposedly materialistic and temporal Jews. It is perhaps not surprising that some Arab fundamentalists who are struggling with modernity project what they reject on "the Jew," "the Zionist," or "the American."

37. *DAGS*, vol. 3, Ludwig Heck I, 2.

38. Abel #545, 2.

39. The power of millennial rhetoric for both community building and localizing evil is best seen in Stephen O'Leary, *Arguing the Apocalypse: A Theory of Millennial Rhetoric* (New York: Oxford University Press, 1994).

40. Abel #179, 1. Hitler likewise claimed to follow an "inner voice," which he believed came from transcendent sources. See Redles, *Hitler's Millennial Reich*, 132–34.

41. *DAGS*, vol. 3, Peter Weber, 1.

42. *DAGS*, vol. 4, Franz Madre, 1.

43. Abel #163, 6.

44. Abel #207, 6.

45. Abel, *Why Hitler*, 116–17.

46. Abel #526, 3.

47. *DAGS*, vol. 4, L. Eifert, 3–4.

48. *DAGS*, vol. 3, Elisabeth Kranz, 26.

49. Ibid. Nazi party rallies, with pronounced symbolism of national rebirth through collective unity, became important tools for imparting the millennial message of National Socialism. See Yvonne Karow, *Deutsches Opfer: Kultische Selbstauslöschung auf den Reichsparteitagen der NSDAP* (Berlin: Akademie Verlag, 1997); Sabine Behrenbeck, *Der Kult um die toten Helden: Nationalsozialistische Mythen, Riten und Symbole* (Vierow: SH-Verlag, 1996); Klaus Vondung, *Magie und Manipulation: Ideologischer Kult und politische Religion des Nationalsozialismus* (Göttingen: Vandenhoeck & Ruprecht, 1971); Hans-Jochen Gamm, *Der braune Kult: Das Dritte Reich und seine Ersatzreligion* (Hamburg: Rütten & Loening, 1962).

50. *DAGS*, vol. 2, Johannes Christ, 12.

51. *DAGS*, vol. 2, Hans Grün, 1.

52. Abel #50, 4.

53. This oneness was of course limited to those of Aryan blood. All others were excluded from the Nazi community. The dualism inherent in Nazi apocalyptic cosmology necessitated an anticommunity, a group whose separation from the Aryan community was a key element in restoring that community and, ultimately, creating the Nazi millennium. The limited nature of this oneness, the Nazi *Volksgenossen*, is a crucial factor leading to the Holocaust. On the intimate relationship between building a national community and demonizing German Jews, see Frank Bajohr, "The 'Folk Community' and the Persecution of the Jews: German Society under National Socialist Dictatorship, 1933–1945," *Holocaust and Genocide Studies* 20 (2006): 183–206; Moritz Föllmer, "The Problem of National Solidarity in Interwar Germany," *German History* 23 (2005): 202–31.

54. Quoted in Wagener, *Memoirs of a Confidant*, 212.

55. Abel #24, 9.

56. Karl Schworm, "Vor Zehn Jahren!," NSDAP Hauptarchiv, Hoover Institution, microfilm roll 26, folder 513, 6.

57. Descriptions of this speech can be found in Adolf Hitler, *Sämtliche Aufzeichnungen: 1905–1924*, ed. Eberhard Jäckel and Axel Kuhn (Stuttgart: Deutsche Verlags-Anstalt, 1980), 378–79.

58. Schworm, "Vor zehn Jahren," 6.

59. *DAGS*, vol. 4, Heinz Hermann Horn, 20.

60. On the infusion of a sense of power after conversion, see Rambo, *Understanding Religious Conversion*, 85–86.

61. See Uriel Tal, *"Political Faith" of Nazism Prior to the Holocaust* (Tel Aviv: Tel Aviv University Press, 1978).

62. *DAGS*, vol. 2, M. Hetzel, 2; Abel #41, 1; *DAGS*, vol. 2, Karl Dörr, 5.

63. Abel, *Why Hitler*, 145.

64. The essential linkage of attempts to build utopias resulting in genocide is discussed in Omer Bartov, *Mirrors of Destruction: War, Genocide, and Modern Identity*

(Oxford: Oxford University Press, 2000); Eric D. Weitz, *A Century of Genocide: Utopias of Race and Nation* (Princeton, NJ: Princeton University Press, 2003).

65. Armin Pfahl-Traughber, *Der antisemitisch-antifreimaurerische Verschwörungsmythos in der Weimarer Republik und im NS-Staat* (Vienna: Wilhelm Braumüller, 1993).

66. Dietrich Eckart, "Immer lächeln, und doch ein Schurke!," *Auf gut deutsch*, February 7, 1919, 83–84.

67. Dietrich Eckart, "Die Schlacht auf den Katalaunischen Feldern," *Auf gut deutsch*, February 20, 1920, 86.

68. Quoted in Claus-Ekkehard Bärsch, "Der Jude als Antichrist in der NS-Ideologie," *Zeitschrift für Religions und Geistesgeschichte* 47 (1995): 173, 174, 175–76. The dangerous and potentially violent coalescence of nationalism, racism, and anti-Semitism has a long and unfortunate history in Europe. On the German experience, see Helmut Walser Smith, *The Continuities of German History: Nation, Religion, and Race across the Long Nineteenth Century* (Cambridge: Cambridge University Press, 2008), and the many examples discussed in Christhard Hoffmann, Werner Bergmann, and Helmut Walser Smith, eds., *Exclusionary Violence: Antisemitic Riots in Modern German History* (Ann Arbor: University of Michigan Press, 2002).

69. Cited in Claus-Ekkehard Bärsch, *Der junge Goebbels: Erlösung und Vernichtung* (Munich: Boer, 1995), 123.

70. Gottfried zur Beek, ed., *Die Geheimnesse der Weisen von Zion* (Charlottenberg: Verlag Auf Vorposten, 1919).

71. See David Redles, "The Turning Point: *The Protocols of the Elders of Zion* and the Eschatological War between Aryans and Jews," in *Reconsidering the Protocols: 100 Years after the Forgery*, ed. Steven T. Katz and Richard Landes (New York: New York University Press, forthcoming).

72. Adolf Hitler, *Mein Kampf*, trans. Ralph Mannheim (Boston: Houghton Mifflin, 1971), 382.

73. Adolf Hitler, *Die Rede Adolf Hitlers in der ersten grossen Massenversammlung (Münchener Bürgerbräu-Keller vom 27. Februar 1925) bei Wiederausrichtung der Nationalsozialistischen Deutschen Arbeiter Partei* (Munich: Ehrer, 1925), 8.

74. Louis L. Snyder, ed., *Hitler's Third Reich: A Documentary History* (Chicago: Nelson-Hall, 1981), 51–52.

75. This radical dualism, its apocalyptic conceptualization, and its continuing relevance in contemporary anti-Semitism is best seen in Robert Wistrich, *Hitler's Apocalypse: Jews and the Nazi Legacy* (New York: St. Martin's Press, 1985).

76. Abel, #35, 1. The Spartacists were one of the leading German communist groups. Many were former sailors who had mutinied or had been dismissed from service and still wore their uniforms during protests.

77. *DAGS*, vol. 3, Emil Hofmann, 1–2.

78. Abel #579, 14–15.

79. Ibid., 13.

80. *DAGS* vol. 1, Willi Altenbrandt, 1. By "November-Germany" Altenbrandt meant the Weimar Germany that resulted from the loss of the war and subsequent Social Democratic government that took power in November 1918.

81. Abel #60, 5–6.

82. Ibid., 7–9.

83. Abel #263, 4.
84. August Reise, *DAGS*, vol. 1, 4.

CHAPTER 14

1. The term is used extensively by François Furet (discussed below) and means the dualism of revolutionary thought: right and wrong, patriot and traitor, revolutionary and counterrevolutionary, and so forth.

2. The political organization of the French kingdom was in estates. The first estate was the clergy, the second the nobility, and the third everyone else. When the king called the Estates General into session—which had last been done in 1614—they were chosen by order (only those in holy orders could vote for first estate deputies, etc.), met separately, and each cast one vote, in order of social precedence. In theory each estate had privileges, but in fact the most important privileges—social distinction, access to office, freedom from taxes—were reserved for the first two estates.

3. Berthier de Sauvigny was the intendant of Paris, the most important royal official in the capital.

4. Georges Lefebvre, *The Great Fear of 1789*, trans. R. R. Palmer and Joan White (Princeton, NJ: Princeton University Press, 1973). He is the most important historian of the peasantry in the French Revolution and this little book remains a classic.

5. Le Bon (1841–1931) was a physician and a sociologist and the first popularizer in France of ideas about collective psychology. Two works are involved: *Les Lois psychologiques de l'évolution des peoples* (1894) and *Psychologie des foules* (1895).

6. See the tables in Donald Greer, *The Incidence of the Terror in the French Revolution* (Cambridge: Cambridge University Press, 1935).

7. See Bronislaw Baczko, *Comment sortir de la Terreur* (Paris: Gallimard, 1989) for an account of the rumors that swirled around Robespierre in the last weeks of his life.

8. Donald Greer, *The Incidence of the Terror in the French Revolution* (1935; Gloucester, MA: Harvard University Press, 1966) is the first systematic statistical study of the Terror, and his figures are widely accepted.

9. Perhaps most chilling of all in the Prairial Laws was the regulation that allowed the jury to stop hearing further testimony whenever they believed they had enough evidence to reach a verdict. The Prairial Laws where a panicky reaction to a couple of assassination attempts on members of the Committee of Public Safety. The six weeks during which these laws were in effect were the bloodiest of the Terror.

10. There is a massive literature on the Terror. Here let me suggest just a few books. On Robespierre, see David P. Jordan, *The Revolutionary Career of Maximilien Robespierre* (Chicago: University of Chicago Press, 1985). For the Committee of Public Safety, who virtually ruled France during the Terror, see R. R. Palmer, *Twelve Who Ruled* (Princeton, NJ: Princeton University Press, 1941). For a revisionist view of why there was a Terror—the Jacobins always argued it was circumstance that forced Terror upon them—see François Furet, "The Revolution Is Over," in *Interpreting the French Revolution*, trans. Elborg Forster (Cambridge and Paris: Cambridge University Press and Editions de la maison des sciences et de l'homme, 1981). On one of the more colorful provincial terrorists, see Colin Lucas, *The Structure of the*

Terror (Oxford: Oxford University Press, 1973), and in general see Richard C. Cobb, *The Police and the People* (Oxford: Oxford University Press, 1970) and his many essays; and most recently, David Andress, *The Terror* (New York: Farrar, Straus, and Giroux, 2006).

11. See David Bell, *The First Total War* (Boston: Houghton Mifflin, 2007) for the best and most recent discussion of this debate.

12. Edmund Burke, *Reflections on the French Revolution* (Hafner Classics), 46.

13. The language of Left and Right comes from the French Revolution. It originally referred to those who sat, at Versailles when the Estates-General first met, to the left or the right of the president of the Assembly. As it turned out those who sat on the left had the more republican and radical politics, those on the right the more monarchical and conservative, and the distinction, originally spatial, soon became political.

14. *Archives parlementaires*, series L, vol. 37, p. 418.

15. *Archives parlementaires*, series L, vol. 36, p. 403.

16. *Archives parlementaires*, series L, vol. 36, p. 440.

17. The most recent statement of this view is Patrice Gueniffey, "Robespierre," in *Dictionnaire critique de la Révolution française*, ed. François Furet and Mona Ozouf (Paris: Flammarion, 1988). Ruth Schurr, *Fatal Purity: Robespierre and the French* Revolution (New York: Henry Holt, 2006) is the most recent biography and attempts to reveal the secrets of Robespierre's personality, a perennial quest. But see a less determinist portrait that concentrates on the role of ideology in the Revolution, in Jordan, *The Revolutionary Career.*

18. Robespierre, *Discours*, VIII, 36 (December 9, 1791).

19. Robespierre, *Discours*, VIII, 40 (December 12, 1791).

20. Robespierre, *Discours*, VIII, 47 (December 18, 1791).

21. Robespierre, *Discours*, VIII, 57 (December 12, 1791).

22. Quoted by M.J. Sydenham, *The French Revolution* (Putnam, NY: Capricorn Books, 1965), 91.

23. Robespierre, *Discours*, VIII, 81 (January 2, 1792).

24. Robespierre, *Discours*, VIII, 86 (January 2, 1792).

25. Robespierre, *Discours*, VIII, 89–90 (January 2, 1792).

26. See Lucien Jaume, *Le discourse Jacobin et la démocratie* (Paris: Fayard, 1989).

27. Quoted in Jordan, *The Revolutionary Career*, 227.

28. *Marat dit L'Ami du Peuple, collection complète du Journal* (Tokyo: Society for Reproduction of Rare Books, 1967), XIII, 271 (April 19, 1792).

29. *Marat dit l'Ami du Peuple*, XIII, 273 (April 19, 1792). This same argument would come back during the king's trial at the end of 1792, when several deputies proposed that an ultimatum be made to the Austrians and Prussians that if they did not leave French soil within a specified time Louis would answer with his head.

30. *Marat dit l'Ami du Peuple*, XIII, 318–19 (April 25, 1792).

31. He was stopped at Varennes on June 21, 1791, and returned a virtual prisoner to Paris. He left behind a declaration of his opposition to the Revolution. The flight to Varennes not only made the Revolution international, but it also snapped the last remaining threads that bound a thousand-year-old monarchy to its subjects. The king's biographer, John Hardman, doesn't think that the king planned to flee France, but even he admits, "Whatever his intentions, if a king leaves his capital at dead of

night and heads East and is stopped within 50 miles of the frontier, it is a reasonable assumption that he is planning to cross it and enlist foreign troops. One way of determining criminal intent today is to ask what a reasonable man would deduce if a silent film were made of the activities concerned." See his essay "The Real and Imagined Conspiracies of Louis XVI," in *Conspiracy in the French Revolution*, ed. Peter R. Campbell, Thomas E. Kaiser, and Marisa Linton (Manchester, UK: Manchester University Press, 2007), 82.

32. The most fantastic of these is Fabre d'Eglantine's West Indies Company plot. Fabre was a minor poet who in fact designed the names of the months and days for the Revolutionary calendar. He was also a scoundrel deeply tainted by fiduciary scandal. As the authorities got closer and closer he began telling them a convoluted story of counterrevolution among the investors in the West Indies Company. This sent several to the guillotine and was concocted to save Fabre's own skin. In this it failed.

33. There are a number of Jacobins who make this argument. René Levasseur, a devoted second-tier Jacobin from LeMans in the Sarthe, makes it as well as anyone. See *Mémoires de R. Levasseur (de la Sarthe)* (Paris: Editions Sociales, 1989).

34. The full development of this argument is in François Furet, *Penser la Révolution française* (Paris: Gallimard, 1978), translated as *Interpreting the French Revolution*, referenced in note 10. The essay is titled "August Cochin: The Theory of Jacobinism."

35. Again there is a rich philosophical literature. Isaiah Berlin, the most eloquent and brilliant opponent of monism, and his essays on Machiavelli and the Romantics are the best place to see the arguments laid out. On Rousseau's ideas of democracy any number of books are worth consulting, but I would recommend above all Keith Baker, *Inventing the French Revolution* (Cambridge: Cambridge University Press, 1990), the best work on the ideology of the French Revolution and the forces that formed it in the eighteenth century.

CHAPTER 15

1. For identifying this pattern and for other ideas, this chapter owes a special debt to Sudhir Kakar, *The Colours of Violence* (New Delhi: Penguin Books India, 1995).

2. Tapan Basu et al., *Khaki Shorts and Saffron Flags: A Critique of the Hindu Right* (New Delhi: Orient Longman, 1993), 3.

3. Christophe Jaffrelot, *The Hindu Nationalist Movement in India* (New York: Columbia University Press, 1996), 11–79, discusses the twin Hindu nationalist strategies of emulating and stereotyping.

4. Among the many accounts of the movement's strategic incorporation of Hindu gods and heroes are Jaffrelot, *Hindu Nationalist Movement*, and Daniel Gold, "Organized Hinduisms: From Vedic Truth to Hindu Nation," in *Fundamentalisms Observed*, vol. 1, ed. Martin E. Marty and R. Scott Appleby (Chicago: University of Chicago Press, 1991), 531–83.

5. V. D. Savarkar, *Hindutva: Who Is a Hindu?*, 6th ed. (New Delhi: Bharti Sahitya Sadan, 1989), 112.

6. Gyanendra Pandey, *Remembering Partition: Violence, Nationalism and History in India* (Cambridge: Cambridge University Press, 2001).

7. Nicholas Dirks, *Castes of Mind: Colonialism and the Making of Modern India* (Princeton, NJ: Princeton University Press, 2001).

8. Nirad C. Chaudhuri, *The Autobiography of an Unknown Indian* (New York: Macmillan, 1951), 225.

9. Richard Eaton, *The Rise of Islam and the Bengal Frontier* (Berkeley: University of California Press, 1993), chapter 2, note 12 suggests that the first band of two hundred was simply "an advance detachment from [the main invading] force of ten thousand."

10. Partha Chatterjee, *The Nation and Its Fragments: Colonial and Postcolonial Histories* (New Delhi: Oxford University Press, 1994), 70.

11. Joseph S. Alter, *Gandhi's Body: Sex, Diet, and the Politics of Nationalism* (Philadelphia: University of Pennsylvania Press, 2000), 150.

12. Sumit Sarkar, *The Swadeshi Movement in Bengal, 1903–1908* (New Delhi: People's Publishing House, 1973), 16–19.

13. Quoted in Mushirul Hasan, "The Myth of Unity: Colonial and National Narratives," in *Contesting the Nation: Religion, Community and the Politics of Democracy in India*, ed. David Ludden (Philadelphia: University of Pennsylvania Press, 1996), 200.

14. John R. McLane, ed., *The Political Awakening in India* (Englewood Cliffs, NJ: Prentice Hall, 1970), 43–47.

15. Susanne Hoeber Rudolph and Lloyd I. Rudolph, *Gandhi: The Traditional Roots of Charisma* (Chicago: University of Chicago Press, 1983), 8–15.

16. Javeed Alam, "Composite Culture and Communal Consciousness," in *Representing Hinduism: The Construction of Religious and National Identity*, ed. Vasudha Dalmia and Heinrich von Stietencron (New Delhi: Sage, 1995), 342–43.

17. John R. McLane, *Indian Nationalism and the Early Congress* (Princeton, NJ: Princeton University Press, 1970), 271–331.

18. Personal communication from Christopher Pinney, October 27, 2008.

19. McLane, *The Political Awakening*, 52–57.

20. Mrinalini Sinha, *Colonial Masculinity: The "Manly Englishman" and the "Effeminate Bengali" in the Late Nineteenth Century* (Manchester, UK: Manchester University Press, 1995).

21. Vinayak Damodar Savarkar, *My Transportation for Life* (Bombay: Veer Savarkar Prakashan, 1984).

22. Jaffrelot, *Hindu Nationalist Movement*, 19–25.

23. Walter K. Andersen and Shridhar D. Damle, *The Brotherhood in Saffron: The Rashtriya Swayamsevak Sangh and Hindu Revivalism* (Boulder, CO: Westview Press, 1987), 92–94.

24. Ibid., 48–49.

25. Christophe Jaffrelot, ed., *The Sangh Parivar: A Reader* (New Delhi: Oxford University Press, 2005), 3–4.

26. Peter van der Veer, "Hindu Nationalism and the Discourse of Modernity: The Vishwa Hindu Parishad," in *Accounting for Fundamentalisms: The Dynamic Character of Movements*, vol. 4, ed. Martin E. Mary and R. Scott Appleby (Chicago: Chicago University Press, 1994), 653–68.

27. Jaffrelot, *The Sangh Parivar*, 5–11.

28. Prime Minister's High Level Committee, *Social, Economic and Educational Status of the Muslim Community of India: A Report* (New Delhi: Government of India, 2006), 67, 166.

29. Gold, "Organized Hinduisms," 531.

30. "A Symbol of Identity," *India Today*, December 31, 1992.

31. Van der Veer, "Hindu Nationalism," 662.

32. *India Today*, December 15, 1989.

33. Anuradha Kapur, "Deity to Crusader: The Changing Iconography of Ram," in *Hindus and Others: The Question of Identity in India Today*, ed. Gyanendra Pandey (New Delhi: Viking, 1993), 74–75.

34. Kakar, *Colours*, 64.

35. Ibid., 210–11.

36. Ibid., 204–14.

37. Basu et al., *Khaki Shorts*, 87–92, also argue that the supporters of the BJP were particularly threatened by the Mandal promise of reservations for OBCs.

38. Kakar, *Colours*, 210.

39. Ibid., 205.

40. Tanika Sarkar, "Women's Agency within Authoritarian Communalism: The Rashtrasevika Samiti and Ramjanmabhoomi," in Pandey, *Hindus and Others*, 27.

41. Kakar, *Colours*, 212–13.

42. Ibid., 62–64.

43. *New York Times*, December 14, 2000.

44. *India Today*, December 31, 1992; *New York Times*, January 15, 1993.

45. Human Rights Watch, *"We Have No Orders to Save You": State Participation and Complicity in Communal Violence in Gujarat* (New York: Human Rights Watch, April 2002), 27, 31, 36.

46. Ashis Nandy, "Obituary of a Culture," *Seminar*, no. 513 (May 2002): 15–18.

47. Human Rights Watch, *Behind the Kashmir Conflict: Abuses by Indian Security Forces and Militant Groups Continue* (New York: Human Rights Watch, 1999).

48. *New York Times*, November 24, 2007; *The Times*, July 28, 2008; *The Economist*, July 31, 2008; *New York Times*, December 5 and 6, 2008.

49. Kakar, *Colours*, 206–17.

Index

LaVergne, TN USA
21 January 2011
213433LV00002B/5/P

9 780195 379662